# A CENTURY OF MUSIC UNDER THE STARS

With forewords by

**Yannick Nézet-Séguin and**

**Catherine M. Cahill and Christopher L. Bruner**

# A CENTURY OF MUSIC UNDER THE STARS

*A History of the Mann Center for the Performing Arts and Robin Hood Dell*

**JACK McCARTHY**

TEMPLE UNIVERSITY PRESS
Philadelphia | Rome | Tokyo

TEMPLE UNIVERSITY PRESS
Philadelphia, Pennsylvania 19122
tupress.temple.edu


Published 2025

Book design by Kate Nichols

Library of Congress Cataloging-in-Publication Data

Names: McCarthy, Jack (Archivist) author | Nézet-Séguin, Yannick, 1975– writer of foreword | Cahill, Catherine M. writer of foreword | Bruner, Christopher L. writer of foreword
Title: A century of music under the stars : a history of the Mann Center for the Performing Arts and Robin Hood Dell / Jack McCarthy ; with forewords by Yannick Nézet-Séguin and Catherine M. Cahill and Christopher L. Bruner.
Description: Philadelphia : Temple University Press, 2025. | Includes bibliographical references and index. | Summary: "Traces the history of two Philadelphia outdoor music venues, the Mann Center for the Performing Arts and the Robin Hood Dell"— Provided by publisher.
Identifiers: LCCN 2025012688 | ISBN 9781439924334 cloth
Subjects: LCSH: Mann, Fredric R. (Fredric Rand), 1903–1987 | Mann Center for the Performing Arts (Philadelphia, Pa.)—History | Mann Music Center (Philadelphia, Pa.)—History | Robin Hood Dell West (Philadelphia, Pa.)—History | Robin Hood Dell (Philadelphia, Pa.)—History | Centers for the performing arts—Pennsylvania—Philadelphia—History | Outdoor concert facilities—Pennsylvania—Philadelphia—History | Music—Social aspects—Pennsylvania—Philadelphia—History
Classification: LCC PN1588.P545 M33 2025 | DDC 790.0974811—dc23/eng/20250609
LC record available at https://lccn.loc.gov/2025012688

The manufacturer's authorized representative in the EU for product safety is Temple University Rome, Via di San Sebastianello, 16, 00187 Rome RM, Italy (https://rome.temple.edu/). tempress@temple.edu

♾ The paper used in this publication meets the requirements of the American National Standard for Information Sciences—Permanence of Paper for Printed Library Materials, ANSI Z39.48–1992

Printed in Canada

9 8 7 6 5 4 3 2 1

*This book is dedicated to the memory of*

FREDRIC R. ("FREDDIE") MANN (1903–1987),

*someone I never met but feel I have come to know*

*through writing this book—an intriguing, paradoxical figure*

*whose contributions to the cultural life of Philadelphia*

*were enormous and enduring.*

# Contents

# Foreword

*Yannick Nézet-Séguin*

At a great musical institution like The Philadelphia Orchestra, history is handed down from one generation to the next, one musician to another, one leader to their successor, one idea of community to many more.

Although I had only been on this earth for a year when the Mann Center we know today was created in 1976, I feel its past, and I know intuitively how deeply the Mann is part of the present musical life of Philadelphia as an ever more inclusive, open, and welcoming space to gather and revel in the infinite pleasure of music.

The musicians of the Orchestra have performed for Philadelphians at the Mann summer after summer since its creation (and at its previous location, the Robin Hood Dell, since its opening in 1930). There are so many indelible collective memories that make up this important bond with the people of Philadelphia, ranging from picnics with friends and romance under the stars to solemn occasions, such as the September 11 Tribute Concert, conducted by Music Director Wolfgang Sawallisch just five days after that catastrophic event in 2001.

I have had the pleasure of conducting the incredible Philadelphia Orchestra at the Mann in a vast array of music: beautiful Beethoven, Margaret Bonds's proud and poignant *The Montgomery Variations*, Mendelssohn's exquisite Violin Concerto performed by Maria Dueñas, and more.

But because the Mann is, in its essence, a civic gathering place, a musical town square for Philadelphians, perhaps my most profound memory is "Hail to the Heroes: A Concert of Gratitude," The Philadelphia Orchestra's first post-pandemic concert with a live audience, on May 15, 2021. With vocalist Laurin Talese we performed "Lift Every Voice and Sing." Continuing our journey of uplifting the music of Florence Price, we performed her Piano Concerto in One Movement with Michelle Cann. We offered new musical horizons with works by Carlos Simon and Vivian Fung and Valerie Coleman's *Seven O'Clock Shout*, her anthem for the heroic frontline workers who saved lives and spirits in the depths of the pandemic. The concert also included beloved favorites from Tchaikovsky and Beethoven and, of course, Bill Conti's theme from *Rocky*. What joy everyone at the Mann, onstage and in the audience, felt that evening to be together again.

This is what the Mann exists for: to bring people together—for occasions; for remembrance; for celebration; for friendship and love; for music, outdoors, on a hot summer Philadelphia evening in West Fairmount Park.

Photograph by Landon Nordeman

**Yannick Nézet-Séguin**
*Music and Artistic Director*
*The Philadelphia Orchestra*

# Foreword

*Catherine M. Cahill and Christopher L. Bruner*

**We're celebrating 50 years! Five decades of glorious music . . .** of world-class artists and rapt audiences . . . of championing the arts, Fairmount Park, and the City of Philadelphia. That is the story of the Mann Center for the Performing Arts.

It's a story that belongs to all of us.

For those of us with the great honor of stewarding the Mann today, we do so with many of the same aspirations that inspired our predecessors. The Mann opened its doors in 1976, but our predecessor, the Robin Hood Dell, dates to 1930. Over all those years, we've known this to be true: Music and the performing arts enrich—even transform—those who experience them. Season after season, we work to connect people with those experiences, presenting a diverse range of artists, outdoors, under the stars, surrounded by the nature and grandeur of our spectacular campus nestled within one of the nation's largest urban parks.

Along the way, our patrons build their own stories here. You picnic on our Great Lawn anticipating an evening with The Philadelphia Orchestra, as generations of classical music audiences have done for decades. You gather in the architectural and acoustical wonder that is the TD Pavilion to see incredible touring artists perform music of all genres on the city's largest stage—the Presser Foundation Stage. The artists are a musical "Who's Who" of favorite stars—James Taylor, Smokey Robinson, Bob Dylan, Sarah McLachlan, Phish, Diana Ross, Willie Nelson, John Legend, and countless more. You watch iconic films with Movies @ the Mann, as orchestras play the scores live. You dance and sing to indie artists on our open-air Highmark

Skyline Stage. You celebrate summer with tens of thousands at our signature, major music festivals such as the Roots Picnic.

Throughout it all, memories are made. Maybe a night at the Mann marked a first date, a marriage proposal, the first time your young family experienced a concert, the discovery of a new favorite artist, or the realization that there is no better place to see fireworks light up the Philadelphia skyline. We're here for all of it.

And we continue to evolve. While our stages are active spring through fall, our work happens year-round with robust education and community engagement programming that develops skills and affinity for the performing arts among young people, particularly those in our own Parkside neighborhood. Beyond education, we're now developing a workforce among our young people through mentorship and apprenticeships that are the first of their kind for a music venue like ours in Philadelphia.

None of this work would be meaningful without you as guests, partners, donors, and our great patrons. None of it would have been possible without the vision of those who came before us, most notably the indefatigable Fredric R. Mann, our namesake.

We invite you to get lost in these pages, in our grand history, and to join us as we herald our future.

**Catherine M. Cahill**
*President and*
*Chief Executive Officer*

**Christopher L. Bruner**
*Chair, Board of Directors*

# Preface

In late July 1966, Patsy Baxter, a young voice student at the Philadelphia Musical Academy, attended a concert with a friend at the Robin Hood Dell, The Philadelphia Orchestra's outdoor summer home in East Fairmount Park. There she was introduced to another aspiring local musician, violinist Booker Rowe, a Yale University graduate student who was home for the summer. Both were lovers of classical music and, like thousands of other Philadelphians that summer, were taking advantage of what the Robin Hood Dell offered, which was unique in America: a six-week summer season of world-class symphonic music in a beautiful outdoor setting entirely free to the public.

Booker Rowe had come up through the School District of Philadelphia's nationally recognized music program, earned a bachelor's degree in music at Temple University, and played with the Nashville Symphony Orchestra for two years before leaving for graduate study at Yale. After he received a master's degree in music from Yale in 1968, Philadelphia Orchestra Music Director Eugene Ormandy invited him to join the Orchestra to replace a violinist who had recently died. While it was a temporary appointment, Booker Rowe made history in November 1968 by becoming the first Black musician to play in the renowned Philadelphia Orchestra.

Booker and Patsy reconnected soon after Booker's return to Philadelphia, began dating, and married in 1970. In 1971, Booker was given a permanent position with The Philadelphia Orchestra and remained with the ensemble for 49 years. During that time, he played the Orchestra's annual summer concert series, first at the original

Robin Hood Dell, where he had first met Patsy, then at the new summer home the Orchestra occupied in 1976 in West Fairmount Park. Initially called Robin Hood Dell West, the new venue was renamed the Mann Music Center in 1979 and then the Mann Center for the Performing Arts in 1998. Patsy regularly attended those concerts while pursuing her own distinguished career in music. She earned two bachelor's degrees from the Philadelphia Musical Academy and a master's in music history and doctorate in music education research from Temple University. She then served as associate professor and chair of the Music Department at Lincoln University; taught at Community College of Philadelphia; managed music and performing arts programs for community organizations; and founded her own musical academy.

When Booker retired from The Philadelphia Orchestra in 2020, he and Patsy had been married for 50 years, had children and grandchildren, and had built a rich musical life together in Philadelphia. And it all started with a chance meeting at a Robin Hood Dell concert in 1966. "The Robin Hood Dell and the Mann Center have made a tremendous contribution to the musical and cultural life of Philadelphia," Patsy notes. "They have allowed budding musicians to easily hear live professional performances, as my husband and I did when we met at a Philadelphia Orchestra concert at the Dell in 1966."[1]

Fourteen years later, the Mann Center played a role in the courtship of another important couple in Philadelphia cultural circles: financier Richard Worley and attorney Leslie Anne Miller. One of their first dates was a picnic on the lawn at a Philadelphia Orchestra concert at the Mann in 1980. "She brought the picnic supper; I brought the blanket and a bottle of wine, and it was just heavenly lying out under the stars," Richard recalled years later. As Leslie Anne remembered on a separate occasion, "That's where he and I jointly learned to love the Orchestra."[2] Married in 1987, the two would become important leaders in Philadelphia arts and culture. Richard was a longtime board member and chair of The Philadelphia Orchestra Association, while Leslie Anne was an early board member of the Kimmel Center for the Performing Arts and chair of the board of the Philadelphia Museum of Art.

Such stories illustrate the enduring role the Robin Hood Dell and Mann Center have played in the lives of countless music lovers over the years. Idyllic settings to enjoy fine music, hear celebrated performing artists, and nurture friendships (and perhaps romances), the venues hold a special place for those in the Philadelphia area and beyond for whom live music is an important part of their lives. For such music lovers, "the Dell" and "the Mann" are places of cherished memories—of inspiring performances, of seeing famous artists in their prime or new artists early in their careers, or of just enjoying picnics under the stars with friends and great music for atmosphere.

Affection for the Robin Hood Dell and Mann Center runs deep in Philadelphia. In early 2009, when The Philadelphia Orchestra announced that it was reducing its number of summer concerts at the Mann for financial reasons (it was the height of

■ "An Evening at Robin Hood Dell," *The Sunday Bulletin*, June 18, 1967. (Scrapbook, Mann Center for the Performing Arts Archives)

the 2008–2009 Great Recession), a longtime patron, Terez Giuliana of Northwest Philadelphia, told *The Philadelphia Inquirer*: "I am heartbroken. I went ever since I was a little kid. I used to go to the Robin Hood Dell with my best friend. My husband and I mark the season by the things we do. Penn basketball in fall. Spring is baseball. And it's not summer until we get the lineup for the Mann. . . . It's the highlight of the summer for me."[3]

Beyond personal attachments, the Dell and the Mann have played important roles in the cultural history of Philadelphia and the history of concert music in America. The venues have launched the careers of many renowned artists and hosted a number of significant musical milestones—from Judy Garland's first public concert to Duke Ellington's first performance with a symphony orchestra; from Zubin Mehta's American conducting debut and Benny Goodman's symphonic conducting debut to world premieres of works by Samuel Barber and Igor Stravinsky.

The Mann gained a whole new audience when it began transitioning from a primarily classical to a contemporary and popular music venue in the 1970s, part of a broader trend in the concert industry as venues nationwide adapted to changing musical tastes and audience expectations. The new patrons developed their own loyalties and traditions. Many longtime fans have rarely missed a show by James Taylor or Bonnie Raitt, perennial favorites who have played the Mann numerous times since their debuts in 1976 and 1981, respectively. Among a younger generation, thousands of loyal followers of the jam band Phish have gathered faithfully for the group's dozens of sold-out Mann concerts since 1992, concerts that have become epic communal gatherings over several nights. More recently, the Roots Picnic, the eclectic, multiday festival at the Mann curated by Philadelphia's beloved hometown band The Roots, has become an iconic, nationally recognized annual event in the world of contemporary Black music.

What distinguishes the Robin Hood Dell and Mann Center from most other major outdoor performing arts centers in America is that they are both *in* and *of* the city of Philadelphia. Whereas other venues often are well outside the home cities of their orchestras—Saratoga and Tanglewood are more than a hundred miles from New York City and Boston; Ravinia and Wolf Trap are in the suburbs of Chicago and Washington, DC—the Dell and the Mann are located in Philadelphia and are part of the urban fabric of the city. The spectacular view of the Philadelphia skyline from the Mann Center connects its patrons to the city in a very tangible way, as do the Mann's multifaceted community engagement programs with its West Philadelphia neighbors.

Both the Dell and the Mann are on city land and have received city funding while being managed by a private nonprofit (the Dell from 1930 to 1975, the Mann from 1976 to the present). Thus, their histories provide a unique perspective on the intersection of Philadelphia's cultural, political, civic, and philanthropic worlds. As revealed in this book, key movers and shakers from these worlds came together to establish the Dell in 1930 and the Mann in 1976. While ultimately successful, they faced many challenges along the way. The book recounts their many successes but also the tense moments—mostly behind the scenes, sometimes in public—in their pursuit of the noble goal of offering Philadelphians great music in a beautiful natural setting.

Looming large in this story is Fredric R. "Freddie" Mann, businessman, philanthropist, civic leader, and government official but, most of all, classical music–loving impresario who rescued the Dell from financial crisis in 1948 and guided the venue and its successor, which now bears his name, for 40 years. Mann's passion for classical music, his powerful influence in civic and political circles, and his hands-on management (not to mention his mostly unpublicized personal generosity) were key factors in the success of the Dell and the Mann. In the 1960s and 1970s, faced with a dwindling audience for his beloved classical music and calls for more diverse programming, Mann was labeled an elitist as he sought to preserve the venues as sanctuaries for symphonic music. It was a challenging period, as he and his colleagues grappled with fundamental cultural changes unfolding throughout American society. How they adapted to these changes is detailed in these pages.

Also described here is the evolving relationship over the years between the venues' management and their chief resident ensemble, The Philadelphia Orchestra, a

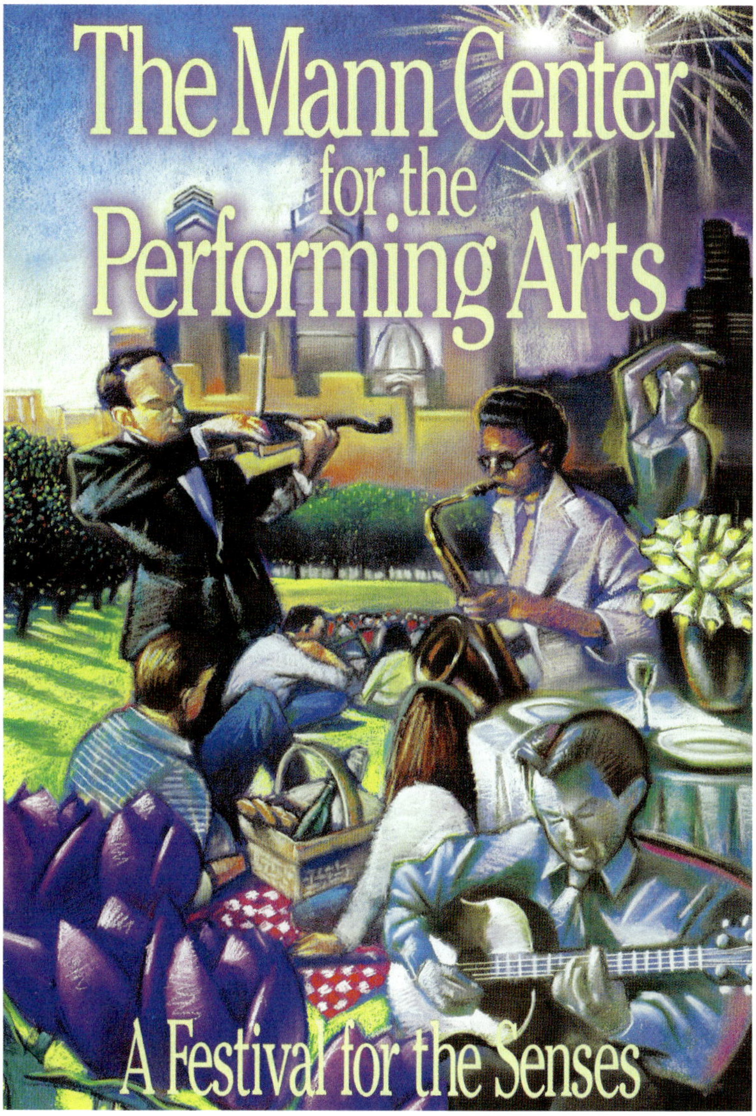


■ 1998 poster promoting a wide-ranging performing arts festival at the Mann Center that year. (Mann Center for the Performing Arts Archives)

relationship that, while generally harmonious, has had its difficult moments. The rich history of the Orchestra, one of the world's great symphonic ensembles, has been covered in depth in many other sources. Some behind-the-scenes aspects of this history are revealed here for the first time, however.

There is an element of confusion to this history due to the changing name of the venue and its sponsoring organization, as well as its move from one location to another in 1976. The organization that is now the Mann Center for the Performing Arts was founded in early 1930 as the Philadelphia Summer Concerts Association, with the mission of building a summer home for The Philadelphia Orchestra. That home, the Robin Hood Dell, opened in July 1930 in East Fairmount Park. In 1935, the organization was rechartered as Robin Hood Dell Concerts Inc. In 1976, it moved to a new home in West Fairmount Park, which, as noted earlier, was initially called Robin Hood Dell West. The venue was renamed the Mann Music Center in 1979 in honor of Fredric Mann, and then the Mann Center for the Performing Arts in 1998 to reflect an expanded mission that had grown to include offering a wide range of educational and community engagement programs in addition to presenting performing arts.

This is a history of the organization under its various names and at its two venues: the Robin Hood Dell from 1930 to 1975 and the Mann Center from 1976 onward. The book does not cover the post-1975 history of the original Robin Hood Dell, renamed the Dell Music Center in 2010. When the organization moved in 1976, the original Dell came under the management of the Philadelphia Department of Recreation, which took over summer-season bookings, offering primarily jazz, rhythm and blues (R&B), soul, and gospel music. These concerts, which continue to this day, are separate from Mann Center programming. The two venues share a history but have been managed by different entities since 1975.

The book is divided into three parts. "Part I: Setting the Stage" traces the rich, centuries-old tradition of outdoor concerts in Philadelphia and tells the story of the enterprising people and organizations that came together to build the Robin Hood Dell in 1930. "Part II: Robin Hood Dell" focuses on the Dell from 1930 to 1975: its notable concerts and artists, major milestones, trials and tribulations, and factors that prompted its leaders to seek a new location. "Part III: Mann Center" covers 1976 to 2024, highlighting the opening of the Robin Hood Dell West in 1976, as well as its transition to the Mann Music Center a few years later and to the Mann Center for the Performing Arts in 1997. Part III concludes with the Mann's expanding profile in the millennial and early 21st-century period: the many great concerts it presented, new programs and activities it initiated, and challenging issues it faced. Those issues included a financial crisis during the Great Recession of 2008–2009 and the unprecedented phenomenon of the COVID-19 pandemic, which resulted in the cancellation of the entire 2020 season of in-person concerts. The book concludes with the Mann's triumphant emergence from these challenges as a much stronger, more dynamic institution than ever as it prepared to celebrate its 50th anniversary in 2026.

# Note on Sources

This book is based largely on primary sources, especially information uncovered in archival collections and gathered from interviews with those who played a role in the history of the Mann Center and Robin Hood Dell. Newspaper accounts were another major source, while other published sources such as biographies, autobiographies, and topical histories were also consulted. Occasionally, older historical sources use language that would be considered inappropriate to contemporary readers. The original wording of these sources has been retained for the sake of accuracy, and while nothing in the book rises to the level of being offensive, a few passages here and there may seem archaic or poorly worded in modern context.

# TIMELINE: MILESTONE EVENTS

## Robin Hood Dell and Mann Center for the Performing Arts

| | |
|---|---|
| **April 10, 1930** | Nonprofit Philadelphia Summer Concerts Association established to build summer home for Philadelphia Orchestra |
| **July 8, 1930** | Robin Hood Dell opens with inaugural concert; Philadelphia Orchestra plays to its largest audience ever |
| **March 1935** | Robin Hood Dell Concerts Inc. established, replacing Philadelphia Summer Concerts Association |
| **July 1942** | Ensemble renamed Robin Hood Dell Orchestra |
| **July 17, 1948** | Season suspended early due to lack of funds; Fredric R. Mann assumes presidency, initiates rescue plan |
| **July 2, 1952** | Children's Concerts series inaugurated |
| **June 22, 1953** | Opening night of the 1953 season, the first season in which all concerts are free |
| **1955–1956** | Robin Hood Dell undergoes complete renovation |
| **August 8, 1967** | First rock concert at Robin Hood Dell |
| **June 17, 1970** | Robin Hood Dell Orchestra name retired; The Philadelphia Orchestra name reinstated |
| **July 31, 1975** | Last symphonic concert in original Robin Hood Dell |
| **June 14, 1976** | Robin Hood Dell West opens with inaugural Philadelphia Orchestra concert |

| | |
|---|---|
| **July 17, 1976** | Electric Factory Concerts begins producing rock and pop shows at Robin Hood Dell West |
| **June 13, 1979** | Robin Hood Dell West renamed Mann Music Center |
| **February 26, 1987** | Fredric Mann dies |
| **January 2, 1997** | Mann Music Center renamed Mann Center for the Performing Arts |
| **2002–2006** | Mann campus dramatically expanded and renovated |
| **July 29, 2012** | Skyline Stage opens |
| **June 1, 2019** | Roots Picnic moves to Mann Center |
| **June 2020** | COVID-19 pandemic forces cancellation of entire 2020 concert season |
| **May 5, 2021** | Mann reopens with Opera Philadelphia performance, the first in-person concert since 2019 |
| **April 29, 2022** | Mann introduces new, intimate Downstage at the Mann concert setting |
| **2023** | Mann establishes Community Artist-in-Residence and Jazz Curator positions and begins hosting biennial Historically Black College and University (HBCU) Festival |

# A CENTURY OF MUSIC UNDER THE STARS

# I. Setting the Stage

1.

# Early Outdoor Music Venues and Musical Institutions

As in most great success stories, a number of fortuitous circumstances came together to make the Robin Hood Dell and its successor, the Mann Center for the Performing Arts, a reality. These include a long-standing tradition of outdoor concerts in Philadelphia, going back to the city's 18th-century pleasure gardens; the establishment in the mid-19th century of Fairmount Park, one of the nation's largest municipal parks, giving the City of Philadelphia control over an expansive landscape with several natural amphitheaters; the U.S. Centennial Exhibition of 1876, which drew millions of visitors to Fairmount Park, thousands of whom flocked to one such amphitheater for daily concerts by renowned ensembles of the time; and the establishment of the Fairmount Park Band in 1899 and the Fairmount Park Symphony Orchestra in 1922, both of which offered a series of nightly summer performances at park sites that further cultivated a public taste for outdoor concerts. Another key factor was the enormous popularity in this period of trolley parks, amusement parks operated by trolley companies where outdoor band and orchestra concerts were a major attraction.

By the 1920s, before the new technologies of recorded music and radio began to challenge the supremacy of live music, there was a great demand for outdoor summer concerts in park settings in Philadelphia. Several Philadelphia musical institutions established in the late 19th and early 20th centuries sought to meet this demand and would come together to build a new, permanent outdoor music venue for the city. Local No. 77 of the American Federation of Musicians (AFM), chartered in 1896, was the Philadelphia musicians' union that gave critical approval to a flexible compensation arrangement for the musicians who would perform at the proposed venue; without such approval, the endeavor would not have been feasible financially. The Philadelphia Orchestra, founded in 1900, rose to worldwide acclaim in the late 1910s under its brilliant, innovative conductor Leopold Stokowski and looked to broaden its local audience and create summer employment opportunities for its musicians. The Sesquicentennial Music Committee, created to produce musical activities for the nation's 150th anniversary celebration in Philadelphia in 1926, brought together the key individuals who would collaborate again four years later in establishing an outdoor venue for symphony concerts. Lastly, the Philadelphia Bureau of Music, established in 1928, was the short-lived but effective municipal agency that would take the early lead in planning and promoting the new venue.

The synergy of these groups and developments laid the groundwork for a nucleus of civic leaders, musicians, elected officials, and others who sought to create a summer home for the city's renowned Philadelphia Orchestra, an outdoor concert venue where citizens from all backgrounds and circumstances could enjoy world-class symphonic music at reasonable prices in a beautiful natural setting. In 1930 such a group came together to build the Robin Hood Dell; 46 years later, a new group, led by an influential, resourceful leader, moved the concerts to a new venue, the Robin Hood Dell West, later renamed the Mann Center for the Performing Arts.

An examination of these interrelated contributing factors, starting with music at Philadelphia's early pleasure gardens, reveals a city that has long valued music and natural spaces, and that has produced visionary leaders who worked to bring the two together for the public's benefit.

## Philadelphia Pleasure Gardens

Philadelphians have been enjoying concerts in outdoor settings since the late 18th century. The city was the political and cultural capital of America at this time, an important center of arts and entertainment in the young nation. Among the diversions available to residents and visitors to the bustling metropolis around the turn of the 19th century were "pleasure gardens," landscaped sites where patrons could stroll well-manicured grounds; take in botanical displays; and enjoy refreshments and entertainment, including outdoor concerts. There were popular pleasure gardens featuring music at Harrowgate, a mineral spring resort about four miles north of down-

**(facing page, bottom)** ▪ Detail from Charles P. Varles's 1802 Map of Philadelphia, as illustrated in the Fall 2023 issue of *Extant*, a publication of Preservation Alliance for Greater Philadelphia, showing Gray's Gardens on the west side of the Schuylkill River. (Original map from the David Rumsey Map Collection, David Rumsey Map Center, Stanford Libraries; illustration courtesy of Preservation Alliance for Greater Philadelphia)

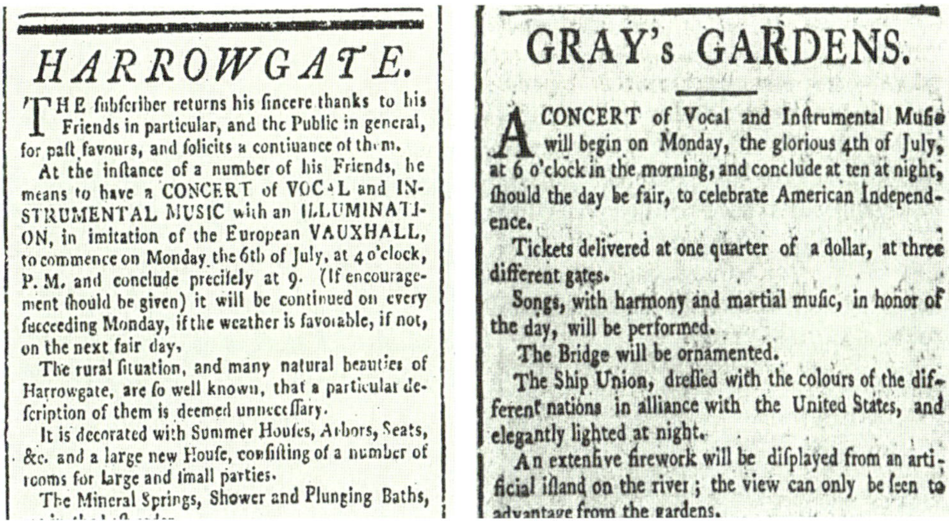

# HARROWGATE.

THE ſubſcriber returns his ſincere thanks to his Friends in particular, and the Public in general, for paſt favours, and ſolicits a contiuance of them.

At the inſtance of a number of his Friends, he means to have a CONCERT of VOCAL and INSTRUMENTAL MUSIC with an ILLUMINATION, in imitation of the European VAUXHALL, to commence on Monday the 6th of July, at 4 o'clock, P. M. and conclude preciſely at 9. (If encouragement ſhould be given) it will be continued on every ſucceeding Monday, if the weather is favorable, if not, on the next fair day.

The rural ſituation, and many natural beauties of Harrowgate, are ſo well known, that a particular deſcription of them is deemed unneceſſary.

It is decorated with Summer Houſes, Arbors, Seats, &c. and a large new Houſe, conſiſting of a number of rooms for large and ſmall parties.

The Mineral Springs, Shower and Plunging Baths,

# GRAY's GARDENS.

A CONCERT of Vocal and Inſtrumental Muſic will begin on Monday, the glorious 4th of July, at 6 o'clock in the morning, and conclude at ten at night, ſhould the day be fair, to celebrate American Independence.

Tickets delivered at one quarter of a dollar, at three different gates.

Songs, with harmony and martial muſic, in honor of the day, will be performed.

The Bridge will be ornamented.

The Ship Union, dreſſed with the colours of the different nations in alliance with the United States, and elegantly lighted at night.

An extenſive firework will be diſplayed from an artificial iſland on the river; the view can only be ſeen to advantage from the gardens.

■ Newspaper notices announcing concerts at the 18th-century Philadelphia pleasure gardens Harrowgate and Gray's Gardens. *Left*: July 1, 1789, notice in *The Independent Gazetteer* of a "Concert of vocal and instrumental music with an illumination" at Harrowgate. *Right*: July 2, 1791, notice in *The Gazette of the United States* of a July 4 "Concert of Vocal and Instrumental Music" at Gray's Gardens. (Retrieved from Newspapers.com)

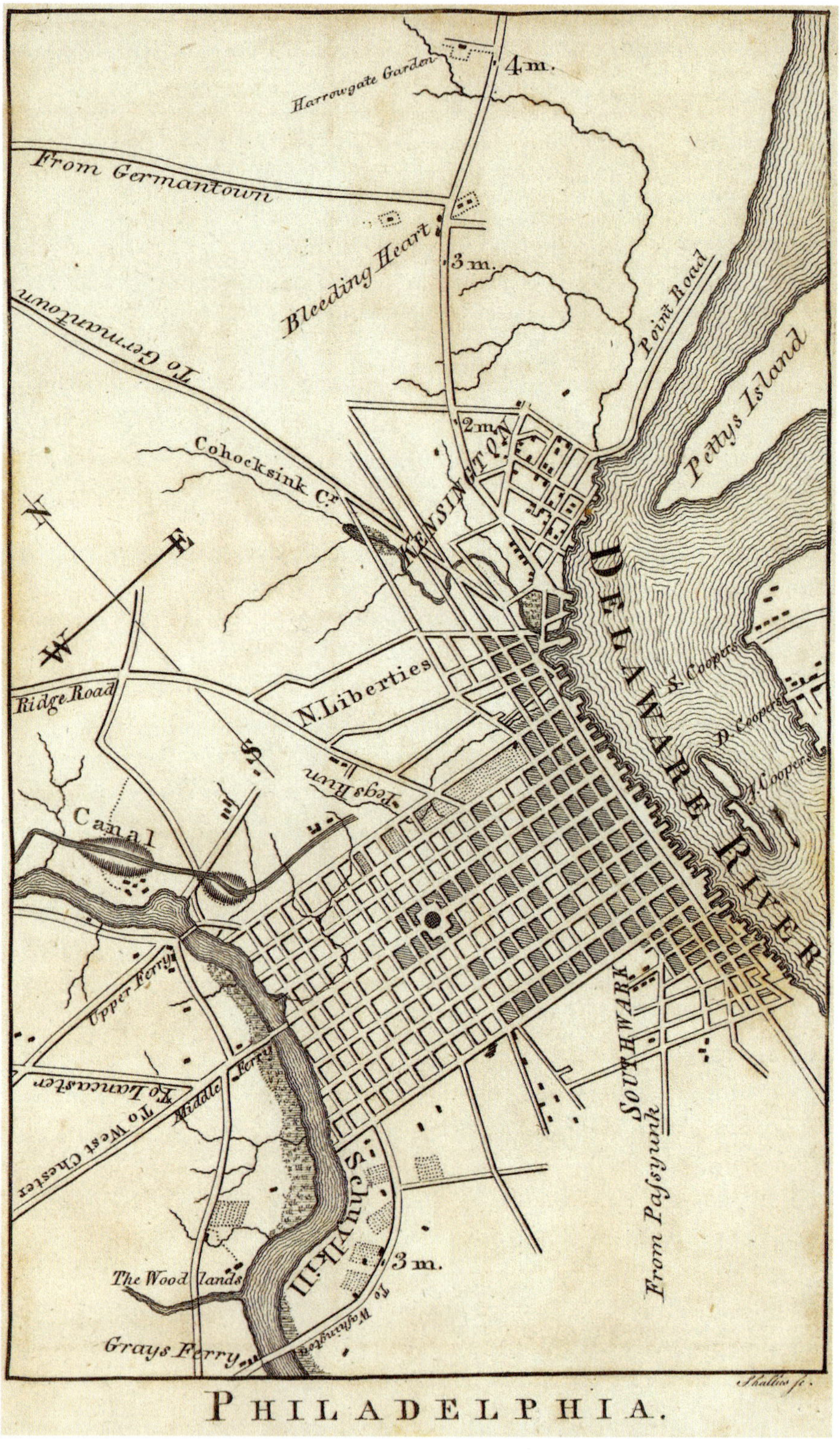


Map of Philadelphia published in 1802 in *The Traveller's Directory, or A pocket companion: shewing the course of the main road from Philadelphia to New York*. Harrowgate Garden is at the top, four miles north of the city center. (Lionel Pincus and Princess Firyal Map Division, New York Public Library Digital Collections)

An illustrated 1930 holiday greeting card from Fidelity-Philadelphia Trust Company, showing an 1819 view of Vauxhall Garden, which stood on the east side of Broad Street between Walnut and Sansom streets, where the Fidelity-Philadelphia building was erected in 1928. (Free Library of Philadelphia, Print and Picture Collection)

town Philadelphia; at Gray's Gardens, a botanical and entertainment venue built around a ferry service the Gray family operated on the west bank of the Schuylkill River (now the neighborhood of Gray's Ferry); at Vauxhall Gardens, a large outdoor entertainment complex at Broad and Walnut Streets; and at other locations in and around the city.

Perhaps the most popular Philadelphia pleasure garden in the early 19th century was Vauxhall Gardens, which opened in 1814 at the northeastern corner of Broad and Walnut streets, then a largely undeveloped part of the city (most residents and businesses were concentrated closer to the Delaware River in this period). Modeled on the famous garden of the same name in London, Vauxhall Gardens occupied an entire city block and featured an illuminated garden, with a large temple-like structure for an orchestra and an audience of up to 1,000. Prominent Philadelphia businessman and politician Samuel Breck visited Vauxhall Gardens on August 23, 1814. As he noted in his diary that day, he was impressed with the setting, if not the concert: "In the afternoon . . . I went to the Vauxhall Gardens. The gardens are pretty, and well illuminated. In the centre stands a handsome temple, with orchestra, boxes, etc. for the accommodation of 1,000 people. We had a concert, which was so so."[1]

## Fairmount Park

Fairmount Park, the vast expanse of nearly 2,000 acres of city-owned open space, recreational areas, and historic estates straddling the Schuylkill River in West Phila-

■ "Music Stand at Lemon Hill," published in *A Century After: Picturesque Glimpses of Philadelphia and Pennsylvania*, 1875. *Inset*: Lemon Hill Mansion, circa 1870. (Both images from Free Library of Philadelphia, Print and Picture Collection)

delphia, was home to a number of outdoor concert venues in the 19th and early 20th centuries. The park began to take shape in the 1840s when the City of Philadelphia started acquiring large tracts of land along the Schuylkill River, primarily to protect the domestic water supply, which was drawn from the river and pumped to an elevated reservoir known as Fair Mount, but also to provide citizens with places to enjoy nature and engage in recreational activities. The first such tract, purchased in 1844, was Lemon Hill, an 1800 riverfront mansion and garden estate near the Fair Mount reservoir. Lemon Hill would figure prominently as a site for outdoor music over the years. Philadelphia's German community gathered there in the 1840s and 1850s for "Sangerfest" concerts of German choral music, and the estate hosted national Sangerfest festivals in 1850 and 1857 that drew some 10,000 choral music enthusiasts from throughout the country. In the 1920s, thousands would gather at Lemon Hill for concerts by the Fairmount Park Symphony Orchestra.

Lemon Hill was dedicated as Fairmount Park in 1855, and in 1867 an act of the Pennsylvania Assembly created the Fairmount Park Commission, a semiautonomous municipal agency whose governing members were leading citizens of Philadelphia. With a mandate to acquire and manage parkland, the commission expanded Fairmount Park dramatically in the late 1860s and 1870s while sponsoring a range of recreational and entertainment activities. From the beginning, the commissioners had big plans for concerts in the park. Their report for 1870 noted that "during the

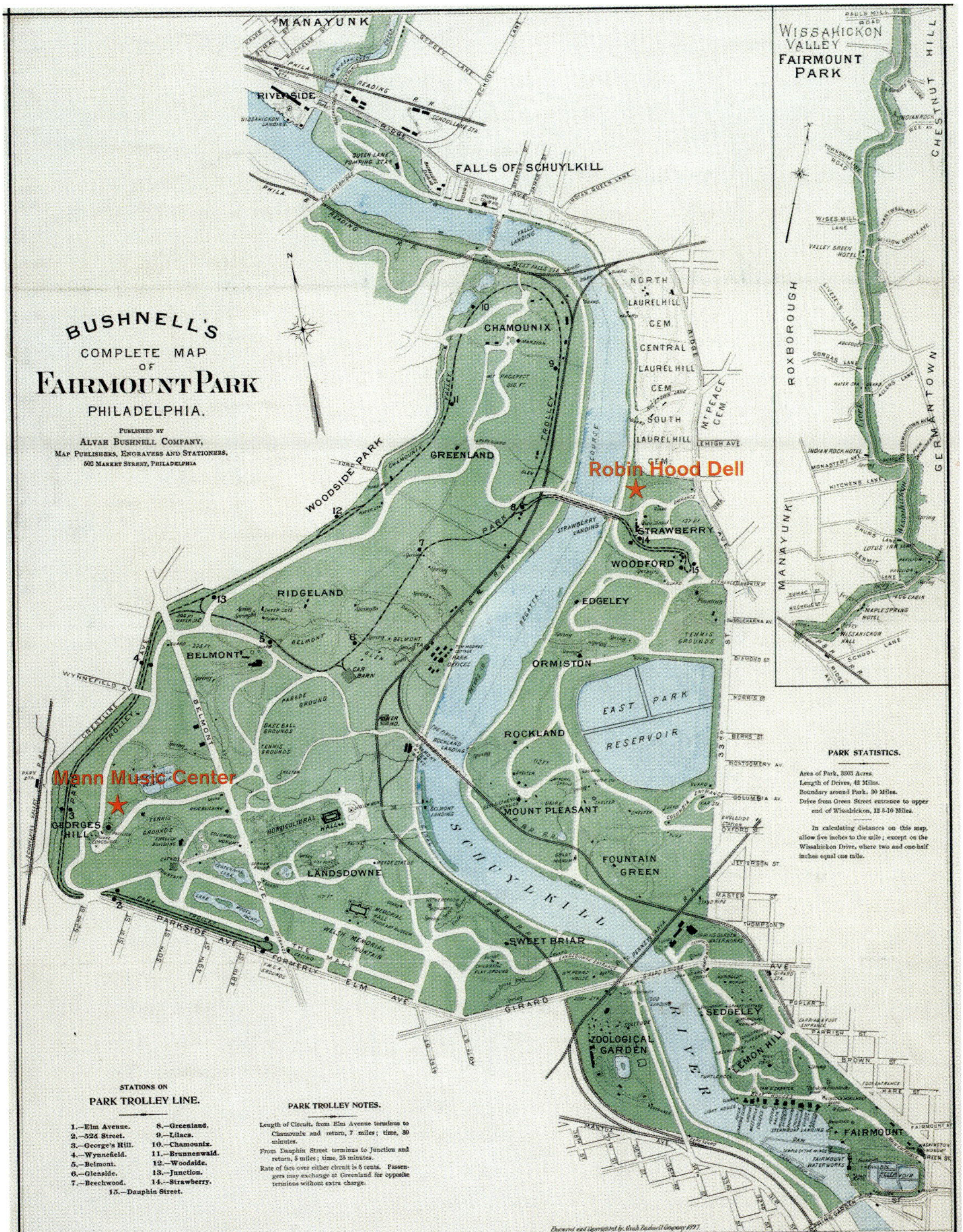


■ 1897 map of Fairmount Park, the sprawling, nearly 2,000-acre public park in West Philadelphia that was established in the mid-19th century. Future locations of Robin Hood Dell and Mann Music Center, which opened in 1930 and 1976, respectively, are marked.
(Free Library of Philadelphia Map Collection)

past summer the Commissioners inaugurated a series of afternoon concerts, which though neither upon so large a scale nor as often repeated as they could have wished, proved eminently successful, and will stimulate to renewed exertions in furtherance of the same object." The same report notes expenditures of $885.69 for building a "Music-stand" and $1,098 for "Concerts in Park."[2] True to their word, the commissioners increased concert expenditures significantly in the ensuing years; the 1874 report notes $8,378.75 allocated for "Music—Concerts in the Park."[3]

In the mid-1870s there were outdoor concerts at the new Philadelphia Zoological Garden, the nation's first zoo, which opened in July 1874 on the west bank of the Schuylkill River in West Fairmount Park. An August 22, 1874, notice in *The Philadelphia Inquirer* for the new zoo announced, "Concerts every Wednesday and Saturday afternoon, during August, by Mr. CARL SENTZ and a band of sixteen musicians."[4] The zoo discontinued the concerts two years later when attendance dropped off due to public focus on the activities of the 1876 Centennial, the huge national celebration that took place nearby.[5]

## The Centennial

The 1876 Centennial—officially the International Exhibition of Arts, Manufactures, and Products of the Soil and Mine—was perhaps the largest, most spectacular event in Philadelphia's history. An ambitious, wide-ranging, and enormously popular celebration of the 100th anniversary of the founding of the United States, the Centennial was based in West Fairmount Park and ran from May to November 1876. It drew some 10 million visitors who came to see the latest technological marvels, displays of new products and services, and exhibitions of arts and culture. Among the featured events were twice-daily concerts by celebrated ensembles of the time, starting in May with Gilmore's Band, led by the nation's foremost bandleader, Patrick S. Gilmore. At first, the concerts were held on a large circular stage in the center of the Main Exhibition Hall, but the crowds grew so large that they blocked access to the exhibits. After a few weeks, the concerts were moved to the outdoor Music Pavilion in Lansdowne Ravine, a grassy area that ran through the center of the exposition grounds and sloped down to a small creek, the two hillsides forming a natural amphitheater that could accommodate several thousand listeners. In addition to Gilmore's Band, the Music Pavilion hosted the U.S. Marine Band and other ensembles throughout the summer.

Gilmore's concerts made a strong impression on a young musician who was part of another ensemble performing during the Centennial, a talented and ambitious instrumentalist who would become an important figure in American music history: John Philip Sousa, a Washington, DC, native, was then a 21-year-old violinist in the orchestra of Jacques Offenbach, the famous French composer and impresario who came to Philadelphia to headline a series of Centennial concerts.

■ Depiction of the Centennial Music Pavilion in Landsdowne Ravine, published in *Harper's Weekly*, July 29, 1876. (Courtesy of Jack McCarthy)

These concerts were held downtown in the evening, after the Centennial grounds had closed for the day, in a new purpose-built venue at Broad and Cherry streets called Offenbach's Concert Garden. Following the Centennial, Sousa remained in Philadelphia for several years, playing in the pit orchestras of local theaters, where he learned to conduct. Like Gilmore before him, Sousa would go on to become America's premier bandleader, celebrated in particular as the nation's "March King," composer of a body of march tunes that have become perennial favorites in the American musical canon. In the early 20th century, Sousa and his band were

**(following spread)** ■ The Music Pavilion is shown in the center in this illustration titled *The Centennial—Balloon-View of the Grounds*, published in *Harper's Weekly*, September 30, 1876. The only buildings in this image still standing are Memorial Hall, the domed building above and to the right of the Music Pavilion, and Ohio House, the uppermost building in the group of smaller state buildings along the curved road at the lower left. (Free Library of Philadelphia, Print and Picture Collection)

SINGER'S SEWING MACHINE
LANSDOWNE
MUSIC PAVILION
VALLEY
AGRICULTURAL BUILDING
U.S. GOVERNMENT
EX. BUILDING
TEMPERANCE FOUNTAIN
WISCONSIN
GEORGE'S HILL RESERVOIR
BELMONT DRIVE
STATE AVENUE

MAIN EXHIBITION BUILDING
AVENUE OF THE REPUBLIC
MACHINERY BUILDING
LAKE
ANNEXES
PRINTING PRESSES
BOILER HOUSE

The Music Pavilion for the public in Lansdowne ravine, between the Lafayette restaurant and Horticultural Hall, erected for the use of Gilmore's Band, will open to-day, when the first open-air concert by the Gilmore Cornet Orchestra will be given. The principal reason for removing the concerts from the Main building, where they have been so successful, was that the traffic in the building was almost entirely interrupted during the continuance of a concert by the congregating of the crowds.

The programme at the Music Pavilion for to-day is as follows:

Morning—10.30 to 12 M.

Overture—Linda di Chamounix..................Donizetti
Song—"Ye Merry Birds"...... ......................Gumbert
Scena—"Ocean, Thou Mighty Monster" (from Oberon), Weber
Waltz—"Wine, Women and Song"..................Strauss
Caprice Heroique—"The Awakening of the Lion." Kontsky
Grand Descriptive March—"Picture of a Wedding Day"..............................................Heinemann

Afternoon—from 3 to 5.

Overture—"Raymond"....................Ambroise Thomas
Cornet Solo—"Attila," with variations...............Verdi
Mr. M. Arbuckle.
Grand Selection—Reminiscences......................Rossini
Saxophone Solo—"Reverie"...........................Savari
Mr E. A. Lefebvre.
Waltz—"Bright Star"......................................Lanner
Rhapsodie Hongroise, No. 2..............................Liszt
Polka, Mazourka—"Gliding Away"..................Strauss
Grand Centennial Quadrille, including the "Airs of All Nations," with variations for the principal instruments, and closing with "Star Spangled Banner."

**(left)** ■ Patrick S. Gilmore, America's leading bandleader in the late 19th century, whose twice-daily performances at the Music Pavilion were a major attraction at the 1876 Centennial. (Library of Congress Prints and Photographs Division)

**(below left)** ■ June 1, 1876, article in *The Philadelphia Times* announcing the opening of the Music Pavilion that day, explaining why the concerts were moved there, and giving the program for the morning and afternoon performances. (Retrieved from Newspapers.com)

one of the main attractions at Willow Grove Park, a popular amusement park a few miles outside Philadelphia.

Competing with Offenbach's ensemble for evening audiences during the Centennial was a concert series led by German immigrant Theodore Thomas, America's most esteemed symphonic conductor (as opposed to Gilmore, who was a bandleader). Thomas had performed often in Philadelphia since the 1850s and had led a series of popular summer concerts in Central Park Garden in New York City from 1868 to 1875. He served as musical director for the elaborate Centennial opening ceremonies in Philadelphia on May 10, 1876, where, before an audience of more than 100,000, he led an orchestra of 150 and chorus of 800 in an open-air concert featuring a mix of traditional pieces and new works he commissioned. Most of the latter were, appropriately, by American composers, but Thomas had also arranged for the Women's Centennial Committee to commission the famous German operatic composer Richard Wagner to compose a "Centennial March" for the occasion, for a fee of $5,000. Despite some initial praise, the piece was largely panned and rarely heard after 1876. Wagner

■ Women's Centennial Music Hall and Garden (*at left*) was built as an addition to the mansion of the late actor Edwin Forrest (*at right*) at Broad and Master streets in North Philadelphia to host evening concerts during the 1876 Centennial. (Free Library of Philadelphia, Print and Picture Collection)

himself reportedly later said that "the best thing about the March [was] the money I got for it."[6]

The Women's Centennial Committee hired Thomas to lead a series of evening symphonic concerts during the Centennial. The concerts were held in a newly constructed auditorium adjacent to the mansion of the late celebrated actor Edwin Forrest, located on Broad Street in North Philadelphia, about a mile and a half above the more centrally situated Offenbach's Concert Garden. Thomas eventually assumed financial responsibility for the series, which drew limited audiences and was a commercial failure, due partly to the remote location and partly to the "serious" symphonic works Thomas programmed, as opposed to the lighter fare Offenbach offered. As Thomas noted later in his memoirs, the series put him in debt for many years, subjecting him to "twelve year's [*sic*] experience with sheriffs and scoundrels."[7] To help alleviate his financial distress, the Women's Centennial Committee sponsored a series of "Ten Grand Concerts" that Thomas led at the Academy of Music in fall 1876. In keeping with the grand scale of all-things Centennial, the concerts were touted as being offered "on a scale of COMPLETENESS and GRANDEUR never before attempted in Philadelphia." The 10 concerts in late September featured Thomas's Orchestra, the 400 voice Women's Centennial Chorus, and numerous vocal and instrumental soloists.[8] Unlike Thomas's summer series, these concerts were successful.

Thomas remained a towering figure in American music into the early 20th century and was a frequent conductor in Philadelphia through 1891. That year, he was the founding musical director of the Chicago Symphony Orchestra, a position he

Theodore Thomas, photograph published in *History of Music and Art in Illinois*, edited by Frances Cheney Bennett, published by Société Universelle Lyrique, 1904.

held until his death in 1905. When The Philadelphia Orchestra was established in 1900, there was a serious attempt by some of the organizers to have Thomas appointed the ensemble's inaugural conductor, but the effort failed. Thomas is remembered in particular for championing the music of Richard Wagner and is largely responsible for the popularity of the German composer's music on American concert programs in the late 19th and early 20th centuries, including at Philadelphia outdoor symphonic concerts.

## Trolley Parks

Philadelphia had an extensive network of privately run trolley services, known as streetcars, in the late 19th century. Prominent local families such as the Elkinses and Wideners made their fortunes in this business. Originally horse-drawn, these trolley lines were electrified in the 1890s, allowing for expansion of their routes to the outer reaches of the city and into the suburbs. To increase business, particularly on the weekends when ridership was low, the companies built amusement parks at the ends of their major routes. These parks proved very popular, enticing many thousands of Philadelphians to ride the trolleys to take in the amusements at the end of the line. Outdoor symphony and band concerts were among the main attractions the parks offered. Willow Grove and Woodside parks were the most prominent, but there were popular amusement parks elsewhere in the city and on its outskirts.

### *Willow Grove Park*

Willow Grove Park, near Philadelphia in eastern Montgomery County, opened in 1896 and was operated by the Philadelphia Rapid Transit Company. Living up to its slogan "Life Is a Lark at Willow Grove Park," the park drew large crowds, due in no

Advertisement for "Nine Days of Gala Music" by John Philip Sousa and His Band at Willow Grove Park in late August/early September 1906. (Historical Society of Pennsylvania)

small part to John Philip Sousa's long tenure there. At the height of his fame, Sousa led a series of outdoor concerts at Willow Grove Park every summer but one from 1901 to 1926. Other popular conductors and bandleaders who performed regularly at Willow Grove Park in the early 20th century include Frederick Innes, Walter Damrosch, and Arthur Pryor, all well-known names in American band and concert music at the time.

*Woodside Park*

Operated by the Fairmount Park Transportation Company, Woodside Park opened in 1897 just outside West Fairmount Park, not far from where the Centennial had taken place 21 years earlier. Concerts were a big attraction at Woodside, and while they would not rival those of Willow Grove in popularity, they would nevertheless prove very consequential in Philadelphia music history. In 1899, Woodside Park engaged Fritz Scheel and the New York Orchestra for a series of concerts in July and August. Scheel was a German-born conductor who had immigrated to America in 1893 and made a name for himself conducting in San Francisco, Chicago, and New York. His expert musicianship and well-received programs at Woodside came to the attention of a group of influential people who were then working to establish a

August 12, 1899, *The Philadelphia Times* ad promoting the attractions at Woodside Park. Fritz Scheel and the New York Orchestra shared the bill with diving horses and a high-wire act. (Retrieved from Newspapers.com)

Torresdale Park

POPULAR PLEASURE GROUNDS FOR THE PEOPLE.

A 15-MILE TROLLEY RIDE FOR 8 CENTS.

WONDERFUL SCENIC RAILWAY

A ride through grottos of ice and rock to the land of the dragon and gnome.

Afternoon and Evening Concerts by the

GERMANIA BAND

Only Park at which Local musicians play.

GRAND DISPLAY OF FIREWORKS EVENING OF

JULY 4th

Beautiful $5000 Soda Fountain and electric lighted Carrousel.

Casino and Restaurant, Bowling Alley, Shooting Gallery and Shuffle Boards.

Take cars on Third and Fifth streets to Frankford, connecting with Bristol Pike line, direct to Park.

ADMISSION FREE!

■ June 28, 1896, advertisement announcing July 4 activities at Torresdale Park, built by the Holmesburg, Tacony, and Frankford Railway Company and located at the far northeastern edge of Philadelphia, in the Torresdale neighborhood. Attractions included afternoon and evening concerts by the Germania Band. (Retrieved from Newspapers.com)

**(facing page, bottom)** ■ Fritz Scheel (*center, holding baton*) and the New York Orchestra at Woodside Park in 1900. Later that year, Scheel was appointed conductor of the newly established Philadelphia Orchestra. (Philadelphia Orchestra Association Digital Library)

permanent professional orchestra in Philadelphia. When The Philadelphia Orchestra was founded in November 1900, Scheel was engaged as its first conductor (not Theodore Thomas, to the chagrin of some of the organizers).

## Fairmount Park Band

Outdoor music was seemingly everywhere in and around Philadelphia in the summer months at the turn of the 20th century. Live performance was still the main form of musical entertainment, as the recording industry was then in its infancy and radio did not come into widespread use until the 1920s. To satisfy public demand and ensure the quality of city-sponsored musical entertainment, in 1899 the Fairmount Park Commission established the Fairmount Park Band. As explained in a February 11, 1899, *Philadelphia Inquirer* article, the commissioners were "dissatisfied with the quality of music secured under the present system . . . , and also tired of being importuned by [City] Councilmen and others in favor of certain musical organizations."[9] Establishing their own band freed the commissioners from such political pressure and allowed them to better manage musical entertainment throughout the park system.

From 1899 to about 1930, the Fairmount Park Band performed seven nights a week in the summer season at various park sites. The commissioners built substantial music pavilions for these concerts at three historic park estates—Strawberry Mansion, Lemon Hill, and Belmont Mansion—along with less elaborate stages and gazebos at other park locations.

## CONCERT

UNDER THE DIRECTION OF THE COMMISSIONERS OF FAIRMOUNT PARK

# GEORGE'S HILL

BY THE

**FAIRMOUNT PARK BAND**

RICHARD SCHMIDT, Bandmaster

**MONDAY, JUNE 17, 1929**

**AT 8 O'CLOCK**

1. March—"Washington Post" .......... *Sousa*
2. Overture—"Zampa" .......... *Herold*
3. Suite—"Americana" .......... *Thurban*
   (1) March—"The Tiger's Tail" (2) Serenade—"When Malindy Sings" (3) Sketch—"The Watermelon Fete"
4. (a) "La Paloma" .......... *Yradier*
   (b) "Ciribiribin" .......... *Pestalozza*
5. "Grand Hungarian Fantasy" .......... *Tobani*
6. Selection—"Il Trovatore" .......... *Verdi*
7. Tenor Solo—Mr. Joe Manion.
   (a) "I'll Tell the World" .......... *Ahlert*
   (b) "Louise" .......... *Whiting*
8. Waltz—"Dreams of Childhood" .......... *Waldteufel*
9. Excerpts—"The Bells of Cornwall" .......... *Planquette*

"Star Spangled Banner"

**Visitors are warned not to scatter, drop or leave any piece of paper, dead flower or other rubbish, except in the waste receptacles, under a penalty of five dollars for each violation of this regulation.**

## CONCERT

UNDER THE DIRECTION OF THE COMMISSIONERS OF FAIRMOUNT PARK

# STRAWBERRY MANSION

MUSIC PAVILION

BY THE

**FAIRMOUNT PARK BAND**

RICHARD SCHMIDT, Bandmaster

**TUESDAY, JUNE 18, 1929**

**AT 8 O'CLOCK**

1. March—"Semper Fidelis" .......... *Sousa*
2. Overture—"The Consecration" .......... *Keler-Bela*
3. Motives from "Les Huguenots" .......... *Meyerbeer*
4. Cornet Solo—"Fantasy Metropole" .......... *Hochs*
   Mr. Sante Martorano
5. Ballet Suite—"Coppelia" .......... *Delibes*
   (a) "Fanfare et Marche de la Cloche" (b) "March des Guerrieres" (c) "Czardas Hongroise"
6. Fantasy—"Gems of Stephen Foster" .......... *Tobani*
7. Tenor Solo—Mr. Joe Manion.
   (a) "I'll Tell the World" .......... *Ahlert*
   (b) "Louise" .......... *Whiting*
8. "Waltz—"Vienna Beauties" .......... *Ziehrer*
9. Selection—"The Grand Mogul" .......... *Luders*

"Star Spangled Banner"

**Visitors are warned not to scatter, drop or leave any piece of paper, dead flower or other rubbish, except in the waste receptacles, under a penalty of five dollars for each violation of this regulation.**

Programs of Fairmount Park Band concerts at George's Hill and Strawberry Mansion on June 17 and June 18, 1929, respectively. George's Hill (the current site of the Mann Center) had a gazebo for band concerts, while Strawberry Mansion had a large music pavilion. The Fairmount Park Band performed seven nights a week at various park locations during the summer months in the early 20th century. (Both images: Records of Fairmount Park Commission, City of Philadelphia, Department of Records, City Archives)

■ Photograph in the August 26, 1906, *Philadelphia Public Ledger* of the new music pavilion at Strawberry Mansion, "Fairmount's Most Popular Resort." (Philadelphia Parks and Recreation Archive)

■ 1913 view of the Lemon Hill music pavilion, noting that the Fairmount Park Band performed there Thursday evenings, June through August. (Philadelphia Parks and Recreation Archive)

## Fairmount Park Symphony Orchestra

In 1922, the city rebuilt the Lemon Hill music pavilion and allocated funding for a new Fairmount Park Symphony Orchestra to give a series of free orchestral concerts there. Separate from the wind instrument–based Fairmount Park Band, the new 50-member symphonic ensemble was composed primarily of Philadelphia Orchestra musicians and was intended to present more "serious" music—that is, orchestral works of the great European masters. Announcements for the new series specified that "music of the finest type only will be rendered." However, *The Philadelphia Inquirer* diplomatically noted that, "while the men [i.e., orchestra musicians] are of the highest musical type, it does not mean that nothing but the so-called classical compositions will be given. There will be a profusion of numbers of the lighter variety, such as operatic selections, overtures, and miscellaneous pieces, and an effort will be made to suit every taste and at the same time develop a desirable discrimination in music."[10]

The Fairmount Park Symphony Orchestra debuted on July 17, 1922, and performed every weekday night and Sunday afternoon for seven weeks. Among the conductors who led the new ensemble in its first season was Thaddeus Rich, then concertmaster of The Philadelphia Orchestra. The concerts were a great success, at times drawing audiences of 20,000. Some of the concerts were broadcast on local radio.[11]

The appeal to popular tastes notwithstanding, the program for the final concert of the season on September 9, an all-request concert determined by audience ballot, consisted almost entirely of "serious" symphonic works by Richard Wagner, Franz Liszt, Hector Berlioz, Pyotr Ilyich Tchaikovsky, Ludwig van Beethoven, Felix Mendelssohn, and Jean Sibelius. The one popular concession was Johann Strauss's perennial favorite, "On the Beautiful Blue Danube" waltz. In a headline previewing the concert, *The Philadelphia Inquirer* noted the "High Taste of Philadelphians Expressed in Park Concert."[12]

The summer concerts by the Fairmount Park Symphony Orchestra at Lemon Hill lasted only through 1925. The following year, most of the musicians were engaged in events for the Sesquicentennial, the large-scale celebration of the nation's 150th anniversary that was held in South Philadelphia. Neither the Fairmount Park Symphony Orchestra nor the orchestral series at Lemon Hill was revived thereafter, but the Orchestra's three-year run at Lemon Hill gave Philadelphians a taste of nightly concerts of high-quality symphonic music in a natural setting. The popularity of the series was often referenced when serious efforts began in 1930 to build a permanent outdoor venue for The Philadelphia Orchestra. Fond memories of the idyllic musical experience at Lemon Hill aside, modern life did sometimes intrude, as one regular attendee noted in a letter to the editor of the *Public Ledger* in 1930: "We

■ Photograph of the September 9, 1922, concert of the Fairmount Park Symphony Orchestra at Lemon Hill, the final concert of that year's summer series, published in *The Philadelphia Inquirer*, September 13, 1922. (From *The Philadelphia Inquirer*. © 1922 Philadelphia Inquirer, LLC. All rights reserved. Used under license. Image from Philadelphia Parks and Recreation Archive)

had good music at Lemon Hill, but the horrible screeching of the railroad whistles was tremendous."[13]

## Key Musical Institutions

As Philadelphians enjoyed outdoor summer concerts in a variety of settings in the late 19th and early 20th centuries, four musical institutions were founded that, each in its own way, would play a significant role in establishing the city's first major public outdoor music venue in 1930. Two of the organizations, The Philadelphia Orchestra and Local No. 77 of the AFM, would evolve into permanent, influential institutions; the other two, the Sesquicentennial Music Committee and the Philadelphia Bureau of Music, were short-lived but important in making the new venue a reality.

### *Local No. 77, American Federation of Musicians*

An industrial powerhouse since the early 19th century, Philadelphia was a key center in the birth and development of the labor union movement in the United States. Growing out of this movement, the Philadelphia Music Society was established in the 1860s as a local musicians' protective association. In 1896, the society was chartered as Local No. 77 of the American Federation of Musicians, one of the 26 original union locals nationwide that united in 1896 to form the AFM. Although Local No. 77 members identified themselves more as "artists" than as the "laborers," they shared concerns with factory workers and manual laborers in matters of compensation, job security, and working conditions. Philadelphia Orchestra musicians were members of Local No. 77, and the union had a vested interest in supporting the establishment of an outdoor concert venue that would provide employment opportunities for its members in the off-season summer months.

### *The Philadelphia Orchestra*

Philadelphia was relatively late in establishing a permanent professional symphony orchestra, as compared with other major U.S. cities. Within 20 years of its founding in 1900, however, The Philadelphia Orchestra was acknowledged as one of the world's great symphonic ensembles. Fritz Scheel led the Orchestra in its early years and brought it growing acclaim, but "worn to a nervous wreck by ceaseless work," he collapsed prior to a concert in February 1907 and died several weeks later.[14] His replacement, Carl Pohlig, a German Bohemian conductor, had an undistinguished

Leopold Stokowski poses on the Academy of Music stage with The Philadelphia Orchestra and assembled choirs for the Orchestra's March 1916 U.S. premiere of Gustav Mahler's Symphony No. 8, the "Symphony of a Thousand." The event brought Stokowski and the Orchestra worldwide acclaim. (Philadelphia Orchestra Association Digital Library)

five-year tenure and was replaced in 1912 by the charismatic visionary Leopold Stokowski. Stokowski was born in England and came to the United States in 1905. His appointment in 1912 as the conductor of The Philadelphia Orchestra was the beginning of an extraordinary 29-year tenure marked by artistic excellence, adventurous programming, and technological innovation that brought the Orchestra international notoriety.

The incentive to secure employment for Orchestra musicians during the summer off-season, along with a desire to broaden the Orchestra's audience beyond those privileged enough to attend concerts in its regular-season home in the Academy of Music, led the Orchestra's governing body, The Philadelphia Orchestra Association, together with the Orchestra musicians, to actively support the initiative to establish an outdoor summer home for the ensemble. The Orchestra's Women's Committees, a highly organized group that did much to support the Orchestra overall, were particularly effective in raising money and public awareness for the summer concerts. Stokowski was a major supporter of the effort as well, going as far as to offer suggestions on the design of the facility, including the lighting. He had long been interested in the visual as well as the aural aspects of the concert experience and suggested a specific lighting system for the venue, which was ultimately adopted.

### *Sesquicentennial Music Committee*

Fifty years after the 1876 Centennial, Philadelphia hosted the Sesquicentennial International Exposition, the official celebration of the nation's 150th anniversary. Unlike the Centennial, the 1926 Sesquicentennial was based in South Philadelphia, not in Fairmount Park or, as many had advocated, along the Benjamin Franklin Parkway, the recently completed downtown cultural thoroughfare. The Sesquicentennial was pretty much a failure, a victim of poor planning and bad weather, as well as the city's notoriously corrupt politics at the time. While it did feature a wide range of concerts and musical activities, they mostly took place indoors in a large purpose-built auditorium on the festival grounds. There were a few major outdoor musical events held in the new 102,000-seat Municipal Stadium, later renamed John F. Kennedy (JFK) Stadium, also built specifically for the exposition, but overall, the Sesquicentennial did not fuel Philadelphia's appetite for outdoor concerts in natural settings as had musical events of the Centennial, the concerts at Lemon Hill, or other summer musical programs throughout the region.

However, the Sesquicentennial was important in that its Music Committee, composed of leading figures in Philadelphia's musical and civic life in the mid-1920s, brought together the core group of individuals who would be the prime movers a few years later in establishing a permanent outdoor music venue for the city. The working relationships forged among the movers and shakers on the Sesquicentennial Music Committee would prove pivotal in that later endeavor.

*Philadelphia Bureau of Music*

The final institution that proved essential in securing a major outdoor concert venue was the Philadelphia Bureau of Music, created by Mayor Harry A. Mackey in late 1928, the first such municipal music bureau in the nation. (No doubt the mayor's decision to establish the bureau was influenced by his wife, Ida Boner Mackey, a music teacher and leader of local music clubs.) The creation of the Bureau of Music represented a milestone in terms of the municipal government's support for music and was part of a long tradition in Philadelphia of musical organizations whose missions were to elevate public taste and bring "fine" music to wider audiences. From the Musical Fund Society of Philadelphia, established in 1820 with the dual purpose of supporting older musicians in need and improving the quality of music in the city, to the dozens of local musical societies, clubs, and associations active throughout the 19th and early 20th centuries, Philadelphia was home to many institutions focused on musical edification and dissemination.*

The Philadelphia Bureau of Music was led by two women who were veterans of these musical institutions. Clara Barnes Abbott, director of the bureau, was a prominent figure in Philadelphia music circles who had been a leading member of the Sesquicentennial Music Committee as well as president of the Matinee Musical Club and the Philadelphia Music League. Her annual salary as director of the Bureau of Music was $5,000.[15] Serving as assistant director of the bureau was Helen Pulaski Innes, whose previous experience included serving as manager of the New York Symphony Orchestra, assistant supervisor of music for Philadelphia public schools, and Philadelphia's first female radio program director in the early 1920s, when live music was a major part of radio programming.

Under the direction of these experienced women, and operating out of offices in City Hall Annex, the bureau sponsored a variety of activities to promote music in Philadelphia, including producing concerts and festivals, offering music education programs, sponsoring municipal bands and orchestras, distributing sheet music and radios around the city, and providing music on the go by means of a "Municipal Music Car" equipped with speakers and records to play. Along with this full slate of activities, in early 1930 the bureau became the primary promoter of establishing an outdoor summer home for The Philadelphia Orchestra.

Prior to the bureau's formation, Abbott, at Mayor Mackey's request, had toured other cities to observe their outdoor concert facilities. Informed by her findings, as well as by data from a survey of Philadelphia music and musicians the bureau conducted in its first year, the bureau issued a report in 1929 that, among other things, noted:

---

* While most of these organizations have long since gone out of existence, the Musical Fund Society is still active, the oldest continuing musical organization in the United States.

> An impartial study of the facts proves the paramount need of more and better summer music. A national survey of the summer-time music, given in the most representative cities of the country, reveals the fact that the most acceptable offering a metropolitan and cosmopolitan city like Philadelphia can present to its citizens is a series of high-class concerts at popular prices by our own Philadelphia Orchestra. To make these series of summer concerts entirely successful, there should be a bowl, a stadium, or amphitheatre erected in one of Fairmount Park's natural ravines.[16]

Highlighting the need for "more and better" music puts the Bureau of Music squarely in the tradition of the Musical Fund Society and other local institutions that had long been pursuing a similar agenda. But the approach was more egalitarian now; Abbott and her colleagues spoke of the need to "democratize" music and bring it to the "masses." Their aim was to be inclusive in providing "ordinary" citizens, as opposed to those who could afford Philadelphia Orchestra concerts at the Academy of Music, opportunities to hear good music. And it was understood that "better" music meant the works of the European masters (or Americans who composed in that tradition); there were no plans for jazz or popular music at the new venue Abbott was promoting. The aim was the same as that which *The Philadelphia Inquirer* had espoused eight years earlier in announcing the Fairmount Park Symphony Orchestra concerts at Lemon Hill: to "develop a desirable discrimination in music."

When serious efforts began in early 1930 to build a summer home for The Philadelphia Orchestra, the Bureau of Music took the early lead, serving as the primary organizing agency until the nonprofit Philadelphia Summer Concerts Music Association was established in April of that year to assume official sponsorship of the initiative. Thereafter, the bureau coordinated publicity and ticket sales.

The Bureau of Music lasted only through 1931. It was abolished when a new mayoral administration assumed office in early 1932, just as the effects of the Great Depression on the city's finances were becoming particularly acute. During

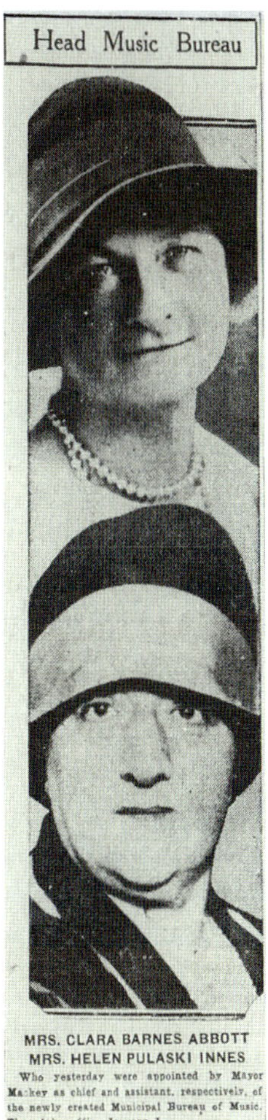
Head Music Bureau

MRS. CLARA BARNES ABBOTT
MRS. HELEN PULASKI INNES
Who yesterday were appointed by Mayor Mackey as chief and assistant, respectively, of the newly created Municipal Bureau of Music. They take office January 1.

■ Notice in the December 29, 1928, *Philadelphia Inquirer* of the appointments of Clara Barnes Abbott (*top*) and Helen Pulaski Innes (*bottom*) as director and assistant director, respectively, of the new Philadelphia Bureau of Music. (From *The Philadelphia Inquirer*. © 1928 Philadelphia Inquirer, LLC. All rights reserved. Used under license. Retrieved from Newspapers.com)

▪ Photograph of the Bureau of Music's Municipal Music Car parked at City Hall, published in *Philadelphia: Historic in the Past, Inviting in the Present, Superb in the Future* (ca. 1930). (Image from collections of Philadelphia Museum of Art)

its brief, highly active existence, the bureau played a critical role in promoting music throughout the city and building a venue to serve as a summer home for The Philadelphia Orchestra.

## Racial Realities

Not surprisingly for the era, the foregoing institutions were all exclusively White; no people of color were included in the initiative to build a summer home for The Philadelphia Orchestra. Despite a history extending back to the early 19th century as an important center of African American arts and culture, Philadelphia was still very much a racially divided, highly segregated city in the early 20th century. Philadelphia's Black population stood at 220,000 in 1930, a little more than 11 percent of the total population, but the leadership and memberships of the city's major civic institutions rarely, if ever, included African Americans or other people of color. Efforts toward diversity and inclusion that characterized much of Philadelphia's civic life later in the 20th century had not really taken hold early in the century.

A prime example are the city's music unions in the 1930s. The powerful White musicians' union, Local No. 77, would not admit African Americans, which led the city's Black musicians to form their own union, Local No. 274, in 1935. (Both locals were affiliates of the national AFM.) Thereafter, Local No. 77 controlled The Philadelphia Orchestra and the city's high-end theaters, hotels, and cafes, while Local No. 274 controlled theaters, dance halls, and clubs that catered to Black audiences. Like the city itself, Black and White musicians in Philadelphia operated largely in separate, segregated worlds in the early 20th century.

## Great Depression and the Temple of Music

The timing of The Philadelphia Orchestra's summer home initiative was indeed fortuitous. Had the project started a year or two later, economic conditions would likely have made it impossible to accomplish. Major planning for the new venue got underway a few months after the stock market crash of October 1929 that marked the start of the Great Depression, but the worst of the Depression was still several years off. The venue was completed in July 1930, a few years before the Depression's most severe effects would set in.

By contrast, the timing for another, much more ambitious plan for a new regular-season home for The Philadelphia Orchestra in the early 1930s was disastrous. By the late 1920s, many (but by no means all) of those in leadership positions with the Orchestra, including Leopold Stokowski, had begun to view the ensemble's home, the venerable Academy of Music, then more than 70 years old, as an outmoded facility for such a world-class institution. Planning began in 1929 for a new home in a massive, state-of-the-art "Temple of Music" to be built on the Benjamin Franklin Parkway, the recently completed grand boulevard in downtown Philadelphia that was emerging as the city's main cultural thoroughfare.*

In 1930, Cyrus Curtis, founder of the Philadelphia-based Curtis Publishing Company (whose daughter, Mary Louise Curtis Bok, had established the city's renowned Curtis Institute of Music in 1924), paid $2 million for a lot at 19th Street and the Parkway on Logan Circle to serve as the site for the new building. A new non-profit organization, the Philadelphia Arts Association, was formed to raise funds to build and manage the facility, which was to house multiple concert halls and theaters and serve as home to several local performing arts organizations, The Philadelphia Orchestra being the most prominent. In early 1931 a New York City architectural firm was hired to design the building. The firm's renderings show a bold, modern design, in sharp contrast to the neoclassical and beaux arts architectural styles of the buildings that had recently been completed or were under construction on the

* One person adamantly opposed to abandoning the Academy of Music was longtime Philadelphia Orchestra Association Board member and prominent preservationist Frances Anne Wister, who publicly rebuked Stokowski for advocating the move. A traditionalist, Wister is reported to have commented that perhaps Stokowski thought his modern music would sound better in a modern building. "Stokowski 'Out of Order' in Music Temple Promise, Miss Wister Tells Women," *Philadelphia Record*, May 1, 1931.

1932 artist's rendering of the proposed "Temple of Music" at Logan Circle on the Benjamin Franklin Parkway at 19th Street, designed to serve as a new home for The Philadelphia Orchestra and other performing arts organizations. The massive multiuse building was never built due to financial difficulties of the Great Depression. (Philadelphia Arts Association Records, The Athenaeum of Philadelphia)

Parkway. It would have been a landmark building in Philadelphia's arts and culture landscape.[17]

By the time architectural plans were completed in 1932, however, the Great Depression was reaching its height, and the estimated $5 million–$6 million it would take to build the enormous facility made the project untenable. The death in 1933 of Cyrus Curtis, one of the initiative's chief benefactors, was another blow to the project. By the mid-1930s, the whole enterprise had been abandoned. While The Philadelphia Orchestra occupied its new summer home in 1930, it would not get a new regular-season home until 2001.

# II. Robin Hood Dell

# 2.

# 1930

## *Summer Concerts Under the Stars*

The Philadelphia Bureau of Music's call to action in 1929 to build a summer home in Fairmount Park for The Philadelphia Orchestra was part of a nationwide movement in the early 20th century that saw high-profile outdoor orchestra venues constructed in a number of major U.S. cities. The two most frequently mentioned as models for Philadelphia were Lewisohn Stadium in New York City, which opened in 1915 and became the summer home of the New York Philharmonic in 1922, and the Hollywood Bowl, which opened in Los Angeles in 1922 and hosted various incarnations of the Hollywood Bowl Orchestra in its early years. Chicago and Boston, whose orchestras rivaled Philadelphia's in stature, also had popular summer venues. Ravinia Park in Chicago, opened in 1904, began hosting orchestra concerts in 1905 and from 1919 through 1931 was known as the "summer opera capital of the world." Ravinia became the summer home of the Chicago Symphony Orchestra in 1936. A new band shell in Boston's Charles River Esplanade hosted its first concert on July 4, 1929, featuring Arthur Fiedler and the Boston Pops, and was later replaced with a more substantial pavilion for the Boston Symphony Orchestra. Surely, local civic and music leaders asserted, Philadelphia, then the nation's third-largest city and home to one of the world's great symphony orchestras, deserved a first-class summer concert venue of its own.

Clara Barnes Abbott took the early lead in pursuing the initiative. Not long after assuming her position as director of the new Philadelphia Bureau of Music, Abbott met with Arthur Judson, manager of The Philadelphia Orchestra, at his office in the Packard Building at 15th and Chestnut streets. Arguably the most pow-

■ The two key initiators of the idea for a Philadelphia Orchestra summer concert series and venue. *Left*: Arthur Judson in a 1946 advertisement for Lord Calvert whiskey; *right*: Clara Barnes Abbott, director of the Philadelphia Bureau of Music. (Left image: Lord Calvert—Valentino Sarra, 1946, Wikimedia Commons; Right image: *The Philadelphia Record*, March 17, 1930, Robin Hood Dell scrapbook, Philadelphia Orchestra Association records, Kislak Center for Special Collections, Rare Books, and Manuscripts, University of Pennsylvania)

erful man in American classical music, Judson wielded enormous influence in the concert world. In an arrangement that would be unthinkable in modern times, he was simultaneously manager of two of America's greatest symphony orchestras, The Philadelphia Orchestra and the New York Philharmonic; founder and president of Columbia Concerts Corporation, the nation's premier concert artist management agency, which booked conductors and soloists with major orchestras throughout the country, including the two he managed; and cofounder of what became the CBS radio network. (Judson's partner in the latter two ventures was William S. Paley, who was then based in Philadelphia and at the beginning of a career that would eventually make him the longtime, powerful head of the CBS media empire.) Notably, Judson had instituted and managed the New York Philharmonic's outdoor concerts at Lewisohn Stadium in the early 1920s.

Abbott sounded Judson out on the idea of an outdoor summer concert series for The Philadelphia Orchestra. Judson was enthusiastic, telling Abbott that he had long dreamed of instituting such a series, but conditions had not been favorable. Now, with a city agency actively supporting the project, he thought it could be done. Together, Abbott and Judson worked out a strategy for what would be an ambitious, multifaceted undertaking. First, Judson discussed the idea with members of the Orchestra, who were very supportive. The musicians offered to approach their union, Local No. 77, with a proposal that, to make the series feasible financially, the union agree to a flexible payment arrangement for the musicians who would be performing in the concerts. As detailed later, the union agreed to the proposal in early 1930.[1]

With this critical initial step accomplished, Abbott and Judson moved to form a new nonprofit organization, the Philadelphia Summer Concerts Association, to sponsor the concert series. The plan was for the association to serve as fiscal sponsor and managing agency for the initiative, the city to supply the site and architectural services, the Bureau of Music to coordinate publicity and ticket sales, and Judson and his Orchestra staff to manage the artistic programming for the concerts.

## Common Goal, Different Agendas

The various institutions that came together in early 1930 to support the summer concerts initiative all had a common goal, but each had a different agenda. The city, through its Bureau of Music, wanted to increase access to and promote appreciation of fine music while enhancing Philadelphia's reputation as a world-class musical center. The Philadelphia Orchestra Association Board and the Orchestra musicians wanted to secure employment for the musicians during the summer off-season, expand the Orchestra's audience base, and maintain the ensemble's high artistic standards year-round. The Fairmount Park Commission wanted to encourage public use and enjoyment of the park.

Local No. 77's agenda was quite different. As previously noted, to make the summer concert series possible financially, Orchestra members proposed to Local No. 77 an unusual arrangement in which the musicians would accept a percentage of the ticket sales as compensation rather than receiving a regular salary for the summer season. This was a risky proposition, but one that the musicians and others spearheading the initiative believed was the only way to make the concerts work from a financial standpoint. None of the sponsoring organizations was in a position to guarantee a regular summer salary for the musicians.

At the February 4, 1930, membership meeting of Local No. 77, Paul P. Lotz, trombonist and personnel manager for The Philadelphia Orchestra, proposed a resolution for the union's adoption that outlined the special compensation arrangement but gave an unusual rationale for it. The resolution, which was approved at the meeting, read:

> WHEREAS The American Federation of Musicians is at this time conducting an extensive campaign to make the public realize the harm mechanical music is doing to music as an art and as a profession, and

> WHEREAS We believe that the most effective way to get the public to realize the value of real (humanized) music is to give the public an opportunity of hearing the very best orchestral music;
>
> We, the members of the Philadelphia Orchestra respectfully ask permission to organize a Symphony Orchestra of 110 men composed of members of Local 77, to find employment in giving a series of concerts in July and August in this city on the basis of a cooperative plan, each member of the orchestra to receive a pro rata compensation from the net proceeds, it being understood that this engagement does not interfere with any other summer engagement in the public parks and public squares for which members of Local 77 are engaged.[2]

Thus, the union's primary motivation for supporting the flexible payment arrangement was to increase live performance opportunities for its members to counter the negative impact the union believed recorded music was having on live performance. The technology for recording music was developed in the late 19th century, and by the turn of the 20th century, listening to recorded music was gaining a foothold as a form of entertainment. Live music still predominated in the 1920s, but recorded music was emerging as serious competition. The issue hit very close to home for Local No. 77 in that Victor Records, the nation's largest record company, was established in Philadelphia in 1901 and in 1907 moved across the Delaware River to Camden, New Jersey, where it grew into an enormous enterprise. In addition to manufacturing and selling millions of its iconic Victrola record players annually, Victor's record label and recording studios were home to some of the most popular recording artists and ensembles of the early 20th century, including The Philadelphia Orchestra.

The original acoustical recording process that Victor and other early record companies employed did not offer very good sound quality, but the advent of the electrical recording process in the mid-1920s improved audio fidelity dramatically. Leopold Stokowski and The Philadelphia Orchestra made the world's first electrical recordings of a symphony orchestra for Victor Records in Camden in 1925. The new technology made listening to recorded music much more enjoyable, and as it became an increasingly popular pastime, the American Federation of Musicians (AFM) initiated a nationwide campaign to promote live musical performance to counter the threat recorded, or "canned," music posed to the livelihood of its members.

Of more immediate concern to Local No. 77 was the serious impact recorded music was having on employment opportunities for musicians in theater orchestras in Philadelphia. In the silent movie era of the early to mid-1920s, major theaters employed full orchestras that accompanied the feature films and provided musical entertainment before and after the showings. Local No. 77 had contracts with 133 Philadelphia-area theaters that employed 486 musicians in their orchestras in the

Cartoon published in the February 1930 edition of *International Musician*, the journal of the American Federation of Musicians, as part of the American Federation of Musicians' national campaign against recorded or "canned" music. (Courtesy of American Federation of Musicians)

1920s. When sound movies with recorded soundtracks—"talkies"—began replacing silent films in the late 1920s, theater owners sought to eliminate or reduce the size of their in-house orchestras. A labor struggle ensued between Local No. 77 and the city's major theater owners, with union strikes against the theaters in 1930 and 1931. The union won some concessions in the settlement of these strikes, but eventually the owners prevailed, and live orchestras were downsized or eliminated entirely in most area theaters over the course of the 1930s.[3]

It was against this backdrop of diminishing job prospects and threats to local musicians' livelihoods that Philadelphia Orchestra members proposed, and Local No. 77 endorsed, a flexible payment arrangement for Orchestra musicians who would be performing in the planned summer concert series.

## Orchestra for All

With the key players and organizations, whatever their motivations, on board in early 1930, events moved swiftly. The *Public Ledger*, Philadelphia's most widely circulated newspaper during this period, had a regular column titled "Now My Idea Is This! Daily Interviews with Interesting People on Subjects They Know Best." The guest columnist on March 15, 1930, was Clara Barnes Abbott, who began her article by stating, "The Philadelphia Orchestra is about to go democratic and for the first time in history it will belong to all the people in the city and not the few who are able to afford Academy of Music prices." She went on to outline plans for the very reasonably priced summer concert series—22 cents per ticket if purchased as part of a season subscription—and the need for the public to support the concerts and take advantage of the unique opportunity at hand:

> The Orchestra men have placed their faith in the workers of Philadelphia and the citizens dare not fail them. . . . Perhaps never again will the Orchestra men volunteer [to play for a percentage of ticket proceeds]. Perhaps never again will the Musicians Union make such a concession.
>
> We are offering the citizens of Philadelphia an evening with the world's greatest entertainers at the astoundingly low price of twenty-two cents, an opportunity to leave the noise and heat of the city this summer and relax under the stars with soothing symphonies.
>
> Two hours of enjoyment for about the price of an ice cream sundae!

Three days after Abbott's newspaper column, The Philadelphia Orchestra Association's Board, at its March 18, 1930, meeting, approved Arthur Judson's recommendation for the loan of "such music, instruments, trunks, etc., as might be necessary to assist the men [i.e., Orchestra musicians] to carry out their summer concert plan."[4] Officially, the Orchestra Association was not involved in the summer concerts initiative—it was a project of the Orchestra musicians themselves, along with the Philadelphia Bureau of Music and others—but several members of the association's Board were deeply involved in the endeavor, Judson and other association employees worked on it, and the association endorsed it.

## Philadelphia Summer Concerts Association

The Philadelphia Bureau of Music was the primary sponsoring organization of the project initially, but that changed with the establishment of the nonprofit Philadelphia Summer Concerts Association, which filed incorporation papers on April 2, 1930; held its first meeting on April 10; and received its charter of incorporation on June 16.[5] As proposed by Judson, Abbott, and their colleagues, the association's Board of Directors would be composed of three representatives from each of the following four groups: The Philadelphia Orchestra Association, Philadelphia Orchestra musicians, the City of Philadelphia, and a committee of "outstanding citizens." Local No. 77's leadership insisted that three members of its executive committee also serve on the Board, but Judson and the three Orchestra musicians, who were Local No. 77 members themselves, countered that this would give the union six seats on the Board, putting the new organization in an unfavorable light with prospective wealthy donors, many of whom were strongly anti-union. Local No. 77's leaders were not swayed by this argument and continued to demand executive committee representation on the Board, but Judson and the others held firm, and the union eventually relented.[6]

The Board of the Summer Concerts Association was a formidable team. Its president was Dr. Herbert J. Tily, civic leader, musician, and president of the Strawbridge & Clothier department store, one of Philadelphia's largest retail establishments. Tily was a member of The Philadelphia Orchestra Association's Board, had chaired the Music Committee for the 1926 Sesquicentennial, and was a director and active patron of several Philadelphia music organizations, in some cases serving as resident conductor and composer. The other officers were Paul Lotz, serving as vice president; Judson, serving as secretary; and Henry G. Brengle, president of Fidelity-Philadelphia Trust and board member of several major financial institutions, serving as treasurer.

Representing the City of Philadelphia on the association's Board were Mayor Harry A. Mackey, City Council President Edwin R. Cox, and Bureau of Music Director Clara Barnes Abbott. Representing Philadelphia Orchestra musicians, in addition to Lotz, were violinist and violist Alfred Lorenz, a member of the Orchestra since 1901, and violist William S. Greenberg. Lorenz would serve as concertmaster for the inaugural summer season.

The Philadelphia Orchestra Association representatives were an especially influential group. Alexander Van Rensselaer, Frances Anne Wister, and William Curtis Bok were all from wealthy Philadelphia families and were prominent in local cultural circles and music institutions. Van Rensselaer, a philanthropist and sportsman, as well as the son-in-law of Drexel University's founder, Anthony Joseph Drexel, was the founding and longtime president of The Philadelphia Orchestra Association. Wister had leading roles in several area musical organizations, including serving as the founding member and longtime president of the Women's Committees for The Philadelphia Orchestra, and she had written the first history of the ensemble, *Twenty-Five Years of the Philadelphia Orchestra, 1900–1925*. She was also a pioneer in the historic preservation movement in Philadelphia. Bok, who went by "Curtis," was the grandson of Cyrus Curtis, founder of the Curtis Publishing Company, and the son of Mary Louise Curtis Bok, who founded the Curtis Institute, and her husband, Edward Bok, also a major philanthropist, Board member, and chief benefactor of The

In addition to Clara Barnes Abbott and Arthur Judson, key members of the Philadelphia Summer Concerts Association Board included association president Dr. Herbert J. Tily (*top*) and members Frances Anne Wister (*middle*) and William Curtis Bok (*bottom*). All were also board members of The Philadelphia Orchestra Association. (Top and bottom photographs: *The Philadelphia Bulletin* photograph collection, Special Collections Research Center, Temple University Libraries; Center photograph: Philadelphia Orchestra Association Digital Library)

Philadelphia Orchestra. Curtis Bok, who was serving at the time as a Philadelphia assistant district attorney, was active in city politics, civic life, and legal affairs. (He later became a Pennsylvania Supreme Court justice.) He had served on the Sesquicentennial Music Committee and, like his parents, was on the boards of the Curtis Institute and Philadelphia Orchestra Association (where he was one of Leopold Stokowski's staunchest supporters).

Rounding out the Summer Concerts Association Board were "outstanding citizen" representatives George W. Elliott, former director of public safety for the City of Philadelphia and general secretary of the Chamber of Commerce of Greater Philadelphia; Morris Wolf, a prominent lawyer, founder of one of the city's most prestigious law firms, and leading member of numerous civic boards and associations; and Carrie E. (Mrs. Benjamin) Maschal, president of the Matinee Musical Club of Philadelphia.

At its April 10 founding meeting, the powerhouse Board established the organizational framework for the Summer Concerts Association and the responsibilities of the various parties. Judson and Louis A. Mattson, manager and associate manager, respectively, of The Philadelphia Orchestra, offered their artistic management services for the summer concerts, which were over and above their regular Orchestra duties, gratis. Judson also promised to secure the services of visiting conductors and soloists, many of whom he managed, on a volunteer basis. Alexander Smallens, who had recently been appointed assistant conductor of the Orchestra, agreed to serve as chief conductor for the summer series and to work under the same flexible compensation arrangement as the Orchestra musicians. (Stokowski, the Orchestra's music director, did not spend his summers in Philadelphia and would not be available to conduct the concerts.) As previously noted, the Bureau of Music would coordinate publicity and ticket sales for the concert series, while the city would supply the site and architectural services for the facility.

Judson, who chaired the initial meeting and did much of the organization's early foundational work, informed the Board at a subsequent meeting that he would be in Europe for about six weeks in April and May with the New York Philharmonic, which was about to embark on its first overseas tour. He would use the opportunity to evaluate outdoor concert venues abroad, but others would have to take the lead in his absence. All would have to move quickly if the concerts were to begin in early July, as intended.[7]

## Robin Hood Dell

With support of key institutions secured, a new sponsoring organization established, and a strong leadership team in place in early April 1930, the next steps were to select a site for the concert venue and raise the money to build and operate it. While the original plan was for a site somewhere in Fairmount Park, the Summer Concerts Association entertained other suggestions, including a site in Wister Woods near Germantown (proposed by Frances Wister) and a site adjacent to the Woodlands Estate in West Philadelphia. Neither was deemed suitable. An intriguing offer came from real estate mogul John McClatchy, who was then developing the area around the busy 69th Street Terminal of the Market-Frankford Elevated transit line in Upper Darby, bordering West Philadelphia. McClatchy, who had recently built the Tower Theater in Upper Darby, not only offered a site near 69th Street, but committed to building and equipping a band shell. As Abbott later reported, "This enticing proposition was reluctantly declined for the reason that the site presented too commercial an aspect in a very congested part of the city."[8]

The site the Summer Concerts Association eventually selected, at the suggestion of the city's architect, Walter H. Thomas, was a much more idyllic location, a natural amphitheater known as Robin Hood Valley, situated on the east bank of the Schuylkill River in East Fairmount Park. The valley extended down from Ridge Avenue to the river, between Strawberry Mansion, the 18th-century estate that gave the neighborhood its name, and Laurel Hill Cemetery, the expansive 19th-century burial ground and public garden. As noted previously, the Fairmount Park Commission had built a large music pavilion at Strawberry Mansion in the early 20th century and sponsored regular concerts there. Robin Hood Valley took its name from the Hood family who had acquired the land in the late 17th century and in the 18th century operated the Robin Hood Tavern, which stood at the top of the valley on the Ridge Road (later Ridge Avenue). The *Public Ledger* described it as "one of the coolest spots in the park," one that was easily accessible by both car and trolley.[9]

The April 15, 1930, minutes of the Fairmount Park Commission's Committee on Superintendence and Property note that The Philadelphia Orchestra requested and was granted permission "to erect a shell and seating accommodations in Robin Hood Valley in Fairmount Park, without cost to the commissioners, for the projected Philadelphia Orchestra summer concerts."*[10] The commission's influential vice president, Eli Kirk Price II, having recently facilitated such major civic landscape and building projects as the Benjamin Franklin Parkway and Philadelphia Museum of Art (of which he was then president), lent his support to the initiative and participated in the site selection process. (Price's grandfather, also named Eli Kirk Price, was one of the original Fairmount Park commissioners in 1867, directly responsible for acquisition of thousands of acres of land that constituted the park.)

After finalizing the site, which it renamed Robin Hood Dell, the Summer Concerts Association announced the location at its April 25 meeting, noting that "the Fairmount Park Commission, the Philadelphia Bureau of Music and the city are cooperating in making the site available and in preparing plans for equipment, but none of these groups is in a position to provide the funds needed." The association

The Picturesque Setting of the Amphitheatre in Robin Hood Dell is indicated in this drawing made in the city architect's office. The dell slopes gently toward the Schuylkill River, at which end, a short distance from East River drive, the temporary shell will be placed. It will be built at a cost of about $20,000 and will easily seat more than 100 musicians. It will also contain facilities for stage spectacles and pageantry. The dell is large enough to accommodate 25,000 persons, but seats for only 6,000 will be provided this season. These permanent wooden benches, arranged in semi-circular rows, will be installed on an inclined concrete floor. Bids for the construction work are to be asked shortly.

■ Artist's rendering of the proposed Robin Hood Dell concert venue, published in *The Evening Bulletin*, May 15, 1930. (Robin Hood Dell scrapbook, Philadelphia Orchestra Association records, Kislak Center for Special Collections, Rare Books, and Manuscripts, University of Pennsylvania)

* The wording of the minutes is misleading: Members of the Orchestra and Summer Concerts Association requested permission to build the shell. The Philadelphia Orchestra Association did not make the request.

also reiterated that "members of the Philadelphia Orchestra, with the consent and approval of the Philadelphia Orchestra Association and the musicians' union, have volunteered to demand no guaranteed remuneration and have agreed to accept as payment the receipts from the sales of tickets."[11]

With a site selected and agreement by the principal parties on critical aspects of the project, it was time for a high-profile fundraising and ticket sales campaign. However, two other major cultural campaigns were commencing in Philadelphia at that time: a $5 million effort to build a new Franklin Institute building on the Benjamin Franklin Parkway and a $200,000 endowment campaign for the Settlement Music School, the South Philadelphia community music school established in 1908. Summer Concerts Association President Herbert Tily was deeply involved in the Franklin Institute campaign, and Mary Louise Curtis Bok, the music-loving philanthropist who was one of the association's target donors for the Robin Hood Dell project, had recently pledged $25,000 to Settlement's 1930 endowment campaign. (She had made a foundational donation of $150,000 to Settlement in 1917.) Despite the competition, and the worsening national economy as the Great Depression set in, the Philadelphia Summer Concerts Association forged ahead with its fundraising plans.

## Getting Down to Business

On April 30, 1930, *The Philadelphia Inquirer* reported that "more than 100 men and women—leaders in the social and business life of Philadelphia—gathered yesterday at a luncheon in the Bellevue-Stratford [Hotel] to hear plans for the presentation this summer of a series of outdoor concerts in Fairmount Park." The city's movers and shakers heard Mayor Mackey, Tily, and others outline a vision for the concerts, their importance to the city, and the financial support necessary to bring the series to fruition. "We have been a little asleep in Philadelphia in the matter of music for the masses," Tily told the attendees. "The idea is to play for a greater number of different people, for in the Academy of Music [with a seating capacity of about 2,500] the orchestra plays only to a limited number."[12]

As detailed at the luncheon, the cost to build and operate the new facility in its first year was estimated at $81,000, of which $55,000 was needed for construction and equipment. Responding to requests from the various speakers for support, attendees pledged a total of $22,500. The Women's Committees for The Philadelphia Orchestra, led by Wister, pledged $1,000 immediately and committed to raising a total of $10,000; Cyrus Curtis pledged $5,000; and $1,000 pledges came from the Matinee Musical Club, Tily, Morris Wolf, and other prominent figures in Philadelphia business and industry. Mayor Mackey and his wife pledged $500.[13]

On May 11, Clara Barnes Abbott announced that ticket sales to the summer series would begin the following day, noting:

> We are forced to call upon every citizen to help us make this movement a success. . . . Unless we can guarantee a reasonable monetary return the project will be unfair to the members of the orchestra who have been good sports enough to gamble on the response of their new and untried audience. . . . Let everybody enjoy Philadelphia's pride. The Philadelphia Orchestra is recognized as the greatest in the world and it is appalling to realize that only one-half of one percent of our city have the opportunity of hearing this great institution. The successful sale of tickets is imperative.[14]

A few days later, the Bureau of Music sponsored a meeting at the Bellevue-Stratford for the presidents of more than 150 area women's clubs. Women's clubs were a powerful force in America in the early 20th century; there were thousands of such groups throughout the nation, organized around a wide range of interests and causes. In Philadelphia, local clubs banded together in 1922 to establish the Philadelphia Federation of Women's Clubs and Allied Organizations to "unite Women's Clubs and other organized groups of women existing in Philadelphia and adjacent territory for purposes of mutual benefit and to promote their common interests in civic, educational and moral measures which make for individual and community welfare."[15]

The 150 women's club presidents at the meeting, representing some 80,000 women, heard several speakers promote the summer concerts. Mrs. Charles Irving Purnell, president of the Philadelphia Federation of Women's Clubs, asserted, "The concerts . . . , will help Philadelphia culturally, commercially, and civically." Paul Lotz offered unique insights as an Orchestra member, telling the group:

■ Members of the Matinee Musical Club of Philadelphia pose on April 30, 1930. The group was one of the many local women's clubs at this time that supported the Robin Hood Dell initiative. (Free Library of Philadelphia, Print and Picture Collection)

> It is not good for the members of any orchestra to be apart during the summer season. Certain qualities are lost by the orchestra breaking up in May and the members playing with other musical groups during the warm weather. . . . Most of them refuse to take well-paying positions in musical bodies that produce inferior music, such as bands. They consider it degrading, and so financially they are at a loss during the long vacation of the orchestra from May to October. Hence the members of the orchestra are glad to play on a cooperative basis. Even if no money is made . . . [or] they get a very small amount of it, they will give the same standard of music that they give at the high-priced winter concerts.[16]

Other speakers included Abbott and Carrie Maschal of the Matinee Musical Club of Philadelphia and Summer Concerts Association Board. The assembled club presidents pledged their united support for the endeavor.

## Music for the Multitudes

With more than a quarter of the necessary funds pledged by mid-May and a large corps of women's club volunteers at the ready, the next step was a public campaign to sell subscriptions to the summer concert series. On May 18, 1930, Mayor Mackey issued a proclamation designating the week of May 25 "Music for the Multitudes" week, an intensive citywide campaign to sell subscriptions to the concerts. A new Central Committee of the Summer Concerts Association, composed of prominent men and women in Philadelphia music circles, was established to promote the ticket sales and coordinate plans for dozens of women's club members to fan out across the city with the goal of selling 15,000 subscriptions to the proposed series, which would consist of 24 concerts over an eight-week season. The cost was $5 per subscription, which came out to about 21 cents per concert. On May 25, 1930, *The Philadelphia Inquirer* reported:

> Senior and junior clubwomen of the city will co-operate in what has been designated as "Music for the Multitudes" Week, starting tomorrow. The week has been set aside to press the sale of tickets for the summer concerts of the Philadelphia Orchestra, . . . in Robin Hood Dell, Fairmount Park. . . . Every day this week a different event has been planned to enlist every type of woman in the city in the city-wide project.[17]

The week kicked off with young women releasing balloons at City Hall, posing in Robin Hood costumes, and working ticket booths downtown. In the days that followed, club women drove around the city in cars festooned with banners promoting subscription sales for the series. Philadelphia newspapers covered the subscription drive extensively, as expected, but the drive also received national attention, with

■ Women's group volunteers fanned out across the city in late May 1930, promoting subscription sales to the Robin Hood Dell concerts. *Left*: *The Public Ledger*, May 20, 1930; *Above*: *The Evening Bulletin*, May 29, 1930. (Both images: Robin Hood Dell scrapbook, Philadelphia Orchestra Association records, Kislak Center for Special Collections, Rare Books, and Manuscripts, University of Pennsylvania)

*The New York Times*, the national magazine *Musical America*, and other out-of-town publications tracking its progress.

The goal of bringing high-quality symphonic music to the masses was a central theme throughout the campaign. Edith Rhetts, former educational director for the Detroit Symphony, joined the Philadelphia Bureau of Music in May to help coordinate the Robin Hood Dell initiative. As she told *The Evening Bulletin*:

> To me, one of the most thrilling things that has happened to modern civilization is the democratization of music. For the first time, the symphony will play for the people. . . . The winter concerts in the cities are still under sway of the old regime. There are a thousand and one traditions that still bind them to the old order of things. In the last five years, music has taken a step toward democratization in daring to emerge from concerts and auditoriums and walk among the people.[18]

## Women's Committees for The Philadelphia Orchestra

The most effective group by far in fundraising for the summer concerts was the Women's Committees for The Philadelphia Orchestra. Established in 1904 to support the Orchestra during its financially precarious early years, the original Women's Committee was the nation's first such female-managed orchestral support organization. To the surprise of some of the male members of The Philadelphia Orchestra

Association's Board, who doubted whether a group of women could be effective in such a role, the Women's Committee proved very adept at fundraising, helping to sustain the Orchestra through some of its most difficult times.

Founded as a single committee, the group by 1930 had grown to encompass a central committee and several neighborhood committees, collectively under the umbrella of the Women's Committees for The Philadelphia Orchestra. The group's president since 1912 was the indefatigable Frances Anne Wister, who, as noted, was also a member of The Philadelphia Orchestra Association and Summer Concerts Association Boards. The group's vice president was another influential woman in Philadelphia music circles, Adele Gilpin Yarnall, generally referred to by her married name, Mrs. Harold Ellis Yarnall. In addition to being a Philadelphia Orchestra Association Board member, Yarnall was a cofounder (with Arthur Judson) and president of the Philadelphia Chamber Music Association and a partner in Judson's artist management company, Columbia Concerts Corporation. Both Yarnall and Wister were from wealthy "Old Philadelphia" families that had long been supporters of city arts and culture institutions. Their roots in Philadelphia society ran deep, and their close ties to the city's wealthy class and cultural community proved valuable in garnering support for the Robin Hood Dell.

Putting the Women's Committees' 25 years of fundraising experience to work, Wister, Yarnall, and their colleagues eventually brought in more than $19,000, almost double the $10,000 they had originally committed to raising. (Mary Louise Curtis Bok contributed $5,000.) The group's corresponding secretary Elizabeth Hancock Arnett, another formidable figure in local music and charitable circles (she had been a Philadelphia Orchestra Association Board member from 1903 to 1928), personally wrote more than 2,300 letters requesting $2 donations, an effort that raised $2,315.

Miss Frances Anne Wister (*left*) and Mrs. William (Elizabeth Hancock) Arnett (*right*) in 1953. Both played an important role in fundraising for the Robin Hood Dell in 1930. (Adrian Siegel photographs, Kislak Center for Special Collections, Rare Books, and Manuscripts, University of Pennsylvania)

## Mayor Mackey

Philadelphia's Mayor Harry A. Mackey was an especially enthusiastic supporter of the initiative. Having created the Bureau of Music a year and a half earlier, he had a vested interest in the success of its chief endeavor and used the power of his office to promote the summer concerts whenever possible. Mackey hosted three luncheons in spring 1930 with influential Philadelphians to garner support for the concerts. One such luncheon, for some 250 members of city commissions and committees, was held on May 29, 1930, on the eve of Mackey's departure for a European trip. The mayor urged the attendees to support the summer series while lavishing praise on the work of the Bureau of Music in bringing together Philadelphians of all backgrounds:

> The Bureau of Music, in my opinion, is the most effective, the most useful and the greatest of all the city's bureaus. We want to give the people of Philadelphia an unparalleled opportunity to hear the Philadelphia Orchestra in summer. We have a spot in Fairmount Park that seems to have been made by nature for that very purpose. The problem of finances alone is worrying us.

He reassured the attendees, however, that "if the money to build the Robin Hood Dell . . . is not available by the time I return, I will see to it that it is procured."[19]

■ Mayor Harry A. Mackey (*center*) at a Matinee Musical Club of Philadelphia luncheon and concert in January 1928. Third from the right is his wife, Ida Boner Mackey, a music teacher who was active in local music organizations. At the far left is Dr. Herbert J. Tily, who would become president of the Philadelphia Summer Concerts Association in 1930, and at the far right is Carrie E. Maschal, president of the Matinee Musical Club, who would also become a member of the Summer Concerts Association Board. (*The Evening Bulletin* photograph collection, Special Collections Research Center, Temple University Libraries)

## Groundbreaking

The weeklong Music for the Multitudes campaign reached only half of its goal of selling 15,000 subscriptions to the concert series, but enough funds had been pledged and subscriptions sold by the end of May to proceed with the project. Groundbreaking took place on June 2, 1930. Summer Concerts Association President Herbert Tily turned the first ceremonial spade of dirt, observing that "the inauguration of the first summer concerts of the Philadelphia Orchestra marks an innovation in the musical life of our city." Repeating a common project refrain, Tily noted that, "in recent years, music has dared to emerge from the cloister and walk boldly and simply among the people. The greater public has responded amazingly."[20] Other Summer Concerts Association Board members and dignitaries took turns with the shovel, including Judson, who had recently returned from his European tour with the New York Philharmonic.

The next day, Tily and Judson, on behalf of the association, signed a contract with Wark Company, a high-profile local construction firm, for the "Erection & Completion of Music Shell & Bowl in Robin Hood Dell, Strawberry Mansion, Fairmount Park, Philadelphia" at a cost of $54,500.[21] The first concert was announced for

Photograph of June 2, 1930, groundbreaking for the Robin Hood Dell, published in *The Philadelphia Inquirer*, June 3, 1930. *Front row, left to right*: Arthur Judson, Adele (Mrs. Harold Ellis) Gilpin Yarnall, Herbert J. Tily (*holding shovel*), and Clara Barnes Abbott. (From *The Philadelphia Inquirer*. © 1930 Philadelphia Inquirer, LLC. All rights reserved. Used under license. *The Philadelphia Inquirer* photograph collection, Special Collections Research Center, Temple University Libraries)

July 7, a little more than a month away. Such a quick turnaround seems impossible by modern standards, but the association wanted the season to begin in early July, and Wark, highly experienced in much more complex Philadelphia construction projects, from hospitals and factories to downtown high-rises, committed to the deadline and completed the project on time.

## The Dell Rises

The Dell facility was designed by City of Philadelphia Architect Walter H. Thomas, who had recently been appointed to the position by Mayor Mackey. Thomas had done a range of projects in and around the city, specializing particularly in churches. His firm had recently designed the iconic Girard College Chapel, then under construction. As designed by Thomas, the Robin Hood Dell was an oval-shaped band

Aerial view of Robin Hood Dell (*circled at the bottom*) published in *The Philadelphia Record*, June 29, 1930, as the venue was nearing completion. Looking east from above the Schuylkill River (*at lower right*), the image shows trolley and bus routes to the venue, Laurel Hill Cemetery immediately to the left of the Dell, and the Philadelphia skyline in the background. (Robin Hood Dell scrapbook, Philadelphia Orchestra Association records, Kislak Center for Special Collections, Rare Books, and Manuscripts, University of Pennsylvania)

shell made of structural steel with wood facing. The stage would accommodate an orchestra of 110 musicians, with an orchestra pit in front for the ensemble if the stage were needed for opera or dance productions. Rows of wooden benches in the sloped seating area—folding chairs were deemed too noisy—would hold an audience of some 6,000, with room for thousands more in the adjacent (unpaid) lawn areas. One thousand seats in the front, the premium seating area, were to be reserved at $1 each; the remaining 5,000 seats were for season subscribers and single ticket purchasers. Adhering to the goal of keeping prices as affordable as possible, subscribers paid about 21 cents per seat; single ticket buyers, 50 cents.

With the facility nearing completion in late June, the campaign to sell subscriptions to the upcoming season intensified. The Bureau of Music enlisted the help of schools, churches, hotels, department stores, factories, and government agencies to promote the concerts. With the approval of Local No. 77, the bureau also arranged

STADIUM FOR SUMMER CONCERTS BEING BUILT IN PARK

Workmen are assembling the shell and stadium in Robin Hood Dell, Fairmount Park, for the series of con-certs to be given by the Philadelphia Orchestra, starting July 8. The picture shows how the structural steel keleton is gradually taking shape. The stadium will house 6,000 listeners, and the shell will accommodate 110

■ Photograph in the June 28, 1930, *Evening Bulletin* showing progress on the Robin Hood Dell structure. The first concert was only 10 days away at that point. (Robin Hood Dell scrapbook, Philadelphia Orchestra Association records, Kislak Center for Special Collections, Rare Books, and Manuscripts, University of Pennsylvania)

for a series of promotional radio concerts on local stations during the week of June 22. The programs featured performances by Philadelphia Orchestra members and other musicians, along with prominent speakers encouraging listeners to patronize the concerts. Hundreds of free tickets were distributed to schools and deserving music students in the area.

Work was finished in time for a July 8 opening, one day later than originally announced—a remarkable 36 days from groundbreaking to completion.

## Alexander Smallens

As work on the facility and the ticket sales campaign continued, Judson planned the concert programs with Philadelphia Orchestra Assistant Conductor Alexander Smallens, who would serve as Robin Hood Dell's music director and chief conductor in the venue's early years. A Russian native who immigrated to America with his family as an infant, Smallens was a well-established conductor of symphonic music, opera, and ballet in both the United States and Europe when he was appointed music

■ Conductor Alexander Smallens (*left*), who served as music director and chief conductor, and violinist Alfred Lorenz (*right*), who served as concertmaster, for the inaugural Robin Hood Dell season. (Both images: Free Library of Philadelphia, Print and Picture Collection)

director of the Philadelphia Civic Opera Company in 1923. He held the position until 1930, and during that time he began working with Leopold Stokowski and The Philadelphia Orchestra. In May 1929, he was officially appointed the Orchestra's assistant conductor. It was in this capacity that he was tapped to serve as the inaugural music director for the summer concerts at the Robin Hood Dell, since Stokowski would not be available. The national magazine *Musical Courier* described Smallens as "one of the brilliant young conductors of the day, and thoroughly up to date. He is, in fact, pretty near to being a modernist, and is closely associated with the driving and ambitious modernist societies which Philadelphia supports."[22] As previously noted, Smallens agreed to work under the same compensation arrangement as the Orchestra musicians, accepting a percentage of ticket sale revenues rather than a regular salary.

## The Musicians

Although the Robin Hood Dell was conceived and promoted as a summer home for The Philadelphia Orchestra, it was not, in strict terms, the full, regular-season Orchestra that performed in the Dell concerts. Rank-and-file Orchestra musicians made up the majority of the 110-member summer ensemble, but most of the Orchestra's first-chair players, the "star" instrumentalists of the ensemble, took the summer off from the Orchestra. It was still The Philadelphia Orchestra, to be sure, but the summer version of the ensemble was missing many of the best players from the regular-season lineup. Violinist and violist Alfred Lorenz, a member of the Orchestra since 1901 and one of its representatives on the Summer Concerts Association Board, served as concertmaster for the inaugural season.

One disgruntled Orchestra patron expressed his dismay with the absence of the principal players in a letter to the editor of the *Philadelphia Record*, published on May 27, 1930:

> I would like to know whether the people [behind the summer concerts] . . . take the musical public for a bunch of those creatures which, according to Barnum, are born every minute. They call it the Philadelphia Orchestra, but as a matter of fact the men who hold the solo chairs in the orchestra and make it what it is will be absent from it. I refer to Kincaid, Tabeteau, Bonade, Simons, and other solo players. . . . [The public] are not being given the complete Philadelphia Orchestra (about one third being outside players).[23]

The writer is referring to first-chair players flutist William Kincaid, oboist Marcel Tabuteau, bassoonist Daniel Bonade, and trombonist Gardell Simons. Simons did perform in the Dell concerts; the others did not.

In addition, the Orchestra's celebrated conductor, Leopold Stokowski, never appeared at the Robin Hood Dell on a regular basis. While he supported the creation of the venue and was involved in its design, he spent his summers in New England or Europe and was unavailable for the Dell concerts. He agreed to conduct the opening piece of the inaugural program in 1930 (although he had to cancel at the last minute), and he made brief, unscheduled appearances in 1931 and 1933, but he never conducted a complete, regularly scheduled concert at the Robin Hood Dell during his tenure as The Philadelphia Orchestra's conductor. (He did lead full concerts at the venue when he returned as a guest conductor in the 1960s.)

The ensemble was often referred to as "the Men of the Philadelphia Orchestra" in this period, and it was, indeed, an all-male institution, as it had been since its founding in 1900. But this would soon change: The first female member, harpist Edna Phillips, would join the Orchestra in fall 1930, just after the initial Dell season concluded. She would be in the Orchestra for the following Dell season. The Orchestra would remain an all-White ensemble for much longer; as detailed later, it hired its first member of Asian descent in 1958 and its first Black musician in 1968.

## Final Preparations

On July 7, as workers put final touches on the Dell for opening night the following evening, Smallens and the Orchestra rehearsed in the space for the first time. During a break, Smallens gushed about the new venue: "I am simply crazy about it. No other

**(above)** ■ Alexander Smallens leads The Philadelphia Orchestra in one of its first rehearsals at the new Robin Hood Dell, in July 1930. (*The Philadelphia Inquirer* photograph collection, Special Collections Research Center, Temple University Libraries)

**(left)** ■ 1930 poster advertising the inaugural concert series. (Administrative Records, Philadelphia Orchestra Association records, Kislak Center for Special Collections, Rare Books, and Manuscripts, University of Pennsylvania) city in the country has anything so distinctly beautiful. The stadium concerts in New York and even the opera season at Ravinia Park in Chicago cannot compare with this. . . . I really cannot express adequately how pleased I am."[24]

## Opening Night

Years of laying the groundwork and months of intense planning and fundraising finally came to fruition on Tuesday evening, July 8, 1930, when an audience of some 10,000–12,000 (estimates varied) came to hear The Philadelphia Orchestra's inaugural concert at the new Robin Hood Dell. "From all directions came men, women, children," *The Evening Bulletin* reported, "in sports costumes, in business suits, in mohair and flannels, crepe de chine and cotton print—all kinds and classes of people."[25] The *Daily News* noted, "They came in droves, afoot, in taxis, in trolleys, in buses, in machines, motorcycles, and bicycles."[26] (Abbott later reported that the Philadelphia Rapid Transit Corporation had "promised a special line service to Robin Hood Dell, but in this respect they disappointed us lamentably."[27])

The National Osteopathic Convention, meeting in Philadelphia at that time, purchased all 1,000 reserved seats for opening night, while subscribers and individual ticket purchasers occupied the other 5,000 paid seats. Perhaps an equal number of nonpaying listeners crowded the areas outside the gates.

■ Cartoon published in the July 21, 1930, issue of *Town Crier of Philadelphia*. (Robin Hood Dell scrapbook, Philadelphia Orchestra Association records, Kislak Center for Special Collections, Rare Books, and Manuscripts, University of Pennsylvania)

SUMMER NIGHT CONCERTS

SEASON 1930

ALEXANDER SMALLENS } Conductors
LEOPOLD STOKOWSKI }

PROGRAM

TUESDAY EVENING, JULY 8, 1930

*OPENING CONCERT*

DEDICATION CEREMONIES

The Star Spangled Banner

Presentation to the City........................DR. HERBERT J. TILY

Acceptance on Behalf of the City—
HON. HARRY A. MACKEY, *Mayor of Philadelphia*

Prelude, "Die Meistersinger" ................................*Wagner*
(Conducted by Leopold Stokowski)

Nocturne and Scherzo from "Midsummer Night's Dream"....*Mendelssohn*

"Death and Transfiguration" ................................*Strauss*

INTERMISSION

Symphony No. 7, in A Major ...............................*Beethoven*

(Programs subject to change without notice)

*The Steinway is the Official Piano of these Concerts*

(Continued on page 10)

■ Opening night program, July 8, 1930. Leopold Stokowski was scheduled to conduct the first piece but had to cancel, so Alexander Smallens conducted the entire program. (Robin Hood Dell programs, Philadelphia Orchestra Association records, Kislak Center for Special Collections, Rare Books, and Manuscripts, University of Pennsylvania)

The evening began with "The Star-Spangled Banner," followed by presentations by Summer Concerts Association President Tily and Mayor Mackey. Tily acknowledged the many individuals and organizations that made the night possible: Wister and the Orchestra Women's Committees; Orchestra musicians and Local No. 77; Judson and his associates; Smallens and Stokowski; Mayor Mackey and Bureau of Music staff; City Architect Walter Thomas; Fairmount Park Commission Vice President Eli Kirk Price II; the Wark construction firm; and the workmen who completed the facility in record time. "All of these join with the Summer Concerts Association in this presentation to the City of Philadelphia."[28]

Mayor Mackey followed by thanking all those involved as well, again singling out the work of the Bureau of Music. Then came the musical portion of the evening. The plan was for Stokowski to conduct the opening piece and then hand the baton to Smallens for the rest of the program. However, Stokowski had to cancel at the last minute, as his wife, Evangeline Johnson Stokowski (heiress to the Johnson & John-

**(following spread)** ■ Opening night audience, as shown in *The Philadelphia Inquirer*, July 13, 1930. (From *The Philadelphia Inquirer*. © 1930 Philadelphia Inquirer, LLC. All rights reserved. Used under license. Robin Hood Dell scrapbook, Philadelphia Orchestra Association records, Kislak Center for Special Collections, Rare Books, and Manuscripts, University of Pennsylvania)

Rotogravure Section
July 13, 1930

# The Philad

PHILADELPHIA ORCHESTRA BEGINS OUTDOOR SUMMER CONCERTS

The scene was photographed in Robin Hood Dell, Thirty-third and Dauphin streets, Fairmount Park, last Tuesday evening during the initial outdoor concert given by the Philadelphia Orchestra under the direction of Alexander Smallens.

Inquirer Photo

hia Inquirer

Rotogravure
Section
July 13, 1930

son fortune), was about to give birth to their second child at their summer home in Connecticut. Instead, Smallens led the entire program, which opened with Richard Wagner's Prelude to "Die Meistersinger von Nürnberg," followed by Nocturne and Scherzo from Felix Mendelssohn's "A Midsummer Night's Dream," and Richard Strauss's *Death and Transfiguration*. After intermission, the concert concluded with Beethoven's Symphony No. 7.

Both the concert and the venue received high praise from the local and national press. Commentators noted in particular the eager, overflowing audience, the largest ever to hear The Philadelphia Orchestra in person. Engaging in some serious hyperbole, the *Public Ledger* called the concert "probably the most auspicious event of its kind that has ever taken place in the United States."[29] *The Philadelphia Inquirer* was effusive in its description of the opening night scene:

> The huge natural amphitheatre, rising smoothly from the base of the splendid music shell that has sprung into existence almost by magic, and surrounded by leafy tree-topped banks, was largely filled before the opening exercises. . . . Before the concert was half over, the aisles were blocked with eager seat seekers, nearly two thousand additional seats perched in nooks on the banks at the sides and above the floor were also crowded, while besides the nine thousand officially admitted on tickets, a bootleg brigade of almost another thousand would-be bearers clustered outside the fence, and dozens of enterprising urchins, eluding park guards, hopped the fence and even crowded in front of august guests of honor in front rows.
>
> It was a record-shattering occasion on more than one count. Not only was it the first outdoor concert officially to be given by the Philadelphia Orchestra, but the audience, which sat spellbound . . . , was the largest audience that has ever heard any concert by the Philadelphia Orchestra. The only disgruntled auditors [i.e., listeners] were a few dozen dazed and dazzled birds that flitted about the treetops. . . . [The program was] played with flawless finish by the city's great orchestra under the crisp and compelling conducting of Alexander Smallens.[30]

The national magazine *Musical America* also gave high marks to the concert and the facility, with one caveat:

> An audience of at least 12,000 heard the opening program in the Summer Concerts Association series by the Philadelphia Orchestra under Alexander Smallens last night, which dedicated the al fresco auditorium at Robin Hood Dell in Fairmount Park. The new convex shell, illuminated with a novel lighting system, has simple dignity. Evenly rising tiers of specially constructed benches give excellent sight of the players from every point. Acoustically

> the bowl is satisfactory with the exception of a few "dead spots." . . . Mr. Smallens chose a very substantial program for the opening concert. He gave a spirited and sparkling reading of the [pieces on the program].[31]

The novel lighting system, as designed by Stokowski, came into full effect when darkness descended, as *The Philadelphia Inquirer* described:

> The concert began in the deepening dusk under a cloudless sky. As the daylight slowly departed, the indirect, invisible lighting placed at the sides of the music shell brilliantly illuminated the stage and sharply silhouetted auditors in the front rows, gradually merging into the velvety darkness of the night towards the rear of the Dell.[32]

The *Evening Public Ledger* gave an especially evocative description of nightfall at the concert:

> As the sun went down behind the orchestra shell in almost theatrical splendor, dusk came quickly into the dell and fireflies were out and about the trees. Sleepy birds awoke now and then to sing a brief opinion of the music. A family of owls drifted silently from tree to tree. It was a scene of magic.[33]

Summing up the inaugural concert, *The Evening Bulletin* noted: "There cannot be any shadow of a doubt, in the light of the auspicious opening night, that the experiment of giving Philadelphia symphonic music in the open air is from all points of view an emphatic success."[34]

There were two main complaints with the new facility, both of which were quickly addressed. First, there were only two entrances and too few ticket takers, causing an enormous backup on opening night. Additional entrance facilities and staff were added for subsequent concerts. Second, as noted by *Musical America*, was that the sound did not carry well to the rear of the seating area, particularly soft string passages, which in some places were barely audible. Facilities staff installed a microphone on the stage and speakers in the trees, which, after a few days of fine tuning, apparently rectified the problem.

## Artists and Repertoire

The inaugural season ran for eight weeks, July 8–September 1, with concerts scheduled seven nights a week. There were to be 56 concerts in all, consisting of 24 different programs, usually three separate programs per week. However, in a scenario that would bedevil Dell managers for the next 46 years, rain forced the postponement or cancellation of some concerts, and the threat of bad weather reduced attendance at others. Smallens conducted the majority of the concerts, with six guest conductors, several of international renown, leading 16 other concerts. Some of the guest conductors were clients of Judson and provided their services gratis.

The Orchestra performed more than 150 compositions by 70 different composers. Music by the European masters predominated, especially that of Beethoven and Wagner, the two most frequently performed composers in the inaugural season. Concerts usually included a full symphony and a mix of other pieces. There were several "All" programs—all-Beethoven, all-Wagner, all-Tchaikovsky, all-Russian. The all-Beethoven program featured his First and Ninth symphonies, the latter monumental work an ambitious undertaking for the Dell's first season.

Initially, Sundays were reserved for lighter fare—overtures, preludes, and dance pieces rather than symphonies or large-scale works—but the Orchestra changed this policy after receiving hundreds of letters requesting that it eliminate the "hodgepodge" of shorter pieces on Sundays. As Judson explained, "Many music lovers called attention to the fact that the mood created musically was broken too frequently with the former miscellaneous assortment we offered. The citizens of Philadelphia are recognized as intelligent music lovers and their keen interest in the type of programs offered sustains this reputation."*[35]

While the repertoire tended heavily toward standard works of the European classical tradition, some modern and American music was presented, including works that were new at the time but have since become standards in the repertoire. They included Ottorino Respighi's *Pines of Rome* and Maurice Ravel's *Bolero*, written in 1924 and 1928, respectively, and George Gershwin's *An American in Paris*, which had had its world premiere in December 1928 and received its first Philadelphia performance at the Dell on August 15, 1930. As revealed later, Ravel's *Bolero* was the most popular piece during the inaugural season.

Undoubtedly the most modern piece of the season, chronologically and stylistically, was *Lysistrata Suite* by Leo Ornstein, performed on August 29. Ornstein, a Russian native, was an avant-garde composer then living in Philadelphia and teaching at the Philadelphia Musical Academy. His *Lysistrata Suite* was based on the music he wrote for the musical comedy *Lysistrata*, which had opened at Philadelphia's Walnut Street Theatre just three months earlier. *The Philadelphia Inquirer* critic had this to say about Ornstein's *Suite*, as heard at the Dell: "It is marked [by] maddening monotony of repetition, conspicuously more eccentricity than originality, and by more bizarre effects of instrumentation than thematic vitality. But it was received with open-minded cordiality, and the composer was called to the stage for two bows."[36]

---

* Modern-day artistic directors of symphony orchestras, who are increasingly programming popular-leaning works to attract audiences, would find it ironic that Philadelphia audiences requested more serious, large-scale works and less light orchestral fare in 1930.

The same critic had a more favorable impression of a new piece by another local composer the previous evening, when Smallens and the Orchestra premiered "Scherzo Grotesque," written in 1925 by Otto Mueller, a former Philadelphia Orchestra violinist. The piece had "freshness of fancy, engaging instrumental effects, especially in the use of percussion, and a genuine and spontaneous melodic facility. It was well received, and the composer, called before the audience, was presented with a floral tribute."[37]

The majority of the concerts were orchestra only, but seven of the 24 programs featured guest soloists or ensembles, including four vocalists, a pianist, a choral group, and a dance troupe. Of the vocalists, two were Philadelphians: contralto Kathryn Meisle, who would perform with the Metropolitan Opera a few years later (and whose husband was an executive in Judson's artist management agency), and the popular baritone Nelson Eddy, who was then primarily an opera singer but would soon be a major star of Hollywood musicals. The dance troupe, the Humphrey-Weidman Group, was co-led by a Philadelphian, as well: Doris Humphrey, a noted modern dancer and choreographer, who on August 19, 1930, premiered her work *La Valse*, a ballet set to Ravel's well-known piece, at the Dell. There was a "no encores" policy at the Dell, although, as reported in the September 1930 issue of *Musical Digest*, the "rule was nearly broken the night Kathryn Meisle sang an aria from [Wagner's opera] 'Rienzi' and a [French composer Léo] Delibes song."[38]

Yet another Philadelphian featured in the inaugural Dell season was none other than Dr. Herbert J. Tily, who in addition to being president of the Philadelphia Summer Concerts Association and president of Strawbridge & Clothier, was a composer and conductor. On July 15, Tily led the Strawbridge & Clothier Chorus in two choral pieces: a "Choral Fantasia," written by British composer Percy Fletcher and based on Wagner's opera *Lohengrin*, and "The Call to Freedom," by American composer Victor Herbert (which Herbert had dedicated to Tily).

The other featured soloists in 1930 were tenor Paul Althouse, contralto Sophie Braslau, and pianists Muriel Kerr and Isabelle Yalkovsky. Guest conductors included Albert Coates, Ernst Knoch, Karl Krueger, Josef Pasternak, Willem Van Hoogstraten, and a 30-year-old violinist-turned-conductor who was starting to make a name for himself in New York City, Eugene Ormandy.

## Ormandy Debuts in Philadelphia

Ormandy was a client of Arthur Judson, and in one of the more consequential bookings in Philadelphia music history, Judson arranged for him to be the first guest conductor at the Robin Hood Dell on July 21, 1930, leading three concerts in the third week after Smallens had conducted the first two weeks. It was Ormandy's first appearance in Philadelphia. Little could anyone have known that night what would be in store for the young conductor and The Philadelphia Orchestra in the years to come.

Undated (probably 1930) photograph of Eugene Ormandy, inscribed to Adrian Siegel and his wife, Sofie. (Adrian Siegel photographs, Philadelphia Orchestra Association records, Kislak Center for Special Collections, Rare Books, and Manuscripts, University of Pennsylvania)

Born in Hungary in 1899, Ormandy immigrated to the United States in 1921 and was working in New York theaters when he came to the attention of Judson, who began managing him in 1927. Judson booked Ormandy for three nights at the Dell in 1930: July 21, 22, and 23. On the first night, Ormandy led The Philadelphia Orchestra in what *The Philadelphia Inquirer* called a "most ambitious programme" of Johannes Brahms's Symphony No. 1, Strauss's *Till Eulenspiegel's Merry Pranks*, and Wagner's Prelude and "Liebestod" from *Tristan und Isolde* and the Prelude to *Die Meistersinger von Nürnberg*. The *Public Ledger* began its review of the concert by stating, "It may as well be said at once that Mr. Ormandy showed himself to be one of the finest young conductors that have appeared in Philadelphia in many years."[39] At the conclusion of the three-night series, the same paper reported, "When Eugene Ormandy ended his program last evening, . . . the orchestra cried 'bravo!' The orchestra refused to obey his appeal to rise in response to the great applause of the audience, thus indicating they wanted him to have every handclap for himself; and when the audience called him back a third time the Orchestra members burst into a veritable yell of approbation."[40]

The success of Ormandy's concerts and his obvious rapport with the Orchestra led to frequent guest appearances in Philadelphia over the next few years, at both the Robin Hood Dell and the Academy of Music. As detailed later, this, in turn, led to his appointment as permanent Philadelphia Orchestra conductor in 1936, following Stokowski's resignation. (The two conductors actually overlapped for several years as Stokowski made a gradual exit from Philadelphia.)

Ormandy's auspicious debut at the Dell almost did not happen. As he recalled years later, he was nearly felled by sunstroke at his first rehearsal with the Orchestra the morning of his opening concert. The sun was blazing, and while the Orchestra was positioned in the shade, Ormandy was not. When the rehearsal was over and the musicians had left, he realized he was not well. "Adrian [cellist Adrian Siegel] found me sitting on the stage and got me to a doctor," he recalled. Ormandy recovered enough to go on that night, but as he remembered: "I was scared to death of this orchestra. I knew if I didn't do well, I'd never be back."[41] He and Siegel would become lifelong friends.

## The Audience

The Robin Hood Dell was intended as a place where ordinary Philadelphians of modest means could hear fine classical music at reasonable prices. Promotional materials for the venue touted the very affordable ticket prices and listed trolley and bus routes to the venue from different parts of the city. So who actually attended concerts in the inaugural year? There is no known demographic information, but extant photographs indicate that the audiences were overwhelmingly White, which is not surprising. While there were no overt racial discrimination policies at the Dell—technically, all were welcome—Philadelphia, as previously noted, was a segregated city in 1930. It was generally understood that Black and White people had their separate places. The Dell was basically a White venue, a bastion of music of the European masters. This changed over time, to be sure—particularly when Black artists began to be featured a few years later—but by and large, Robin Hood Dell audiences were predominantly White in the early years.

The city's weekly African American newspaper, *The Philadelphia Tribune*, did occasionally promote the concerts to its readers in the Dell's first season. A June 5, 1930, *Tribune* column entitled "Symphonies Under the Stars" extolled the venue's bucolic setting and the unique opportunity it presented for democratizing classical music:

> Cloistered in a cathedral-like setting of trees, with the hills, the river and sky for accompanying background, the finest orchestra in the world for the first time will perform for thousands of workaday people the music gems of the masters. . . .
>
> This new audience, . . . will be a transition from the few restricted patrons, who have enjoyed the music in the winter months. It will be democracy's first audition. It will be a meeting between Philadelphia's workers

> and the masters of melody. It will be a wedding of the orchestra and the community.
>
> At last the orchestra will become an integral part of city life, and the symphonies which have been imprisoned within the hallowed halls of the Academy [of Music] will be whistled in the by-ways.
>
> Music for the Multitudes! How it fires the imagination!

The *Tribune* ran a column a month later previewing the inaugural season as it was about to start, but otherwise it did not report on the concerts. This was in contrast to Philadelphia's major daily newspapers, which routinely ran feature articles on upcoming concerts, gave daily program listings, and published critical reviews of the concerts.

The Strawberry Mansion neighborhood where the Dell was located was predominantly Jewish in 1930. Given the strong European classical music tradition in Jewish American culture at the time, and the fact that the Dell was within easy walking distance, it is reasonable to assume that many in the audience were Jewish.

Regardless of their ethnicity or place of residence, music lovers came in large numbers, often waiting in long lines to get in. As *The Evening Bulletin* reported:

> Standing in line on a hot summer's night. Elbows pressing in one's side, hot arms pressing against one, beetles and mosquitoes pricking the back of one's neck. It is hardly an amusing pastime. Yet so great is the enthusiasm of men, women, and children of Philadelphia for this city's newest diversion, that they consider it a privilege, apparently, to stand huddled together, ladies in breezy chiffons next to homey little women in house frocks, waiting for the gates of Robin Hood Dell . . . to open.[42]

Along with the "regular" citizens the Dell was intended to serve, Philadelphia's social elite patronized the summer concerts. Major newspapers had "social pages" in this period that tracked the comings and goings of the upper class. *The Philadelphia Inquirer* social page for July 20, 1930, reported, "[With] the great success of the summer concerts being given by the Philadelphia Orchestra in Robin Hood Dell, [young socialites] have formed a committee which is arranging a series of supper dances to follow the Wednesday evening performances. . . . They are to be held at Belmont Mansion, a fascinating spot at this season and quite accessible to the Dell. . . . They are bound to be delightful affairs." Local newspapers reported on these high-society supper dances periodically thereafter. "Dainty Frocks Worn at Dell Supper Dances" ran a headline in the August 14, 1930, *Philadelphia Record*, while an August 17 *Public Ledger* headline proclaimed, "Park Supper-Dance Is the Scene of Much Entertaining—Fourth of Belmont Mansion Series Follows Dell Concert."[43]

## First Season Finales

The final week of the inaugural season began with violinist Alfred Lorenz, who had served as concertmaster for the summer series, as soloist in Norwegian composer Johan Svendsen's Romance for Violin and Orchestra on August 30, followed the next night by hometown favorite baritone Nelson Eddy, the season's final guest artist, who sang a set of operatic arias. *The Philadelphia Inquirer* praised Lorenz's "poetic performance," noting "the purity and depth of his tone marked by a lovely legato," while the *Public Ledger* noted that Eddy "scored the most emphatic success of any of the soloists of the season. . . . He was splendid in voice and exhibited great artistry and that clear enunciation which always features his work."[44]

The final concert on September 1 was an all-request program. As reported in the newspapers, a light but persistent rain fell as Smallens conducted Cesar Franck's Symphony in D minor, Tchaikovsky's *Romeo and Juliet*, Wagner's Prelude and "Liebestod" from *Tristan und Isolde*, and Ravel's *Bolero*—the last the most requested piece, with the Franck symphony a close second. Johann Strauss's "On the Beautiful Blue Danube" waltz was programmed as an encore but was not performed; "The Star-Spangled Banner" closed the program instead. At the concert's conclusion, Smallens was presented with a basket of flowers as a token of appreciation for his leadership of the summer series, and he made a brief speech in which he noted that the first season was one of experimentation to determine what the public liked best and that next season would be even better.

## Inaugural Season in Review

The inaugural season was deemed a great success by all concerned and brought Philadelphia national acclaim. "That Philadelphia's experiment in outdoor symphonic performances has been a remarkable success nobody can deny," declared *Musical Digest* in its September 1930 issue. That same month, *Musical America* noted: "In the eight weeks of nightly programs, approximately 225,000 have heard the members of the Philadelphia Orchestra under Alexander Smallens, the regular conductor, and a series of notable guest conductors. . . . In addition to being a boon to the regular public . . . this pioneering enterprise has been a remarkable force for musical propaganda and a missionary influence of great benefit for the orchestra."[45]

Notes of appreciation for the principal organizers came from many sources. At its October 21, 1930, meeting, The Philadelphia Orchestra Association Board noted "the exceedingly good work contributed by Mr. Judson who, with his wide and comprehensive knowledge of things musical hitherto obtained in such efforts, gave unsparingly of his knowledge, experience, time, and effort, . . . with the results flowing therefrom considered most satisfactory."[46] Clara Barnes Abbott later offered her appreciation of Judson's indispensable contributions in her 1930 annual report on the work of the Bureau of Music: "From the first favorable reaction [to her initial proposal for the summer concerts] to the close of the very successful season," she reported that she benefitted from "the fine business acumen, the splendid managerial experience, and the years of musical contacts" that Judson brought to the endeavor.[47]

The Orchestra Association also acknowledged the efforts of its two Board members, Frances Wister and Herbert J. Tily. The association's secretary wrote a letter to Wister expressing the Board's "gratification at the successful outcome of your very great efforts toward the establishment of what will doubtless prove to be in Philadelphia a very notable addition to its cultural facilities. Your every thought, energy, and business capacity were all expended on this effort which the public of Philadelphia so largely appreciated as to render the continuance of these concerts a certainty which will redound to the benefit of all who in Philadelphia love the better things." The Board also noted that "Dr. Herbert J. Tily had joined Miss Wister in all the planning and execution of the work leading the Summer Concerts."[48]

Statistical and financial analysis of the inaugural season was provided in the May 1931 annual report of the Women's Committees for The Philadelphia Orchestra, in Abbott's year-end report for the Bureau of Music for 1930, and in an informational document sent to newspaper editors in 1931. The Women's Committees' report, issued as planning was underway for the second Dell season, noted that in the first season, "the attendance [i.e., paid ticket holders] at the 56 concerts was 220,000 people, besides those who listened in free from various parts of Fairmount Park adjacent to the Dell." The report also noted that Orchestra musicians, having agreed to work on a percentage of the ticket sales rather than a set salary, made 89 percent of their usual minimum wage in the 1930 season, and in the upcoming season, "it is hoped the amount will be larger."[49]

The informational document, "For the Information of the Editor—Questions Concerning the Financial Status of the Philadelphia Orchestra's Summer Concerts in Robin Hood Dell," noted that "the approximate amount raised for financing of the Summer Concerts in 1930 was $125,000. This did NOT include the salaries of the musicians; they were paid out of the receipts and sale of season tickets." The document also states that "the season of 1930 closed without a deficit being carried over. This was due to the fact that the appeal for money to build the [band] shell resulted in donations of comparatively large sums."[50]

The source of one of the "comparatively large" donations was revealed in the minutes of Local No. 77's executive committee. The union did not normally allow mixing of amateurs and professionals in its members' playing engagements, but in 1930 it agreed to permit students at the Curtis Institute of Music to play in concerts with its members, rationalizing that doing so would keep the union in the

## *Do You Want These Concerts to Continue?*

The continuance of these concerts every evening for eight weeks depends on the response from the citizens of Philadelphia. These concerts are not subsidized by the city or a few wealthy patrons. They are dependent entirely on voluntary gifts for equipment and paid attendance for orchestra salaries.

Here are the facts:

| | |
|---|---|
| **Cost of building Stadium and stage and general expenses (about)** | **$71,000** |
| **Contributions** | **50,000** |
| **Still needed** | **$21,000** |

The orchestra men receive no guaranteed salaries, but depend on the memberships and paid admissions for their remuneration.

| | |
|---|---|
| **We have sold memberships to the extent of** | **$22,000** |
| **We expect in general admissions** | **42,000** |
| **Total in sight** | **$64,000** |

For these salaries we must have $19,000 in addition to what we have in sight.

For these two funds the Association needs $40,000 more. Unless it receives this amount within the next ten days it will be compelled to conclude that Philadelphia does not want the finest Summer Concerts given anywhere.

To enable the orchestra men to continue, send your check (for any amount) to The Philadelphia Summer Concerts Association, Inc., 811 Packard Building, Philadelphia.

- - - - - - - - - - - - - - - - - - - - - - - - - - - - - - - - - - - -

**Philadelphia Summer Concerts Association, Inc.**
**811 Packard Building**

I enclose my check for $..............................as a contribution to the expenses of the Fairmount Park Summer Concerts.

Insert in late season 1930 Robin Hood Dell program book, detailing the costs of the concert series and asking for donations. (Robin Hood Dell programs, Philadelphia Orchestra Association records, Kislak Center for Special Collections, Rare Books, and Manuscripts, University of Pennsylvania) good graces of philanthropist Mary Louise Curtis Bok. At the executive committee's October 18, 1930, meeting, the committee chairman noted: "Mrs. Bok is very generous to the Musicians, and we do not wish to displease her if we can avoid doing so. She recently paid [the] $25,000.00 deficit for the Summer Concerts at the Dell this past summer, so the Chair was told."[51]

The 1931 Women's Committees report, referencing the deepening effects of the Great Depression while looking ahead to the second Robin Hood Dell season, noted:

> This year it seems to us that the Summer Concerts will be more important to the public than last. People who have passed through or are passing through, moments of depression, financial and mental, need the concerts . . . to keep up spirits and divert minds from troubled thoughts. Also there will be people this year who will not make weekend trips in their automobiles, as they have been doing during the past ten years, and to these the possibility of going to 24 Philadelphia Orchestra Concerts for $5.00 will be a great boon.[52]

The seasons that followed saw continued public enthusiasm for the summer concerts, along with some notable musical triumphs, but the venue's finances would remain precarious, especially as the Great Depression worsened in the early 1930s. As with their founding in 1930, the Robin Hood Dell concerts would require a combination of public patronage, municipal funding, and philanthropic support to continue.

# 3.

# 1931–1935

## *Early Triumphs and Trials*

On opening day of the 1931 Robin Hood Dell season, the *Public Ledger* offered a sobering assessment of where things stood with the year-old venue, now that the excitement of the inaugural season had passed and the effects of the Great Depression were really setting in:

> The second season of summer music is bound to be a difficult one. It will lack the original stimulus of a great idea and the large contributions of those who gave so generously to inaugurate the concerts. The times are troubled, and the mood of economy is unfriendly to the arts. The unquestioned charm of novelty is gone from Robin Hood Dell and the friendly fraternity of last year's regular attendants will take some time to renew.[1]

Indeed, just a week earlier the Philadelphia Summer Concerts Association had announced that the upcoming season might have to be curtailed from eight to four weeks if additional funding was not secured. Ticket sales and fundraising were not as robust as in 1930, and there were new expenses to cover. "We had to put up the biggest awning in the city to protect the men when they are rehearsing," Arthur Judson told the *Philadelphia Record*.[2] He told another newspaper that the success of the 1931 season was critical to the entire enterprise: "This summer season will mark the crucial point in the experiment. Without voluntary cooperation of the Philadelphia Orchestra members [last year,] the Dell concerts could never have been carried out. If failure or curtailment is seen this year, the withdrawal of their cooperation next season appears inevitable."[3]

## Public Appeal

As in 1930, there was a concerted public effort to sell subscriptions to the summer series. Among the high-profile musicians who helped promote the concerts was Olga Samaroff, a respected concert pianist and teacher in Philadelphia and New York City (and the ex-wife of Leopold Stokowski), who told *The Evening Bulletin*, "If city government were to offer the average citizen a trip through beautiful country for the price of a season concert ticket, he would jump at the chance, yet a ticket for Robin Hood Dell offers an excursion into a whole world of beauty which has more lasting effect on one's whole life than any trip in any country."[4]

Again, appeals went out across the city, to many different communities. The *Jewish Exponent* put out a call specifically to its readers: "As the musicians must depend entirely on the gate receipts for their remuneration it is up to lovers of good music, and there are many among our Jewish people, to subscribe at once to the series. . . . There are many Jewish musicians in the orchestra, which is being led by Alexander Smallens, . . . who will be assisted by Sol Cohen."[5] Cohen, longtime first trumpet with the Orchestra, was appointed assistant conductor for the summer concerts in 1931. Listed in later years as Saul Cohen-Caston, and eventually as just Saul Caston, he

Opening night of the second Robin Hood Dell season, July 8, 1931. (Free Library of Philadelphia, Print and Picture Collection)

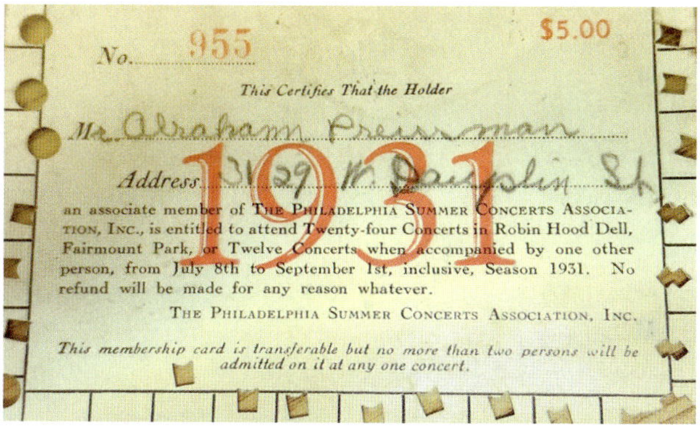

No. 955 $5.00

This Certifies That the Holder

Mr. Abraham Preissman

Address 3129 W. Dauphin St

1931

an associate member of The Philadelphia Summer Concerts Association, Inc., is entitled to attend Twenty-four Concerts in Robin Hood Dell, Fairmount Park, or Twelve Concerts when accompanied by one other person, from July 8th to September 1st, inclusive, Season 1931. No refund will be made for any reason whatever.

The Philadelphia Summer Concerts Association, Inc.

*This membership card is transferable but no more than two persons will be admitted on it at any one concert.*

■ Subscription card for Abraham Preissman for the 1931 Robin Hood Dell season. His $5 subscription entitled him to attend 24 concerts, or 12 concerts for two people. Preissman's address indicates that he lived in Strawberry Mansion, near the Dell. Hole punches on his card show that he attended 22 of the 24 concerts that year. (Administrative Records, Philadelphia Orchestra Association records, Kislak Center for Special Collections, Rare Books, and Manuscripts, University of Pennsylvania)

would conduct at the Dell often throughout the 1930s, serving as assistant conductor and for a time as music director. In 1945 he became music director of the Denver Symphony Orchestra.

In the end, the Summer Concerts Association was able to sponsor a full eight weeks of concerts in 1931. With programs seven nights a week, 56 concerts were scheduled, of which eight were rained out. Total attendance was estimated at 220,000, about 10,000 more than in 1930. However, there were higher operational expenses in 1931, including upgrades to the sound system and physical improvements to the facility, so the musicians ended up making only 77 percent of their regular salary, compared with 89 percent in 1930.[6] But the Dell had made it through the "crucial point" of its second season, and the summer concerts were here to stay, although there would be major financial struggles a few years later.

## Early Conductors

The conductors were the primary stars in the early years of the Dell. There were programs with featured artists—vocalists, instrumentalists, and ensembles—and such artists would play an increasingly prominent role over time, but in the early 1930s the conductors were the main attraction. Smallens led the majority of the concerts again in 1931, with several of the same guest conductors from 1930 returning. Eugene Ormandy, who had recently been appointed music director of the Minneapolis Symphony (as arranged by Judson), conducted seven concerts, and the great Hungarian-born conductor Fritz Reiner, who had recently moved to Philadelphia to become director of the Curtis Institute Orchestra, made his debut and led a week of concerts.

A highlight of the 1931 season for many was when Stokowski made a brief impromptu conducting appearance, his first at the venue. Stokowski did not spend the summer months in Philadelphia, but he was in the city that July to lead a recording session with The Philadelphia Orchestra at the Academy of Music. On the evening of July 15, he came to hear a Dell concert for the first time. Smallens was conducting that night, and following the intermission he invited Stokowski to the stage to conduct the Prelude and "Liebestod" from Wagner's opera *Tristan und Isolde.* "Clad informally in grey, Mr. Stokowski mounted the conductor's stand and made the concert a memorable and exciting one by conducting the orchestra with soaring, passionate beauty," *The Philadelphia Inquirer* reported. After the piece, he told the audience that it was "wonderful to sit in the very last seat where I [had] been sitting and hear perfectly."[7] Apparently, the sound system upgrades were effective.

Stokowski made another brief appearance at the Dell two years later. Alexander Van Rensselaer, the founding and only president of The Philadelphia Orchestra Association since 1900, died on July 18, 1933, at 82. Two days later, Stokowski, in honor of his friend and supporter, traveled from his summer home in Connecticut to lead the Orchestra in "Siegfried's Funeral March" from Wagner's opera *Götterdämmerung.* Stokowski "waited in silence while he was applauded by the audience of 4,500," according to *The Philadelphia Inquirer,* "and then spoke to the crowd. . . . 'We members of the Philadelphia Orchestra would like to invite you to join us in paying tribute to the memory of our beloved president, Alexander Van Rensselaer, who has just left us. . . . This is heroic music that we play, and he was heroic. Our hearts will always be with him.'"[8] Stokowski's two brief appearances in the early 1930s were his only ones at the Dell while he was music director of The Philadelphia Orchestra; he never led a full, regularly scheduled concert at the venue during his tenure in Philadelphia. He left in 1941 and did not return to the city until 1960, when he played to enormous, enthusiastic crowds as guest conductor at the Dell four times from 1960 to 1965.

Meanwhile, Ormandy led 21 Dell concerts from 1931 to 1935, while Reiner led 12. In 1934, a new conductor debuted who would play an important role at the venue for many years: the fiery Spanish pianist and conductor José Iturbi. Born in Valencia, Spain, in 1895, Iturbi made his U.S. debut as a pianist with Stokowski and The Philadelphia Orchestra at the Academy of Music in 1929, to great critical acclaim. A few years later he began what became a very successful conducting career, including frequent appearances with The Philadelphia Orchestra in the mid-1930s, in both regular-season concerts at the Academy of Music and summer concerts at the Dell. "His compelling combination of authority and eloquence found instant and emphatic favor with the audience," wrote *The Philadelphia Inquirer* following his July 18, 1934, Dell debut, "making a most auspicious inaugural for his engagement as guest conductor in the summer symphony season."[9]

Keeping tabs on Iturbi's rise in Philadelphia was Ormandy, monitoring developments from Minneapolis. In early March 1934, as Iturbi was making his conducting debut with The Philadelphia Orchestra at the Academy of Music, Ormandy wrote to his friend, Orchestra cellist Adrian Siegel: "I am most anxious to hear how Iturbi did as a conductor in Philly? I want to know how the Orchestra likes him, how he rehearses, how the concerts were, and finally, how the audience liked him? If he is half as good as people told me in N.Y. then he must be twice as good as Toscanini."[10] (There is no record of Siegel's response.) When Stokowski's relationship with The

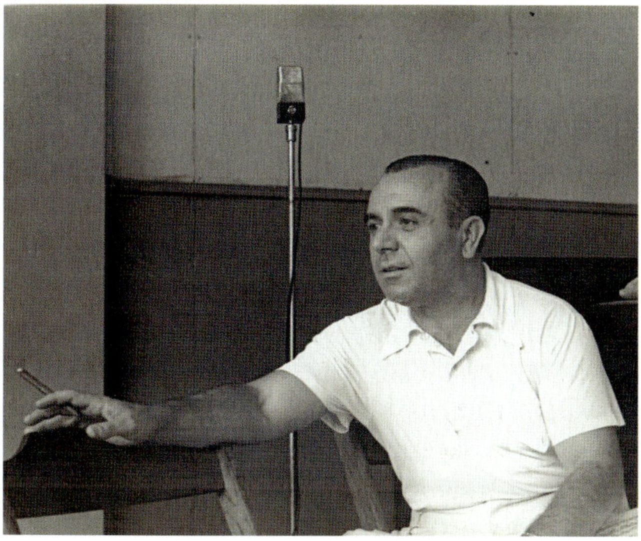

**(top)** ■ Pianist and conductor José Iturbi relaxing at the Robin Hood Dell, undated 1930s photograph. (Adrian Siegel photographs, Philadelphia Orchestra Association records, Kislak Center for Special Collections, Rare Books, and Manuscripts, University of Pennsylvania)

**(bottom)** ■ Adrian Siegel (*left*) and Eugene Ormandy (*right*) on the Boardwalk in Atlantic City in 1931. A member of The Philadelphia Orchestra since 1922, Siegel began taking photographs of Orchestra musicians, conductors, and guest artists in the 1930s and became the Orchestra's official photographer after retiring from the ensemble in 1959. His collection of some 300,000 images is a treasure trove of Orchestra history. (Adrian Siegel photographs, Philadelphia Orchestra Association records, Kislak Center for Special Collections, Rare Books, and Manuscripts, University of Pennsylvania)

Philadelphia Orchestra Association's Board began to deteriorate in the mid-1930s and his resignation as music director seemed likely, Ormandy, Iturbi, and Reiner were reportedly all in the running to replace him. The position ultimately went to Ormandy in 1936. Iturbi became chief conductor at the Dell at that point.

With the introduction of a weekly opera series in 1933 (described later), a new division of conductor duties was created. Smallens continued as music director, while Cohen-Caston was designated "assistant conductor for concerts" and Henri Elkan, who was then conductor of the Philadelphia Grand Opera Company, was appointed "assistant conductor for opera." Elkan, a native of Belgium, also co-owned the local music publishing company Elkan-Vogel with his business partner, Philadelphia Orchestra cellist Adolph Vogel.

## Guest Artists

Singers were the most popular featured soloists in the early 1930s. Baritone Nelson Eddy and contralto Kathryn Meisle—both hometown favorites—made several appearances in this period, as did Metropolitan Opera contralto Sophie Braslau, along with various other American and European singers. Instrumentalists were programmed less frequently early on but became more common over time, particularly pianists and violinists. The usual format when there was a guest artist was for the first half of the program to consist of a symphony or other orchestra-only pieces, with the guest artist appearing after intermission.

On July 13, 1932, the Hilger Trio, three sisters from Czechoslovakia who had been touring the United States and South America since coming to America in 1920, performed Beethoven's Triple Concerto for Violin, Cello, and Piano at the Dell. In 1935, cellist Elsa Hilger became the second woman to join The Philadelphia Orchestra. She would remain with the ensemble for the next 34 four years, during which time she was a fixture at the Robin Hood Dell.

The first female member of The Philadelphia Orchestra, harpist Edna Phillips, debuted as a soloist at the Dell on August 20, 1933, playing Ravel's Introduction and Allegro for Harp and Small Orchestra. Phillips had joined the Orchestra in the fall of 1930, after the initial Dell season had concluded, and began playing the summer concerts in 1931. As she later described to her biographer, "For eight steamy weeks

In a photograph labeled "Ladies of the Orchestra," five female members of The Philadelphia Orchestra pose at the Robin Hood Dell in 1944. *Left to right*: cellist Elsa Hilger, violinist Veda Reynolds, harpist and keyboardist Marjorie Tyre, violinist Lois Putlitz, and harpist Edna Phillips. (Scrapbook, Mann Center for the Performing Arts Archives)

[in 1931], with conductors coming and going and mosquitoes crawling up her arms, [she] played that summer under the stars."*[11] At her featured appearance in 1933, it started to rain at the beginning of her piece, but as *The Philadelphia Inquirer* reported, those "who valued excellent music over safety from a prospective soaking enjoyed one of the most satisfying portions of the program."[12]

## Choral Groups

Local choral groups, including those sponsored by Philadelphia department stores such as the Strawbridge & Clothier Chorus (sometimes led by Herbert J. Tily) and the Lit Brothers' Chorus, appeared regularly at the Dell in the early 1930s. Beethoven's Symphony No. 9, the "Choral" Symphony, was programmed every year but one from 1930 to 1935, providing local choruses opportunities to perform at the venue. The Reading Choral Society, from nearby Reading, Pennsylvania, sang the choral parts for the July 1933 performances led by Smallens, while the Strawbridge & Clothier Chorus did so for the July 1934 performances led by Ormandy.

One of the most popular vocal ensembles to perform at the Dell in the early years was the Hall Johnson Choir, the first Black artists to appear at the venue. Established in New York City in 1925 by composer and conductor Hall Johnson, the choir specialized in performing Johnson's sophisticated arrangements of what were then called Negro Spirituals, the great body of African American religious folk songs created in the pre–Civil War era by enslaved southern Blacks. The Hall Johnson Choir debuted at the Dell on July 24, 1931. It was a three-part program, with the first and third parts consisting of symphonic works and the Hall Johnson Choir featured in between. Ormandy opened the concert leading two pieces by Czech composer Antonín Dvořák, including his Symphony No. 9, "From the New World." This was no doubt intentional, as Dvořák's famous 1893 symphony was heavily influenced by spirituals, and he publicly championed their use as a basis for an American school of composition. After intermission, the Hall Johnson Choir performed eight Johnson arrangements, including such iconic spirituals as "Swing Low, Sweet Chariot," "Go Down Moses," and "Steal Away to Jesus." The evening concluded with Ormandy leading the Orchestra in excerpts from Wagner's opera *Die Walküre*.

The choir performed the following night as well, after which *The Philadelphia Inquirer* reported that "the Hall Johnson Negro Choir scored another tremendous success at . . . the Robin Hood Dell last night, presenting a totally different programme

---

* Phillips remained with the Orchestra until 1942. In 1933, she married attorney Samuel Rosenbaum, an influential member of both The Philadelphia Orchestra Association and Robin Hood Dell Concerts Inc. Boards, the latter the successor organization to the Philadelphia Summer Concerts Association.

Hall Johnson (*at left*) and the Hall Johnson Choir, ca. 1935–1952. (The Hall Johnson Collection, Smithsonian National Museum of African American History & Culture)

from that which marked the debut . . . of these remarkable singers the previous night. As before, they displayed striking range in vocal resources and diversity of numbers, winning prolonged applause."[13]

The Hall Johnson Choir performed every year at the Dell from 1931 to 1934, usually on two consecutive nights, and their concerts drew large, diverse audiences. In 1932, "an audience of 10,000 . . . filled every seat in the Dell," according to *The Philadelphia Inquirer*, "including hundreds of extra chairs squeezed in down front and at the side, . . . augmented by many hundreds of standees on the banks and steps at the rear and sides of the Dell, while many more stood outside the fence."[14] *The Philadelphia Tribune*, the city's Black newspaper, reported in 1933 that the choir "thrilled the huge audiences made up of all races" and named a number of prominent Black Philadelphians who attended the concerts, describing the "well known persons in society, business and professional men [who] were part of the audience that applauded these excellent singers."[15] Renowned contralto (and Philadelphia native) Marian Anderson, who would draw large integrated audiences to the Dell herself beginning in 1940, worked closely with Johnson in later years and recorded a number of his vocal arrangements. Upon Johnson's death in 1970, Anderson wrote a tribute for *The New York Times*, remembering him as "a unique genius. For although he invented no new harmonies, designed no new forms, originated no new melodic styles, discovered no new rhythmic principles, he was yet able to fashion a whole new world of music in his own image."[16]

## Dance

Dance was featured at the Dell from the very beginning; local and national companies performed regularly in the early 1930s, and well-known international troupes made occasional appearances. The Humphrey-Weidman Group performed four times from 1930 to 1935; the Irma Duncan Dancers, led by the foster daughter of pioneering choreographer Isadora Duncan, appeared in 1932; and 1935 saw performances by two groundbreaking ballet companies, George Balanchine's American Ballet and Fokine Ballet. The latter was founded by Russian dancer and choreographer Mikhail Fokine, who in the 1910s had been choreographer for the famous Russian troupe, the Ballet Russes. Two Philadelphia-based dance troupes performed often at the Dell in this period as well: the Littlefield Ballet and the Montgomery Dancers. Catherine Littlefield was an acclaimed dancer, choreographer, and teacher who was a key figure in establishing ballet as an American art form. She formed the Littlefield Ballet in 1934 and later renamed it The Philadelphia Ballet (not to be confused with the modern Philadelphia Ballet). The Littlefield Ballet performed both as a featured ensemble and as part of operatic productions at the Dell in the mid-1930s.

The Montgomery Dancers were formed in 1932 by Mary Binney Montgomery, one of the more compelling figures in the early 20th-century Philadelphia performing arts world. Born in 1907 into a prominent local family—her father founded what became the Janney Montgomery Scott investment company; her sister was the famous socialite Hope Montgomery Scott, on whom Katherine Hepburn's character in the 1939 stage play and 1940 movie *The Philadelphia Story* was based; and the family's suburban Philadelphia home, Ardrossan, is one of the region's most storied Main Line estates—Mary Binney Montgomery studied piano at the Curtis Institute of Music starting in 1924, and later in Vienna. In 1929, she and another pianist recorded Camille Saint-Saëns's "Carnival of the Animals" with Stokowski and The Philadelphia Orchestra. Stokowski, 25 years Montgomery's senior, was smitten with the young pianist and proposed marriage, but her family was adamantly opposed and prevented it. The two remained friends and collaborators, however; when Stokowski created The Philadelphia Orchestra Youth Concert Committee in 1932 to help plan and promote concerts for young people ages 13–25, Montgomery was one of the early leaders of the group.[17]

Montgomery abandoned her piano career in the early 1930s and turned to her other love, dance. She formed the Montgomery Dancers, opened a dance studio on Walnut Street in downtown Philadelphia, and became a champion of modern dance. The Montgomery Dancers made frequent appearances at the Dell, often

■ Mary Binney Montgomery, as shown in a brochure for her ballet company. (Courtesy of Joan W. Mackie, Mary Binney Montgomery's daughter)

performing pieces Montgomery had choreographed and in costumes she designed. "Choreography, Costumes and Lighting Effects by Mary Binney Montgomery," read the program for their July 27, 1934, Dell performance. Her interest in modern dance is evidenced by her piece in that evening's program, titled, "Study in Counter Rhythms for Dancers and Percussion Instruments." *Time* magazine, reviewing the troupe's 1937 performance of Montgomery's adaptation of George Gershwin's *An American in Paris* at the Dell, noted: "In the four years she has been dancing at the Dell, handsome Miss Montgomery has triumphed many times."[18] In August 1935, the company performed selections from Igor Stravinsky's landmark 1913 ballet score *The Rite of Spring* at the Dell, in what *The Philadelphia Inquirer* speculated was probably the world's first outdoor performance of the modern masterpiece.[19] (Stokowski and The Philadelphia Orchestra had given the U.S. premieres of the concert version of *The Rite of Spring* in 1922 at the Academy of Music and the fully staged ballet version in 1930 at the Metropolitan Opera House on North Broad Street.)

## World Premieres

The Dell hosted the world premieres of a number of new works in its early years. Most were by composers who have long since been forgotten, as has their music. Composer and conductor Henry Kimball Hadley, whose music was widely played in the early 20th century, led a week of concerts in July 1932, during which he performed several of his works, including the world premiere of his three-movement *San Francisco Suite*.

One work that had its world premiere at the Dell in 1933 did go on to become a standard in the symphonic repertoire: Samuel Barber's Overture to *The School for Scandal*. Barber was born and raised in West Chester, Pennsylvania, in suburban Philadelphia, and entered the Curtis Institute of Music in 1924 at 14 (along with 17-year-old Mary Binney Montgomery). He completed the Overture, his first orchestral composition, in 1931 while still at Curtis. Much to his consternation, Curtis Orchestra conductor Fritz Reiner had no interest in performing it. Two years later, however, Barber received a $1,200 composition prize for the piece from Columbia University, which allowed him to spend the summer of 1933 studying in Europe. He was in Italy (with his Curtis classmate and romantic partner Gian Carlo Menotti) and did not get to hear the Overture's premiere, led by Smallens at the Dell on August 30, 1933. It was Barber's first orchestral piece to be performed by a major orchestra and was "well received," according to *The Philadelphia Inquirer*, which described it as "marked by a certain melodic facility and a sure sense of design, neither purely freakish in effect in the modern manner

Samuel Barber in 1932 while a student at the Curtis Institute of Music, a year before the world premiere of his Overture to *The School for Scandal* at the Robin Hood Dell. (Curtis Institute of Music Archives)

nor complacently old-fashioned."[20] Years later, Barber remembered that conductor Arturo Toscanini "gave me hell" for missing the premiere of the Overture.[21] In 1938, Toscanini and the NBC Symphony premiered Barber's Adagio for Strings, one of the most beloved and frequently performed works in the symphonic repertoire, including many performances at the Robin Hood Dell and Mann Center.

## Opera

"Carpenters, lighting experts, and stage mechanics are now at work in Robin Hood Dell in Fairmount Park, transforming the music shell into a stage suitable for the production of operas," *The Philadelphia Inquirer* reported on June 4, 1933.[22] In one of the more ambitious undertakings in the Dell's early years, the Summer Concerts Association programmed a series of eight fully staged grand operas to be given on Monday and Tuesday evenings over the course of the eight-week 1933 season. There had been staged opera at the Dell once before, in June 1932, as part of an *Opera and Ballet* benefit concert for both the Dell concerts and The Philadelphia Orchestra Association Pension Fund, but that was a onetime, preseason event. The 1933 series was the first time the Dell presented an entire season of fully staged opera, including many standards in the grand opera tradition: Giuseppe Verdi's *Aida*, *Rigoletto*, *Il trovatore*, and *La traviata*;

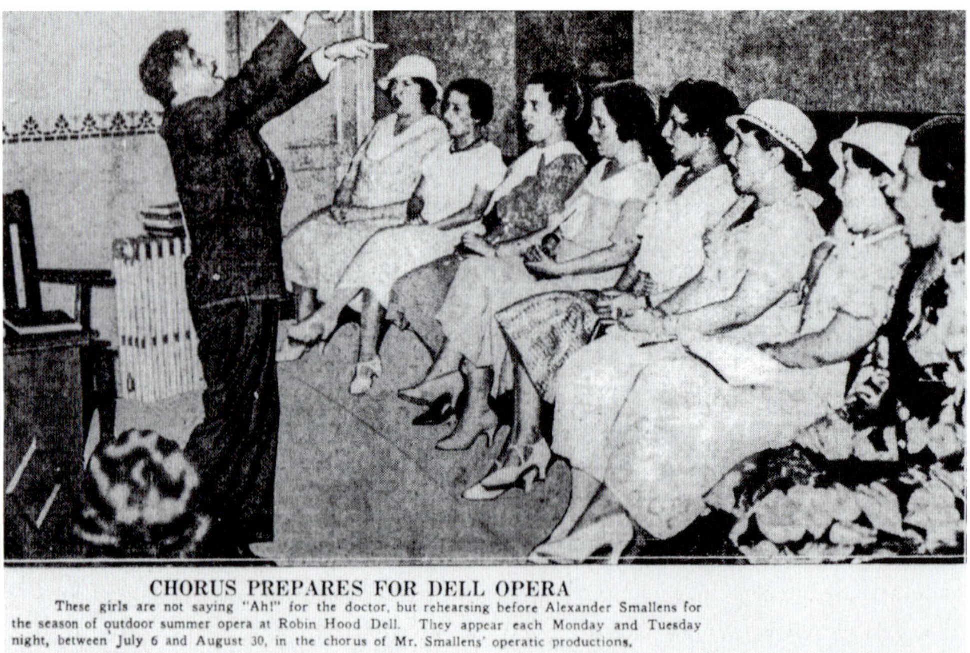

CHORUS PREPARES FOR DELL OPERA

These girls are not saying "Ah!" for the doctor, but rehearsing before Alexander Smallens for the season of outdoor summer opera at Robin Hood Dell. They appear each Monday and Tuesday night, between July 6 and August 30, in the chorus of Mr. Smallens' operatic productions.

■ *The Philadelphia Inquirer*, June 20, 1933. Alexander Smallens rehearsed the chorus singers three times a week for several weeks leading up to the first opera production on July 10. (From *The Philadelphia Inquirer*. © 1933 Philadelphia Inquirer, LLC. All rights reserved. Used under license. Retrieved from Newspapers.com)

These tents were installed directly behind the Dell auditorium in 1934 to serve as dressing rooms for opera productions. (*The Philadelphia Bulletin* photograph collection, Special Collections Research Center, Temple University Libraries)

Charles Gounod's *Faust*; Pietro Mascagni's *Cavalleria rusticana*; Ruggero Leoncavallo's *Pagliacci*; Giacomo Puccini's *Madama Butterfly*; and Georges Bizet's *Carmen*.

Principal singers were engaged from the Metropolitan Opera and other American and European companies. Chorus members came from the former Philadelphia Civic Opera Company, which Smallens had led for seven years; the Philadelphia Grand Opera Company; and other local choral groups. Littlefield Ballet provided the dancers, and scenery and stage sets were lent by the Philadelphia Grand Opera Company and, in later years, by the Curtis Institute of Music. The series was a great success. Attendance was excellent, and critical reviews were mostly positive. The series continued through the 1930s, although not on a weekly basis later in the decade.

## Pops Concerts and Radio Broadcasts

Another new feature in 1933 were Sunday evening "Pops Concerts," weekly programs consisting of lighter symphonic fare, such as overtures, dance pieces, and incidental music, rather than full symphonies or long-form works. As noted previously (see page 62), Dell management tried such programs in the inaugural season but abandoned the idea after patrons indicated that they preferred hearing long-form works at every concert. The 1933 pops series officially lasted for only that one season, but popular repertoire would be programmed with increasing frequency in the years to follow. When Philadelphia Orchestra musicians themselves took over artistic programming for the summer concerts in 1935, they made it a point to program light classics more often, including introducing operetta—a lighter form of musical theater than grand opera—into the Dell opera series.

In May 1931, Orchestra trombonist and Summer Concerts Association Board member Paul Lotz requested and received approval from Local No. 77 for Robin Hood Dell concerts to be broadcast on the radio, leading to local and national broadcasts of many Dell programs.[23] Broadcasts were generally on Philadelphia station WCAU and sometimes distributed nationwide through WABC in New York City. No doubt Arthur Judson helped facilitate the broadcasts, as WCAU was the local affiliate and WABC the flagship station of the national radio network that Judson established in the 1920s and that he and his partner, William S. Paley, would eventually develop into the CBS Radio Network. As noted earlier (see page 34), Paley began his media career in Philadelphia radio before moving to New York City and building CBS into a broadcasting and entertainment powerhouse.

## Finances

Finances were always a challenge in the early years. There were subscription drives, benefit concerts, and other fundraising efforts every year, and the Women's Committees of The Philadelphia Orchestra continued to provide critical support. In her report to the May 24, 1932, annual meeting of The Philadelphia Orchestra Association, Frances Wister waxed poetic in describing the committees' commitment to supporting the summer concerts:

> What place in the world is so romantic as Robin Hood Dell of a summer night with the river below and the stars above and the spell of such music in our ears? So, while many people do not consider money-raising romantic, when Philadelphia Orchestra Concerts in this Dell are at stake, even begging is tinged with romance to us. When you hear the results you will know that the Women's Committees combine sentiment with hard-headed ability.[24]

The women's combination of sentiment and hard-headed ability raised $12,660 for the Dell that year.[25] Over time, however, the Women's Committees turned their attention to other Orchestra needs and reduced their involvement in Dell fundraising. In her May 28, 1935, report, Wister noted: "This year, to our regret, we are not soliciting for the Summer Concerts, not for lack of interest, but because our first duty is to the Board of Directors of the Philadelphia Orchestra Association," which had recently launched its own fundraising campaign.[26]

The worst season for the Dell was 1934, when a combination of bad weather and poor attendance, not to mention the ongoing effects of the Great Depression, prompted the Summer Concerts Association Board to cancel the last two weeks of the season. By late July, attendance was averaging 1,200–1,300 fewer people per concert and receipts were $25,000 below the previous year, prompting the Board to consider its options. During intermission of the July 20 concert led by Iturbi—after "the audience had been electrified by the fire and power of Senor Iturbi's reading of [Rimsky-Korsakov's] *Sheherazade*," according to *The Philadelphia Inquirer*—Benjamin Ludlow, secretary of The Philadelphia Orchestra Association, addressed the audience of some 4,000: "This Dell holds 6,700 people and has on special occasions held as many as 9,000. The thing for you and me to do is to come more frequently and get others to imitate us. The trouble is we have been taking the summer concerts too much for granted. And if we take this Dell for granted, we won't have it with us long."[27]

Three weeks later, the Board issued the following statement:

> The directors of the Philadelphia Summer Concerts Association announce with regret that the present season will be terminated with the concert of Wednesday evening August 15th. Every effort has been made by the directors, the orchestra men, and the Musician's Union, to find some means of continuing the concerts for the full term of eight weeks, but no practical solution has been found. . . . The directors have felt it better to discontinue at the end of the sixth week rather than accumulate a large deficit which might jeopardize the giving of these concerts another year.[28]

The final concert, the second of two scheduled performances of the opera *Tosca* led by Smallens, was actually rained out. Ironically, the previous night, an "enthralled and electrified" record-setting audience of some 9,300 heard Puccini's grand opera in what turned out to be not just the final concert of the 1934 season, but the final concert sponsored by the Philadelphia Summer Concerts Association.[29] The following year, everything would be different.

## Year of Change

After five years of concerts, the 1935 season marked a new era for the Robin Hood Dell, with major changes in the venue's governance, musical leadership, and artistic programming. These changes were closely related to a major shakeup at the time at The Philadelphia Orchestra, revolving around Orchestra Association President W. Curtis Bok, Manager Arthur Judson, and Music Director Leopold Stokowski.* Judson, who had managed The Philadelphia Orchestra since 1915 (and the New York Philharmonic since 1922) and had played a leading role in the creation and management of the Robin Hood Dell, notified The Philadelphia Orchestra Association's Board in October 1934 that he was resigning from his position and would be leaving

---

* The Philadelphia Orchestra used the title "music director" intermittently during the 1930s before making it permanent in 1938 for Eugene Ormandy, but Stokowski had all the responsibilities and privileges of the position during his tenure. See "Ormandy Named Orchestra Aide," *The Evening Ledger*, September 28, 1938.

in May 1935. Bok, who had assumed the association's presidency in 1934 following the death of Alexander Van Rensselaer and was a steadfast supporter of Stokowski, resigned in December 1934 after the Board refused to adopt his plan for sweeping organizational changes designed to ensure that Stokowski stayed in Philadelphia. (Bok's mother, Mary Louise Curtis Bok, also an Orchestra Board member and one of its biggest benefactors, also resigned at this time.) Curtis Bok's support notwithstanding, Stokowski had grown increasingly frustrated with the Board in recent years and had announced publicly several times that he was considering resigning. There was a brief reconciliation in 1935, but his days in Philadelphia were numbered. He officially resigned as chief conductor and music director in January 1936, at which point the Board appointed Ormandy to replace him. Stokowski continued to conduct the Orchestra, however; he and Ormandy were "co-conductors" for five years as Stokowski gradually reduced his time in Philadelphia before leaving completely in 1941. Ormandy would remain sole music director and chief conductor of The Philadelphia Orchestra for the next 39 years, while Stokowski would not return to conduct in Philadelphia until 1960.

What led to these changes was a growing rift between Judson, still one of the most powerful men in the concert industry, on the one side, and Stokowski, widely regarded as one of the world's most brilliant conductors, and his chief supporter, Curtis Bok, one of the richest, most influential men in Philadelphia, on the other. Judson and Stokowski had worked together for 20 years by the mid-1930s and had been responsible for some of the greatest innovations in symphonic music, but Judson had become exasperated with Stokowski's artistic demands and had grown to dislike him intensely. For his part, Stokowski had come to believe that, with the exception of Bok, The Philadelphia Orchestra Association's Board, with Judson as its manager, was much too conservative for such a world-class ensemble—objecting to Stokowski's frequent programming of modern music that challenged audiences; not actively pursuing radio exposure, which he thought was crucial for maintaining the Orchestra's national profile; and settling for second-tier guest conductors rather than engaging the world-class conductors he recommended. Stokowski was also beginning to look beyond Philadelphia at this time; he was building a home in Hollywood and making plans to appear in movies while also pursuing musical and nonmusical activities elsewhere. It all added up to fundamental changes at the Orchestra.[30]

There was a major shakeup at the Robin Hood Dell at this time as well, partly as a result of the changes at the Orchestra and partly due to other factors. With Judson's departure and the elimination a few years earlier of the Philadelphia Bureau of Music, the city agency that Clara Barnes Abbott directed, the Philadelphia Summer Concerts Association, the organization that had created and managed the Dell, lost much of its clout. On the musical front, Smallens resigned as Dell music director after the 1934 season to pursue other activities, necessitating a new approach to programming the summer concerts. With the need for new leadership at the Dell,

# ROBIN HOOD DELL CONCERTS

**Incorporated**

***Under the Stars with the Men of The Philadelphia Orchestra***

**in**

**Symphony Concerts, Grand and Light Operas and Ballets**

Robin Hood Dell, Fairmount Park

**Nightly from June 28 to August 22, 1935**

**Concerts at 8.30** | **Operas at 8**

## OFFICERS

**CURTIS BOK, *President***
**PAUL P. LOTZ, *Vice-President***
**ALEXANDER ZENKER, *Chairman***
**WILLIAM K. HUFF, *Secretary***
**DAVID COHEN, *Treasurer***

## BOARD OF DIRECTORS

**DAVID COHEN**
**ARTHUR BENNETT LIPKIN**
**ALFRED LORENZ**
**EDWARD MURRAY**
**WILLIAM A. SCHMIDT**
**ADRIAN SIEGEL**
**ALEXANDER ZENKER, *Chairman***

---

## CONDUCTORS FOR THE CONCERTS

**Howard Barlow, Frank Black, Saul Caston, Alexander Hilsberg, José Iturbi, Hans Kindler, Hans Lange, Alfred Lorenz, Josef Pasternack, Thaddeus Rich, Fabien Sevitzky, Nathaniel Shilkret, Alexander Smallens, Nikolai Sokoloff, Willem van den Burg, Willem van Hoogstraten, Alfred Wallenstein, Paul Whiteman.**

---

## CONDUCTORS FOR OPERA AND BALLET

**Saul Caston, Boris Goldovsky, Fulgenzio Guerrieri, Sandor Harmati, Sylvan Levin, Josef Pasternack, John Thoms**

---

**WILLIAM K. HUFF, *Manager***

---

**GEORGE T. HALY, *Assistant Manager***
**KARL SCHROEDER, *Stage Director***
**SCHIMA KAUFMAN, *Program Adviser***
**ARTHUR BENNETT LIPKIN, *Technical Adviser***
**EMMA FELDMAN, *Ticket Campaign Manager***
***Opera Ballet Corps*: LITTLEFIELD DANCERS**
**CATHERINE LITTLEFIELD, *Director***

---

***Executive Office*—1300 PACKARD BUILDING—Rittenhouse 6128**
***Ticket Campaign Office*—1717 CHESTNUT STREET—Rittenhouse 2562**

---

■ Title page from the 1935 *Robin Hood Dell Concerts Review*, the Dell program book, listing the officers, Board members, and staff of the newly incorporated Robin Hood Dell Concerts Inc., as well as the conductors to be featured that year. (Robin Hood Dell program books, Music Department, Free Library of Philadelphia) the Philadelphia Summer Concerts Association was dissolved and a new nonprofit, Robin Hood Dell Concerts Inc., was chartered in March 1935 to take over. The president of the new organization was none other than Curtis Bok, with its officers and Board members consisting mostly of Philadelphia Orchestra musicians, some of whom had been on the Summer Concerts Association Board.

On January 8, 1935, two of these musicians—Paul Lotz, who was also the Orchestra's personnel manager at the time, and William Schmidt—petitioned their union, Local No. 77, for permission "to give concerts at the Robin Hood Dell . . . for the season of 1935, on a fully cooperative basis, including conductors and soloists."[31] The latter phrase was key; whereas Judson and his staff, as employees of The Philadelphia Orchestra Association, had been responsible for choosing conductors, soloists, and repertoire at the Dell, the musicians would now be handling this function. This was a unique arrangement in American concert music, having the musicians themselves program concerts at a major venue. The petition was approved, and the musicians formed a committee to plan the concerts. Rather than fill Smallens's position, the musicians arranged for a rotating cast of more than two dozen conductors to lead the concerts, Smallens among them.

Like Judson, Smallens would be based in New York City after 1934, although he returned to Philadelphia often in the mid- to late 1930s to conduct, mostly in operatic productions, at both the Dell and the Academy of Music. His work in New York included conducting summer concerts of the Stadium Symphony Orchestra of New York at Lewisohn Stadium, as well as leading groundbreaking operatic works of the time, such as Virgil Thomson's *Four Saints in Three Acts* and George Gershwin's *Porgy and Bess*. Smallens worked closely with Gershwin on the latter landmark opera and conducted its original Broadway run in 1935. On January 21, 1936, at the Academy of Music in Philadelphia, Smallens, Gershwin, and The Philadelphia Orchestra gave the world premiere of Gershwin's orchestral *Suite from Porgy and Bess*, later retitled *Catfish Row*. Also on the program was Gershwin's Piano Concerto in F, with the composer at the piano.

## New Manager, New Approach

In an article previewing the 1935 season, *The Philadelphia Inquirer* noted:

> This season for the first time the entire responsibility, artistic and financial, is assumed by the musicians of the Philadelphia Orchestra on a wholly cooperative basis. Another innovation is that the musicians themselves have decreed that lighter and more popular types of music are to prevail to [a] greater extent than ever before. "To entertain and not to educate" will be the forthcoming season's keynote. William K. Huff, manager of the concerts, and the [musicians'] committee . . . have been working out the details.[32]

■ The Schmidt Quartet, a local string ensemble, included three musicians who played prominent roles at the Robin Hood Dell in the mid-1930s. Alexander Zenker was chairman and William Schmidt a member of the Robin Hood Dell Concerts Inc. Board, and Henri Elkan was assistant conductor for opera at the venue. (Free Library of Philadelphia, Print and Picture Collection)

William K. Huff, the man Curtis Bok and the musicians chose to replace Judson as manager of the summer concerts, was founding executive director of The Philadelphia Forum, a presenting organization that Curtis's late father, Edward Bok, had established in 1921 and for which Curtis served as president. The Forum presented concerts, recitals, lectures, and other cultural events in the fall and spring months at the Academy of Music. The Robin Hood Dell Concerts Board considered Huff well qualified for the job, as Alexander Zenker, Philadelphia Orchestra violinist and chairman of the Dell Board, attested in a letter to *Time*, after the magazine appeared to slight the manager. In its July 8, 1935, issue, *Time* reported on how Orchestra musicians came together to manage the Robin Hood Dell concerts, and on the local music community's "massed effort . . . to make a success of" the enterprise:

> Since no manager would touch it this year, the orchestra men appointed a committee of their own, got Curtis Bok to be president, chipped in what they could, pledged themselves to give a full season even if they had to play to the shrubs and trees of Fairmount Park. They scheduled opera in English, Gilbert & Sullivan, "pop" and symphony concerts, ballets by Fokine, Humphrey-Weidman, and Philadelphia's Montgomery and Littlefield dancers. . . . When on opening night, 7,000 people filled seats in Robin Hood Dell, gloomy Philadelphians were honestly surprised, cheered themselves hoarse at the end.

> Conductor was José Iturbi who hurried down from Manhattan, played a Beethoven-Wagner program which the musicians had chosen for him.[33]

The article prompted a letter to the editor from Zenker, who called parts of it "incorrect as to the facts and . . . susceptible to serious misinterpretation," asserting that the article

> appears to be a direct reflection upon the management of the concert series by Mr. William K. Huff. So far from being true that no manager would touch it, the Orchestra Committee received and considered numerous applications by well-known managers for the position. When it was ascertained that the services of Mr. Huff would be available, the Committee hastened to take advantage of that opportunity. Mr. Huff is very well known. He has been for 15 years Executive Director of The Philadelphia Forum, and has managed its affairs with conspicuous success.[34]

## Paul Whiteman

As part of its effort to "entertain, not educate," in 1935 the Dell engaged bandleader Paul Whiteman, who led a pair of concerts on July 29 and 30 that were billed as the "Philadelphia Orchestra, augmented by Paul Whiteman's Orchestra." Whiteman occupied a unique place in American concert music at this time, with a foot in both the light classical and jazz worlds. In the 1920s he led one of the nation's most popular dance bands and was dubbed the "King of Jazz." It was an erroneous label, as his band did not play jazz per se but syncopated dance music in a jazz style. However, Whiteman employed some of the top White jazzmen of the era (integrated bands were not accepted in the 1920s), and he did much to popularize jazz with mainstream audiences. He also played symphonic music, and in this realm he holds an important place in the annals of American music for commissioning pianist and composer George Gershwin to write the landmark *Rhapsody in Blue*. Whiteman conducted the world premiere of the piece in 1924 in New York City at a concert he produced entitled "An Experiment in Modern Music."

Whiteman's 1935 Dell concerts featured a mix of light classical, popular, and dance pieces, along with a heavy dose of modern American symphonic music. The latter included a movement from Black composer William Grant Still's 1930 symphonic poem *Africa*; two pieces from the *Grand Canyon Suite*, the popular 1931 symphonic work by Whiteman's longtime arranger, Ferde Grofé; and, of course, *Rhapsody in Blue*, with pianist Roy Bargy. Getting featured spots in the concert were two jazz greats who were in Whiteman's band at the time: trombonist Jack Teagarden and saxophonist Frankie Trumbauer.

■ The Paul Whiteman Orchestra in 1931. (Paul Whiteman Collection, Williams College Special Collections)

Two months later, in an article entitled "Great Music Jeopardized by Jazz?" *The Philadelphia Inquirer* recalled "the sensational, record-shattering attendance that swamped Robin Hood Dell . . . for Paul Whiteman's super-jazz." It noted:

> The spectacular success of Whiteman's jazz boys at the Dell . . . prompted the jocose suggestion in some quarters that it might help to put the Philadelphia Orchestra on its financial feet if he were engaged to "jazz it up a bit." . . . Of course, the suggestion was only offered in a spirit of good, clean fun, . . . though it might be hailed with irreverent relish by the more juvenile generation. Apparently that younger generation is a force increasingly to be reckoned with in the future of the Philadelphia Orchestra.[35]

While there was a good bit of popular fare such as the Whiteman concert in the 1935 season, serious long-form works still made up a significant part of the programming. Wagner and Tchaikovsky were the most performed composers by far, with Beethoven, Johann Strauss, Debussy, Ravel, Mussorgsky, Rimsky-Korsakoff, and Liszt also well represented.

## Men of The Philadelphia Orchestra

Yet another significant development in 1935 was the adoption of the name "Men of the Philadelphia Orchestra" for the Dell ensemble, although the variant "Members of the Philadelphia Orchestra" was used occasionally. The ensemble name had been a thorny issue for the previous few years. The Dell was built as a summer home for The Philadelphia Orchestra, and for the first three years concert programs and promotional literature always referred to the ensemble as "the Philadelphia Orchestra" (the convention of capitalizing the article "The" was not adopted until years later). Things got murkier beginning in 1933, when Dell and Orchestra management sought to differentiate between the regular- and summer-season ensembles while not minimizing the close relationship between the two. Printed matter in 1933 and 1934 generally omitted any mention of the ensemble name, and a promotional flyer for the 1933 season included the following explanatory note: "As heretofore, the Orchestra will consist predominantly of members of the Philadelphia Orchestra and those who have been former members of that organization."

Alexander Zenker brought the issue up with The Philadelphia Orchestra Association's Board several times in early 1935, but each time the association referred the matter to a committee, and there is no record that they ever made a decision.[36] Regardless, beginning in 1935 Dell concert programs opened with the banner "Robin Hood Dell Concerts Incorporated—Under the Stars with the Men of the Philadelphia Orchestra in Symphony Concerts, Grand and Light Operas and Ballets" (see page 87). "Men of the Philadelphia Orchestra" would serve as the working name for the ensemble for the next seven years. Music critics and journalists sometimes took pains to clarify the difference between the regular- and summer-season ensembles, but they usually did not. It remained an issue of ambiguity for many. And while the ensemble was still overwhelming male, harpist Edna Phillips and cellist Elsa Hilger were in the Orchestra at this time, so "Men" was not really an accurate title.

This ambiguity was also reflected in the underlying relationship between The Philadelphia Orchestra Association and Dell management (both Robin Hood Dell Concerts Inc. and its predecessor, Philadelphia Summer Concerts Association). Although the two organizations shared several Board members and their ensembles were composed of mostly the same musicians, there was uncertainty on the part of the Dell as to where it stood with the Orchestra's Board. Seeking clarity, Orchestra violinist and Dell Board member Arthur Bennett Lipkin brought the matter to the Orchestra Association Board's December 30, 1935, meeting. The minutes of the meeting recount the deliberations:

> Mr. Lipkin laid before the Board the matter of the summer concerts. He stated that the Summer Concerts Association never knew the Board's atti-

■ Orchestra musicians relax at a Robin Hood Dell rehearsal in this undated (probably 1930s) photograph. (Adrian Siegel photographs, Philadelphia Orchestra Association records, Kislak Center for Special Collections, Rare Books, and Manuscripts, University of Pennsylvania)

tude about this enterprise. If they were in sympathy with it, he suggested the following motion be approved:

> We, the Board of Directors of The Philadelphia Orchestra Association, having had before us the aims and aspirations of the Robin Hood Dell Concerts, together with its plan of operation, look with favor upon and heartily concur in the efforts of the members of the Orchestra to make possible these concerts.
>
> We recognize very clearly the value of increased activity in their professions, both artistically and financially. We believe that there is here an opportunity to build up a future audience for the regular season, and that these summer concerts in themselves make a definite contribution to Philadelphia's cultural life.
>
> As members of the governing body of the Orchestra we will, as in the past, and as far as we are able, cooperate with the men in realizing their very worthwhile project.

In discussing approval of the motion, Samuel Rosenbaum, a member of the association's Board, noted that the plan of operation for the Dell referenced in the motion had not been presented, so it was agreed that that phrase should be deleted. With that change, the motion passed unanimously.[37] It was a moment of harmony and consensus in a relationship that would have its ups and downs over the years.

## Note of Thanks

Mindful of the contributions of its many partners and supporters in helping to make the inaugural season of Robin Hood Dell Concerts Inc. possible, the Dell Board posted a note of appreciation in the final program of the 1935 season:

> We Thank You! The Administration Committee and the men of the Philadelphia Orchestra wish to express their deep appreciation of the cordial cooperation of Mrs. Mary Louise Bok in allowing us to use the opera scenery and music of The Curtis Institute of Music; of Mr. Edwin Fleisher* in permitting us to call upon the vast resources of his collection of orchestral music [housed in the Free Library of Philadelphia]; of The Philadelphia Orchestra Association in granting us the use of the Orchestra's library; and the Fairmount Park Commission . . . and the personnel of the Fairmount Park Guards for their constant help.[38]

* Philadelphia businessman and philanthropist Edwin Fleisher donated his extensive collection of orchestral scores to the Free Library of Philadelphia in 1929. Still actively used, the Edwin A. Fleisher Collection of Orchestral Music is the largest circulating collection of orchestral music in the world.

# 4.

# 1936–1948

*Auspicious Debuts, Major Milestones*

The years surrounding World War II were heady ones for the Robin Hood Dell. As the nation emerged from the Great Depression in the late 1930s while the threat of world war loomed, the Dell hosted important debuts and milestone events that were significant both in Philadelphia musical life and American concert music at large. The Dell remained one of the nation's premier summer music venues through the war years and into the postwar period, before financial crisis struck in 1948. Its recovery from that crisis set the Dell on a course it would follow for the next 40 years.

## The Late 1930s

The program book for the opening concert of the 1936 season, the second under new Dell management, sounded a note of optimism for the upcoming summer series while sharing a scary story about the new principal conductor, José Iturbi, who had set out on a tour of South America a few months earlier:

> Ladeez 'n genemen! Welcome to a newer and better Dell. During the ten months which have flown by since we last saw you out here, not a day passed that we didn't give some thought to increasing your pleasure and comfort at these concerts. In planning any concert season, without guaranteed financial backing, it is difficult to see blue sky. But encouraged by your support of last year's cooperative undertaking, we have gone ahead to build on top of

what we have already created. Never before were we able to offer you such distinguished soloists, opera casts, ballets, [and] conductors. This at no increase in prices. Never before did we start a season with such confidence in its successful outcome. . . .

We were getting pretty well set when a cable . . . from Port au Spain [Trinidad] informed us that the Brazilian Clipper [airplane], on which José Iturbi—the conductor we had built the season around—was a passenger, had sunk in the harbor. For five terrifying hours we held our breath until reassuring word reached us that Iturbi was safe, the last living person to climb out of the ill-fated airliner.[1]

Three people on the plane were killed in the April 1936 accident. "Fortunately, I had only minor injuries," Iturbi reported. "My left wrist was badly bruised and I suffered body bruises, but I am improving rapidly and hope to conduct in about a week and play [piano] later."[2] He finished his South American tour and was fine for the opening of the Dell season on June 26, 1936. Amazingly, the experience did not deter Iturbi from flying; in the late 1930s he took up flying himself, got a pilot's license, and would fly himself to engagements across the country.

## New Titles

The program for the 1936 opening concert also announced new honorary titles recognizing individuals who played a key role in establishing and supporting the Dell in its formative years: Honorary President Herbert J. Tily and Honorary Vice Presidents Miss Frances Wister and Mrs. Edward (Mary Louise Curtis) Bok. Leopold Stokowski, who had resigned as music director of The Philadelphia Orchestra six months earlier, was given the title of honorary music director. (It was strictly an honorific title; Stokowski had no involvement with the Dell.) Curtis Bok remained president of the Board, with Philadelphia Orchestra musicians again constituting the majority of the Board's membership and making the artistic planning decisions.

In terms of musical leadership, Iturbi was listed as conductor for the 1936 season; Alexander Smallens, as conductor for opera; Henri Elkan, as associate conductor for opera; and Saul Caston, as conductor for ballet. Several guest conductors were also listed. One name not on the list was Eugene Ormandy, who curtailed his conducting at the Dell sharply after his 1936 appointment as Philadelphia Orchestra music director. He did not appear at all at the Dell in 1936 and 1937, led only one concert a year from 1938 to 1942, and led none from 1943 to 1948. He was given the title of honorary music director in 1939, replacing Stokowski in that titular position.

Starting in 1936, there would be six concerts per week, not seven. Wednesday nights were left open unless needed to make up a postponed concert. Also, there

Eugene Ormandy leading a rehearsal at the Robin Hood Dell in the late 1930s, one of his few appearances at the Dell in this period. (Eugene Ormandy photographs, Kislak Center for Special Collections, Rare Books, and Manuscripts, University of Pennsylvania)

would be four fully staged operas during the season, not eight as in recent years. These cutbacks eased the strain somewhat on the Dell's small staff and the musicians who were programming the concerts.

## The Iturbi Years

Prior to the opening of the regular 1936 summer season were two preseason concerts at the Dell on June 23 and 24 with the Paul Whiteman Orchestra, offered in conjunction with the Democratic National Convention that was meeting in Philadelphia that summer. These concerts followed the successful formula of Whiteman's 1935 appearance, with the Whiteman and Dell orchestras combining forces on a mix of symphonic works, light orchestral pieces, and popular songs. Iturbi conducted the season-opening concert on Friday, June 26, but there was no concert on Saturday evening, as The Philadelphia Orchestra performed at the Democratic Party ceremonies that night at Franklin Field on the University of Pennsylvania campus, the event at which President Franklin Delano Roosevelt accepted the party's nomination for another term as president. Dell concerts resumed on Sunday and continued on a regular basis thereafter.

# Hurled Chair Shatters Calm of Dell as Arts Collide

By GEORGE M. MAWHINNEY

ART versus music!

That, folks, was the big debate, placed somewhat temperamentally, and more by action than with words, before the large audience at Robin Hood Dell last night.

It was all very impromptu—not on the program, you must understand—and somebody threw a chair. And, oh, yes, personages no less interesting than Mayor S. Davis Wilson, of the City of Brotherly Love, and Mayor Fiorello LaGuardia, of the big city to the northward, ducked low. Even though the chair was not thrown at them.

Well, folks, it was like this:

In this corner we had a small handful of photographers, representing art. And if you don't think photography is art . . . oh, well, that's another debate.

And in that corner there was Albert Spalding, last night's violin soloist in the Beethoven Concerto, representing music.

As a matter of fact there weren't any corners either. But you get the idea.

Well, up came the moment when

Continued on Page 6, Column 2

JOSE ITURBI

■ *The Philadelphia Inquirer*, August 20, 1936. (From *The Philadelphia Inquirer*.  Retrieved from Newspapers.com)

Iturbi's two years as chief conductor in 1936 and 1937 were marked by exceptional musicianship and public acclaim, along with occasional outbursts of his legendary temper. On August 10, 1937, Philadelphia Orchestra Manager Reginald Allen wrote to Ormandy regarding a number of Orchestra matters and included this note: "As I write this I have just had another outburst of that old ailment, Iturbi. In fact, we have been making the front page of the papers together today. If you ever get like that, I'll break your neck!"[3]

The incident in question was an "All American" concert led by Iturbi at the Dell on August 9 in celebration of the 150th anniversary of the U.S. Constitution. The program included both symphonic works and popular songs by songwriters such as Jerome Kern and Victor Herbert sung by soprano Lucy Monroe and tenor Jan Peerce (who would join the Philadelphia La Scala Opera Company the following year). The first half of the concert was to be broadcast nationally on the NBC radio network, and Orchestra management scheduled the popular songs for this part of the program. Iturbi objected, claiming that it was beneath the dignity of The Philadelphia Orchestra to be heard nationally playing what he described as "compositions of the 'I Love You' and 'Kiss Me' type." Iturbi changed the order and began with the symphonic works, prompting NBC to abruptly stop the national broadcast and switch to other programming. As with other Iturbi incidents at the Dell, the episode made local and national news.[4]

Dell audiences had witnessed Iturbi's temper firsthand a year earlier, at a concert he conducted featuring violinist Albert Spalding, on August 19, 1936. When photographers and audience members began making a commotion over two prominent late arrivals—S. Davis Wilson and Fiorello La Guardia, the mayors of Philadelphia

Violinist Albert Spalding and cellist Alfred Wallenstein rehearse Brahms's Concerto in A minor for Violin, Violincello, and Orchestra prior to their July 8, 1937, Dell concert with conductor José Iturbi. Wallenstein would return as conductor at the Dell several times in the late 1930s. (*The Evening Bulletin* photograph collection, Special Collections Research Center, Temple University Libraries)

and New York City, respectively—Spalding and Iturbi left the stage, and a furious Iturbi reportedly threw a chair from the wings onto the stage.[5]

His volatile nature aside, Iturbi was loved by Philadelphia audiences, and critics praised his musicianship. Attendance was excellent during his two years as chief conductor, in which he led most of the concerts, often performed as piano soloist, and sometimes did both. He also performed with his sister Amparo, a concert pianist. They had performed together in Europe in earlier years, and on June 28, 1937, they gave their first duo performance in America at the Robin Hood Dell, performing Mozart's Concerto for Two Pianos, with José conducting. The following evening, they performed Johann Sebastion Bach's Concerto in C major for Two Harpsichords and String Orchestra, with José leading from the harpsichord, after which he conducted his sister's performance of Robert Schumann's Piano Concerto.

Iturbi did not appear at the Dell at all in 1938 and 1939, as Hollywood had come calling. He moved to California in 1939 and starred in movies throughout the 1940s, always playing himself. His recording career also took off at this time, and he became one of the nation's best-selling classical recording artists. When word leaked out a few years afterward that he had played the piano parts (but did not appear on-screen) in the 1945 movie *A Song to Remember*, a heavily fictionalized biography of Frederic Chopin, his recording of Chopin's Polonaise in A-flat went gold. Despite his film and recording work, he still found time to perform at the Dell during this time. He appeared in a series of three concerts in 1940; seven in 1941; and single concerts in 1942, 1943, and 1948.

## Young Patron

In the summer of 1938, 15-year-old Dorothy Miller, a student at Overbrook High School, attended a series of concerts at the Dell, taking two trolleys from her home in the Eastwick section of Southwest Philadelphia to reach the venue. She had become interested in opera by listening to Metropolitan Opera radio broadcasts on Saturday afternoons and furthered that interest by attending opera, ballet, and symphony concerts at the Dell and the Academy of Music. She made notes of her impressions of the performers and their pieces in her concert programs, which are now housed at the Free Library of Philadelphia. The Dell concerts were apparently her initial exposure to live staged musical performances, as her handwritten notes include comments such as "my first opera" and "my second ballet." In contrast to the "expert" opinions of music critics and cognoscenti, young Dorothy's jottings in her programs contain the spontaneous, unvarnished reactions of a Philadelphia teenager to the world-class music she was hearing that summer.

Her notes in the program for the early August 1938 performance at the Dell of Georges Bizet's opera *Carmen* reveal a young music lover with definite opinions. Led by Smallens, the opera featured Italian mezzo-soprano Bruna Castagna, Armenian tenor Armand Tokatyan, Welsh baritone Mostyn Thomas, and American soprano Lucy Monroe. Writing that "the Dell was terribly crowded!" that night, Dorothy shared that "Armand was magnificent. His acting touching if a little overdone. . . . Bruna Castagna was stout and a little disappointing but had a marvelous voice. . . . Miss Monroe was small and petite and sang better than I had even expected. . . . I did not especially care for Mostyn Thomas." She also noted that Tokatyan was "my favorite tenor" and acts 3 and 4 of *Carmen* were "my favorite acts."[6]

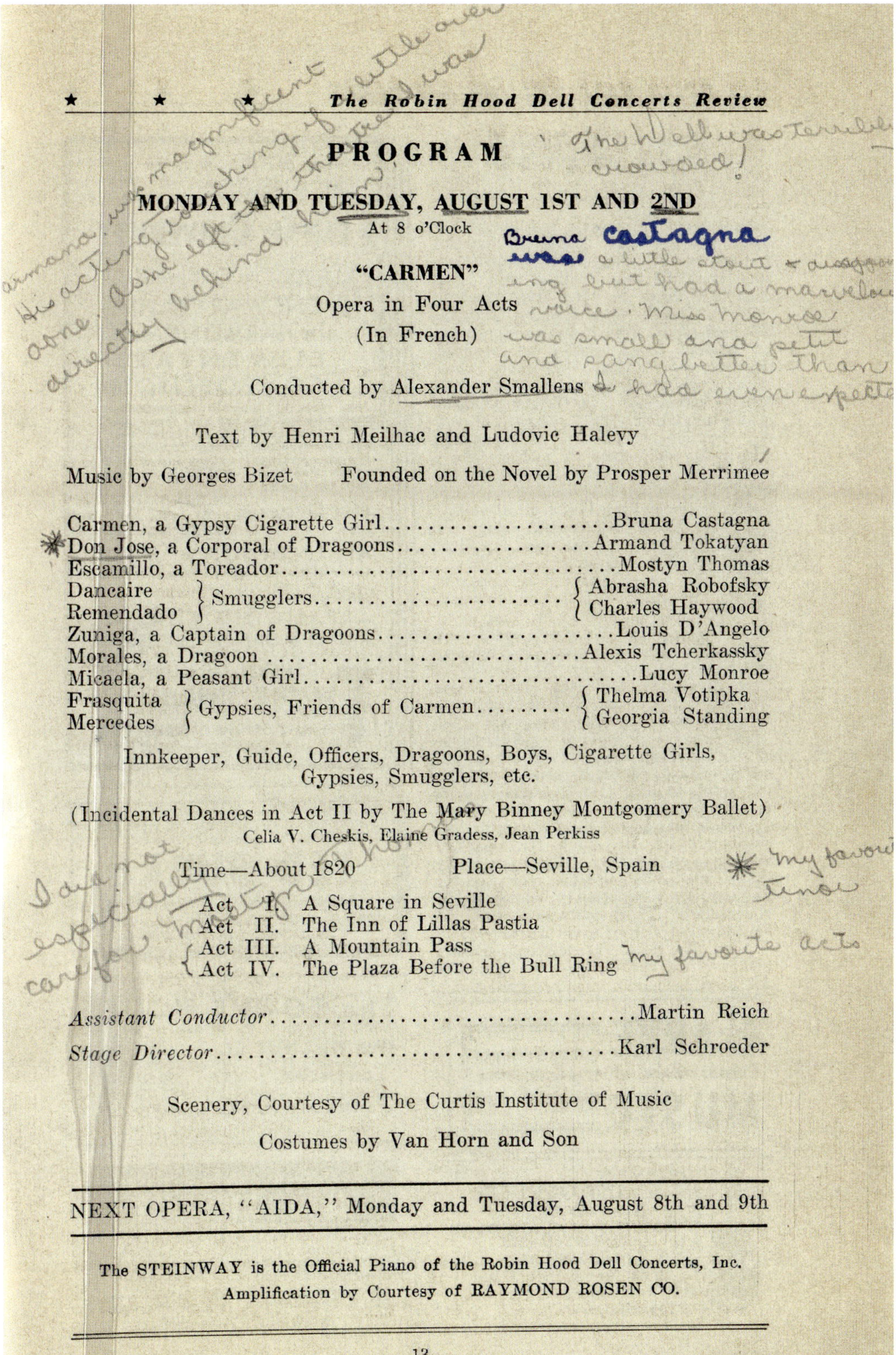

★ ★ ★ *The Robin Hood Dell Concerts Review*

**PROGRAM**

**MONDAY AND TUESDAY, AUGUST 1ST AND 2ND**

At 8 o'Clock

**"CARMEN"**

Opera in Four Acts

(In French)

Conducted by Alexander Smallens

Text by Henri Meilhac and Ludovic Halevy

Music by Georges Bizet Founded on the Novel by Prosper Merrimee

| | | |
|---|---|---|
| Carmen, a Gypsy Cigarette Girl | | Bruna Castagna |
| Don Jose, a Corporal of Dragoons | | Armand Tokatyan |
| Escamillo, a Toreador | | Mostyn Thomas |
| Dancaire | Smugglers | Abrasha Robofsky |
| Remendado | | Charles Haywood |
| Zuniga, a Captain of Dragoons | | Louis D'Angelo |
| Morales, a Dragoon | | Alexis Tcherkassky |
| Micaela, a Peasant Girl | | Lucy Monroe |
| Frasquita | Gypsies, Friends of Carmen | Thelma Votipka |
| Mercedes | | Georgia Standing |

Innkeeper, Guide, Officers, Dragoons, Boys, Cigarette Girls, Gypsies, Smugglers, etc.

(Incidental Dances in Act II by The Mary Binney Montgomery Ballet)

Celia V. Cheskis, Elaine Gradess, Jean Perkiss

Time—About 1820 Place—Seville, Spain

Act I. A Square in Seville
Act II. The Inn of Lillas Pastia
Act III. A Mountain Pass
Act IV. The Plaza Before the Bull Ring

*Assistant Conductor*.................Martin Reich

*Stage Director*.................Karl Schroeder

Scenery, Courtesy of The Curtis Institute of Music

Costumes by Van Horn and Son

NEXT OPERA, "AIDA," Monday and Tuesday, August 8th and 9th

The STEINWAY is the Official Piano of the Robin Hood Dell Concerts, Inc.
Amplification by Courtesy of RAYMOND ROSEN CO.

13

Fifteen-year-old Dorothy Miller's annotated August 1938 Robin Hood Dell program.
(Free Library of Philadelphia, Print and Picture Collection)

## New Leadership, New Labor Agreement

By the late 1930s, the cooperative plan implemented in 1935 by which a group of Philadelphia Orchestra musicians ran the Dell and programmed the concerts was no longer working effectively. The musicians wanted a change. A new plan was needed, along with a new way of supporting the summer concerts, which had been lagging. On April 27, 1939, Samuel R. Rosenbaum, vice president of The Philadelphia Orchestra Association and newly elected president of Robin Hood Dell Concerts Inc., spoke before a group gathered at the Bellevue-Stratford Hotel. The occasion was a celebration of the 35th anniversary of the Women's Committees of The Philadelphia Orchestra and announcement of a new campaign to "Save the Dell." Rosenbaum told the group: "The results of the cooperative arrangement have been declining year after year until the whole thing has reached too low a plane for the Philadelphia Orchestra and for music in Philadelphia."[7] Major changes were unfolding at the 10-year-old venue.

In a series of two meetings, on April 25 and 26, the old Dell Board, including President Curtis Bok and the Orchestra musicians, all resigned and were replaced by a new Board of three: Rosenbaum, Benjamin Ludlow, and William K. Huff. Rosenbaum, in addition to serving as vice president of The Philadelphia Orchestra Association, was president of WFIL Broadcasting Company and chairman of the labor committee of the National Association of Broadcasters. (He was also the husband of Philadelphia Orchestra harpist Edna Phillips.)* Ludlow was a prominent attorney and civic leader who had previously served as a Pennsylvania state representative. Huff, as previously noted, had been executive director of The Philadelphia Forum since its founding in 1921 and had served as manager of the Dell since 1935. He was appointed manager again while also serving on the Board. His salary, as manager, was $2,500 for the eight-week season.

At subsequent meetings in May, the three-member Dell Board elected new members that expanded the group to more than a dozen and hired new staff. Philadelphia Orchestra violinist John Molloy was engaged as assistant manager and orchestra personnel manager, while Emma Feldman, who had worked for the Dell on and off for several years, was hired to do ticket sales and promotion. Feldman would emerge as an important figure in Philadelphia concert life. She began selling tickets to Robin Hood Dell concerts out of her bookstore on Locust Street in the early 1930s. Soon after, with support from Arthur Judson, she started producing small concerts. In 1935, she founded the All Star Concert Series, which produced recitals and concerts at the Academy of Music featuring local and international artists. In 1961, the All

* Five years after assuming the Dell presidency, Rosenbaum wrote a lengthy article titled "The Philadelphia Orchestra and Robin Hood Dell" that was published in the September 1944 issue of *Tempo*, a journal devoted to contemporary concert music. The article traced the history of the Dell and assessed its current status.

Star Concert Series would merge with the Philadelphia Forum, the cultural event series that Edward Bok had founded and William Huff had directed, to create the All Star-Concert Forum. Feldman ran the All Star-Concert Forum series (later just All Star-Forum) until shortly before her death in 1966.

Another major development in the spring of 1939—in all likelihood the underlying issue that precipitated all of the aforementioned changes—was that Robin Hood Dell Concerts Inc. signed a trade agreement on May 16, 1939, with the musicians' Local No. 77 for the summer concert series. The musicians would now receive a guaranteed regular salary and have union protection; no longer would they have to assume the risk of working for a percentage of the ticket sales. The former arrangement, which was crucial in getting the Dell established 10 years earlier, was no longer tenable. The new agreement called for an orchestra of 90, with "present members of the Philadelphia Orchestra musicians to have first choice for employment." The season would be eight weeks, with five concerts a week, Monday through Friday; there would be no performances on Saturdays or Sundays unless needed to make up concerts postponed due to weather. In addition to the nightly five concerts, the workweek would "include three rehearsals not to exceed three hours each, with one fifteen-minute intermission for each rehearsal." The minimum salary for the musicians was $60 per week (the weekly minimum was what the lowest-paid musicians made; first chair and other higher-position players made more).[8]

To support these changes, a new group was established, originally known as the Committee of 400 (based on the goal of lining up 400 Dell subscribers) but later changed to "Friends of the Dell." Composed of contributors of $50 or more whose donation entitled them to seats in the reserved section of the venue, members of the group took an active role in supporting the Dell. This was the beginning of the Friends of the Dell, the subscriber group that would evolve to play a key role in supporting the Dell over many years. In spring 1939, the Friends of the Dell kicked off a campaign with the goal of selling $45,000 in subscriptions to the upcoming summer season. Coupon books were offered at $3 for 12 admissions or $5 for 24 admissions to the unreserved section, or $8 for 20 admissions to the reserved section. (Subscription prices for the least expensive seats—about 24 cents a ticket—were about the same as when the Dell opened in 1930.) Ten balloons were released at the June 5, 1939, kickoff event downtown, each carrying a coupon book for the lucky finder. Friends of the Dell also circulated a citywide petition in support of the Dell and sponsored a "Save the Dell" dinner at the Bellevue-Stratford Hotel.[9]

## The Bombardier

The 1940s began with a bang at the Dell, literally. The opening concert of the 1940 season was an all-Tchaikovsky program on June 18 conducted by Eugene Ormandy, with one of the Russian composer's most popular pieces, the *1812 Overture*, serving as the finale. Tchaikovsky had written the piece in 1882 for the dedication of a cathedral in Moscow that commemorated the country's successful defense against Napoleon's army in the French invasion of Russia in 1812. The stirring symphonic work quotes a Russian folk song and chant and the French National anthem, "La Marseillaise," to depict the opposing forces; it ends with a thrilling orchestral climax accompanied by bells and real cannon fire. That is how Tchaikovsky originally scored the piece, which was premiered in a tent outside the cathedral, but the practicality of using actual cannons made such instrumentation a rarity in performance in later years; percussion instruments generally substituted for the cannon. For the 1940 Dell performance, Ormandy wanted to follow the original score and use a real cannon, for which he enlisted the help of the Pennsylvania National Guard. Upon learning of these plans, A. Rex Riccardi, secretary of Local No. 77, informed the Dell that "if the cannon is to be fired as part of the performance, we will require that it be played by a member of Local 77, as it will, under those circumstances, be an instrument of the Orchestra."[10]

To comply with the union requirement, Dell officials held auditions at the National Guard armory at Broad and Wharton streets in South Philadelphia "to select a performer who can play the cannon with due regard to its musical value." The musician they chose to serve as "bombardier" for the concert was Charles Lemisch,

**NOISE FOR ART'S SAKE** None of these gunners had the title of "symphony bombardier," but they were the boys who made the most noise during the playing of Tchaikowski's "1812 Overture" at Robin Hood Dell last night. For it was they, as members of the 111th Infantry, Pennsylvania National Guard, who fired 37-millimeter guns at the appropriate point in the score. The "symphony bombardier" said when.

■ *The Philadelphia Inquirer,* June 19, 1940. (From *The Philadelphia Inquirer.* © 1940 Philadelphia Inquirer, LLC. All rights reserved. Used under license. Retrieved from Newspapers.com)

a 64-year-old veteran of the Spanish-American War who had played French horn during service in Cuba. Although not a member of The Philadelphia Orchestra, Lemisch was a member of Local No. 77 and would be paid union scale for his services.[11] In actuality, his role was ceremonial; he did not "play" anything. For the concert, a squad of gunners from the 111th Infantry, Pennsylvania National Guard, was set up with a pair of 37-millimeter anti-tank guns on the bank of the Schuylkill River, accompanied by Lemisch and Orchestra Assistant Conductor Sylvan Levin. As the Orchestra played, Levin followed the score with a flashlight and at the appropriate time cued Lemisch, who cued the guardsmen to fire.

While not exactly what Ormandy had envisioned, or Tchaikovsky had written, the unusual configuration had the desired effect. *The Philadelphia Inquirer* described the concert as a "triumphant success," reporting that "the baby cannon were fired alternately, not simultaneously, at five-second intervals, and thus, with the musical reinforcements of the Orchestra under Mr. Ormandy's direction . . . the inaugural all-Tchaikovsky program came to a blaring, enthusiastically applauded end."[12]

## Auspicious Debuts

The year 1940 saw the Dell debuts of two world-famous Black singers with local ties: contralto Marian Anderson, who was born and raised in South Philadelphia, and bass-baritone Paul Robeson, who had family in the city and would spend his final years in West Philadelphia. Each in their own way had become an icon of the Civil Rights Movement by the time of their first appearances at the Dell.

Anderson was 43 when she debuted at the Dell on July 18, 1940, a veteran concert artist 15 months removed from her landmark performance at the Lincoln Memorial in Washington, DC, on Easter Sunday, April 9, 1939. The story behind that historic event is well known: After Anderson was denied the opportunity to perform at the Daughters of the American Revolution's prestigious Constitution Hall in Washington because she was Black, a group of activists, including First Lady Eleanor Roosevelt, arranged for her to give an outdoor concert at the Lincoln Memorial. The concert, which drew an integrated audience of 75,000 and was broadcast nationally on radio, became a signal event in the Civil Rights Movement.

When she performed at Robin Hood Dell the following year, the first of four Dell appearances over the course of the 1940s, Anderson was greeted as a hometown hero. *The Philadelphia Inquirer* reported that the concert set a Dell record of more than 12,000 attendees and that several thousand were turned away. The paper also noted the unusual circumstances of Anderson's arrival at the venue: "There was something of a mob scene when the soloist's chauffeur became confused and Miss Anderson appeared at the general admission entrance. Alert park guards rescued her from enthusiastic fans . . . and directed the chauffeur to the soloist's private entrance at the rear of

Marian Anderson receives the prestigious Philadelphia Award on March 18, 1941, eight months after her July 1940 debut at the Robin Hood Dell. (*The Evening Bulletin* photograph collection, Special Collections Research Center, Temple University Libraries)

the orchestra shell. Inside the Dell the crush was almost as bad, and there were several cases of fainting."[13] Describing Anderson's program of opera arias, spirituals, and one of her signature vocal pieces, *The Philadelphia Inquirer* reported:

> Miss Anderson was at her magnificent best. Dressed in a light blue evening gown, with an orchid at her left shoulder, the great Negro contralto thrilled her listeners with her rich, round-toned voice, and the sonority of her unequaled lower tones, in the famous Handel Largo ("Umbrai [*sic*] Mai Fu") and again in the dramatic recitative and aria "O Mio Fernando" from Donizetti's "La Favorita." [Later in the program], Miss Anderson sang three Negro Spirituals with the Orchestra—"Deep River," "Heav'n, Heav'n" and "Sometimes I Feel Like A Motherless Child." She repeated "Heav'n, Heav'n" as an encore and then . . . sang Schubert's "Ave Maria" as only Marian Anderson can sing it.[14]

A little more than a month later, Paul Robeson made his Dell debut. A true Renaissance man, the multitalented Robeson excelled in many areas—sports, music, theater, film—while working tirelessly for civil rights and racial justice. Like Anderson, Robeson was a veteran concert artist by the time he first performed at the Dell on August 1, 1940, at 42. Also like Anderson, he was known particularly for his interpretations of spirituals, which he featured prominently in his concerts. (Between the Hall Johnson Choir performances in the 1930s and Anderson's and Robeson's concerts in the 1940s, Dell audiences had become quite familiar with spirituals.)

Reporting on the 1940 concert, *The Philadelphia Inquirer* noted that "Robeson's winning stage presence immediately captivated the audience, and his superlative singing endeared him considerably more. . . . Robeson's concert was comprised principally of folk songs [spirituals], all of which were sung in his familiar voice of rich timbre, with

Robin Hood's Men

"THE BETTER TO HEAR YOU WITH . . " Paul Robeson, at rehearsal, cups his hand to his ear to hear how his voice sounds to an audience. The distinguished Negro bass-baritone will be the soloist at Robin Hood Dell on Thursday night.

Notice in the July 25, 1943, *Philadelphia Record* of Paul Robeson's upcoming concert at the Robin Hood Dell on July 29, his last appearance at the venue. (Scrapbook, Mann Center for the Performing Arts Archives)

impeccable fidelity to pitch and exceptional clarity of enunciation." After the main part of the program, "vociferous requests for encores" prompted several more numbers, including "Old Man River," the song from the 1927 musical *Show Boat* that Robeson had made famous on stage and screen, and "Ballad for Americans," a ten-minute patriotic cantata composed in 1939 that became one of his signature concert finales.[15]

Robeson appeared annually at the Robin Hood Dell from 1940 to 1943, drawing large, appreciative audiences each time; "11,000 Acclaim Paul Robeson at Dell" ran the August 1, 1942, headline of the city's Black newspaper, *The Philadelphia Tribune*. While his renditions of spirituals were always a highlight, Robeson's repertoire expanded in this period to include folk songs of other nations and vocal pieces from the Western classical tradition. In his Dell appearance on July 30, 1943, he sang English, German, and Russian folksongs; pieces by Felix Mendelssohn and Modest Mussorgsky; and several spirituals. His multi-song encore concluded, as usual, with "Ballad for Americans." That was Robeson's last appearance at the Robin Hood Dell. By the mid-1940s his increasing political activism, including staunch support of the Soviet Union, had made him a controversial figure, significantly curtailing his musical career.

Like the Hall Johnson Choir concerts of the early 1930s, audiences at the Anderson and Robeson concerts at the Dell in the 1940s were diverse. *The Philadelphia Tribune* listed the names of several prominent Black Philadelphians at Robeson's July 9, 1941, concert, and the following year, under the heading "No Color Bar," the paper reported on "the large mixed audience" at Anderson's July 6, 1942, concert.[16] There was never a "color bar" at the Dell per se—the concerts were open to all—but social norms at the time were such that Black people rarely attended concerts at the venue unless an African American artist or group was featured, in which case it was understood that the audience would be racially mixed.

## Benny Goodman Integrates the Dell Stage

The Dell debut of jazz clarinetist and bandleader Benny Goodman on July 10, 1941, was notable for several reasons: It featured a new work by Igor Stravinsky, with Goodman himself leading the piece in his symphonic conducting debut; it involved a dispute with José Iturbi that made national headlines (again); and it was the first time a racially integrated group performed at the Dell.

Goodman rose to fame in the mid-1930s as the "King of Swing," leading the nation's most popular big band during the height of the swing era of jazz. While not a vocal civil rights activist, he used his popularity to break down racial barriers of the time by featuring small integrated ensembles at his shows. Black and White jazz musicians sometimes played together informally or in small clubs in the 1930s, but societal norms did not allow integrated bands in major venues. Goodman was one of the first to successfully challenge such discrimination by having Black and White musicians play together in his small ensembles—quartets, quintets, sextets—as part of his big band shows. Due to his enormous popularity, he essentially forced major concert and dance halls to book his integrated small groups when they hired his much in-demand big band.

Goodman was still at the height of his fame when he was engaged to play the Robin Hood Dell with his big band and sextet in July 1941. An accomplished classical as well as jazz musician, he did triple duty that evening: He was the featured soloist in Mozart's Clarinet Concerto; he conducted the world premiere of a new orchestral arrangement of *Tango*, a short piece composed by Igor Stravinsky in 1940; and he performed with his sextet and big band. The conductor for the symphonic pieces that constituted the first part of the program, including the Mozart concerto, was supposed to be Iturbi, but when the mercurial conductor and pianist learned that Goodman was to be the soloist, he balked. "[Goodman] is a jazz-band leader. It would be beneath my dignity to conduct for him," he said, insisting that Dell management find another soloist. Upon hearing this, Goodman suggested that the Dell find an American conductor instead, which is exactly what they did, engaging conductor and pianist Edwin McArthur. As with other Iturbi incidents, the dispute made national headlines, reported in *The New York Times*, *Time* magazine, and other publications.[17]

The Stravinsky piece *Tango* was the first work the great Russian-born composer wrote entirely in America. Having recently settled in Hollywood after leaving war-torn Europe, Stravinsky had lost much of the royalty income from his earlier works and reportedly wrote *Tango* to make money. Although the piece was originally written for piano, the version Goodman led at the Dell was scored for chamber orchestra by Felix Guenther, a German-born pianist, arranger, and conductor who had also recently fled Europe. Stravinsky reportedly approved Guenther's arrange-

■ Benny Goodman (*right*) in a light moment with conductor Edwin McArthur (*left*) during rehearsal at the Robin Hood Dell for his July 10, 1941, performance. (Adrian Siegel photographs, Philadelphia Orchestra Association records, Kislak Center for Special Collections, Rare Books, and Manuscripts, University of Pennsylvania)

ment.[18] According to *The Philadelphia Inquirer*, while the rest of the program was very well received, the Stravinsky piece as conducted by Goodman "earned a moderate reception from the audience. Presumably, it was the music."[19]

Following the classical selections, the final part of the program featured Goodman's sextet and big band. The sextet at this time included Black musicians Cootie Williams on trumpet, Big Sid Catlett on drums, and Charlie Christian on guitar, and White musicians Mel Powell on piano, Walter Iooss on bass, and Goodman on clarinet. However, Christian, a pioneer of the electric guitar in jazz, became ill with tuberculosis just before the engagement and was replaced by White guitarist Tom Morgan. (Christian would die in early 1942.) The sextet's appearance at the Dell was groundbreaking. While Black artists had been featured at the venue before, it was always in "separate" capacities: the Hall Johnson Choir performing separately from the Orchestra; Marian Anderson or Paul Robeson accompanied by, but standing apart from, the Orchestra. It was not until Goodman and his musicians took the Dell stage on July 10, 1941, that Black and White musicians actually played together, side by side, as an ensemble. Catlett and Williams also played with the big band, yet another advancement in breaking racial barriers, as it was generally just Goodman's small ensembles that were integrated at this time, not the full band.[20]

While coverage of the concert by Philadelphia's mainstream White newspapers did not make note of this significant development, *The Philadelphia Tribune* did, reporting: "Goodman, the clarinet jazz virtuoso, . . . dominated this program, but not without permitting his sepia members to star on this night, for this was the first time any colored musicians have appeared in an orchestra at the Robin Hood Dell." The article concluded by noting: "Right now, regardless to traditions, it would appear that Mr. Goodman is determined to use colored musicians in his band, whenever and wherever possible."[21]

Two love birds at a 1941 Robin Hood Dell concert, as shown in *The Philadelphia Inquirer*, July 13, 1941. (From *The Philadelphia Inquirer*. © 1941 Philadelphia Inquirer, LLC. All rights reserved. Used under license. *The Philadelphia Inquirer* photograph collection, Special Collections Research Center, Temple University Libraries)

A technician installs a new speaker as part of an upgraded sound system in advance of the 1942 Robin Hood Dell season. (*The Philadelphia Inquirer* photograph collection, Special Collections Research Center, Temple University Libraries)

A month after Goodman's appearance, harmonica virtuoso Larry Adler made his debut at the Dell. Known for his fine musicianship and first-rate performances of the classical repertoire on what was generally considered a folk instrument with limited expressive possibilities, Adler had impressed everyone, from George Gershwin to Maurice Ravel, with his playing of their music. As Adler notes in his autobiography, Ravel gave him special rights to perform the composer's signature piece, *Bolero*, which Adler gave as an encore at his August 7, 1941, Robin Hood Dell concert:

> In 1940 [it was actually 1941] I was soloist with the Philadelphia Orchestra's Robin Hood Dell concerts. Saul Caston, the conductor, suggested an encore; when I chose *Bolero* the librarian objected. Performance fees for one performance were very high, not worth it for an encore. Elkan-Vogel, Ravel's publishers, were in Philadelphia; I went to their office and announced myself. Mr. Elkan [who had conducted at the Dell in the 1930s] came out and told me he knew about me. Ravel had left instructions that I was to have free rights to play the *Bolero* in whatever medium I pleased. That right is unique to me.[22]

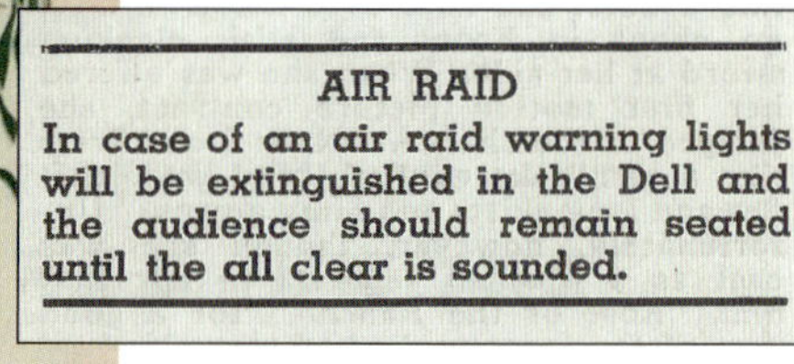
AIR RAID

In case of an air raid warning lights will be extinguished in the Dell and the audience should remain seated until the all clear is sounded.

**(above)** ■ A reminder that the nation was at war, this notice appeared in the program for Robin Hood Dell concerts the week of July 5, 1943. (Playbills, Mann Center for the Performing Arts Archives)

**(left)** ■ 1943 Robin Hood Dell poster. (Mann Center for the Performing Arts Archives)

## Robin Hood Dell Orchestra

The issue of the name of the Dell ensemble was finally resolved with the opening of the 1942 season. As previously noted, the ensemble was called the "Philadelphia Orchestra" for the Dell's first few years, then there was a period of ambiguity before settling on the "Men of the Philadelphia Orchestra" in 1935. That name still generated confusion, however, so starting in 1942 the ensemble was officially designated the "Robin Hood Dell Orchestra." They would play, and occasionally record, under this name for the next 27 years. Music critics and journalists often took pains to explain the difference and note how the Robin Hood Dell Orchestra was essentially, but not exactly, The Philadelphia Orchestra. However, the general public did not make the distinction for the most part, and even guest artists with the ensemble would claim that they had performed with The Philadelphia Orchestra when it was, in fact, the Robin Hood Dell Orchestra with which they appeared.

## Judy Garland's First Concert

Of all the auspicious Dell debuts in the early 1940s, the one that garnered the most national attention was the July 1, 1943, performance by 21-year-old Judy Garland. It was the first public concert of her career. While a veteran of stage and screen and a major star at that time—she had made a series of popular movies with actor Mickey Rooney in the late 1930s and early 1940s and had starred in the iconic film *The Wizard of Oz* in 1939—Garland had never performed as a solo artist in a concert setting. Her 1943 Dell concert with Andre Kostelanetz conducting was a great success and added another dimension to the young entertainer's already multifaceted career.

Garland's star power was such that the concert drew a record crowd, with lines forming at the gates three-and-a-half hours before showtime. "Concert goer and hep cat brushed elbows in a mad scramble for the ticket gate long before curtain time," *The Philadelphia Inquirer* reported. "By trolley and foot they came, the ant-like lines increasing every minute."[23] The final totals were some 15,000 ticket-buying attendees, perhaps an equal number listening on the hillsides outside the gates, and some 5,000 who left when they could not find spots close enough. The concert was in two parts, each of which began with symphonic selections and concluded with Garland

■ Judy Garland rehearsing with the Robin Hood Dell Orchestra in advance of her July 1, 1943, concert at the Dell. (Adrian Siegel photographs, Philadelphia Orchestra Association records, Kislak Center for Special Collections, Rare Books, and Manuscripts, University of Pennsylvania)

■ This profile in the November 1943 issue of *Movie and Radio Guide* recounts the success of Judy Garland's concert at the Robin Hood Dell earlier that year. (Scrapbook, Mann Center for the Performing Arts Archives)

singing with the Orchestra—a medley of Gershwin songs wrapping up the first part and songs she had made famous in her movies the second part. The latter, of course, included "Over the Rainbow" from *The Wizard of Oz*.

As *The Philadelphia Inquirer* reported:

> Judy Garland, pert and pretty miss from Hollywood . . . , sang for the first time with a symphony orchestra. Miss Garland was radiant in a transparent pale organdy blue dress with silver spangles, a small bouquet of white flowers at her waist, her reddish golden hair shining in the stage spotlights.
>
> Frankly nervous at the beginning . . . the songstress gradually warmed to her stint, and the enthusiastic reception accorded that opening group [of Gershwin songs] must have removed her expressed fears that the audience wouldn't like her singing. . . . Things got better as they went along, but in Gershwin's "Strike Up the Band" Miss Garland really injected all that personality which has made her a leading screen songstress.[24]

By the final number of the concert—a spirited version of "The Joint Is Really Jumpin' Down at Carnegie Hall," which she sang in the about-to-be-released movie *Thousands Cheer*—Garland was fully in command, according to the *Inquirer*: "Judy really cut loose here, and apparently enjoyed it as much as the audience, for she said, 'I think it would be sorta fun if we did that last number over again.' In the encore, she substituted the words 'Robin Hood Dell' once for 'Carnegie Hall.'"[25]

Other notable debuts in the early 1940s included the biggest names in concert music at the time: conductors Pierre Monteux, George Szell, Dimitri Mitropoulos, Erich Leinsdorf, William Steinberg, Andre Kostelanetz, and Lorin Maazel, who was a 13-year-old conducting prodigy; pianists Arthur Rubinstein, Rudolph Serkin, Oscar Levant, and William Kapell (Vladimir Horowitz was scheduled but had

The great French conductor Pierre Monteux debuted at the Robin Hood Dell in 1941. He is shown here rehearsing the Robin Hood Dell Orchestra in 1954. Behind Monteux is the tarp the Dell used to protect the musicians from the summer sun during daytime rehearsals. (Free Library of Philadelphia, Print and Picture Collection)

to cancel due to a hand injury); violinists Yehudi Menuhin, Albert Spalding, Isaac Stern, Nathan Milstein, Jasha Heifetz, and Bronislaw Huberman; singers Kirsten Flagstad, Gladys Swarthout, John Charles Thomas, Lawrence Tibbett, Eleanor Steber, Jeanette MacDonald, Robert Merrill, and Richard Tucker; and cellist Gregor Piatigorsky, who had moved to Philadelphia in 1942 to become head of the Cello Department at the Curtis Institute of Music.

Three weeks before young Lorin Maazel's July 23, 1943, Dell debut, he was the subject of correspondence between Frances Wister and Philadelphia Orchestra Manager Harl McDonald. McDonald was considering booking Maazel for an Orchestra Children's Concert at the Academy of Music. On July 1, he wrote to Wister:

> I enclose information on LORIN MAAZEL which I have just received from New York. In all probability we would have to pay the youngster between $250 and $350. Do you think he would be worth any such amount? Frankly, the net earnings from the Children's Series are already so low that I hesitate to spend any sizable amount of money, although I do think it would be very interesting for all of the children to see one of their own on the podium. I shall be interested to see how he is received at Robin Hood Dell.

A few weeks later, after Maazel's Dell concert—which was a regular evening program, not a Children's Concert—Wister replied: "Unfortunately I have not been able to go to the Dell. I think the boy drew a big crowd but I don't remember the figures. [Attendance was 6,000.] The Dell audience has resolved itself mostly into summertime [and] curiosity seekers. . . . It would hardly be a guide for our Children's Concerts. I doubt he would bring in his fee, but perhaps I am wrong."[26]

The Orchestra did engage Maazel as conductor at a Children's Concert on January 7, 1945. McDonald's concerns, and Wister's prediction, turned out to be unfounded. As *The New York Times* reported, "An audience of several thousand saw and heard 14-year-old Lorin Maazel of Pittsburgh conduct the Philadelphia Orchestra in the first children's concert of the season today at the Academy of Music. Thunderous applause followed the . . . performance."[27]

## First Black Conductor

The Dell made another significant step in breaking racial barriers at the venue in 1944 when it engaged Dean Dixon, the first Black conductor to lead the Robin Hood Dell Orchestra. Born in Harlem to parents of Caribbean descent, Dixon studied at the Julliard School and Columbia University. He conducted the NBC Summer Symphony in 1941 and the Philharmonic Symphony Orchestra at Lewisohn Stadium, the summer version of the New York Philharmonic, in 1942, the first Black conductor to lead both ensembles. He had the same distinction when he led the

New fencing is installed at the Dell in advance of the 1944 season. The poster lists the world-famous artists appearing that year, including Arthur Rubinstein, Jasha Heifetz, Marian Anderson, and Gregor Piatigorsky. (Scrapbook, Mann Center for the Performing Arts Archives)

Robin Hood Dell Orchestra on July 17, 1944, in a program featuring two other Black artists: soprano Anne Brown and baritone Todd Duncan. Brown and Duncan had starred in the original 1936 production of the landmark Gershwin opera *Porgy and Bess* (conducted by Alexander Smallens), and songs from the opera formed a major part of their 1944 Dell program. As reported in *The Philadelphia Tribune*, members of the E. Gilbert Anderson Symphony Orchestra, Philadelphia's Black symphony, gave a dinner in honor of Dixon the night after the concert.[28]

## Sinatra at the Dell

Robin Hood Dell patrons were treated to an unexpected delight when Frank Sinatra made a brief, unscheduled appearance at the venue in July 1945. Sinatra first came into prominence in 1940 as a featured singer with Tommy Dorsey's big band. He left Dorsey after two years and embarked on a very successful solo career. In May 1945, he set out on an eight-week United Service Organizations (USO) tour to entertain the troops in Europe. Immediately upon his return, he accepted an invitation to attend the July 6 concert of his good friend, singer Dinah Shore, who was appearing that evening at the Robin Hood Dell with Kostelanetz.

Billed as the "First Lady of Popular Song," Shore was enjoying great popularity at the time as well. "Golly, this is the biggest thrill I've ever had in my life, singing at the Dell and with Andre Kostelanetz," she told the audience. Following the usual format for Dell concerts with popular singers, each half of the two-part program began with symphonic pieces by the Orchestra, followed by vocal selections by the featured artist with orchestral accompaniment. Shore sang a medley of songs by Richard Rodgers and Lorenz Hart to close the first half and a selection of songs by George and Ira Gershwin, Cole Porter, and Jerome Kern for the second half.[29]

Sinatra had arrived toward the beginning of the concert and was escorted to a seat in the fourth row to enjoy his friend's performance. After finishing her final song, Shore called Sinatra to the stage, to "a wild howl of approval" from the audience. Before singing, he asked for quiet, telling the audience: "I don't want to sound pampered, but I just entertained the greatest audience in the world—our fighting men. And I guess I'm spoiled because you could hear a pin drop. They appreciate any entertainment over there." Sinatra sang Gershwin's "Embraceable You" and Kern's "Old Man River," then he and Shore finished with a duet on Gershwin's "Summertime," which "was received with wild applause."[30] It was the only time Sinatra would appear at the Dell or its successor, the Mann Music Center.

Two weeks after the Dinah Shore concert, another popular female singer made her debut at the Dell: hometown favorite Jeanette MacDonald. Born and raised in West Philadelphia, MacDonald began as a singer and dancer in musical theater before becoming a singing film star in Hollywood musicals beginning in the late 1920s. She made several movies with French actor Maurice Chevalier, then was paired

■ Frank Sinatra sings during an impromptu appearance at a Dinah Shore concert at the Robin Hood Dell on July 6, 1945. Shore is at right. Published in *The Philadelphia Inquirer*, October 16, 1949. (From *The Philadelphia Inquirer*. © 1945 Philadelphia Inquirer, LLC. All rights reserved. Used under license. *The Philadelphia Inquirer* photograph collection, Special Collections Research Center, Temple University Libraries)

with Nelson Eddy in a series of highly successful MGM musicals starting in 1935. Eddy began his singing career as a young man in Philadelphia and performed at the Dell several times in the early 1930s. He and MacDonald became popular romantic partners in eight lavish musicals MGM produced in the late 1930s and early 1940s. By the time she appeared at the Dell on July 6, 1945, with Dimitri Mitropoulos conducting, MacDonald was a big star. "[Sixteen thousand] of her admirers thronged

Jeanette MacDonald with Dimitri Mitropoulos and the Robin Hood Dell Orchestra, July 20, 1945. (Oliver Daniel research collection on Dimitri Mitropoulos, Kislak Center for Special Collections, Rare Books, and Manuscripts, University of Pennsylvania)

the Dell last night to welcome her back to her home town," *The Philadelphia Inquirer* reported. "The crowd not only broke the season's record, but was one of the largest in Dell history. . . . Wild applause broke out at the close of the program, augmented by cheers and whistles, and, naturally, Miss MacDonald responded with a more than generous supply of encores."[31]

## More Board and Staff Changes

C. David Hocker, general manager of the Philadelphia Opera Company, served as manager of the Dell from 1940 to 1948. He worked under two presidents: Frederic H. Strawbridge, son of one of the founders of the Strawbridge & Clothier department store chain, who was president from 1942 to 1943, followed by Henry E. Gerstley, who was president from 1944 to 1948. Gerstley, owner of a manufacturing company, was president of the Philadelphia Opera Company at the time and later would serve as president of the Settlement Music School for many years. In 1943, Hocker hired Helen Martin as his assistant and secretary. Except for a brief hiatus for marriage and the birth of her son, Martin worked at the Dell for more than 50 years, eventually rising to president herself.

With little fanfare, Fredric R. Mann joined the Dell Board in 1941, an appointment that would have enormous implications for the venue in the years to come. Mann had made a fortune in business, but his passion was classical music. He had studied piano seriously in his youth and later, as a successful businessman and philanthropist, developed close friendships with many of the world's greatest conductors and soloists while actively supporting the careers of emerging musicians. He served as chairman of the Dell finance committee in 1943 and then as vice president in 1944 and 1945, before leaving due to a disagreement over management of the venue. He would return three years later to rescue the Dell from financial crisis and lead it as president for 40 years.

## Evolving Relationship

Robin Hood Dell Concerts Inc. maintained cordial relations with The Philadelphia Orchestra Association in the early 1940s for the most part, although there were occasional testy exchanges between their respective managers, David Hocker and Harl McDonald. The Orchestra was supportive of the Dell in a number of ways: lending it music, instruments, and equipment every summer; allowing the Dell to use the Orchestra's mailing list for its annual fundraising campaign; and even contributing $1,000 to the campaign itself for several years.[32]

On May 4, 1942, five months after the United States entered World War II, Dell President Frederic Strawbridge wrote to Philadelphia Orchestra Association President Orville Bullitt, outlining plans for the coming Dell season and seeking the Orchestra's support:

> Feeling that the need for fine music at this time will be greater than ever before, the Board of Directors of Robin Hood Dell has made plans for another Summer Season, and I hope that the Board of Directors of the Philadelphia Orchestra will give us another generous contribution as you have in years past. . . . Although we face the coming Summer Season without a deficit for the first time there is . . . an absolute necessity for a pre-Season Campaign, . . . and this year we hope to secure approximately $15,000.

McDonald responded two weeks later, informing Strawbridge that when his letter was presented to the Orchestra Board at its recent meeting, "the Board voted a contribution of $1,000 to the Robin Hood Dell Concerts for the 1942 season." But in a cryptic note that perhaps indicated some friction between the two organizations, McDonald noted that the Board also asked him "to express the following to the Board of Directors of Robin Hood Dell Concerts, Inc.":

> We are glad to assist the Dell in any way we can, but hope that in future years proper recognition of the men of the Philadelphia Orchestra is shown. We suggest that in the future they consider the employment of our Assistant Conductors, and that, in general, the affairs of the Dell may be so conducted as to maintain the cordiality of feeling which we wish to have.[33]

In his reply, Strawbridge assured McDonald that "complete and wholehearted cooperation is [the] earnest desire" of the Dell Board, but that in regard to using Orchestra assistant conductors, the Dell preferred having top-name conductors who would draw big audiences, noting that the Dell's policy was "toward the engagement of performers and conductors universally recognized for their notable achievements, or others from outside our City whose qualifications are known to be outstanding."[34]

Occasionally, McDonald would refuse Hocker's request for the loan of certain instruments or musical scores due to their poor condition or for some other reason. Such was the case when he wrote to Hocker in May 1945 that some of the scores Hocker had requested would not be available because they "have been very considerably re-edited by Mr. Ormandy and he has requested that these materials be used by no other conductor due to the fact that changes in bowings, phrasings, dynamics, etc., would make it impossible for him to use the material again without great loss of time in rehearsal."[35]

## Recordings

Another area of occasional contention between McDonald and Hocker concerned a new recording program the Dell embarked on with Columbia Records in the mid-1940s. Kostelanetz and Mitropoulos led the Robin Hood Dell Orchestra in recordings made in this period in the Academy of Music that were issued on Columbia's Masterworks label. Kostelanetz, who specialized in popular and light classical works, had appeared regularly at the Dell since his debut in 1939, often with his wife, soprano Lily Pons. He had also led the Judy Garland and Dinah Shore concerts at the Dell in 1943 and 1945, respectively. Mitropoulos, who debuted in 1944 and would be named the Dell's music director in 1945, was known for championing modern works. The conductors and the Robin Hood Dell Orchestra got equal billing on these recordings. Dell and Orchestra management worked out an agreement that the Dell would not record works that were in the Orchestra's active repertoire or recording catalog, but there were sometimes disagreements as to which pieces fell into that category.[36]

## Mitropoulos

Conducting duties in 1944 were mostly split among three well-known conductors, each of whom led an extended series of concerts that year: Dimitri Mitropoulos, who was then music director of the Minneapolis Symphony (having succeeded Ormandy in 1937, an appointment also arranged by Arthur Judson) and was a frequent guest conductor of the New York Philharmonic; George Szell, who was then based in New York City but in two years would begin his celebrated 25-year tenure with the Cleveland Orchestra; and Vladimir Golschmann, who was then in the midst of his 28-year term with the St. Louis Symphony Orchestra. There were also two guest conductors that year: Dean Dixon, the Dell's first Black conductor, as detailed earlier, and Sigmund Romberg, known primarily as a composer of musicals and operettas. On August 3, 1944, Romberg led an "American Composers' Night" featuring the music of a number of famous songwriters, many of whom were in attendance and were brought onstage for a salute. The interracial group included Oscar Hammerstein II, Richard Rodgers, Harold Arlen, Dorothy Fields, W. C. Handy, Herman Hupfeld, Luckey Roberts, and several others.

The Mitropoulos, Szell, and Golschmann concerts in 1944 were well received, but the Mitropoulos concerts were especially popular with audiences and critics. In September of that year, the Dell Board appointed him music director and chief conductor of the summer concert series, beginning in the 1945 season. "Three lusty cheers and then some more for the management of the Robin Hood Dell in getting Dimitri Mitropoulos as music director and conductor for the 1945 season!" wrote one music fan to the editor of *The Philadelphia Inquirer.* "Mitropoulos is in the forefront of the world's greatest conductors and Philadelphia is thrice-lucky in having him come here to take charge of our Fairmount Park open-air concert hall next summer."[37]

The Greek-born Mitropoulos was a most unusual individual in the high-profile conducting positions he held. Deeply religious, ascetic in appearance and lifestyle, he lived simply, had few possessions, and was exceptionally generous with his time and money. Also, unlike other prominent musical artists of the era in similar circumstances, he did not go to great lengths to hide the fact that he was gay, a decision that reportedly cost him prominent appointments.[38] And he was an exceptionally gifted conductor, with a demonstrated ability to lead orchestras in inspired performances.

David Amram, later a successful composer and instrumentalist in both classical music and jazz, was a teenager living in the Philadelphia area when he got to know Mitropoulos in 1946. Amram's mother was a friend of Dell President Henry Gerstley, through which connection Mitropoulos spent time with the Amram family, and young David got to attend Dell concerts and meet with the conductor backstage. Years later, Amram recalled his first encounter with Mitropoulos in June 1946:

> I noticed immediately that there was a constant electric energy that seemed to emanate from him. . . . He seemed to be able to see everything at a glance. At the same time there was a hint of a smile that played constantly about the corners of his mouth. He seemed to have life all figured out, with a kind of

Dimitri Mitropoulos conducts the Robin Hood Dell Orchestra on opening night, June 23, 1947. (*The Philadelphia Inquirer* photograph collection, Special Collections Research Center, Temple University Libraries)

Olympian chuckle about it all. He seemed totally aware of everything that was happening.

Soon after that first meeting, Amram attended a concert at the Dell, in which Mitropoulos conducted Claude Debussy's *Iberia* and Johannes Brahms's Symphony No. 1:

> When Mitropoulos walked out on stage to conduct, you could tell the musicians were glad to see him there. There was no looking at the floor, no zombie-like stares as if they were being humiliated by someone who was presumably going to lead them. They were glad he was there. And from the first downbeat to the last there was a kind of excitement I had never seen before at a concert. . . . I had never realized the fire and passion that lay in Debussy's music until I heard this performance.

Amram was equally moved by Mitropoulos's interpretation of the Brahms symphony:

■ Dimitri Mitropoulos in a pensive moment at the Dell. (Adrian Siegel photographs, Philadelphia Orchestra Association records, Kislak Center for Special Collections, Rare Books, and Manuscripts, University of Pennsylvania)

> The great torrents of energy, the contrasting pastoral and reflective moments sounded completely different. . . . I had the uncanny feeling that Brahms would have liked this performance more than any so-called Brahms experts, who made him drip with lugubrious, Germanic, pedantic, heavy-handed sentimentality. Mitropoulos interpreted this as a free piece.[39]

Mitropoulos programmed standard symphonic repertoire and conducted occasional pops concerts during his four years as music director, but he also gave audiences a heavy dose of new music. On opening night of the 1947 season, he led one of the early performances in Philadelphia of Sergei Prokofiev's Symphony No. 5, a piece written just three years earlier. "The Greek conductor seems like the ideal man for this work," wrote *The Evening Bulletin*. "His drive and energy kept the long curving line of the score moving . . . , and who but he could so well have realized the long, slow, tortured *Adagio* which forms the work's third movement."[40] Nine days later, conducting from the piano, Mitropoulos led the Philadelphia premiere of Austrian American composer Ernest Krenek's Piano Concerto No. 3, a work that Mitropoulos had commissioned and given its world premiere in Minneapolis the year before. It was a challenging piece that, at one point, had Mitropoulos reaching inside the piano to pluck the strings. "Dissonance is freely employed," wrote *The Philadelphia Inquirer*, "and on first hearing the composition sounded cerebral rather than inspired."[41]

## Broadcasting

The Dell began a new series of national radio broadcasts in 1948 while also exploring possibilities with the increasingly popular medium of television. Television ownership skyrocketed across the nation in this period; in Philadelphia, the three main stations—affiliates of CBS, ABC, and NBC—were all operating by 1948. Dell management initiated discussions with these stations about broadcasting concerts, but Local No. 77 required a fee of $12 per musician per broadcast ($1,080 per concert for the 90-piece orchestra). As noted in the June 24, 1948, meeting minutes of the Robin Hood Dell Concerts Inc. Board, the union demand "made it impossible to go forward with plans to televise the Dell concerts."[42]

The Dell's contract with the union did give it the right to broadcast up to two concerts a week on radio, however. At that same June 24 meeting, the Board approved an agreement with WFIL radio to broadcast concerts on Mondays and Thursdays, "with a contribution to the Dell of $200.00 per broadcast with a minimum guarantee of $1,200." Twelve such broadcasts were planned over the seven-week season, and WFIL made arrangements to have the Monday evening concerts broadcast nationally.[43]

The first national broadcast was scheduled for Monday, June 28, featuring the Dell debut of pianist and singer Hazel Scott, with conductor Paul Strauss. Unfortunately, the concert was postponed to the following night due to rain, so the broadcast did not happen. Scott, a Black musician who was adept at both classical music and jazz, was also a civil rights activist who was married at the time to prominent New York City Baptist minister and U.S. Congressman Adam Clayton Powell. At the Dell she performed Beethoven's Piano Concerto No. 1 in the first half of the program, then did a segment with her piano, bass, and drums trio in the second half. In the latter, "the pianist . . . was all over the keyboard . . . doing fantastic embroideries and variations," *The Philadelphia Inquirer* reported. The set included an original boogie-woogie Scott called "A Rainy Night in G."[44] Two years later, Scott would be the first African American to have her own television show, *The Hazel Scott Show*.

## Season Suspended

There were some successful seasons during Mitropoulos's tenure at the Dell. The 1946 season was the best attended in the venue's 17-year history, for example, with more than 200,000 tickets sold. But 1948 was disastrous. Ticket sales were lower going into the season, then a combination of bad weather and Philadelphia hosting the Republican National Convention that summer severely limited attendance. The venue's financial condition grew increasingly precarious as the season unfolded. "Our concerts here so far have been very unsuccessful," Mitropoulos wrote to friends in Minneapolis on July 13, "partly because of the weather and partly because people are more interested in conventions and in having a grand time than in coming to listen to our long-beard expressions in music."[45] Mitropoulos had recently made a $2,240 donation to Robin Hood Dell Concerts Inc. in support of the Board's efforts to keep the concerts going.[46]

Faced with a looming financial crisis—the deficit was estimated at $50,000—the Dell Board met several times in July 1948 to consider ways to both save the current season and sustain the venue over the long term. Board members approached powerful Philadelphia media mogul Walter Annenberg, whose holdings included *The Philadelphia Inquirer*, the *Daily News*, and WFIL television and radio stations, about his philanthropic organization, Inquirer Charities, taking over the concerts. Inquirer Charities had recently taken on sponsorship of the Philadelphia Forum series, which had also been struggling financially, and the Board hoped that Annenberg would consider doing the same for the Dell concerts. He expressed interest but declined because he did not think his organization was in a position to solicit funds from Friends of the Dell, who had already contributed substantially to the summer concert series. The Board also discussed approaching The Philadelphia Orchestra Association about taking over the concerts, but the timing was bad. The association was about to enter what were anticipated to be difficult labor negotiations with Local No. 77 regarding a new musicians' contract and was seriously preparing for the possibility of having to cancel the Orchestra's 1948–1949 season if the parties could not come to terms. (The association and the union did eventually agree on a new contract.)[47]

With no savior willing to step in and an immediate cash crisis at hand, the Board debated at its July 15 meeting whether to attempt to complete the season and run up a large deficit or end the season early to minimize its losses. They opted for the latter, voting to suspend the season after the July 17 program and cancel the last three weeks of concerts.[48] Management informed Mitropoulos and the orchestra musicians at intermission of the July 16 concert and asked them not to share the news until after the Board released a formal statement the next morning. Mitropoulos did not wait, however. At the conclusion of the concert that night, he told the audience, "You might as well enjoy it. Tomorrow night is the last night. The Friends of the Dell have let us down."[49] Forced to respond, Dell President Henry Gerstley issued the formal statement, which read in part:

> All of us realize what a serious action this is, and we have taken it most reluctantly and unhappily. This summer marked the Dell's 19th season and we entered on it confident it would go through successfully. However, several factors have adversely affected our plans, and we are compelled to terminate present activities at once. But the sudden and unwelcome end of this season does not mean the end of the Dell. We already are looking forward to 1949 and a new season which will witness different policies in purposes and programs.[50]

Predictably, there was a hue and cry from the public over the cancellation of the concerts. Newspaper editorials and letters to the editor decried the situation and questioned why a world-class music city such as Philadelphia could not support such an enterprise. "We people of Philadelphia and vicinity must and shall save Robin Hood

Dell. The trend to allow brutal forces to kill the noble and spiritual best in a community need not overtake Philadelphia," one patron wrote to *The Evening Bulletin*.[51] Several writers called for the city to subsidize the concerts; others called for programming more popular types of music, including one writer who suggested the Dell "look into the so-called 'hillbilly' field for the great American folk-music artists."[52]

Some blamed Mitropoulos's penchant for playing modern music for the drop in attendance, while others praised his adventurous programming. Among the former, one patron found it "incomprehensible that [Mitropoulos] picked such vague, somber, and ultra-classical pieces. It should be evident that people have no desire to pay good money to hear the 11th tone poem of some unknown Russian composer."[53] One despondent admirer of the conductor mused: "I do not wonder that Dimitri Mitropoulos will not be coming back to the Dell next summer. Philadelphians have certainly let him down, and it is a disgrace to our city that we are losing him."[54] The writer was correct: Mitropoulos would never conduct at the Dell, or the Academy of Music, again.

## Freddie Mann to the Rescue

Following its decision to cancel the remaining concerts, the Board met again on July 22, this time with Fredric R. Mann—"Freddie" to his many friends—in attendance. Mann, who had left the Board three years earlier in disagreement over its management of the Dell, was well known as a successful businessman, music lover, and philanthropist. Gerstley had reached out to him after the last Board meeting and asked him to consider rejoining the organization and helping to rescue it. "We were in California for the summer," Mann's daughter, Gilda Rand Mann Ellis, remembered in an interview years later, "and he gets this call that the Dell has folded, and to come home and save it[,] . . . and he came home to save the Dell."[55]

The fateful July 22 Board meeting that changed the direction of the Dell forever took all of 63 minutes, commencing at 4:00 P.M. and adjourning at 5:03 P.M. It began with a review of the organization's finances, followed by a statement by President Gerstley that he had been in consultation with Mann and several Board members and had come to the conclusion that the only way forward was a complete change in the Board of Directors. He then turned the meeting over to Mann.

Mann reported that he had met with the executive committee of the musicians' union—he was a longtime member of the union, although he was not a working musician himself—who informed him that "the present management and Board of Directors [of Robin Hood Dell Concerts Inc.] were to be blackballed by the Union for failure to pay the balance of three weeks' salaries . . . , and that the musicians would refuse to play the Dell in the future unless the Board of Directors resign and the present management be changed." Mann concluded by stating that he would be willing to accept the presidency of the Dell under those conditions.[56]

■ Fredric R. Mann.
(*The Evening Bulletin* photograph collection, Special Collections Research Center, Temple University Libraries)

At that point, General Manager David Hocker resigned. Gerstley followed by resigning the presidency and making a motion that Mann be elected president. The motion was approved unanimously, at which point the entire Board "presented their resignations to Mr. Mann, who accepted them. There being no further business the meeting adjourned at 5:03 P.M."[57]

Mann spent the following weeks and months rebuilding the Board, lining up artists and programs for 1949, and developing plans to stabilize the organization and its finances. As he told *The Philadelphia Inquirer*:

> My first and immediate objective will be to formulate a plan which I hope will be satisfactory to the holders of outstanding coupon books; that will make some provision for those loyal and devoted musicians who have suffered loss of salary and disruption of their plans because of the sudden ending of the Dell season. And finally the plan will set up a sound and solid financial basis for the future—a basis that will assure the public that the Dell is a permanent Philadelphia institution, dedicated to the high purpose of affording our fellow citizens the continued pleasure of great symphonic music and the opportunities to see and hear the outstanding musical artists of the world.[58]

That is exactly what Mann proceeded to do.

# 5.

# 1949–1959

## *The Philadelphia Plan, Free Concerts for All*

Fredric Rand ("Freddie") Mann was profiled in numerous publications, local and national, beginning in the late 1940s, not just for rescuing the Robin Hood Dell, but for his prominent role in Philadelphia civic and cultural life, as well as being a major contributor to Democratic Party politicians. Democrats would begin to seize control of Philadelphia's municipal government in this period, and Mann would be in the middle of the movement.

Born in 1903 to a Jewish family in Russia (like many of the famous musicians he would befriend), Mann came to America with his family as an infant. They settled in New Haven, Connecticut, where Freddie grew up. He studied piano seriously in his youth, including commuting to New York City for lessons and even returning to Russia for study at one point. But he was hit by a car while riding a bicycle in his mid-teens, and the injuries to his arms and shoulders ended any aspirations for a concert career. He attended Yale University for two years in the early 1920s, then moved to Philadelphia to study at the Wharton School of the University of Pennsylvania, from which he graduated in 1924. Philadelphia would be his home and base of operations for the rest of his life.

Soon after graduating from Penn, Mann married his first wife, Henrietta Weber, the daughter of a paper box manufacturer, and joined his father-in-law's firm. By the early 1930s, he had divorced Henrietta and left his father-in-law's firm to start his own cardboard box company, which became very successful. Mann would eventually own 22 factories, seven pulp mills, and forest acreage in five states.[1] In 1932 he met Silvia Rosenberg, a Broadway singer and dancer who was performing in a show at the Forrest

■ Violinist Isaac Stern (*left*) and Fredric Mann (*right*), circa 1950. (Courtesy of the Mann family)

Theatre in Philadelphia. They married later that year and would have four daughters, joining Mann's daughter from his first marriage. Silvia would be Freddie's lifelong partner in their many joint ventures, serving on the Boards and working on behalf of the music and Jewish organizations they supported; cohosting dinners and parties they held for notable musicians and dignitaries; and serving as "Jewish mother" to the many young musicians whose careers they helped advance, financially and artistically.

"I didn't inherit a fortune to distribute," Mann said late in life of his charitable contributions. "This is my hard-earned money I give out. You know the Hebrew

Freddie and Silvia Mann, flanking their good friend, pianist Arthur Rubinstein. (Courtesy of the Mann family)

word for charity is *tzedakah*, which really means justice. If you live opulently, you have to share with the less fortunate. If I eat, somebody else has to eat."[2]

## Philadelphia Mover and Shaker

Mann's wealth and business savvy, combined with his involvement in Philadelphia Democratic politics, put him in the inner circle of the movers and shakers who would transform the city's political landscape in the late 1940s and early 1950s. After some 90 years of iron-clad Republican control, an era marked by cronyism and corruption, Democrats made headway in Philadelphia in the 1948 city elections and then swept into power in 1952. Led by the two key figures in the city reform movement—Joseph S. Clark, who served as mayor of Philadelphia from 1952 to 1956 and U.S. senator from 1957 to 1969, and Richardson Dilworth, who served as district attorney from 1952 to 1956 and mayor from 1956 to 1962—Democrats took the reins of city government and implemented a wide range of municipal reforms. The legal basis for these reforms was a new Home Rule City Charter enacted in April 1951, which fundamentally redefined how city government would be structured and operate. Mann, a close ally of both Clark and Dilworth, was a member of the 15-person Philadelphia Charter Commission that drafted the transformative document.

In October 1951, Mann was appointed to the Fairmount Park Commission, the semiautonomous board of prominent Philadelphians who managed the city's vast park system. This was an advantageous appointment for the Robin Hood Dell, as the venue was part of the Fairmount Park system, and Dell management had to go through the commission for physical changes and improvements to the facility. Mann would remain a Fairmount Park commissioner until shortly before his death in 1987 and would serve as president of the commission from 1963 to 1967.

Upon taking office as mayor in January 1952, Clark appointed Mann as Philadelphia's first recreation commissioner, head of the new Department of Recreation established under the city charter. Previously, recreation had been a bureau in the Department of Welfare; now it was an autonomous department with its own cabinet-level commissioner. Mann had had a key role in creating the department as a member of the charter commission. In a letter to Clark in May 1952, he explained his vision for the department and his rationale for making its commissioner an advocate for both culture and physical recreation in the city:

> When I was active in helping to draft the chapter on the Recreation Department in the new Charter, I fought hard for departmental status for recreation—both cultural as well as physical. This came as a result of personal experience in seeing fine men who gave hours of time unselfishly and much of their means to civic cultural efforts being pushed around and treated to indignities when they came before [City] Council for appropriations on behalf of cultural institutions.
>
> I saw how Orville Bullitt for the Orchestra, Sturgis Ingersoll for the Art Museum, Charles Thompson for [Fairmount] Park, Joe Carson for the Library, and myself for the Dell, had no City Official spear-heading or being protagonist in their search for financial support from Council, which they well deserved.
>
> I felt the City could do a better job for organizations of this type and that having a department head who understood their problems and was sympathetic to their needs would be a great help in furthering their budgetary requirements with a sense of dignity that these institutions deserve.
>
> At that time I had no idea of being your Recreation Commissioner, and I am sure that you, best of all, can attest to this fact. Now that I am Recreation Commissioner I believe that as a practical matter the spirit of the Charter would be invalidated if you permitted the personal feelings of any individual to deter you from carrying out this provision of the Charter.[3]

The last sentence was in reference to Philadelphia Orchestra Association President Orville Bullitt raising objections with Clark about Mann's appointment to the association's Board by virtue of Mann's position as recreation commissioner. Mann urged Clark to hold firm to the new policy of having institutions such as the Orchestra work through the Department of Recreation in their negotiations with the city and not be influenced by back-channel appeals. Clark did hold firm, and Mann would wield considerable influence in the Philadelphia cultural community as a result, although his relationship with the Orchestra would be rocky.

While he knew the city's cultural landscape well, Mann also knew that he did not have the expertise to administer the physical recreation aspects of his department. Soon after his appointment, he recruited Robert W. Crawford, a highly regarded administrator then serving as superintendent of recreation in Oakland, California, to serve as deputy recreation commissioner in Philadelphia. Crawford stayed with the department for nearly 30 years, succeeding Mann as recreation commissioner in 1955 and becoming recognized nationally for his innovative leadership in Philadelphia. Crawford became president of the Fairmount Park Commission in 1970, serving as both commission president and recreation commissioner until his retirement in 1981. He also served on the Board of Robin Hood Dell Concerts Inc., led by his mentor, Mann, for much of that period.[4] (Crawford Circle at the entrance to the Mann Center is named in his honor.)

After three years in the position, Mann resigned as recreation commissioner in January 1955 to focus on his business and music activities, but when Richardson Dilworth took office as mayor a year later, he appointed Mann to the position of city representative and director of commerce. Mann's already high profile grew even higher in this prominent position, which he held until 1966. In addition to overseeing business and industry development in the city, the position entailed representing the city or the mayor at major events, greeting visiting dignitaries, and promoting Philadelphia nationally and internationally. (As detailed later, Mann used his position as director of commerce, with authority over Philadelphia International Airport, to reroute flights around Robin Hood Dell on concert nights to minimize airplane noise.)

Mann held other public positions as well, including serving on the Delaware River Port Authority and the governor's Advisory Council on Recreation. He did all this work pro bono. He even paid Crawford's moving expenses from California and for part of Crawford's salary. When Crawford told Mann that he could not accept the Philadelphia position at the deputy commissioner's salary, Mann offered to pay Crawford the difference between the commissioner's and deputy commissioner's salaries. Mann reasoned that, with his many other responsibilities, he would not be able to run the Recreation Department himself, and since Crawford would essentially be doing the work of the commissioner, he should be paid at that level.[5]

## Friend to Musical Luminaries and Emerging Artists

Even as he was leading city agencies, serving as president and general manager of the Robin Hood Dell, and running his businesses, Mann continued to cultivate close personal relationships with the world's top musical artists while helping emerging musicians early in their careers. His good friends included such giants as pianist Arthur Rubinstein, violinist Jascha Heifetz, and cellist Gregor Piatigorsky. These relationships sometimes extended into the financial realm. Zubin Mehta, the Indian-born conductor who benefited greatly from Mann's support early in his career and became a good friend, recalled the financial dealings of the close-knit group:

> Freddie . . . was a great friend of Rubinstein, Heifetz, and Piatigorsky, the "Million-Dollar Trio." . . . Rubinstein was in and out of his home all the time. Freddie would invest money for Rubinstein and not tell him if the stock went down. He took the loss himself. . . . Through Rubinstein he met Heifetz, and Heifetz was very money conscious. And he invested for Heifetz and took *more* of a loss for him. He didn't invest for Piatigorsky because Piatigorsky was married to Miss Rothschild [Jacqueline Rebecca Louise de Rothschild Piatigorsky, heiress to the French banking family fortune]. He didn't need Freddie's advice financially. . . . They were all great friends.[6]

Other famous musicians with whom Mann was close included violinists Isaac Stern, Yehudi Menuhin, Mischa Elman, Henryk Szeryng, and Itzhak Perlman; cellist Mstislav Rostropovich; pianists José Iturbi, Van Cliburn, William Kapell, and Jerome Lowenthal; and singers Jan Peerce, Robert Merrill, Richard Tucker, and Roberta Peters. Young conductors whose careers he helped advance include Daniel Barenboim, Lorin Maazel, and Mehta. "He loved Zubin," Mann's granddaughter, Jane Gitomer, remembered. "Zubin was like a son almost [to him]."[7]

Barenboim met Mann when he first came to the United States as a young pianist in the late 1950s. He appeared frequently as a pianist and conductor at the Dell in the 1960s and 1970s and grew close to Mann. He remembered Mann's ability to relate to people from all walks of life:

> Although he had been an ambassador [to Barbados in the late 1960s] and he knew presidents and he mixed very easily in high society, there was something very earthy about him [that made him] have a very normal, natural contact with workers, with musicians, with people who one could imagine . . . would be mistrustful . . . of someone who had contacts at the White House. . . . He made everybody feel very much at home with him. He was a very smart fellow, you know. . . . He was very jovial and he was very nice and adorable, but he knew what he wanted and he knew he had to get certain things, . . . so when he felt he needed to, he went as a bulldog. . . . But nobody ever resented it.[8]

Contrary to Barenboim's last statement, many did resent Mann's occasional aggressive style, as we shall see.

## Reviving the Dell

Using his influence and contacts, political and musical, Mann set about reorganizing the Robin Hood Dell after its ill-fated 1948 season. He got the musicians' union to forgive the debt the Dell owed Orchestra musicians for the cancelled 1948 concerts and worked out a plan for patrons to redeem their unused tickets for those concerts. He undertook physical upgrades to the venue, revamped the concert schedule, lowered ticket prices, and lined up world-class conductors and soloists for 1949. His formula for revitalizing the Dell essentially boiled down to fewer concerts with better artists for lower prices for a greater number of patrons. He always insisted that the Dell should cater not to the "carriage trade" (that is, a wealthy clientele) but to everyday people who could not afford regular-season tickets to see The Philadelphia Orchestra at the Academy of Music.[9]

Beginning in 1949, the Dell would present 18 concerts over a six-week season (down from 28 concerts in previous years), with concerts on Mondays, Wednesdays, and Thursdays. Wednesdays, dubbed the "Symphonic Series," would be orchestra-only programs; Mondays and Thursdays, the "Master Series," would feature guest soloists. Mann's two-part strategy for financing the concerts relied, on the one part, on subscriptions from Friends of the Dell, who would contribute $100 or more and receive two seats in the reserved section for every concert, and on the other part from a matching subsidy from the city. Thus was born Mann's celebrated "Philadelphia Plan" (although it was not yet called that), a unique approach to supporting summer symphony concerts that would bring him and the Dell national recognition. The Dell Board set a goal of $50,000 in subscriptions for 1949 (which it actually surpassed by $5,000), and Philadelphia City Council appropriated $50,000 for the Dell that year.[10]

For the final, critical component of his grand plan—the performing artists—Mann got many of his famous friends to perform at the Dell in 1949, some of them for free or for reduced fees. Rubinstein, Heifetz, Piatigorsky, Stern, Peerce, Iturbi, Kapell, violinist Nathan Milstein, and conductor Leonard Bernstein are among the world-famous artists who appeared that year. Bernstein, a 1941 graduate of the Curtis Institute of Music, made his Dell debut conducting all three concerts the first week of the 1949 season. He had been an in-demand conductor ever since his legendary debut with the New York Philharmonic in 1943, when his performance as a last-minute substitute for the ailing Bruno Walter created a sensation. On opening night at the Dell on June 27, 1949, an audience of 10,000 heard Bernstein lead Metropolitan Opera stars tenor Lauritz Melchior and soprano Helen Traubel in the world premiere of a concert version of Richard Wagner's opera *Tristan und Isolde*.[11] The fol-

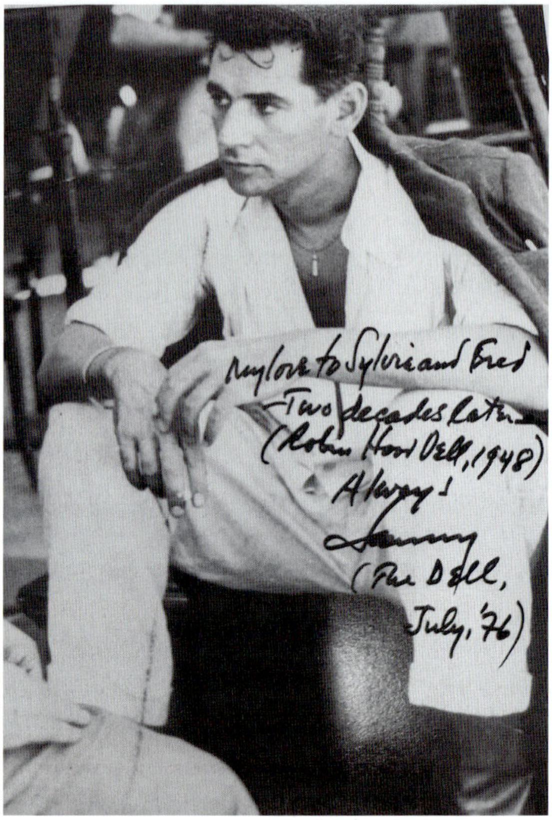


This photograph of Leonard Bernstein was taken at the time of his June 1949 debut at the Robin Hood Dell. Twenty-seven years later, he inscribed it to Silvia and Fred Mann, on the occasion of his appearance at the new Robin Hood Dell West in July 1976. (Bernstein had the wrong year for the photograph—it was 1949, not 1948—and the wrong number of decades: the 1976 inscription was almost three decades later, not two.) (Courtesy of the Mann family)

lowing night, Bernstein appeared as conductor and pianist, leading several symphonic pieces, as well as Beethoven's Piano Concerto No. 1, which he conducted from the keyboard. The third night he led a program with cellist Piatigorsky and violinist Milstein, each playing a concerto and then performing Johannes Brahms's Double Concerto together.

The remainder of the 1949 season was equally star-studded. Attendance was excellent for the most part, and the season was deemed a great success. It concluded on August 5—a Friday, as the Thursday concert was rained out—with Iturbi appearing as conductor and pianist before a crowd of 16,000. At intermission there were tributes and expressions of thanks to Fredric Mann from his fellow Dell Board members, from the city (represented by City Treasurer Ralph W. Pitman, introduced as "the most musical member of city government"), and from the Orchestra musicians.[12] The musicians presented Mann with a framed resolution that read, in part:

> Whereas, the efforts of Mr. Mann and those whom he has inspired to assist him have resulted in the resurgence of the Robin Hood Dell as a civic enterprise and have caused it to receive favorable publicity throughout the entire country so that Philadelphia is once more recognized as one of the leading musical cities of the nation and the world. Now, therefore be it
>
> Resolved, that the members of the Robin Hood Dell Orchestra express their heartiest appreciation, gratitude, and congratulations to Fredric R. Mann, and recognize his magnificent services to music in Philadelphia by a rising vote of thanks.[13]

As *The Philadelphia Inquirer* reported, "In responding, Mann, somewhat overwhelmed, said that without the cooperation of the city government, the Dell Board of Directors, the Fairmount Park Commission, the Orchestra players, the Friends of the Dell, and the general public the season could not have been as successful as it had been."[14] It was a refrain he would repeat often over the next 38 years.

## Duke at the Dell

Along with the world's top classical artists, one of the biggest luminaries in jazz performed at the Dell in 1949: Duke Ellington and his Orchestra were guest artists on July 25, 1949, a most unusual concert that featured rising and established jazz stars and culminated with the Ellington and Robin Hood Dell orchestras combining forces in a medley of Ellington hits. It was the first time Ellington's band ever performed with a symphony orchestra, a milestone he mentioned in his autobiography years later.[15] It was also the first time Black and White orchestras played together on the Dell stage. Some 13,000 were on hand for the historic event.

Edward Kennedy "Duke" Ellington was one of the most popular and respected bandleaders and composers in jazz at that time. He had written and recorded numerous hits, from romantic ballads to swing dance tunes, but was also beginning to experiment with longer-form pieces, including works that explored his African American heritage. He performed several of these works at the Dell in 1949, one of which was written specifically for the occasion and was Ellington's first composition for band and symphony orchestra.

The first half of the program featured just the Duke Ellington Orchestra, with Ellington in the triple role of bandleader, pianist, and composer. The band played all Ellington tunes, along with a song by his longtime writing and arranging partner, Billy Strayhorn. Strayhorn's "Brown Betty" featured a solo by Ellington's great alto saxophonist, Johnny Hodges. The band also played "Liberian Suite," a longer-form piece that the Liberian government commissioned Ellington to write in 1947 in honor of the centennial of the African nation's independence.

It was in the second half of the program that the Ellington and Robin Hood Dell orchestras combined to present their version of "symphonic jazz." Russ Case, an experienced conductor and arranger, directed the merged ensemble—around 117 musicians—in the performance of two Ellington compositions: "New World A-Comin'" and "Grand Slam Jam." "New World A-Comin'" was a rhapsodic piece for piano and orchestra, with the composer at the piano. Duke had premiered the piece at Carnegie Hall in 1943, but just with his band, not with a symphony orchestra as performed at the Dell. "Grand Slam Jam," an adaptation of a riff-based tune on which the Ellington band would sometimes jam, was written specifically for the Robin Hood Dell concert. As such, it is Ellington's first composition for band and symphony orchestra. He was so pleased with how well the two ensembles integrated

There are no known photographs of the July 25, 1949, Duke Ellington concert at the Robin Hood Dell, just this caricature published with *The Evening Bulletin* review of the concert the next day. (Scrapbook, Mann Center for the Performing Arts Archives)

on "Grand Slam Jam" that he later refashioned the piece and recorded it under the new title, "Non-Violent Integration."

Also on the bill with the Ellington Orchestra was singer Sarah Vaughan, then a rising star who would soon become one of the premiere vocalists in jazz. Following the combined orchestra performance, Vaughan sang several songs and, according to some reviewers, nearly stole the show. When Vaughan was finished, the two orchestras combined again for a finale of a medley of Ellington's hits, with Case again conducting and Ellington at the piano.

The concert was covered by both local and out-of-town newspapers, including several Black papers. Among the latter was the following enthusiastic review by the *Pittsburgh Courier*:

> Duke Ellington and Sarah Vaughan enjoyed their finest hours here last Monday night when they became the first beige artists of their ilk to starline [*sic*] . . . [a] Robin Hood Dell Fairmount Park concert. . . . Something to look forward to on the part of serious-minded music lovers, the Dell has nonetheless never slighted talents of the race. In the past such greats as Marian Anderson, Paul Robeson, and Hazel Scott Powell have spiced the evenings with their great ability. This, however, is the first time that its president, the very personable Frederic [*sic*] R. Mann, has dared to mix the popular colored talent with those who adhere to the compositions of the masters.

For real Americans, and there were 13,000 of them niched into the amphitheatre created by nature in a sloping dell in Fairmount Park, it was one of those rare thrills. A star-spangled montage of fine American democracy waving its talent in the breeze to strike the ears and stir the imagination of a humanity that was on this night woven into one because of a one and the same love for music. . . .

And brother, the multitude was moved—into the loudest applause these ears have ever heard. It rang deep into the environs of the airy park and had its resounding effects throughout the city of Brotherly Love.[16]

## The Early 1950s

The early 1950s saw some of the most significant developments in the history of the Dell. Having emerged from the 1948 financial crisis as a more stable, forward-looking institution, Mann and the Dell Board did great things in this period, from instituting the popular Children's Concert series to implementing the groundbreaking policy of making the entire summer concert series free. As *The Philadelphia Inquirer* noted on the eve of the 1950 season, "Under the aggressive direction of . . . new president, Fredric R. Mann, [the Dell] completed a scintillant [1949] season with a 'small operating surplus' for the first time in its history. Mr. Mann achieved this miracle under spectacularly discouraging circumstances."[17] With Mann directing overall operations, day-to-day management was in the steady hands of Morton Howard, who came on as manager in 1949, and his assistant, Helen Martin, who had been at the Dell since 1943. Both would have long tenures at the venue.

Among the early 1950s success stories was the return of Philadelphia native and local favorite Jeanette MacDonald on July 27, 1950, with Vladimir Golschmann conducting. The concert drew an estimated 16,000–18,000, the largest in Dell history to that point. MacDonald's concerts in 1951 and 1952 were also very successful. July 17, 1952, saw the Dell debut of 22-year-old soprano Roberta Peters, the first of her 26 appearances at the Dell and its successor, the Mann Music Center, through 1987. Four months after her Dell debut, Peters began her 35-year tenure with the Metropolitan Opera. Her Dell concerts always drew large audiences.

Other renowned artists who debuted or returned to the Dell in this period include 14-year-old Italian soprano sensation Anna Maria Alberghetti; singers Lily Pons (often with her husband, Andre Kostelanetz conducting), Marian Anderson, Elaine Malbin, Jarmila Novotná, Risë Stevens, Dorothy Maynor, Jan Peerce, Lauritz Melchior, Ezio Pinza, and Robert Merrill; violinists Yehudi Menuhin, Nathan Milstein, Mischa Elman, and Isaac Stern; cellist Gregor Piatigorsky; pianists Claudio Arrau, Rudolph Serkin, William Kapell, Oscar Levant, Eugene Istomin, Alec Templeton, and Rudolph Firkušný; and conductors Leonard Bernstein, Pierre Monteux,

■ Robin Hood Dell box office in 1950. (Free Library of Philadelphia, Print and Picture Collection)

Fritz Reiner, Antal Dorati, William Steinberg, Erich Leinsdorf, Julius Rudel, and Franz Allers.

The Robin Hood Dell Orchestra recording program was revived in the early 1950s as well. Dorati, Reiner, Steinberg, Leinsdorf, and Kostelanetz led the ensemble in a series of recordings done mostly in the Academy of Music. The Kostelanetz recordings were for the Columbia label, but the others were done for RCA Victor Records, based in Camden, New Jersey, and issued on the company's prestigious Red Seal label. The repertoire usually consisted of pieces the conductors had recently performed with the Orchestra at the Dell. It was the same with soloists who recorded concertos with the Orchestra in this period, including Piatigorsky, Milstein, and Kapell.

There was a serious effort in 1950 to raise money to build a retractable roof over the Dell so that concerts could be held regardless of the weather. A new group, the Women's Advisory Committee of Robin Hood Dell, cochaired by Silvia Mann, initiated a fundraising drive and held promotional events for the project, which was estimated to cost $200,000. The kickoff event was a fashion and music show in the Wanamaker Auditorium, the event space in Philadelphia's grand John Wanamaker department store, on October 10, 1950, with performances by soprano Jarmila Novotná and comedian pianist Victor Borge, among others.[18] There were other

This couple were serious music fans, following the score at a 1950 Dell performance. (*The Evening Bulletin* photograph collection, Special Collections Research Center, Temple University Libraries)

fundraising events, and Fredric Mann tried to get the City Council to appropriate funds for the project, but the initiative was unsuccessful. The Dell would continue to be at the mercy of the weather, which often wreaked havoc with the schedule, until it moved in 1976.

## Children's Concerts

The Dell instituted one of its most enduringly popular series in 1952: Children's Concerts. Presented on Wednesday mornings three times over the course of each season, the free concerts offered music for young people and always featured a promising local artist who auditioned for the privilege to play with the Robin Hood Dell Orchestra. Local dance troupes often performed as well. Philadelphia Orchestra Concertmaster and Associate Conductor Alexander Hilsberg initiated and served as music director of the series from 1952 to 1959. Hilsberg left The Philadelphia Orchestra in 1952 to become music director of the New Orleans Philharmonic but returned to the Dell every summer for the next seven years to lead the Children's Concerts. In 1959, Philadelphia Orchestra Assistant Conductor William Smith took over as music director of the series and would lead it into the early 1990s. The concerts were held during the daytime, with the audiences composed mostly of children with their parents or guardians.

The Children's Concerts were often based on a theme. "Music for the Outdoors" was the theme for the July 15, 1952, concert, which included Handel's *Water Music*, Nikolai Rimsky-Korsakov's *Flight of the Bumblebee*, and a piece titled "The Mosquito." Featured soloist that day was 10-year-old Philadelphia piano prodigy Susan Starr, a student at the Curtis Institute of Music, who played the Rondo movement of Mendelssohn's Piano Concerto in G minor. "After playing the Paganini-Schumann

■ Alexander Hilsberg conducts a Robin Hood Dell Children's Concert on July 8, 1953. (*The Evening Bulletin* photograph collection, Special Collections Research Center, Temple University Libraries)

Caprice as [an] encore," *The Philadelphia Inquirer* reported, the young pianist "rewarded Conductor Hilsberg with a hug and a kiss, but, stage-wise, gave no acknowledgement to her father, Isadore Schwartz, a violinist in the orchestra."[19] Ten years later, Starr would take the silver medal in the International Tchaikovsky Competition in Moscow, which would help launch her long Philadelphia-based performing and teaching career.

The July 10, 1957, Children's Concert led by Hilsberg featured a new piece titled "Adventures of a Zoo" in honor of the recently opened Dietrich Memorial Children's Zoo at the Philadelphia Zoo. The piece was accompanied by a display of live animals from the new zoo, including a baby chimpanzee, a young llama, a guanaco (similar to a llama), a lion cub, a young kangaroo, and several birds. Vying for attention with the menagerie was a local pianist making his Dell debut, 11-year-old André Watts, who performed the first movement of Felix Mendelssohn's Piano Concerto in G minor. Watts was born in Germany in 1946 to a Black father and

White mother who moved to Philadelphia when he was eight. A child prodigy, he studied at the Philadelphia Musical Academy and debuted with The Philadelphia Orchestra in January 1957 at age 10, followed by his Dell debut seven months later. As detailed later, by the time he next appeared at the Dell in 1964, he had become a national sensation and had won a Grammy for best new classical artist.

## Free Concerts for All

Freddie Mann continued to pursue his lofty goal in the early 1950s of making world-class music available to the masses on an affordable basis. In May 1951 he announced that ticket prices would be lowered for the coming season. Master series concerts featuring special guest artists would go from $1.30 to $1 per ticket, and orchestra-only Symphonic Series concerts would go from 65 cents to 50 cents. "Despite the fact that other costs have risen, the Dell's board of directors feels that this is a people's concert hall," he said. "The new low prices will bring the work of artists within the means of everyone."[20] Eleven days later, Mann announced that the Dell would offer three free concerts in July, two of which would be led by the great French conductor Pierre Monteux. Patrons would clip out coupons published in local newspapers and send them in with a self-addressed stamped envelope to receive tickets by mail.[21] The Dell offered the three free concerts again in 1952, laying the groundwork for the full realization of Mann's dream the following year.

On February 24, 1953, Mann announced that the entire 1953 Robin Hood Dell season—all 18 concerts, plus three Children's Concerts—would be free. "This program of free concerts, never attempted before by any city on such a scope, will really make the Dell 'the people's concert hall' of Philadelphia," he said. "We have free libraries, schools are free, and music in a big city like Philadelphia should also be free. For many years we have been struggling to bring this program into reality."[22] Mann got the City Council to increase its 1953 subsidy to $75,000 and enlisted 750 Friends of the Dell to subscribe for $100. The $150,000 was enough to present the entire season at no cost to audiences. Twenty thousand tickets were made available for each concert; as before, patrons clipped coupons from the newspapers and mailed them in to get their tickets.

The new policy made national news. On February 25, 1953, the *Chicago Tribune* reported: "In a move described as 'revolutionary,' Philadelphia's Robin Hood Dell has decided to charge no admission this summer." Two weeks later, a *New York Times* headline announced, "Box Office Banished: Philadelphia Dell Tries Cultural Experiment."[23] Eugene Ormandy, who had not conducted at the Dell in 11 years, agreed to come home from his summer vacation in Switzerland to lead the first three concerts of the groundbreaking season. Reflecting on his first performance in Philadelphia at the Dell 23 years earlier, he said, "I owe whatever success I have had to the Dell, having received my start as its conductor in 1930."[24]

■ The audience on June 22, 1953, opening night of the 1953 season, the first concert of the first entirely free season of concerts at the Robin Hood Dell. (*The Evening Bulletin* photograph collection, Special Collections Research Center, Temple University Libraries)

■ Part of a clip-out coupon and a ticket for Robin Hood Dell concerts in 1953. For free tickets, patrons would clip coupons published in local newspapers; mail them in with a self-addressed, stamped envelope; and receive tickets in the mail. (Both images: Scrapbook, Mann Center for the Performing Arts Archives)

An estimated 17,000 people were on hand for opening night on June 22 to hear Ormandy, the Robin Hood Dell Orchestra, vocal soloists, and a chorus perform a concert version of Puccini's opera *Madama Butterfly*. As *The Philadelphia Inquirer* reported:

> The opening . . . was quite a triumph. The weather, hesitant at first, turned to a kindly mood. The surrounding hills were in their gayest garb, all seats were free for the first time in the Dell's history, and Eugene Ormandy was on the podium after an absence of 11 years. Judging by the ovation he received many in the audience doubtless were aware that 23 years ago he conducted his first Philadelphia concert here at the Dell.[25]

The second night was an all-Tchaikovsky program, and the third a Viennese-themed concert featuring the music of Franz Schubert and other Vienna-based composers.

## Young Pianists

Along with veteran pianists such as Rubinstein and Iturbi, the Dell hosted several promising young pianists in the early 1950s, two of whom, William Kapell and Jerome Lowenthal, were especially close to Fredric Mann and benefited greatly from his support.

Born in 1922, Kapell debuted at the Dell on July 25, 1941, performing Beethoven's Piano Concerto No. 3 with conductor Charles O'Connell. Earlier that year, he had appeared with The Philadelphia Orchestra after winning the audition for its Youth Concert series. He was then studying with Olga Samaroff at the Philadelphia

William Kapell and Fredric Mann. (Mann Center for the Performing Arts Archives)

Conservatory of Music. By this time, Mann was helping to support the young pianist and guide his career. Many years later, Mann explained how this had come about:

> [Around 1933], Arthur Rubinstein, who was a close friend of mine, called to say that he had heard a talent so outstanding that it warranted all the assistance possible from anyone who really loved music. Joining Rubinstein in this effort was no less than José Iturbi. They were referring to a boy of eleven named William Kapell. I had helped several young musicians who were in need and was willing to do so again, but naturally wanted to hear this talent for myself. Kapell, at this young age, had already studied with Olga Samaroff, one of the great piano pedagogues of her day, but he was too young, being under sixteen, to be admitted to Julliard. Even then, Kapell had fingers of steel. His technique was incredible and so was his musicianship; he was a total musician whose ability lacked nothing. There was sensitivity, beauty of phrasing, an innate understanding of the different styles of music, and a combination of inner tension and calmness that is difficult to find even in the old masters. In the years to come, even though fate would deem that there would not be many, Kapell developed into an artist of the rarest form. I do not find it an overstatement to say, with utmost sincerity, that Willie Kapell had the technique of Horowitz, the tone of Rubinstein, and the musicianship of Rachmaninoff.[26]

By the mid-1940s, Kapell was touring and recording extensively and was regarded as one of the great young pianists of the era. Following his 1941 Dell debut, he appeared at the venue again in 1943 and then every year from 1949 through 1952. In October 1953, he was returning from a tour of Australia when his plane crashed just minutes from its San Francisco destination, killing everyone on board. He was 31. Mann did not make a public statement on the tragedy, but his personal papers contain numerous heartfelt letters of condolence from friends and musical associates on the loss of his beloved protégé.[27]

The following year, the Dell instituted the William Kapell Memorial Concert, which it presented annually for many years. The inaugural concert on July 13, 1954, featured 22-year-old Philadelphia pianist Jerome Lowenthal, one of Kapell's few students and another budding musician whom Mann took under his wing. Mann described how he helped the young pianist in an interview 20 years later:

> Jerry's father died when he was eleven. A friend of his aunt asked if I couldn't step in and help the boy. I heard him play. That convinced me. I wanted to help. So I invited Olga Samaroff to dinner. . . . While we ate, I had Jerry hidden away in the library. Then, when we were finished, I said, "I want you to hear someone play." Then I brought Jerry in. Well, Madame Samaroff was convinced too; she took him as a student.[28]

Lowenthal credited Mann with his successful career: "I never could have coped with preparation for a musical career on my own, neither financially nor in the sense of knowing of what teachers might be good for me. Mr. Mann helped both financially and in terms of guiding me. He became sort of a surrogate father for me. I spent summers and vacations with the Manns."[29]

"It is eminently fitting that Lowenthal was chosen as the soloist for the memorial concert," *The Philadelphia Inquirer* noted of the 1954 inaugural Kapell memorial, "inasmuch as he was the first pupil and an intimate friend of the late artist and both were proteges of Fredric R. Mann."[30] "It was thrilling, [but] there was grief also," Lowenthal recalled years later of his debut at the Dell that night, performing Tchaikovsky's Piano Concerto No. 1. "[Kapell's] wife was there and we spoke a lot that day."[31] Lowenthal would have a long, successful career, appearing at the Dell frequently and later serving as chair of the Piano Department at the Julliard School for many years.

## Freddie and the Orchestra Board

At the same time that Mann was getting national attention in the early 1950s for his innovative leadership of the Robin Hood Dell, he was appointed to The Philadelphia Orchestra Association's Board. The appointment was the subject of intense internal debate on the part of Board, which accepted it begrudgingly. It was the result of an agreement the city and the association had reached several years earlier. In the late 1940s, the city began making an annual appropriation of $50,000 to the Orchestra in exchange for the Orchestra presenting four free public concerts and the mayor and president of City Council having ex officio seats on the Board. When Joseph Clark became mayor in January 1952 and appointed Mann to the new position of commissioner of recreation, he made Mann his designee on the Board. This did not sit well with many members of the Board, who thought that Mann was controlling and aggressive and would not be a good fit for the association.

There was lengthy discussion of the issue at the June 11, 1952, Board meeting. President Orville Bullitt reported that he taken the matter up directly with Mayor Clark, but Clark would not yield about Mann serving as his designee. (This was the impetus for Mann's May 26 letter to Clark quoted earlier.) Board member William F. Kurtz, chairman of First Pennsylvania Bank, shared his thoughts on the matter, as recorded in the meeting minutes:

> Mr. Kurtz . . . spoke at length on the subject. He said that he had spoken to the mayor and Mr. Mann. He felt the whole difficulty was a matter of personality. He said he agreed with the Mayor and the Director of Recreation that the latter was the logical person to serve on the board. Although we don't want Mr. Mann on our board, and have avoided that for years, he felt that the matter should be considered carefully. Mr. Mann has caused difficulties for the Orchestra Association and Mr. Ormandy in the past. Mr. Kurtz mentioned that he once threw him out of his bank but that he is now doing business with him and he has behaved properly. We must consider two choices: (a) That we take the Director of Recreation on our board, and Mr. Mann has promised Mr. Kurtz on oath that he would not interfere with the Orchestra's operations;—or (b) that, if we refuse to take him on the board we must realize that Mr. Mann would have to oppose the grant to the Orchestra next year or resign his position . . . ; there is danger of the situation being aired in the press; . . . [and] of its hitting the front pages of the newspapers or the gossip columns. . . . If we should refuse to take a city appropriation with the condition of appointing the Director of Recreation to the Board, the Association would have a difficult time raising money in its campaign as the public would not understand. . . . He urged that personal preferences be set aside and that the problem be looked at from the point of view of what is best for the Orchestra. He felt strongly that we would not receive a City appropriation unless we accepted Mr. Mann.

Following Kurtz's statement, Board member Curtin Winsor shared "that he had served with Mr. Mann on the Dell board for two years and that his experience was that he was all right so long as he could run the show. He is extremely difficult to get along with and irritates a great many people. He [Winsor] could not share the viewpoint that Mr. Mann would behave well." After considerable debate, the Board voted, although not unanimously, to accept the city's appropriation for the 1952–1953 season and to "accept whatever appointee, if any, was designated to serve on the Board by the City."[32] Mann was voted onto the Board the following year, at the association's March 23, 1953, meeting.[33]

According to several reports, his tenure did not go well. One Board member confided to a writer doing a socioeconomic case study of the Orchestra 10 years later that "Fred's aggressiveness and outspoken ways offended the Board. He wasn't satisfied to just sit on the Board. He wanted to know about everything that was going on, and he took to calling the office and making suggestions to the manager. The Board was afraid that he was trying to take over."[34]

Mann's tenure ended three years later, after the 1955–1956 season. At its June 25, 1956, meeting, the association's Executive Committee voted not to seek a city appropriation for the coming season. They reasoned that, with the Orchestra's planned transcontinental tour that year, the association could not commit to giving the free concerts the appropriation required, and with the Robin Hood Dell now offering an entire summer of free concerts, there was no longer a need for such concerts anyway.[35] The official rationale notwithstanding, some maintained that the real reason for not pursuing the city grant was the Board's desire to rid itself of Fredric Mann.[36]

This view is borne out in a November 1956 letter written by Mayor Richardson Dilworth, who had assumed office that January and appointed Mann as city representative and director of commerce. Responding to Leonard Dill, secretary of the University of Pennsylvania Alumni Society, who had written Dilworth about the Orchestra situation, Dilworth did not hold back in criticizing what he perceived as the association's elitist, exclusionary management of the Orchestra:

> I still think [the Orchestra] is a tremendous asset to Philadelphia, but doubt whether it will continue to be if the present group long remains in control. Those now in control of the fortunes of the Orchestra seem to regard it as property of individuals, whose viewpoint is strictly limited to the Main Line and the Whitemarsh Valley [wealthy Philadelphia suburbs].
>
> For example, the City's contribution of $50,000 could be of material help in improving the Orchestra's situation, yet it was refused this year purely because the little group of men and women who have such a firm grip on the Orchestra do not enjoy the company of our City Representative. I think what they really object to is the fact that our City Representative shook them out of their complacency.[37]

For their part, some Orchestra Board members felt that since it was, in fact, the elite class who had always supported the Orchestra, they should be entitled to run it

Philadelphia Mayor Richardson Dilworth at the Robin Hood Dell in the late 1950s or early 1960s. (Adrian Siegel photographs, Philadelphia Orchestra Association records, Kislak Center for Special Collections, Rare Books, and Manuscripts, University of Pennsylvania)

as they deemed best. After all, they were the ones who had purchased subscriptions over the years and raised or contributed large sums of money to keep the enterprise going. As one Board member put it in the 1960s, "Look, this organization belongs to the Main Line because that kind of person started it and that kind of person has kept it alive. We're the people who care for and appreciate the Orchestra."[38]

No doubt factoring into the association's feelings about Mann were the views of Orchestra Music Director Eugene Ormandy, whose relationship with the philanthropist and businessman evolved over the years from one of admiration and even warmth early on to outright disdain (on the part of Ormandy, at least) and, later, back again. In 1942, Ormandy wrote to Mann after Mann thanked him for helping a young musician's career along: "You owe me no thanks whatever because it is my duty to further the cause of young talented musicians. You do the same thing and no one thanks you for it. It is a gratifying feeling, isn't it, when your protégé succeeds?"[39]

By the mid-1950s Ormandy's attitude toward Mann had changed significantly. In a series of letters with C. Wanton Balis, who had succeeded Orville Bullitt as president of The Philadelphia Orchestra Association in 1955, Ormandy and Balis complained about Mann's aggressive personality and behavior. In early July 1958, while Ormandy was vacationing in California, Balis attended the opening night concert at the Dell. He wrote to Ormandy that, in his comments from the stage, Mann seemed to imply that he was president of The Philadelphia Orchestra Association. Ormandy replied:

> I had to laugh (with some bitterness) at Freddie Mann's statement from the Dell stage. Of course, he told Willie Kapell more than 10 years ago that he will stop at nothing to become the Orchestra's President, and thus the Musical Czar of Philadelphia. What I cannot understand is that you and the Board are taking this all without hitting back. He reminds me a little bit of Stalin and [Egyptian President Gamal Abdel] Nassir. He will talk and talk until people, who don't hear the other side's story, finally believe him.[40]

A powerful but largely unspoken dynamic in all of this was Mann's status as a "new money" Jewish businessman and philanthropist in the largely Protestant "old Philadelphia money" world of The Philadelphia Orchestra Association. While there were some Jewish members on the association's Board in the 1950s—Paul Rosenbaum being the most prominent—it was overwhelmingly Protestant and largely composed of people whose wealth went back generations in Philadelphia. Quite a number of the Board members were listed in the *Social Register*, the publication that tracked America's traditional elite class.[41] Conversely, the Robin Hood Dell Concerts Inc. Board was mostly, although certainly not overwhelming, Jewish. (Neither Board had any members of color in the 1950s.)

Mann reflected on this dynamic 30 years later in a confidential interview he gave to a consulting firm the Orchestra Association engaged as part of an organizational self-study in 1984. In his early 80s at this time, he was back on the association's Board—and, in fact, was the Orchestra's largest donor at the time—and still ran the summer concert venue that was now named for him. In her notes from the session, the interviewer wrote that Mann "believes that the Orchestra is the premier symphony in the world and he states this very emphatically. . . . However, [he] cannot . . . consider the Orchestra's affairs without considering the Orchestra's relationship with the Mann Music Center. . . . His sense [is] that fellow Orchestra board members don't support the Mann's programs and continue to take a 'we-they' attitude toward the Jewish community."[42]

Joseph Kluger, who served as general manager and, later, president and chief executive officer of The Philadelphia Orchestra Association from 1985 to 2005, and who knew Mann well, confirms that Mann believed that anti-Semitism was a major factor in his relationship with the Orchestra over the years: "Freddie's take on this was that it was a slight because he was Jewish. I don't know whether it was an overt slight on [the Orchestra Board's] part or whether it was just his gruffness, . . . but he

■ The Robin Hood Dell Concerts Inc. Board in 1959. Fredric Mann is in the center.
(Mann Center for the Performing Arts Archives)

certainly perceived it to be discriminatory. And he found that quite ironic, given the amount of money he provided."[43]

## A New Dell

In the midst of all the drama with the Orchestra Board in the mid-1950s, Mann was overseeing a complete rebuilding of the Dell facility, which was 25 years old at that point and badly in need of an upgrade. Mann had begun advocating for major improvements in 1953, and in 1955 the City Council appropriated some $360,000 for the project.[44] What transpired was much more than an upgrade. In the 10-and-a-half-month period from the conclusion of the 1955 season to the opening concert of 1956, the venue was literally demolished and rebuilt from the ground up. The project included a complete reconfiguring of the venue grounds, a new band shell, a new fan-shaped seating arrangement (as opposed to the original rectangular orientation), new aisles, walkways, entrance concourse, concession and restroom amenities, and other improvements. "When the 1956 season opens, Philadelphians not only will hear the world's greatest music—for which the Dell has been famed throughout its (right) ■ *Left to right*: Philadelphia Commissioner of Recreation Robert W. Crawford, Robin Hood Dell Board member Mrs. J. Maurice (Eleanor) Gray, and Fredric Mann in July 1955, examining a model for the rebuilt Robin Hood Dell. (*The Evening Bulletin* photograph collection, Special Collections Research Center, Temple University Libraries)

(below) ■ A concert at the newly rebuilt Robin Hood Dell. (Mann Center for the Performing Arts Archives)

history—but they will listen in one of the world's most beautiful concert halls," Mann told the local press.[45]

On June 18, 1956, an audience of some 20,000—10,000 ticketed attendees inside the venue and an equal number estimated to be assembled outside the gates—was treated to a high-tech ribbon cutting for the newly renovated facility. As the audience "watched in awed silence," conductor Eugene Ormandy took the stage and cued concertmaster Jacob Krachmalnick to sound the note "A" on his centuries-old Guarnerius violin. The vibrations from the instrument triggered a magnesium pellet attached to a tubular ribbon suspended above the stage to explode, dissolving the ribbon into a puff of smoke. The technological display, devised by Dr. I. M. Levitt, director of the Fels Planetarium at The Franklin Institute, was a big hit with the audience, which "burst into long and spirited applause." Everyone then sang "The Star-Spangled Banner" to open the all-Beethoven program, with pianist Rudolph Serkin featured as guest artist.[46]

Unfortunately, three years after the reopening, an unforeseen external development would compromise the new facility's suitability as a symphonic music venue.

## Local and Out-of-Town Ensembles

The Robin Hood Dell continued to present both local and international artists and ensembles in the mid- to late 1950s. The year 1955 saw the Dell debut of Singing City Choir, a remarkable Philadelphia vocal ensemble founded in 1948 as an interracial group with a mission of bringing vocalists of different backgrounds together through singing and fellowship. The group's underlying premise was that people of different races and creeds who sing together can live together in harmony. Founder and longtime director Elaine Brown built Singing City into a formidable presence in the region, performing everywhere, from major concert halls to local churches and community centers. The group also toured nationally and internationally. At Singing City's first Dell concert on June 22, 1955, Dell manager Morton Howard introduced Brown as someone who "was celebrated all over America and Europe."[47] With Erich Leinsdorf conducting, Singing City performed Brahms's *Nänie* for chorus and orchestra and Giuseppe Verdi's *Te Deum*, then Brown led the group in Randall Thompson's a cappella *Peaceable Kingdom*. Singing City Choir performed regularly at the Dell and the Mann Center from the mid-1950s through the late 1970s.

Dell audiences experienced something new in 1958: For the first time in the venue's 29-year history, a symphony orchestra other than the Robin Hood Dell Orchestra or its regular-season version, The Philadelphia Orchestra, performed at the Dell. The Philadelphia Orchestra embarked on an eight-week European tour in May 1958, and the musicians would not be back in time for the beginning of the summer season, so Mann invited George Szell and the Cleveland Orchestra to fill in. Szell was quite familiar with the Dell, having conducted at the venue dozens of times before and after his 1946 appointment as music director in Cleveland. He and the Cleveland Orchestra performed six concerts over 11 days, from June 16 to June 26. "We are proud to present to Robin Hood Dell fans an orchestra and conductor of such high caliber," Mann told *The Philadelphia Inquirer,* "and, at the same time enjoy, as Philadelphia citizens, the unprecedented acclaim which is being given abroad to our own orchestra."[48] Following the Cleveland Orchestra's departure, there were no concerts the week of June 30, then regular concerts with the Robin Hood Dell Orchestra resumed on July 7.

## New Distractions

As the 1950s drew to a close, Mann could look back on a remarkable decade of progress since he assumed the presidency of the Robin Hood Dell in 1948. However, a new, completely unexpected development would present a serious challenge in his second decade. When the 1959 season commenced on June 22, everyone was struck by the distraction of the traffic noise from the Schuylkill Expressway, which had opened seven months earlier just across the Schuylkill River (see page 158). In the 30 years since the Dell opened in 1930, America had become an autocentric society. The Schuylkill Expressway was one of several major highways built in the Philadelphia area in the post–World War II period as part of a regional expressway network created to meet the population's demand for more and better roads. Immediately upon opening, "the Schuylkill" became one of the region's busiest, most congested highways. It ran along the west bank of the Schuylkill River, just several hundred yards across open water from the Dell, and the constant drone of its traffic noise was noticeable and annoying to both the performers and the thousands of music lovers who gathered three nights a week on the east bank.

The late 1950s also saw the beginning of commercial jet travel in the United States, replacing propellor-driven flights. The roar of jet engines in the night sky over the Dell created yet another major distraction. However, jet travel also opened new opportunities for touring concert artists, especially foreign musicians, who could now reach the United Sates much more easily and quickly. The Dell benefited significantly from the wider range of first-rate conductors and concert artists available in the late 1950s but suffered from the noise of the new mode of transportation that brought them there.

# 6.

# 1960–1970

## *The 1960s, Navigating Change*

**Like the nation at large, the Robin Hood Dell would undergo fundamental** changes in the 1960s, in terms of both the venue itself and the music it presented. Fredric Mann and the Robin Hood Dell Concerts Inc. Board entered the 1960s firmly entrenched in the facility the Dell had occupied and the classical music tradition it had espoused since 1930. By the end of the decade, things had changed; the Dell was starting to host other types of music, and Mann and the Board were actively looking for a new home.

In terms of the venue, the vagaries of the weather remained an ongoing problem, compounded by the fact that jet-setting guest artists now had increasingly tight schedules and were reluctant to sign contracts that required rain date carry-overs. There had been discussions over the years about constructing a retractable roof over the Dell so concerts could continue in bad weather, and there was even a fundraising campaign for such a structure in 1950 (see pages 140–141), but the plans never came to fruition. With the opening of the Schuylkill Expressway in 1958 and the resultant traffic noise that diminished the concert experience, investing in improvements at the current location no longer seemed advisable. Although the Dell had been completely rebuilt in 1956, by the early 1960s Mann was exploring options for relocating.

At the same time, America was undergoing a sea change socially with the rise of a new youth-oriented culture that saw an increasing focus on the preferences and buying habits of the emerging baby boomer generation. Entering their teen-

Aerial view of the Robin Hood Dell in the June 18, 1961, issue of *The Philadelphia Inquirer Sunday Magazine.* The Strawberry Mansion Bridge crosses the Schuylkill River in the center; the Schuylkill Expressway, whose traffic noise was a major irritant, is at the upper right. (From *The Philadelphia Inquirer.*  Scrapbook, Mann Center for the Performing Arts Archives)

■ Children of Robin Hood Dell Orchestra musicians pose on the Dell stage. *The Philadelphia Inquirer Sunday Magazine*, June 19, 1960. (From *The Philadelphia Inquirer*. © 1960 Philadelphia Inquirer, LLC. All rights reserved. Used under license. Scrapbook, Mann Center for the Performing Arts Archives)

age and early adulthood years in the 1960s, this massive wave of young people was reshaping American life. Nowhere was this transformation more evident than in music, where the rock-and-roll explosion of the mid-1950s continued to reverberate through American society. The national epicenter of this youth music movement was just a few miles from the Robin Hood Dell, at the WFIL-TV studios at 46th and Market streets in West Philadelphia, the home of the enormously popular teen music and dance program *American Bandstand*. Roger Clipp, the general manager of WFIL Radio and TV who was responsible for launching the program, was a Dell Board member in this period.

With the ascent of this new youth culture, the audience for classical music slowly but surely began to shrink. Young people wanted their own music, not that of their parents and grandparents and certainly not that from centuries ago. For Mann, raised on and devoted to the music of the great European masters, the Robin Hood Dell was a sacred space for the classical music he loved so dearly, a refuge for "fine" music in an often crass world. He staunchly opposed deviating from the Dell's long-established symphonic programming to appease prevailing tastes. He and the Dell Board held on to the venue's strictly classical artists and repertoire policy as long as they could. By the late 1960s, however, pressure to expand the Dell's musical offerings had become too powerful to resist.

Mann and the Dell Board had to navigate other calls for change in the 1960s as well, from elected officials questioning the benefit of allocating taxpayer money to a venue that catered to an increasingly narrow segment of the population to negotiations with The Philadelphia Orchestra Association over its union contracts with the musicians who constituted the Robin Hood Dell Orchestra. The latter issue went to the heart of the Dell's operations and had the potential to disrupt everything. At the same time, other summer music venues and concert series were being established in the Philadelphia area, challenging the Dell's supremacy as the region's premier summer music venue. Such challenges notwithstanding, the 1960s saw some of the Robin Hood Dell's greatest triumphs, with record-setting audiences attending concerts by many of the world's preeminent performing artists.

## Financier in the Dell

In June 1960, *The New York Times* ran a preview of the Robin Hood Dell's upcoming season that included a profile of Mann, focusing specifically on the "Philadelphia Plan," the financial arrangement he devised in 1949 that continued to sustain the Dell. The article, "Financier in the Dell," recounted how Mann had assumed control and rescued the Dell after the 1948 season had ended early due to lack of funds. Noting that "it was Mr. Mann's 'Friends of the Dell' plan that saved the summer concerts," the *Times* explained Mann's rationale behind it:

> Mr. Mann's reasoning was that the summer concerts would not and could not be expected to pay their own way [through ticket sales]. But if 750 generous Philadelphians would pay $100 each for a pair of box seats for the season, this would raise $75,000. With an equal grant from the city, the Dell concerts would have financial breathing room. . . . [The] arrangement has worked smoothly from the start.

The article noted that the budget for the 1960 Dell season had increased to $180,000.[1]

By the end of the decade, the budget had nearly doubled, with the same cost-sharing arrangement of half the expenses being funded by Friends of the Dell subscriptions and half by the city. As it had since 1953, Mann's "Philadelphia Plan" allowed the general public to enjoy an entire summer season of world-class symphonic music completely for free. Dell promotional brochures noted that the concerts were "conducted under the joint sponsorship of the City of Philadelphia and Friends of the Dell."

## The 1960 Season

In May 1960, Robin Hood Dell Concerts Inc. signed a two-year contract with the musicians' union, Local No. 77, that called for weekly increases of $7.50 per musician in 1960 and $10 in 1961 for members of the Robin Hood Dell Orchestra. This brought the weekly minimum to $165 per musician in 1961, a total of $990 for the six-week season. (Again, the weekly minimum was what the lowest-paid musicians made; first-chair and other higher-position players made more.) The contract called for an orchestra of 91 musicians, plus two additional players as needed. Conductors' fees for the season were projected to be $14,450; soloists' fees, $22,950.[2] Actual total expenses for the season ended up being $179,000.

In previewing the season, Mann proclaimed: "It promises to be one of the most exciting schedules the Dell management has ever programmed." Local newspapers touted the "great diversity of programs" and how "musical variety will spice the 1960 season."[3] A writer for the *Philadelphia Jewish Exponent* had a decidedly different take, however, lamenting what he perceived as the Dell's overreliance on standard programming and sensing changes in the air:

> During the next six weeks we will be treated to 18 concerts by members of the Philadelphia Orchestra under leading conductors . . . with top-rank soloists . . . as well as rising talents. . . . But with this summer's programs we sense a trend toward the tried and true that ought to be opposed. . . . Must all . . . works be familiar "standards" of the classical repertory? Evidently the Dell management thinks so, . . . [but] people who make a habit of keeping their ears to the musical ground will tell you there are significant changes taking place. It isn't that audiences are "demanding" new things, rather that they are vaguely dissatisfied with the same old things.[4]

Major changes were indeed brewing, but they would take a while. For the foreseeable future, it would be mostly business as usual. In terms of programming, the 1960 season continued to rely mostly on the "tried and true," leaning especially heavily on standard Western European repertoire of the 19th and early 20th centuries, a repertoire that generally calls for large-scale orchestral forces, such as the 91-piece Robin Hood Dell Orchestra, as opposed to smaller orchestral ensembles for which symphonic works from earlier periods are scored. Late Beethoven, Brahms, Tchaikovsky, and Ravel were well represented on the 1960 schedule, and several nights were devoted to opera selections, which were always popular. As the *Philadelphia Jewish Exponent* article noted, "The two lonely pre-19th century works (both Mozart Concertos) indicate a policy of using the full orchestra consistently in order to fill the outdoor air."[5]

The featured guest artists tended toward the tried and true as well. Beloved Metropolitan Opera tenor Jan Peerce and star pianist-conductor José Iturbi made their 18th and 14th Dell appearances, respectively, in 1960, while longtime Metropolitan Opera soprano Roberta Peters made her seventh. Other familiar conductors and soloists filled out the schedule. The few departures from the standard

Music

SUMMER MUSIC UNDER THE STARS: Jan Peerce, popular Metropolitan Opera tenor, makes his 18th Robin Hood Dell appearance for the opening of the six-week concert season tomorrow night. Laurel Hurley (right) Allentown soprano from the Met, co-stars in the operatic program that same evening.

**(above)** ■ Notice of the opening of the 1960 Robin Hood Dell season. (*The Sunday Bulletin*, June 19, 1960, Scrapbook, Mann Center for the Performing Arts Archives)

**(left)** ■ A young fan gets an up-close look at a member of Ballet Trianon, a local dance troupe that performed at the June 29, 1960, Robin Hood Dell Children's Concert. (*The Philadelphia Inquirer* photograph collection, Special Collections Research Center, Temple University Libraries) artists and repertoire included pops conductor Arthur Fiedler leading an all-Gershwin program; Cuban-born conductor Alberto Bolet leading a Latin American program; and the Robin Hood Dell Chorus and vocal soloists featured in "An Evening of Gilbert and Sullivan." The U.S. Air Force Band presented a "Patriotic Jubilee" on July 4.

Concerts were scheduled three times a week—Monday, Tuesday, and Thursday—for six weeks, from June 20 to July 28. Guest conductors usually appeared twice in a week, leading two different programs. Featured soloists generally appeared just once. The Children's Concerts also continued, held monthly on Wednesday mornings and led by Philadelphia Orchestra Assistant Conductor William Smith. As before, these always included a young featured soloist from the area, who was selected through an audition process. Local ensembles and dance troupes frequently performed at the Children's Concerts, as well. On July 19, 1961, a Children's Concert alumni party was held at the Dell celebrating the tenth anniversary of the series and honoring some of the local musicians who had been featured over the years and gone on to successful careers. They included three rising concert pianists: 19-year-old Susan Starr, who would take the silver medal in the International Tchaikovsky Competition in Moscow the following year, and a 21-year-old duo, the Marlowe Twins, who had been touring since adolescence and had appeared on a number of national TV shows.[6]

## Modern Life Encroaches

For the regular evening concerts, new measures were implemented in the 1960 season to try to mitigate the ever-encroaching noise of modern life. Little could be done about the Schuylkill Expressway traffic, but Mann flexed his muscle as Philadelphia director of commerce, with jurisdiction over Philadelphia International Airport, to reduce airplane noise. As *The New York Times* reported on the June 20 opening night concert, "A new feature of the Dell . . . made its appearance tonight. A pair of searchlights, eight miles apart and visible to a height of 3,000 feet, pinpoint the location of the Dell for the benefit of pilots nearing or leaving Philadelphia. Aircraft are instructed to stay outside this eight-mile zone between 8:30 and 10:30 o'clock on concert nights."[7]

Another offender was the Reading Railroad, whose tracks ran along the western bank of the Schuylkill River (adjacent to the expressway) and whose train whistles and horn blasts were especially disruptive. In July, Reading President E. P. Gangewere, probably at Mann's request, issued a directive for engineers to "go easy on whistling while passing through Fairmount Park during Dell performances."[8] As detailed later, this directive was not always followed.

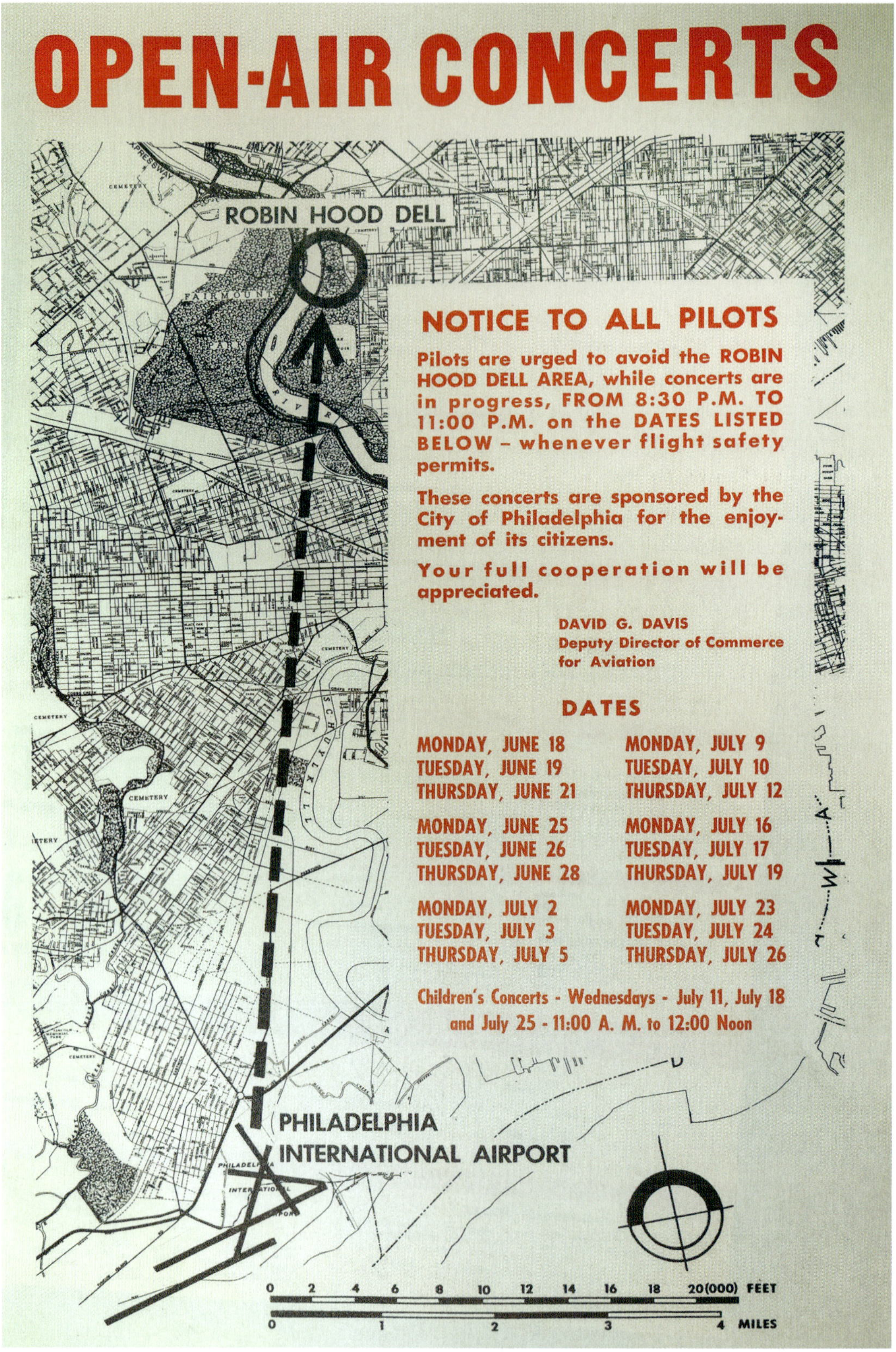


■ 1962 poster advising airplane pilots to avoid the Robin Hood Dell area during concert times. As director of commerce for the City of Philadelphia, Dell President Fredric Mann had authority over Philadelphia International Airport. (Scrapbook, Mann Center for the Performing Arts Archives)

## Tuesday Night Showcases

While most of the guest artists in 1960 were well-established audience favorites, there was a notable programming innovation that year that turned out to be quite significant. Tuesday nights were reserved for emerging artists, musicians in the early stages of promising careers who would benefit from an appearance at the Dell. These concerts would launch or enhance the careers of several renowned artists.

The first such Tuesday night artist was violinist Anshel Brusilow, appearing as conductor. A Philadelphia native who had studied at the Philadelphia Musical Academy and Curtis Institute of Music, Brusilow was an accomplished orchestral violinist with conducting aspirations. He had been concertmaster of the Cleveland Orchestra from 1955 to 1959, when Eugene Ormandy lured him home to take the same position with The Philadelphia Orchestra. Brusilow had studied with two of the great conductors of the era, Pierre Monteux and George Szell, and was eager to develop this aspect of his career. He had conducted one piece in a Philadelphia Orchestra Youth Concert in 1949 after being runner-up in a young conductors contest a year earlier, and had led a Philadelphia Orchestra Children's Concert in 1954, but otherwise had never conducted the Orchestra in a regular or summer season concert. On June 21, 1960, the 31-year-old Brusilow led the Robin Hood Dell Orchestra in Tchaikovsky's *Capriccio italien*; Max Bruch's Violin Concerto No. 1, with South African violinist Hyman Bress as soloist; and Anton Dvořák's Symphony No. 9, the

■ Published August 2, 1960, in *The Philadelphia Tribune*, this photograph shows (*left to right*): Robin Hood Dell Manager Morton Howard, mezzo-soprano Shirley Verrett, and Marian Anderson, with the score of Manuel de Falla's *El amor brujo*, which Verrett sang at the Dell on July 26, 1960, with Anderson in attendance. (Used by permission of *The Philadelphia Tribune*, Philadelphia, PA, Scrapbook, Mann Center for the Performing Arts Archives)

famous "New World" Symphony. The concert was the first of many Brusilow would conduct at the Dell over the next six years.

The Tuesday night July 26, 1960, concert saw the Dell debut of another rising star: mezzo-soprano Shirley Verrett, a graduate of the Julliard School who had been a recipient of the Marian Anderson Award in 1957. Verrett was part of the generation of Black operatic singers who were benefiting from Anderson's trail-blazing successes 20 years earlier. In 1959, Leopold Stokowski, then music director of the Houston Symphony, tried to engage Verrett for a performance in Houston of Spanish composer Manuel de Falla's *El amor brujo* but was denied because Verrett was Black. Stokowski had her sing the pieces when he conducted The Philadelphia Orchestra in February 1960 at the Academy of Music, and she reprised them five months later at the Dell, with José Iturbi conducting an all-Spanish program. *The Philadelphia Inquirer* praised Verrett as "an impressive new talent" who gave a "stunning account" of the Falla vocal pieces.[9] Like Anderson, who was in attendance at the Dell concert, Verrett went on to sing in the world's great opera houses and concert halls.

## Mehta's American Debut

The most notable Tuesday evening emerging artist showcase of the season was the July 5 appearance by 24-year-old Indian-born conductor Zubin Mehta, making his American debut. "Indian Conductor Bows," read a *Philadelphia Inquirer* headline the next day, reporting on the concert that would jumpstart Mehta's celebrated six-decade career. Zubin's father, Mehli Mehta, a violinist, was the founder and concertmaster of the Bombay Symphony Orchestra. Growing up in India, young Zubin was steeped in Western classical music, especially recordings of The Philadelphia Orchestra, which his father prized. Zubin studied conducting in Vienna in the mid-1950s and subsequently won high-profile conducting competitions in Europe and the United States, leading to Mann's invitation for him to conduct at the Robin Hood Dell in 1960. Coincidentally, Mehta's parents had moved to Philadelphia the year before, when his father joined the Curtis String Quartet in 1959. Mann became close friends with Zubin and would be among the conductor's major benefactors early in his career.

Mehta's debut at the Dell was actually the result of maneuvering by Stokowski's agent, Siegfried Hearst. Hearst had recently taken on Mehta as a client and was looking to get him engagements. Stokowski was booked to conduct two concerts at the Dell in the summer of 1960, followed a few weeks later by four concerts with the Stadium Symphony Orchestra of New York at Lewisohn Stadium in New York City. (Similar to the relationship between The Philadelphia Orchestra and Robin Hood Dell Orchestra, the Stadium Symphony Orchestra was the summer version of the New York Philharmonic.) The elderly Stokowski wanted to lessen his workload and suggested to Mann that Mehta take one of his Philadelphia dates. Hearst had actually

Zubin Mehta in 1965, five years after he made his American debut at the Robin Hood Dell. (Adrian Siegel photographs, Philadelphia Orchestra Association records, Kislak Center for Special Collections, Rare Books, and Manuscripts, University of Pennsylvania)

engineered the whole scenario by intentionally overbooking Stokowski to create substitution opportunities for Mehta, who also ended up being booked to conduct three of the four Lewisohn Stadium concerts Stokowski was scheduled to lead.[10]

Mehta was thrilled at the prospect of conducting the Robin Hood Dell Orchestra, which was essentially The Philadelphia Orchestra minus many of the first chair players. "I was tutored by my father in Bombay to believe that the Philadelphia Orchestra was the greatest orchestra in world," Mehta recalled years later. "I couldn't believe I was standing there in front of that orchestra rehearsing."[11] His American debut at the Dell was a great success, generating an enthusiastic audience response and very favorable critical reviews. He received $500 for his appearance. As Mehta tells it in his autobiography, he and his wife and two young children were staying with his parents in Philadelphia not long after the concert when he received an offer to conduct the Montreal Symphony.[12] This led to Mehta's appointment as music director in Montreal later in 1960, which, in turn, led to the same position with the Los Angeles Philharmonic and then the New York Philharmonic.

Mehta became one of the first international "jet-set" conductors, leading orchestras throughout the world. In 1961, Mann helped arrange for Mehta to substitute for Ormandy when Ormandy had to cancel an engagement with the Israel Philharmonic. This started a relationship that eventually led to Mehta's 50-year tenure as music adviser and director of the Israel Philharmonic from 1969 to 2019. For most of this time, Mehta and the Philharmonic performed in the Fredric R. Mann Auditorium in Tel Aviv, which opened in 1957 and was named for his early benefactor, who was one of the founders and financial supporters of the Israel Philharmonic.*

* The venue was renovated and reopened in 2013 as the Charles Bronfman Auditorium.

Mehta conducted often at the Robin Hood Dell and its successor, the Mann Music Center, due in large part to his allegiance to Mann. In 1975, he conducted the final Philadelphia Orchestra concert at the Dell before the move to the new location in 1976. In 1978, his father, Mehli Mehta, conducted the Orchestra at the new venue the year before it was renamed the Mann Music Center.

## Stokowski Returns

If Zubin Mehta's July 5, 1960, debut at the Dell signaled the beginning of a young conductor's brilliant career, Leopold Stokowski's appearance two weeks later marked the triumphant return of a veteran in the late stages of such a career. On July 21, Stokowski took the podium at the Dell after a 27-year absence. It was his first full, regularly scheduled concert at the venue; other than two brief impromptu appearances in the early 1930s in which he led one or two pieces (see pages 73–74), he had never led a complete Dell concert during his tenure with The Philadelphia Orchestra. After leaving the Orchestra in 1941, Stokowski did not conduct in Philadelphia for 19 years. He returned in February 1960 to lead The Philadelphia Orchestra in a series of regular-season concerts in the Academy of Music, including the one with Shirley Verrett. It was a celebrated reunion that was met with a rapturous reception. Now, five months later, at 78, he was returning to the Robin Hood Dell, where he had last appeared in 1933.

Not surprisingly, given Stokowski's star power and history in Philadelphia, the concert was a big hit with the audience and Orchestra musicians. "The season in Robin Hood Dell came to a peak of glamour and excitement," *The Philadelphia Inquirer* reported, "when a throng estimated at 31,000 jammed the outdoor auditorium in Fairmount Park to hear Leopold Stokowski conduct in his first Dell appearance in 27 years. . . . [An] inspired Dell Orchestra (of whom almost one third had played under Stokowski in bygone decades) outdid itself in sheer glitter, virtuosity and splendor."[13]

Unfortunately, the concert was marred by railroad and airplane noises. Previously described efforts to mitigate these disturbances apparently did not work that night. Blasts from train horns were especially egregious. Stokowski stopped the music several times due to the distractions and even left the stage at one point. Backstage, he reportedly fumed, "Do something about it. You have the greatest orchestra and the people are entitled to hear it."[14] Later, adopting a more resigned tone, he told the audience, "We must be patient with modern civilization." At the end of the concert, after multiple bows, he announced that he would like to play an encore "if it would not disturb the Reading Railroad."*[15]

* Stokowski reportedly had an even worse time with airplane noises while conducting the Stadium Symphony Orchestra of New York at Lewisohn Stadium. See "Stokowski vs. the Jet Age," *The Philadelphia Inquirer*, August 4, 1960.

Leopold Stokowski faces an overflow audience at the Robin Hood Dell on July 21, 1960. (*The Evening Bulletin* photograph collection, Special Collections Research Center, Temple University Libraries)

View of the record-breaking audience at the July 21, 1960, Leopold Stokowski concert. (*The Philadelphia Inquirer* photograph collection, Special Collections Research Center, Temple University Libraries)

Mann reported afterward that, despite the interruptions, Stokowski was delighted with the record-breaking audience. "He thought the crowd was wonderfully behaved and appreciative of the music," Mann relayed, "and said he'd love to come back."[16] True to his word, Stokowski returned to conduct at the Dell three more times through 1965.

## Positive Notes

Financially, 1960 was an excellent season. Total receipts were $188,000, against expenses of $179,000. While the surplus was welcome news, the Robin Hood Dell Concerts Inc. Board cautioned that expenses were expected to rise $6,000 in 1961 due to the raises called for in the new musicians' contract.[17]

The 1960 season ended on a positive note in terms of the weather as well. On August 3, 1960, the *Philadelphia Daily News* reported, "For the first time in its 31-year history, the Dell completed its season last week without one concert postponed because of rain." This positivity was tempered by the paper expressing hope that "the Dell can solve the problem of noisy Reading Railroad freight trains that bothered Leopold Stokowski during his appearance."[18]

The parents of pianist William Kapell stand before a tree planted in his memory at the Robin Hood Dell in July 1960. Kapell, who had appeared often at the Dell before perishing in a plane crash in 1953 at 31, was honored with the annual William Kapell Memorial Concert at the Dell for many years. Photograph published in *The Philadelphia Inquirer*, July 20, 1960. (From *The Philadelphia Inquirer*. © 1960 Philadelphia Inquirer, LLC. All rights reserved. Used under license. *The Philadelphia Inquirer* photograph collection, Special Collections Research Center, Temple University Libraries)

At the conclusion of the 1960 season, *The Philadelphia Inquirer* reported:

> In looking forward to 1961, Fredric Mann says he wants to outdo the past season although he feels that will not be an easy achievement. He hopes to stage a complete opera in concert form next year if he can get a cast of national stature. He also wants to schedule a ballet at the Dell—it has been unusually successful in past seasons. [Neither happened.] Mann also pointed out that it has become annually more expensive to maintain high musical standards at the Dell.[19]

Mann had bold plans, to be sure, but money was always a factor. The minutes of the Robin Hood Dell Concerts Inc. Board meetings record his urgent pleas throughout the 1960s to enlist more Friends of the Dell subscribers to meet the venue's rising costs and his ambitious agenda. Not noted in the minutes, or at all publicly, is the fact that he gave generously of his own money in support of the concerts.

## The 1960s Unfold

Opening night concerts in the early 1960s were often vocal music extravaganzas, featuring singers and programs that were audience favorites. The 1960 season opener was an "Operatic Gala," with arias sung by Jan Peerce and his fellow Metropolitan Opera principal artist, soprano Laurel Hurley; 1961 opened with Giuseppe Verdi's *Requiem*, with star vocal soloists and Philadelphia's Singing City Choir; and in 1963, it was Carl Orff's famous cantata, *Carmina burana*, again with noted vocal soloists and the Singing City Choir. Otherwise, programming in the early 1960s was largely the same as in years past. A few novel concerts and emerging artists excepted, the seasons offered a rotating cast of mostly familiar conductors, each usually leading two or three programs over the course of a few days, along with a dozen or so featured soloists during the six-week season, many of them Dell veterans. As had become tradition, the repertoire leaned heavily on 19th- and early 20th-century classics in the Western concert tradition.

## Anshel Brusilow

In June 1962, Mann appointed Anshel Brusilow, then in the middle of his seven-year tenure as regular season concertmaster of The Philadelphia Orchestra, concertmaster and assistant conductor of the Robin Hood Dell Orchestra, the latter a newly created position. As previously noted, Brusilow made his Dell conducting debut in 1960 and was looking to advance this aspect of his career. Mann enticed Brusilow, who had chosen not to play at the Dell in the summer of 1961, by promising conducting opportunities and the new title if he agreed to serve as concertmaster of the Robin

■ *Left to right*: Anshel Brusilow, Leopold Stokowski, and Fredric Mann backstage at the Robin Hood Dell, June 28, 1962. (Mann Center for the Performing Arts Archives)

Hood Dell Orchestra for the summer seasons. Brusilow recalled the circumstances years later in an interview, in which he also revealed Ormandy's disdain for conducting in the summer heat and the uneasy relationship between Mann and Ormandy, who was noticeably absent from the Dell for much of the 1950s and 1960s:

> The only way I could conduct, really, was that I had to promise Fred I would be concertmaster [for] the summer. If I promised Fred to be concertmaster, then he would let me conduct. At first it was one concert, then it got to be two, and I did a whole week. I was a very good accompanist [with guest soloists]. . . . So everybody wanted to play with me.
>
> I did a lot of conducting at the Robin Hood Dell. Freddy Mann was very good to me in that respect, but only because I was with the Philadelphia Orchestra. Once I left the Orchestra, that was the end of Fred. As far as he was concerned with me, it was over.
>
> Ormandy and Freddy never got along well, and I don't know what the reason was, but Ormandy didn't like him. He didn't like Freddy Mann. Fred tried to cultivate Ormandy. He . . . tried every way to get . . . Ormandy to conduct at the Robin Hood Dell, and Ormandy didn't want it, because he hated summers. He didn't want to get out there and sweat. And it was hot. The old Dell, particularly, rehearsals were awful. But eventually he got Ormandy to come and do a concert outdoors. . . . They became sort of "friends" . . . , but there was never any love lost there.[20]

In 1962, Brusilow cofounded and conducted the Chamber Orchestra of Philadelphia, a 30-member ensemble composed primarily of Philadelphia Orchestra musicians that played five or six concerts annually in its early years. Ormandy was apparently not happy with the new group, viewing it as competition. In 1966, a "no moonlighting" clause in the contract between The Philadelphia Orchestra Association and Orchestra musicians went into effect that barred the musicians from playing in ensembles larger than six members. Brusilow was given an ultimatum: give up the Chamber Orchestra or The Philadelphia Orchestra. He chose the latter, leaving The Philadelphia Orchestra after the 1965–1966 season to focus on conducting the chamber orchestra, which was rechristened the Chamber Symphony of Philadelphia and was now composed of non–Philadelphia Orchestra players. Under Brusilow's leadership, the ensemble played more than 100 concerts a year locally and throughout the United States before folding after two years due to financial problems (despite major support from local philanthropist Theodore Pitcairn). Brusilow later became music director of the Dallas Symphony Orchestra and had a long teaching career in Texas. His last appearance at the Robin Hood Dell was as conductor for a pair of concerts in July 1966. As he noted, once he left The Philadelphia Orchestra, Mann was no longer interested in his conducting services.[21]

## Pension Fund Concerts of the Stars

For a few years beginning in 1962, the Robin Hood Dell hosted an annual benefit concert in support of the Philadelphia Orchestra Pension Foundation. (Mann was treasurer of the foundation.) Not part of the regular Dell season, these concerts were special events held just after the season concluded. They were especially high-profile events, featuring a famous soloist. Everyone donated their services. The first such concert, on July 31, 1962, starred comedian Jack Benny, who, in addition to his highly successful career in radio, television, and film, was an accomplished violinist who was doing a series of benefit concerts throughout the nation that summer.*

The following year's Pension Fund Concert, on August 1, 1963, marked the Robin Hood Dell debut of arguably the most popular artist ever to appear at the

* Two years earlier, plans for Benny to appear with Ormandy and The Philadelphia Orchestra at the Academy of Music in a benefit for Children's Hospital of Philadelphia were scrapped when The Philadelphia Orchestra Association Board questioned "the wisdom of permitting Mr. Ormandy to appear with Mr. Benny": Minutes of Board of Directors of The Philadelphia Orchestra Association, November 28, 1960, Organizational Governance records, Philadelphia Orchestra Association records, Kislak Center for Special Collections, Rare Books, and Manuscripts, University of Pennsylvania. A few years later, the association's manager, responding to an offer from entertainer Danny Kaye to appear with the Orchestra, suggested that Kaye "consider performing at Robin Hood Dell, Philadelphia's summer-concert facility. . . . a much more meaningful location for a tremendous crowd": Boris Sokolov to Danny Kaye, letter, October 27, 1964, Danny Kaye and Sylvia Fine Collection, Music Division, Library of Congress.

■ Jack Benny performing with the Robin Hood Dell Orchestra at a July 31, 1962, benefit concert for The Philadelphia Orchestra Pension Foundation. (Mann Center for the Performing Arts Archives)

venue: Texas-born pianist Harvey Lavan "Van" Cliburn. Five years earlier, Cliburn had stunned the world with his gold medal victory at the inaugural International Tchaikovsky Competition in Moscow. Given the geopolitical context of his accomplishment—the Soviet Union and United States were in the midst of a Cold War and nuclear arms race and the Soviets had recently sent shock waves through the world by launching the first artificial satellite to orbit the Earth—winning the Tchaikovsky medal in Russia made Cliburn an instant American hero. He enjoyed a level of adulation few classical musicians have ever achieved, before or since—from being honored with a ticker-tape parade on Broadway in New York City to being featured on the cover of *Time*.

By the time he debuted at the Dell, Cliburn was a star attraction, a seasoned touring artist who drew huge crowds everywhere he played. Cliburn donated his services for the pension benefit concert, serving as both conductor and pianist. While he had conducted individual pieces before, this was the first time he had ever conducted an entire concert. It was an all-Russian program, starting with symphonic pieces by Dmitry Kabalevsky, Tchaikovsky, and Rachmaninoff, followed in the second half by Cliburn conducting Prokofiev's Piano Concerto No. 3 from the keyboard. (Dimitri

■ Poster for Van Cliburn's August 1, 1963, debut at the Robin Hood Dell, in which he appeared as both pianist and conductor. (Mann Center for the Performing Arts Archives)

**(above)** ■ Van Cliburn conducting a rehearsal at the Robin Hood Dell, undated, probably on or around August 1, 1963. (Adrian Siegel photographs, Philadelphia Orchestra Association records, Kislak Center for Special Collections, Rare Books, and Manuscripts, University of Pennsylvania)

**(right)** ■ The Dell audience bathed in moonlight at the August 2, 1963, Van Cliburn concert (a repeat of the partially rained-out concert on August 1). (*The Evening Bulletin* photograph collection, Special Collections Research Center, Temple University Libraries)

Mitropoulos had led the same piece from the piano at the Dell in 1944 and recorded it with the Robin Hood Dell Orchestra in 1946.) Cliburn played from a specially made piano with a transparent plastic top that allowed him to see the orchestra from the keyboard. The concert was cut short due to rain, so the program was repeated in its entirety the following night. During intermission, Mann presented Cliburn with an engraved silver baton and a framed photograph of the venue signed by all of the Orchestra musicians. "I shall always treasure these gifts," Cliburn told the audience, "but one of the greatest gifts you have already given me—your willingness to come out a second night—and this great orchestra, one of the greatest orchestras the world has ever known." Both the audience and critics loved the performance.[22]

## Mid-1960s

The mid-1960s was the real beginning of the era of profound change in America that would come to be known as "the Sixties." While change had been brewing for some time, major events in 1963 and 1964, occurring just as the massive baby boomer generation was coming of age, would trigger a fundamental reshaping of American society: dramatic events in the Civil Rights Movement, the assassination of President John F. Kennedy, The Beatles' debut on *The Ed Sullivan Show*, and the escalation of the Vietnam War, among other signal developments. At the same time, the nation was experiencing a publicly funded "culture boom" in the mid-1960s, with the establishment of government agencies such as the National Endowment for the Arts and National Endowment for the Humanities (and, closer to home, the Pennsylvania Council on the Arts), and groundbreaking for major performing arts centers, including the John F. Kennedy Center for the Performing Arts in Washington, DC; the Saratoga Performing Arts Center in upstate New York; and Wolf Trap National Park for the Performing Arts in the Washington, DC, suburbs. The underlying goal of these public initiatives was to make the arts available to broader audiences, not just the elite, something the Robin Hood Dell had been doing since 1930 and for free since 1953.

As these larger societal developments unfolded in the mid-1960s, Mann and the Robin Hood Dell Board began to face their own intense calls for change. Inevitably, they had to adapt, but for a few years it was business as usual. On June 22, 1964, the Robin Hood Dell offered a performance of Verdi's *Requiem* in a "John Fitzgerald Kennedy Memorial" concert, a special event that was not part of the regular summer schedule. Philadelphia Mayor James H. J. Tate introduced Pierre Salinger, Kennedy's former press secretary, who gave a eulogy.* Other notable concerts of the

* Mann had written to several members of the Kennedy family that he knew, including the late president's mother, Rose Kennedy, inviting them to the concert. They all responded personally with notes of appreciation but declining the invitation: Correspondence, Fredric R. Mann papers, Irving S. Gilmore Music Library, Yale University.

1964 season included Brusilow conducting Igor Stravinsky's modern masterpiece *The Rite of Spring*. Brusilow had recently conferred with Stravinsky about the piece, and Mann promised Brusilow he would find the money for the extra players the piece required.[23] The season also included Stokowski conducting Sergei Rachmaninoff's *Rhapsody on a Theme of Paganini*, featuring pianist (and Philadelphia native) Jerome Lowenthal (Stokowski and The Philadelphia Orchestra had given the world premiere of the piece in 1934 at the Academy of Music, with Rachmaninoff at the piano) and concert versions of Georges Bizet's opera *Carmen* and Johann Strauss Jr.'s operetta *Die Fledermaus*. As always, opera was a crowd favorite at the Dell.

Another local pianist, André Watts, returned to the Dell in 1964, his first appearance since his debut at a Children's Concert at age 11 in 1957. In the time in between, he had become a star. His big break came in January 1963 with Leonard Bernstein and the New York Philharmonic. After winning an audition to appear with Bernstein and the orchestra on their nationally televised Young People's Concerts series, 16-year-old Watts made a great impression playing Franz Liszt's Piano Concerto No. 1. Two weeks later, Bernstein asked Watts to fill in at a regular Philharmonic concert for pianist Glen Gould, who was scheduled to perform the same Liszt concerto but had fallen ill. Watts was a huge success, earning standing ovations from both the audience and the orchestra. The hastily scheduled performance launched Watts's decades-long concert and recording career. When he returned to the Dell on July 6, 1964, at 18, an audience estimated at 23,000 heard him perform Camille Saint-Saëns's Piano Concerto No. 2 with conductor Izler Solomon. "From the opening, unaccompanied section to the end, there was a sense of ease and joy in the playing, a feeling that communicated itself instantly to the listeners," *The Philadelphia Inquirer* reported.[24] Watts would return to his hometown many times over the years to perform at the Robin Hood Dell and the Mann Center.

Another hometown favorite debuted at the Dell in 1964: soprano Anna Moffo. Born to Italian immigrant parents in suburban Wayne, Pennsylvania, and a graduate of the Curtis Institute of Music, Moffo was 32 when she debuted on July 2, 1964. In an interview prior to the concert, she remembered attending Dell concerts as a child: "My family was never wild about opera, but we did love those concerts under the stars."[25] She sang four programmed arias and several encores, to the delight of the audience of 18,000.[26] Despite her personal connection to the Dell, Moffo performed at the venue only twice in her celebrated 30-year career. She appeared more frequently at the region's other major outdoor music venue, the Temple University Music Festival in Ambler, Pennsylvania, which opened in 1968.

## Friends of the Dell

Friends of the Dell continued to provide critical support in this period. Subscribers were entitled to two reserved seats for each concert of the season. In 1961, a subscription cost $110; by 1965, it had risen to $150, with a $300 option for special box seats. There were usually some 800–900 regular Friends of the Dell subscribers and about two dozen box seat purchasers annually in the mid-1960s. A few years later, Mann and the Friends would be publicly criticized as an elitist group of classical music lovers who wanted to keep the city-funded Dell for themselves, but the reality was that "free concerts for all"—that most democratic of principles—would not have been possible without them. To be sure, their subscriptions bought them special privileges—the best seats in the house, preferred parking—but without their support, it is highly unlikely the city would have made the substantial annual appropriations necessary to sustain the Dell concerts as free events. The entire enterprise—more than 400,000 music lovers attending six weeks of summer concerts each year for free—was made possible by the 800–900 patrons willing and able to pay for an annual Friends of the Dell subscription.

## Finance and Administration

In early 1964, the Robin Hood Dell Inc. Board negotiated its next two-year contract with Orchestra musicians. The agreement called for a $167.50 minimum per week for each player in 1964, rising to $175 in 1965. The Orchestra would consist of 91 musicians, plus three additional as required, and the season would be reduced from seven to six weeks. As it turned out, this would be the Board's final contract with the musicians; everything would change in the 1966 season.

At the end of the 1964 season, General Manager and Executive Vice President Morton Howard retired after 16 years at the Dell. Reflecting on his tenure, he noted that he had not missed a single concert in all that time, not even a Children's Concert, and could only remember three emergencies. Two were last-minute replacements of soloists due to illness and one was a situation in which a well-known diva and conductor simply could not work together and the diva's concert had to be rescheduled with another conductor. (Although Howard would not name them, it was soprano Hilda Gueden and conductor Josef Krips in 1958. Howard did note that he found conductors to be more temperamental than soloists.)[27] Replacing Howard was Assistant Manager Helen Martin, who started at the Dell in 1943 as personal secretary and assistant to General Manager David Hocker. Martin was given the new title of executive director; together, she and Mann would manage the Dell for the next 23 years.

## Dell Women's Committee

Playing a key role in supporting the Dell in this period was the Robin Hood Dell Women's Committee, whose primary mission was to sell Friends of the Dell subscriptions. Like The Philadelphia Orchestra Women's Committees during the founding of

NEW PRESIDENT---Mrs. J. Maurice Gray, (right) has been named president of the women's committee of the Friends of the Robin Hood Dell. The selection of Mrs. Gray to her new post was announced at a luncheon of the committee held at the home of Mr. and Mrs. Mann at the Parkway House. From left, Mrs. David C. Martin of Haverford, executive director of the Robin Hood Dell, Mrs. Fredric R. Mann, member of the Women's Committee of the Dell, and wife of the president of the Dell, and Mrs. J. Maurice Gray.

*Left to right*: Robin Hood Dell Executive Director Helen Martin; Silvia Mann, wife of Fredric Mann; and Mrs. Maurice J. (Eleanor) Gray, Robin Hood Dell Women's Committee Board member, pose at a Women's Committee luncheon at the Manns' home. (*The Main Line Times*, March 15, 1965, Scrapbook, Mann Center for the Performing Arts Archives)

the Dell 30-some years earlier, the Robin Hood Dell Women's Committee was a well-organized, highly effective group. Each year it ran a campaign that included sponsoring teas, luncheons, and musicales to promote subscription sales. The two longtime cochairmen (as they were called) of the committee, Mrs. Morris (Rebecca) Wenger and Mrs. Nicholas G. (Emily) Roosevelt (whose husband was a cousin of Franklin Delano Roosevelt), were involved in a number of local arts and culture organizations and used their considerable connections to help sell Dell subscriptions. Wenger and Roosevelt cochaired the Women's Committee from 1950 to 1965 while also serving as Board members of Robin Hood Dell Concerts Inc.

In 1965, the Women's Committee was dissolved and replaced by a new Robin Hood Dell Guild, which had a similar but broader mission. Whereas the Women's Committee came together for several months each year for a focused subscription campaign, the guild was active year-round and sponsored other activities, including a scholarship program. An all-female organization like the Women's Committee, the guild would prove essential in generating support for the Dell. Mrs. Maurice J. (Eleanor) Gray would serve as inaugural president of the guild.

## The Board

Wenger and Roosevelt's joint leadership of the Dell Women's Committee, a partnership between a Jewish and a non-Jewish woman, is representative of the overall makeup of the Robin Hood Dell Inc.'s Board of Directors in this period. Freddie Mann and his wife, Silvia, were highly active in Jewish organizations and enlisted their friends and colleagues from these circles to serve on the Dell Board. While the Board was mostly Jewish, it was not overwhelmingly so; it was very much a mix. This was in contrast to The Philadelphia Orchestra Association Board, which had a few Jewish members but was composed primarily of individuals from "Old Philadelphia" Protestant families (see pages 152–153).

High-profile Jewish members of the Robin Hood Dell Concerts Inc. Board in the mid-1960s included Benedict Gimbel Jr., scion of the Philadelphia-based Gimbels department store chain and onetime owner of radio station WIP; Lawrence Katz, a prominent manufacturer, arts patron, and sportsman whose international business expertise led to consulting for presidential commissions on foreign trade relations; Harry Shapiro, former Pennsylvania state senator and secretary of welfare; and Bernard M. Guth, a lawyer and budding real estate mogul who was married to the granddaughter of Philadelphia's most powerful real estate developer, Albert M. Greenfield.

Non-Jewish Board members from Philadelphia's political and business worlds included Roger Clipp, general manager of WFIL Radio and TV; Matthew McCloskey, head of a large construction firm that built landmark buildings in Philadelphia and Washington, DC, and was a major national Democratic Party fundraiser, U.S. ambassador to Ireland, and member of President John F. Kennedy's so-called Irish Mafia; and Mann's protégé Robert Crawford, longtime Philadelphia commissioner of recreation who would become chair of the Fairmount Park Commission in 1970. As per Dell policy, Philadelphia Mayor James H. J. Tate and City Council President Paul D'Ortona were ex officio Board members—as long as the city continued its annual Dell appropriation.

Freddie Mann moved freely in these circles. As previously noted, in addition to his business interests and international music connections, he held high-profile positions in Philadelphia government, including commissioner of recreation from 1952 to 1955, city representative and director of commerce from 1956 to 1966, and president of the Fairmount Park Commission from 1963 to 1967. Like his friend Matthew McCloskey, Mann was a major donor and player in Democratic politics, locally and nationally, which led to his appointment by President Lyndon B. Johnson as U.S. ambassador to Barbados, a position he held from 1967 to 1969.

While the Robin Hood Dell Concerts Inc. Board was mixed in terms of Jews and non-Jews and men and women, it did not have any people of color in the 1960s, which was typical of most high-profile Philadelphia cultural and civic Boards in this period. The Dell Board would welcome its first Black member in 1971.

## 1965 Season

Opening night of the 1965 season on Monday evening, June 21, featured Stokowski leading the Robin Hood Dell Orchestra in what turned out to be the 83-year-old conductor's final Dell appearance. At Stokowski's suggestion, the preconcert rehearsal was opened to the public. Normally, rehearsals are held earlier in the day of an evening concert, but at Stokowski's age, he required that rehearsals be held the day before. On Sunday afternoon, some 5,000 people came to the Dell to see the renowned conductor lead the rehearsal. Unfortunately, the heat was excessive that day, and Stokowski asked that the tarp the Dell used to cover the stage during especially hot rehearsals be unfurled to shield everyone onstage, making the attendees very unhappy.[28]

As was often the case, the opening night program included a vocal music extravaganza—in this case, a cantata for mezzo-soprano, chorus, and orchestra that Russian composer Sergei Prokofiev adapted from his 1938 film score, *Alexander Nevsky*. It featured opera singer Elaine Bonazzi, who specialized in contemporary repertoire, and the Philadelphia Chorale. Also on the program was local composer Vincent Persichetti's 1946 piece *The Hollow Men*, an evocation of a T. S. Eliot poem scored for solo trumpet and strings.* A lifelong Philadelphian, Persichetti studied at Combs College of Music, the Philadelphia Conservatory of Music, and the Curtis Institute of Music and was a longtime faculty member of both the Philadelphia Conservatory and the Juilliard School of Music in New York City.

## Marian Anderson Final Bows

Beloved Philadelphia contralto Marian Anderson made her final singing appearance at the Dell on June 28, 1965, part of her international farewell tour. The concert was conducted by her nephew, James DePreist, also a Philadelphia native, who had studied at the University of Pennsylvania and Philadelphia Conservatory of Music, studying composition with Persichetti at the latter. Making his debut at the Dell that night, DePreist was in the early stages of a remarkable career that would see him become one of the first major Black conductors on the world stage. An estimated 35,000 attended the concert, including both ticketed patrons and those listening outside the gates. The concert featured Anderson's well-honed repertoire of Italian arias, German Lieder, and spirituals, concluding with the enduring favorite, Franz Schubert's "Ave Maria."

Two years later, on July 3, 1967, Anderson returned to the Dell, this time in a non-singing role, narrating Aaron Copland's *Lincoln Portrait*, with Arthur Fiedler conducting the Robin Hood Dell Orchestra. Fiedler, the longtime director of the Boston Pops and a frequent guest conductor at the Dell, was then at the height of his fame, a best-selling concert and recording artist who had become a popular TV personality. This concert, on the eve of July 4, featured the kind of patriotic and popular music that was Fiedler's specialty, with Anderson providing a sense of gravitas. "It was a popular concert in all senses of the word," noted *The Philadelphia Inquirer*.

---

* An unreleased recording of the 1965 performance of *The Hollow Men* by Stokowski and the Robin Hood Dell Orchestra exists on tape in the New York Public Library's Vincent Persichetti collection of noncommercial recordings, 1940–1987.

Fredric Mann, Marian Anderson, and James DePreist pose at the Robin Hood Dell on June 15, 1965, prior to Anderson and DePreist's June 28 concert. (Marian Anderson Collection of Photographs, Kislak Center for Special Collections, Rare Books, and Manuscripts, University of Pennsylvania)

"Fiedler gave his audience all the tried and true standards that never fail. . . . Of course, the main drawing card was Miss Anderson. This great contralto, already a legend, seems unchanged by the inexorable years. She is still tall, regal, and her magic voice retains its thrilling timbre although she no longer sings."[29]

## Cliburn Triumphs Again

Van Cliburn's eagerly awaited second appearance at the Dell, on July 29, 1965, set an all-time attendance record. He appeared as soloist with the Robin Hood Dell Orchestra under Eugene Ormandy, who had recently returned from a five-week guest conducting tour of Europe. It was Ormandy's first appearance at the Dell since 1956. The all-Rachmaninoff program featured a Cliburn staple, the Russian composer's Piano Concerto No. 3, one of the pieces with which Cliburn had won the Tchaikovsky Competition in 1958. The newspapers reported on the enormous crowd, both inside the venue and in the surrounding area. "Park guards estimated some 35,000 jammed . . . the famed Dell to hear Cliburn play," noted *The Philadelphia Inquirer*.* "Another 3,000 flocked to bordering drives and settled in solid masses of humanity on nearby hillsides hoping to catch a few notes of the music. . . . Some

* Such crowd estimates in the newspapers are not really reliable and could well be inflated, as there was no way to gauge the number of attendees outside the Dell gates with any degree of accuracy.

■ *Left to right*: Fredric Mann, Eugene Ormandy, and Van Cliburn relax at the Robin Hood Dell around the time of Cliburn's record-setting July 29, 1965, concert. (Mann Center for the Performing Arts Archives)

visitors—many from distant areas—parked their cars across the Strawberry Mansion Bridge and walked about two miles, only to find they couldn't gain entrance."[30]

The Cliburn-Ormandy concert closed the 1965 season. In an editorial note on August 10, 1965, the *Philadelphia Daily News* noted: "The season just completed was the most successful, from an attendance standpoint, in the Dell's 36-year history. Nearly 450,000 persons attended the 19 evening and three children's concerts. Any season that includes Leopold Stokowski, Marian Anderson, and Van Cliburn must also be considered an artistic success."[31]

## Fewer Conductors, More Time

Back in July 1964, *The Evening Bulletin*'s music critic James Felton wrote an opinion piece that questioned the wisdom of the established Dell practice of having so many different conductors in a single season, usually 12 conductors in the six-week series:

> When a conductor flies in for a one-night stand and leads a concert after a single rehearsal, how can anyone reasonably expect a monumental performance? . . . A member of the orchestra has expressed his candid opinion that

> the men know the standard works so well (and most Dell fare is standard) that they feel them and play them together as a unit almost independently of any but two or three conductors who ever stand before them. . . . The cavalcade of conductors is bound to be distracting. . . . Why not establish a permanent music director at the Dell[?] A man of the highest caliber, . . . who could establish rapport with the orchestra and have a whole season to develop it.[32]

The *Bulletin* critic was essentially calling for a return to the 1930s and 1940s, when conductors such as Alexander Smallens, José Iturbi, and Dimitri Mitropoulos led the majority of concerts and served as music director for the season, whether formally given the title or not. While the Dell did not return to that format, it did make a major change in the mid-1960s that resulted in fewer conductors per season, allowing more time for conductors and the musicians to work together.

Beginning in 1966, there would be one conductor leading an entire week of concerts—concerts were still on Mondays, Tuesdays, and Thursdays in this period—for each of the six weeks of the season. Also, two more rehearsals were added per week. As Mann explained, "We have always had six services (three rehearsals and three concerts) a week, but now we are paying for eight. It will mean that a conductor can try new music. We haven't been able to do much of that in the past because there was no time to prepare it."[33]

## de Pasquale Brothers

In another new development in 1966, violinist William de Pasquale replaced Anshel Brusilow as concertmaster of the Robin Hood Dell Orchestra. Part of a unique Philadelphia family, William and his three brothers—violinist Robert, violist Joseph, and cellist Francis—were all trained by their father, a violin teacher and cabinetmaker by trade, and went on to study at prestigious conservatories and join major orchestras. Francis joined The Philadelphia Orchestra in 1943, while his brothers played with other top-tier orchestras until 1964, when Ormandy brought them all home to join The Philadelphia Orchestra. In addition to playing for the Orchestra, they formed the highly acclaimed de Pasquale Quartet.

William de Pasquale's appointment as concertmaster of the Dell Orchestra was actually a maneuver by Ormandy in response to an issue Mann had raised about the Orchestra's Associate Concertmaster David Madison, who was in line to replace Brusilow at the Dell. Following Brusilow's departure as regular season concertmaster, Norman Carol, also a Philadelphia native, was appointed to the position, beginning in the fall 1966 season. With Carol's appointment, Madison normally would have taken the concertmaster position at the Dell, but a letter from Ormandy to Mann in March 1966 reveals another dynamic at work:

■ De Pasquale brothers, *left to right*: Robert, Joseph, Francis, and William. William was concertmaster for most Robin Hood Dell concerts from 1966 to 1969. (Adrian Siegel photographs, Philadelphia Orchestra Association records, Kislak Center for Special Collections, Rare Books, and Manuscripts, University of Pennsylvania)

> When you and I talked . . . I told you I had someone in mind for the concertmastership at the Dell, since you so vehemently opposed David Madison, claiming that all your guest conductors complained about him (incidentally, this statement came as a surprise to me because I think Madison is a first-class violinist and an excellent concertmaster). Knowing how you felt about Madison, I decided that William de Pasquale, . . . will make a very fine concertmaster for the Dell.[34]

William de Pasquale was concertmaster for most Robin Hood Dell concerts from 1966 through 1969, although Carol occasionally filled that role. The de Pasquale brothers played at the Dell for many years, with the exception of Francis, who died in 1972. William and Joseph were featured soloists several times at Dell concerts.

## Young People at the Dell

The Dell was a popular place for young people in the 1960s. Frank Hoeber began attending concerts there in 1959, when he was 16 and living in West Mount Airy:

"It was the place to be for the [young] people we knew. This was the place in the summertime. It sounds funny to think of kids hanging out . . . with the Philadelphia Orchestra."[35] In 1960, Frank began selling ice cream at Dell concerts: "I had to wear a white jacket and a white hat, and I had big box with a strap going over my shoulder and it was loaded up with Dixie Cups, cups of ice cream. . . . [I] would walk around yelling, 'Ice Cream, Ice Cream, 25 cents!'" One of his best customers was young Ditta Baron, from Wynnefield Heights. "I bought ice cream several times, at several concerts," she said. "It took quite a while for Frank to realize that I wasn't really interested in ice cream." Frank: "There was this really pretty girl who was a great customer." Ditta: "And there was this cute guy who wasn't very smart." They eventually began dating and married in 1967.

Interviewed at the Dell in 2023, 63 years after first meeting there, Frank and Ditta remembered the venue in the early 1960s. The Dell "had a particular atmosphere," Frank recalled:

> It was a wonderful place to come in the summer. It was free, although you had to have a ticket. . . . It was packed most nights, with rare exceptions. It was incredibly hot most of the time, good Philadelphia summer weather. The atmosphere is hard to imagine. Everybody smoked, although you couldn't smoke during the performance. It was a great place for a high school kid to hang out. Over on the side [was] a hill and there were trees on the hillside. . . . All the kids from Central [High School] and Girls High and other schools in Philadelphia would come . . . and gather on the hill. It was the social thing that we did. Some of us would come by car, but most of us came by public transportation to get here. We had our own private community going, up there on the hill, . . . watching these wonderful concerts for free. I don't think we appreciated then how fabulous these concerts were. With one of the greatest orchestras in the world, with some of the greatest conductors in the world and greatest soloists in the world. It was a fabulous experience that seemed so ordinary.

"People listened to the music," said Ditta. "The music . . . was soothing and quieted you." Frank remembered that "everybody was very respectful. In between [pieces], there was lots of talking and socializing, but when the music was on, we all quieted down and knew that this was the same as being in a concert hall."

Frank and Ditta were both at the Dell for the infamous 1960 concert in which Stokowski stopped the performance due to train noises, as Ditta remembers:

> My parents had always gone to the Academy of Music for the concerts, for most of their lives, and I heard about Stokowski all the time; he was just the most wonderful conductor. So, of course, I was going to be there [when he

returned to the Dell in 1960]. I was up on the hill and we were listening to the concert and the train came past, and . . . he stopped the orchestra and waited until the train was finished passing. And while that was happening, if you looked up—it was dark by then—I was on this side [of the hill] and there were people sitting on the other side and you'd see a light, and then another light, and then another light. And it looked like fireflies. It was cigarettes; everybody lit a cigarette. It was an intermission! And it was so beautiful! It was part of what made it so memorable.

Frank recalls:

For those of us who were there, it was a tremendous lesson in respect for the music—when one of the greatest conductors in the world stops the entire

**(above)** ■ Young ladies find a comfortable spot to stretch out on the hill on opening night at the Dell, June 21, 1966. (*Daily News* photograph collection, Special Collections Research Center, Temple University Libraries)

**(left)** ■ Opening night of the 1962 season, June 18. In the background in the center is "the hill" where young people gathered for concerts. (Mann Center for the Performing Arts Archives)

> Philadelphia Orchestra and says, "We're not playing while that damn train across the river is going by," it made a tremendous impression on all of us as high school students that this was a very important thing that we were listening to. . . . He just stopped; he didn't make any announcement. He just left [the stage]. That was very impactful, as well.

## Landmark Contract

In November 1960, *McCall's* magazine published an article titled, "Trouble in Our Symphony Orchestras." The article opened by noting that, "for lack of a living wage, musicians are beginning to quit, and our cities and towns can lose much of their cultural value and charm." The vexing issue was that orchestra musicians were generally employed for only 30-some weeks per year, since orchestra seasons ran from fall through spring and did not include summer months. Eugene Ormandy, who was among those interviewed for the article, predicted that "the time will have to come when a symphony orchestra musician will receive a fifty-two week salary. It can be arranged. It will have to be arranged. The performer may get a little less per week, but he will be a man with a feeling of security. You can't expect musicians to divide thirty weeks' pay into fifty-two weeks."[36] Six years later, it would be Ormandy's own Philadelphia Orchestra that would lead the way in offering its musicians a 52-week contract, a groundbreaking development that would have major repercussions for the Robin Hood Dell.

When the 1966 Robin Hood Dell season opened on June 20, for the first time in more than 30 years the musicians who composed the Robin Hood Dell Orchestra no longer worked for Robin Hood Dell Concerts Inc. but were now year-round employees of The Philadelphia Orchestra Association. The tangled tale of how this foundational change unfolded began three years earlier. On September 9, 1963, Philadelphia Orchestra musicians, with the approval of their union, Local No. 77, signed a new three-year contract with The Philadelphia Orchestra Association that, among other things, gradually increased the musicians' number of paid weeks of employment each year from 35—which was essentially the fall-through-spring regular season, with a few extra concerts here and there—to a full 52 paid weeks by the year 1966. It was a landmark agreement, the first 52-week contract for a major orchestra in American history.*

For Robin Hood Dell Concerts Inc., which traditionally had negotiated its own, separate two-year contracts with the musicians' union, this changed everything. Mann and the Dell Board were apparently not informed in advance of the terms of the Orchestra Association's new contract and were quite upset when they learned the details. The minutes of the October 23, 1963, Dell Board meeting reveal Mann's consternation, when he reported:

> The Philadelphia Orchestra Association had entered into an agreement with the Musicians Union as a result of which it obtained exclusive services of the Musicians for the entire 1966 season. This in effect would preclude the Dell from obtaining and entering into an agreement directly with the Musicians beginning with the 1966 season. The [Robin Hood Dell] Directors view with dismay the action of The Philadelphia Orchestra Association, particularly because the Orchestra Association did not see fit to consult with the Dell before concluding such arrangements. This presents a very serious problem

* Seven months after the contract was signed, the New York Philharmonic signed a new contract with its musicians, instituting a 52-week schedule that went into effect in September 1964. Thus, The Philadelphia Orchestra was the first major orchestra to sign a 52-week contract, while the New York Philharmonic was the first to have a 52-week schedule go into effect.

to the Dell, and it could very well affect the activities of the Dell beginning with the 1966 season. Mr. Mann appointed a Committee to meet with the Executives and the Board of Directors of the Philadelphia Orchestra Association for a discussion of the matters pertaining thereto.*[37]

A month earlier, shortly after the contract had been signed, Mann had met with Philadelphia Orchestra Association President C. Wanton Balis Jr. to address the situation. Balis subsequently reported at The Philadelphia Orchestra Association's September 23 Board meeting that "he discussed with Mr. Mann the basis on which the Philadelphia Orchestra would be available for the Robin Hood Dell Concerts in 1966, when the 52-week program becomes effective." At the meeting, the association adopted a motion that "any contract negotiated [with the Dell] should include the provision that if Robin Hood Dell Concerts Inc. uses the name 'Philadelphia Orchestra,' the conductors, soloists, and programs shall be subject to the approval of the Philadelphia Orchestra Association."[38]

This was a huge issue. Mann had had personal artistic control at the Dell since the late 1940s, choosing the conductors and featured soloists and working with them in selecting the programs and setting the schedule. He had developed good working relationships and, in many cases, close personal friendships with the world's top concert artists who regularly appeared at the Dell, often out of loyalty to him. How would the new arrangement work? How much artistic control would Mann be willing to relinquish? And what would the Dell ensemble be called?

It actually took until 1970 to resolve all these issues completely, but by the fall of 1964, the two institutions had a formal agreement for how things would work beginning with the 1966 season. The negotiations took eight months and were at times tense. Representing the Dell in the talks was federal Judge J. Cullen Ganey, a longtime Dell Board member. The Philadelphia Orchestra Association originally wanted the Dell to employ the full 106-musician ensemble and pay the musicians the full regular-season rate by 1966. Mann publicly characterized these terms as "stiff" and said that the Dell was being asked to suffer for the Orchestra's "affluence." He noted that the two organizations had always had a constructive relationship but warned that "the Orchestra cannot deny the Dell its rights."[39]

The final terms agreed on for the 1966 season ended up being more favorable to the Dell than the Orchestra had originally proposed. Dell musicians would work for The Philadelphia Orchestra Association, but the ensemble would still be called the "Robin Hood Dell Orchestra," and the Dell, in the person of Fredric Mann, would have "complete freedom of choice in the selection of soloists, conductors, and programs." The Orchestra would consist of 94 musicians and include at least one-third of the first-

* Dell board minutes are usually perfunctory reports of the proceedings, with little opinion or editorializing; the frankness in these minutes is striking.

■ *Left to right*: C. Wanton Balis, Eugene Ormandy, and Orville Bullitt, undated 1960s photograph. Bullitt was president of The Philadelphia Orchestra Association from 1938 to 1955, followed by Balis from 1955 to 1969. Balis led the negotiations with Robin Hood Dell Concerts Inc. on behalf of the association. (Adrian Siegel photographs, Philadelphia Orchestra Association records, Kislak Center for Special Collections, Rare Books, and Manuscripts, University of Pennsylvania)

chair players. Robin Hood Dell Concerts Inc. would reimburse the association for 87.5 percent, not 100 percent, of the cost of the musicians for the summer concerts.[40] After negotiations were completed, Balis wrote to Judge Ganey, "I commend you on your patience in having achieved a constructive solution of a thorny problem."[41]

Other provisions in the 1963 contract between The Philadelphia Orchestra Association and Orchestra musicians and their union that took effect in 1966 included the aforementioned "no moonlighting" clause that prompted Anshel Brusilow to leave the Orchestra, and, of particular significance to the Dell, restrictions on musicians opting out of performing in the Dell summer series. Now, musicians who wished to take off from Dell concerts had to request an unpaid leave of absence for the entire six-week season; no longer could they pick and choose which summer concerts they would play. At the December 27, 1965, association Board meeting, 10 musicians requesting such a leave for 1966 were given approval. An exception was made for two cellists who, at Ormandy's request, had worked out a special arrangement in which they would each play three consecutive weeks of the six-week season. Balis told the Board at the meeting that the association "would furnish a well-balanced orchestra to the Dell in which not less than one-third of the first-desk players would perform."[42] This was a far cry from the early days of the Dell, when the first-chair players traditionally took the summer off and many of the orchestra musicians were summer replacements.

Under the previous contract, the minimum weekly salary for Philadelphia Orchestra musicians had been $190 for the regular season and $165 for the Dell season. The new contract, by its third year in 1966, factoring in new income from recordings and four weeks of paid vacation to which the musicians were now entitled, guaranteed them a $238 weekly minimum income for 52 weeks (unless they requested and received approval to take the six-week Dell season off).[43]

## Other Venues

With its musicians now under a 52-week contract, The Philadelphia Orchestra Association needed to secure additional summer performance opportunities to ensure that its musicians had year-round work. Combined, the ensemble's regular and Dell seasons, along with occasional tours and short engagements, did not total 52 weeks. There were serious discussions about building a new facility and establishing a summer residency for the Orchestra in the Pocono Mountains in northeastern Pennsylvania, but the idea never came to fruition.[44] It would be in upstate New York that The Philadelphia Orchestra would find a second permanent summer home.

The Saratoga Performing Arts Center in Saratoga Springs, New York, in the Adirondack Region, was a pet project of Governor Nelson Rockefeller and originally intended as a summer home for the New York Philharmonic. However, the Philharmonic had gotten funding in the early 1960s to give a series of summer concerts in Central Park in the city and opted out. The Philadelphia Orchestra was offered the opportunity instead. With Ormandy's enthusiastic support, in March 1964—while still deep in negotiations with Robin Hood Dell management over the terms of the Orchestra's Dell residency—The Philadelphia Orchestra Association committed to a three-week residency in Saratoga every August, after the Dell season had concluded. (Presumably, the weather in upstate New York in August was more tolerable to Ormandy than the sweltering Philadelphia summers he detested.) At the groundbreaking on June 30, 1964, Ormandy noted that "the seeds have been planted for what we hope will grow into one of the great summer festivals of our time."[45] The facility opened in July 1966.

Ormandy and the Orchestra inaugurated the Saratoga concert series on August 4, 1966, after the venue's other resident company, the New York City Ballet, finished its opening series. Freddie Mann was probably not pleased to hear Ormandy quoted during opening week as saying, "In no way do I want to belittle any other theatre, but [Saratoga] is the greatest, most beautiful festival I have ever seen or participated in in my whole life."[46] Mann knew he had to redouble his efforts toward new, better facilities to keep the Orchestra in Philadelphia in June and July. (The Philadelphia Orchestra has continued its August Saratoga residency ever since.)

In reviewing the recently concluded 1966 Dell season and thinking ahead to a new home, Mann offered his perspective on the summer homes of other major orchestras, as well as the Dell's focus on offering music to urban dwellers who did not have the means to travel to remote locations to see their home orchestra. "Personally, the Saratoga and Tanglewood [the Boston Symphony Orchestra's summer home, more than 130 miles from the city] theaters are not to my taste. . . . The way I see it, this is the era of the urbanite. The rich fellow can buy a ticket to Tanglewood or Saratoga, but my concern is with the man who lives in the city. We can't give them less than the best. We can't play down cultural values."[47] It would take Mann 10 years to realize his vision of a new Dell home for the Philadelphia urbanite.

Saratoga did not really represent competition for the Dell; the two venues were in different markets more than 250 miles apart, and The Philadelphia Orchestra's Saratoga residency began after its Dell season concluded. Much closer to home, and a more serious rival, was the music festival that opened in 1968 at Temple University's suburban campus in Ambler, Pennsylvania, just 15 miles from the Dell. Officially the Temple University Music Festival and Institute, the Ambler facility hosted both a summer concert series and a music institute for some 300 students. Situated on beautiful landscaped grounds with attractive amenities, ample parking, and a new 3,000-seat amphitheater that was covered but open on the sides (performances were in a

■ Temple University Music Festival campus. (Templana Photograph Collection, Special Collections Research Center, Temple University Libraries)

tent for the first three years; a permanent amphitheater was built in 1971), the new Ambler venue had many modern features the 38-year-old Robin Hood Dell lacked.

The inaugural six-week Temple Music Festival ran from June 24 to August 4, 1968, with 42 concerts featuring a wide variety of musical genres and styles. Brusilow's Chamber Symphony of Philadelphia was the resident ensemble; the Pennsylvania Ballet and Lenox String Quartet gave multiple performances; and top-name artists as diverse as Van Cliburn, Benny Goodman, Ella Fitzgerald, soprano Eleanor Steber, and flamenco guitarist Carlos Montoya performed. This diversity of musical offerings was a hallmark of the festival during its 13-year existence. Beginning in 1970, the Pittsburgh Symphony Orchestra, with Music Director William Steinberg, became the resident ensemble and remained so until Temple University discontinued the entire enterprise after the 1980 season.

While it lasted only 13 years, the Temple University Music Festival was a major summer cultural attraction in the region. For 11 of those years, Philadelphia-area classical music lovers could hear two major American symphony orchestras on a regular basis in the summer months. The Robin Hood Dell survived competition from the Temple festival, and by the time the festival closed in 1980, the Dell concerts had moved to a new modern, covered facility and had been offering popular and contemporary music along with symphonic repertoire for five years.

Much closer to the Robin Hood Dell, but not really representing competition, was Playhouse in the Park, a city-owned theater near Belmont Mansion in West Fairmount (very close to where the Dell concerts would move in 1976). Erected in 1952 as an open-air tent theater, which was replaced by a permanent theater-in-the-round building in 1958, Playhouse in the Park was championed by prominent Philadelphia businessman and civic leader John B. Kelly Sr., who was president of the Fairmount Park Commission. Kelly's daughter Grace, a budding actress and future movie star and princess of Monaco, performed at the venue in its early years. Playhouse in the Park offered traditional summer stock theater and musicals for much of its existence, although in the late 1960s and 1970s it occasionally presented popular singers, jazz artists, and performing arts groups. Such fare did not vie for the Dell's symphonic music audience for the most part, although there may have been some minor competition for audiences. Several different entities operated the theater over the years—some nonprofit, some commercial (in the 1960s, the commercial entities included the group that owned and managed the Valley Forge and Camden County Music Fairs). By the late 1970s, Playhouse in the Park was no longer profitable or sustainable. It closed in 1979, and the building was demolished in the 1990s.

## Open the Dell

In June 1967, the Philadelphia Transportation Company (PTC) announced that it would begin providing special bus service to the Robin Hood Dell on concert nights. Three routes with buses marked "Dell Concert Special" would link different sections of the city directly with the venue.[48] While this was welcome news in terms of broadening access to the Dell on a geographic basis, Mann and the Robin Hood Dell Board were grappling at that time with serious calls from influential quarters to open the Dell to other types of music and audiences.

There had been such calls in the past, but they reached a pitch in 1967. That spring, a local promoter tried to book a festival at the Dell featuring Count Basie and Duke Ellington, among others. The festival would be held in late summer, after the orchestral season had concluded. The promoter was shot down by the Fairmount Park Commission, of which Mann was then president. "The Dell is being kept a sacrosanct enclosure for the benefit of the Friends of the Dell," the anonymous promoter was quoted as saying, "and I wonder how many of them actually live in Philadelphia. They seem to have set some cultural qualifications for admission."[49] *The Philadelphia Tribune*, the city's Black newspaper, also weighed in:

> Although more people listen to jazz than any other music in the world, and the taxpayers of Philadelphia are taxed for support of the Robin Hood Dell, Mr. Mann, it seems, is of the opinion that the city's Robin Hood Dell is for the chosen few—those music lovers interested in classical music only. . . . All attempts by lovers of jazz and other forms of music who have repeatedly petitioned Frederick [*sic*] Mann to schedule jazz concerts such as are annually presented in Central Park in New York, Cleveland, Boston, and Los Angeles, have failed.[50]

Protests from promoters and journalists were one thing, but when Philadelphia's City Council got involved, things got serious. On June 20, 1967, Councilman Thomas M. Foglietta wrote Mann a scathing letter demanding that the Dell be made available for other types of music from early August through mid-September. "Robin Hood Dell belongs to the citizens of Philadelphia and not to you or any other member of your elite set of friends," wrote Foglietta, warning Mann that if appropriate action was not taken, a citizen's group was ready to take legal action "to enjoin you from depriving the citizens of Philadelphia of their taxpaying rights."[51]

No one was advocating inserting popular or jazz concerts into the six-week orchestral season or forcing Robin Hood Dell Concerts Inc. to produce nonclassical concerts; rather, the protesters wanted the Dell to be available for other producers to present other kinds of music after the Orchestra's season had concluded, usually around August 1. For his part, Mann usually left to travel abroad when the Dell season ended and was fearful of what would happen to his beloved venue in his absence. In his view, and that of his colleagues on both the Robin Hood Dell Concerts Inc. Board and the Fairmount Park Commission, the Dell was built as a summer home for The Philadelphia Orchestra and should be reserved for that use.

After all the public posturing, the matter was resolved fairly quickly—or so it seemed. The *Philadelphia Daily News* reported on June 27 that Mann and Foglietta met over lunch and agreed that "there was no reason why musical events other than the annual Dell [i.e., orchestral] series could not be presented at the Park facility, provided there were guarantees against damage." Mann contended that the Dell had always been available for other events, but the *Daily News* disputed this, citing two years of unsuccessful attempts to open the venue for different music.[52]

There was some progress in scheduling other types of music at the Dell as a result of the meeting between Mann and Foglietta, but not enough to satisfy Foglietta. A rock-and-roll show was booked for early August, but by late July only one other new event had been scheduled: a concert by the U.S. Army Band. Foglietta expressed disappointment "that Mr. Mann has not carried through on his promise to do everything possible to keep the Dell open" and noted that he attempted to contact Mann about the situation, "only to find that he is out of the country."*[53] The Dell did eventually open for a number of nonclassical late summer events in subsequent years. In the meantime, however, it was about to rock out in a big way for one night in 1967.

## Geator's Rock 'n Roll Jamboree

On August 8, 1967, 20,000–35,000 young people gathered at the Robin Hood Dell for a "Rock 'n Roll Jamboree." (Audience estimates varied widely, but more than 19,000 tickets were sold and thousands listened from outside the gates.) The event was produced and emceed by local disc jockey (DJ) Jerry Blavat and was sponsored by the Philadelphia Department of Recreation and Fairmount Park Commission in partnership with WFIL-TV. The concert was part of a broader effort by the city that summer to provide entertainment for young people. In an initiative dubbed the "Total Teen Scene," the department and the commission jointly staged a series of dances and concerts at various locations throughout the city, from historic Fairmount Park estates to local parks and recreation centers. The Rock 'n Roll Jamboree at the Dell was to be the grand finale of the series.† Blavat, 37 and a ubiquitous figure in Philadelphia popular music at the time, was well positioned to produce and host the concert. He began as a dancer on *Bandstand* in 1955 (before it went national and became *American Bandstand*), went on to manage the successful Philadelphia vocal group Danny and the Juniors, and from there built a high-profile career as a DJ, TV host, producer, and emcee at dances throughout the greater Philadelphia area—all under his widely known moniker, "the Geator with the Heater."

---

* Ironically, Mann became a financial supporter of Foglietta's successful campaign for U.S. Congress in the 1980s. See Fredric R. Mann papers, Irving S. Gilmore Library, Yale University.

† According to Blavat, when there was resistance to staging the concert at the Dell, it was Walter Annenberg, the powerful owner of WFIL-TV and radio, *The Philadelphia Inquirer*, and the *Daily News*, who interceded to ensure that the show went on at the venue.

**(above)** ■ DJ Jerry Blavat, "the Geator with the Heater," onstage at the Rock 'n Roll Jamboree he produced and hosted at the Robin Hood Dell on August 8, 1967. (Courtesy of Keely Stahl)

**(right)** ■ View of the audience at the August 8, 1967, Rock 'n Roll Jamboree at the Robin Hood Dell. (*The Evening Bulletin* photograph collection, Special Collections Research Center, Temple University Libraries)

The Geator put together an impressive lineup for the jamboree. The show featured 16 acts, a mix of Black and White groups and singers, both national and local. Local performers included the Soul Survivors, Bunny Sigler, Jay and the Techniques, the Tymes, Patti LaBelle and the Bluebelles, and Billy Harner, all of whom were riding high with hit records that summer or had had hits in the recent past. The Soul Survivors closed the show with their big hit "Expressway to Your Heart," written and produced by the emerging Philadelphia songwriting and producing team of Kenny Gamble and Leon Huff.[54]

Photographs of the concert show a racially mixed crowd, all packed tightly together. According to *The Evening Bulletin*, the "teenagers . . . danced on their seats and yelled continually during every song." City Representative Abe S. Rosen, who was in attendance, observed: "If there were a roof on the Dell, they would have raised it." After the show, Blavat noted that the concert "gave the kids what they want. That in itself is fantastic. Because of that there was an easing of racial tensions—no incidents, no problems."[55]

The minutes of the Robin Hood Dell Concerts Inc. Board a couple of months later offer a less positive assessment, at least in terms of the concert's impact on Dell facilities. As Mann reviewed plans for the 1968 season at the Board's October 16, 1967, meeting, he called attention to recent "comments [in the newspapers] on expanded use of the Dell facilities. In that connection, Mr. Mann pointed out the damage to the physical facilities which occurred during the 'Rock Jamboree' following the close of the regular season in the summer of 1967."[56] Damage or no, the days of the Dell as a venue exclusively for symphonic music were numbered.

## Changing Face of the Orchestra

As the Dell was opening up to new audiences in the 1960s, The Philadelphia Orchestra was beginning to integrate, albeit ever so slowly. The first members of Asian descent were Chinese violinist Ling Tung, who joined the Orchestra in 1958, and his brother, cellist Yuan Tung, who joined the following year. Yuan left after one year, but Ling remained until 1964. Both played in the Robin Hood Dell Orchestra. Black players would join a few years later. While the Orchestra had been accompanying Black featured soloists for many years, it did not hire its first Black orchestral musician until 1968, when violinist Booker Rowe began playing with the ensemble as a substitute (see page xiii). Rowe left the Orchestra after a year, and in 1970 violist Renard Edwards was the first Black musician to be given a permanent position. Rowe returned that year and received a permanent appointment in 1971.

These appointments were part of a coordinated effort on the part of The Philadelphia Orchestra Association in the late 1960s to hire musicians of color. At the June 23, 1969, association Board meeting, Orchestra Manager Boris Sokolov noted that "the Association is making every effort to seek out competent black musicians to audition for vacancies in the Orchestra. . . . Last season a post in the Orchestra was offered to a negro violist, but he turned it down because his salary in New York was higher."[57]

## Face of the Audience

There was serious public discussion in the 1960s about the racial makeup of the Dell audience. This was an especially fraught time in race relations in Philadelphia, and America at large. In the summer of 1964, there was a major race riot on Columbia Avenue (now Cecil B. Moore Avenue) in North Philadelphia, less than two miles from the Dell. The following year, the city drew national attention for the organized Black-led protests to desegregate Girard College, the high-profile private boarding school in North Philadelphia that had been restricted to White boys since its founding in 1848. (Despite its name, Girard College was and is an elementary and high school.) The protests ultimately proved successful when, in May 1968, the U.S. Supreme Court upheld a lower court's order that Black students be admitted to the school. However, this ruling came just weeks after the assassination of Dr. Martin Luther King Jr. on April 4, 1968, which sparked a wave of unrest nationwide. Philadelphia was spared the major rioting that many cities experienced at this time, but tensions ran high. It was against this backdrop that discussions took place in the late 1960s on the racial makeup of the Dell audience.

The Strawberry Mansion neighborhood in which the Dell was located had become primarily Black by this time, yet few people of color attended the Orchestra concerts. In a letter to the editor of *The Evening Bulletin* in 1965, a writer noted:

> I had the delightful pleasure of attending [a recent] Robin Hood Dell concert. . . . It was a vast, attentive assemblage, overflowing the whole area, filling the benches and covering the grass. . . . Only one thing was wrong! . . . There was not one Negro in a hundred! Here was a sincere opportunity to show the true worthwhileness of integration. Here, there was no discrimination, no admission fee and for thousands living nearby, no transportation [obstacles]. What was the problem?[58]

The issue came up again in the same newspaper three years later. In July 1968, the New Jersey Symphony gave a series of what were called "Ghetto Concerts" in Black neighborhoods in Newark, New Jersey, in tribute to Dr. King. Longtime *Evening Bulletin* music critic James Felton wrote about the concerts, noting that in Philadelphia, while the population was more than one-quarter Black, this percentage was not reflected in audiences at Philadelphia Orchestra concerts at the Dell or the Academy of Music. Felton expressed surprise that so few Black people from the Strawberry Mansion neighborhood attended the free Dell concerts. The article brought a sharp reply from conductor James DePreist, who, like his aunt, Marian

Anderson, was a racial trailblazer forging a successful career as a Black man in the predominately White world of classical music. In a rebuttal piece titled "Concerts in Ghettos: A Musician's View," published in *The Sunday Bulletin* the following week, DePreist took exception to Felton's implication that Black people do not care for "the white man's music," warning that the "concept of 'the white man's music' . . . is not only inaccurate and misleading but also dangerous." DePreist questioned how classical music could be called the White man's music when only a tiny fraction of the White population attended classical concerts:

> I maintain there are just as many ghetto Negroes at the Dell concerts as there are ghetto whites, it's just that the latter are not as easily identifiable. Ghetto concerts are nice but they don't deal with the real problem. I recently conducted the Chicago Symphony at two Ravinia Park [Chicago Symphony's outdoor summer venue] concerts for young people from ghetto areas and the thought came to me that unless the persisting racial barriers to a good education, to admission to the trades and professions and to substantial income are fully destroyed, these children would have neither the inclination, time nor money to attend concerts as adults. The end of discrimination is the obvious answer to most of Mr. Felton's questions because concert attendance should be understood in a socio-economic context and not as an isolated phenomenon.[59]

## 1968 Season

On November 29, 1967, Recreation Commissioner Robert Crawford testified before the City Council on the city's recreation budget for the coming year, which included funding for the Robin Hood Dell. Among other things, he reported that the city would not support extending the Dell orchestral season by several weeks, as Council President Paul D'Ortona and others had proposed (both D'Ortona and Crawford were Dell Board members), but that the city was increasing its annual appropriation to the Dell from $130,000 to $160,000 and was developing plans for a series of eight special events at the venue in August and early September. The special shows were to include "jazz, rock 'n roll, and possibly a few nationally known artists," with tickets to be made available at a nominal charge.[60] The series ended up being four shows, not eight, that were billed as "Dell Jamborees." They featured pop, rock, and soul recording artists—some local, some national—but no jazz.

Two days before Crawford's testimony, Fredric Mann was in Barbados, presenting his credentials to begin service as U.S. ambassador to the Caribbean Island nation, having recently been appointed to the post by President Lyndon B. Johnson. Mann would fly back and forth between Barbados and Philadelphia frequently over the next 18 months, until his ambassadorship concluded in April 1969. As he later told a Philadelphia reporter, he conducted much of his work for the Dell from Bar-

1968 Dell season brochure. (Mann Center for the Performing Arts Archives)

bados—not an easy task, given the state of communication technology at the time. "I do most of it by telephone," he said. "I contact the British Virgin Islands by radio and from there the call to America is completed by cable. You should see my telephone bills. And I pay them, not the U.S. government."[61]

Mann was back in Philadelphia for the scheduled June 17 opening of the 1968 Dell season, a concert that featured the ever popular Van Cliburn. Rain caused postponement of the concert to the following night, the first of several postponements that season. Additional highlights of the season included appearances by pianists Jerome Lowenthal and Vladimir Ashkenazy, cellist Jacqueline Du Pré, and opera singers Richard Tucker, Robert Merrill, Roberta Peters, and Jan Peerce; a performance of Hector Berlioz's dramatic choral symphony *Romeo and Juliet*, with vocal soloists and the Philadelphia Chorale; and all-Beethoven, Brahms, and Richard Strauss programs. In keeping with the "fewer conductors, more time" policy implemented in 1966, there were six conductors, each of whom led a full week of concerts—Stanislaw Skrowaczewski, Antal Dorati, Josef Krips, Werner Torkanowsky, Charles Munch,* and Daniel Barenboim—while Lawrence Foster led the final concert, with Barenboim as featured pianist.

The concerts led by Barenboim, the young Argentinian-born Jewish pianist and conductor who had made his Dell debut two years earlier, included accompanying his wife Du Pré (they had married the year before in Israel) in Camille Saint-Saëns's Cello Concerto No. 1, then his good friend Ashkenazy in Beethoven's Piano Concerto No. 5, before closing the season as a soloist himself in Beethoven's Piano Concerto No. 3. While Barenboim and Ashkenazy performed several times at the Dell in the 1960s and 1970s, Du Pré's 1968 concert at 23 was her only appearance at the venue. Considered one of the greatest cellists of all time, she developed multiple sclerosis in the early 1970s and was forced to end her promising playing career a few years later.

## Dell Jamborees

Part of the broader effort begun the previous year to open the Dell to other types of music, the Dell Jamborees ran for four consecutive Thursday evenings beginning in mid-August 1968. Sponsored by WFIL-TV and Radio in conjunction with the city Department of Recreation's "Action Summer '68" activities program, the concerts

* Two Robin Hood Dell Orchestra musicians, associate principal clarinetist Donald Montanaro and violinist Herbert Light, recalled a daytime rehearsal prior to an evening concert with the esteemed French conductor Charles Munch in 1966 or 1967. It was extremely hot during the rehearsal, prompting Munch to declare, "Gentlemen, you know the music, I know the music. Let's go home." Light remembered that the concert received an excellent review by a Philadelphia music critic, who wrote that the brilliant playing must have been the result of much extra rehearsal. The incident is recounted in Tom DiNardo, *Listening to Musicians: Forty Years of the Philadelphia Orchestra* (La Crescenta, CA: Jaygale, 2016), 164.

were emceed by WFIL DJs, known as "Boss Jocks," and television personalities, including Jerry Blavat. The shows featured a variety of local and national pop, rock, and soul acts, many of whom had best-selling records. Tickets were only $1. Headlining the first show was Philadelphia singer Barbara Mason, who had a big hit in 1965 with the romantic ballad "Yes, I'm Ready." Also on the bill were singer Jeannie C. Riley, who had just released a record, "Harper Valley P.T.A," that was about to become a smash hit, and the Ohio Express, who had a hit in 1967 with "Beg, Borrow, and Steal." Subsequent weeks featured the Angels ("Till," "My Boyfriend's Back"), local group Brenda and the Tabulations ("Dry Your Eyes"), and B. J. Thomas ("Hooked on a Feeling").

## Crisis Averted

A crisis loomed in early 1969 as the Dell prepared for its 40th season of concerts. In February, the Pennsylvania State Supreme Court rejected an emergency tax increase the City of Philadelphia had enacted to address its looming budget deficit, leaving the city with a projected $44.5 million shortfall. Mayor Tate subsequently announced drastic cuts to city subsidies for arts and culture organizations, including the elimination of the city's annual $160,000 allocation to the Dell. Speaking from Barbados in mid-February on the prospect of having to cancel the season, Mann sounded a concerned but optimistic note: "It would be a blow to culture in Philadelphia if these concerts were cancelled, and I have confidence that the people of our city will not allow that to happen."[62] About 10 days later, Mann, a close ally of Mayor Tate, told *The Philadelphia Inquirer*: "We'll have a Dell. I personally think the city's announcement is part of a political program to bring the tax problems to the attention of the public."[63] Coincidentally (or not), just at this time Mayor Tate and his wife vacationed in Barbados, where he visited with Mann. In early March, Tate announced that the Dell funding would be restored.

## 40th Anniversary

At the June 16 opening-night concert of the 1969 season, the Dell marked its 40th anniversary by honoring seven musicians who had been with the Orchestra since opening night in 1930. Six were still playing with the ensemble; the seventh, cellist Adrian Siegel, had retired but was serving as the Orchestra's official photographer.* (It was Siegel who, in 1930, found Ormandy suffering heat stroke after his first rehearsal with the Orchestra on a hot day and got the conductor to a doctor [see page 65].)

* As previously noted, Siegel began taking photographs of Orchestra musicians, conductors, and guest artists in the 1930s. His collection of some 300,000 images is a phenomenal resource that is now part of the Philadelphia Orchestra Association records at the University of Pennsylvania's Kislak Center for Special Collections, Rare Books, and Manuscripts.

*The Sunday Bulletin*, June 22, 1969. (Scrapbook, Mann Center for the Performing Arts Archives)

Orchestra members who were with the ensemble on opening night of the Dell in 1930 are honored on opening night of the venue's 40th season, June 16, 1969. *Left to right*: Manuel Roth, Paul Ferguson, Leonard Mogill, Meyer Simkin, David Madison, Sol Ruden, and Adrian Siegel. Roth was the Orchestra's assistant personnel manager in 1969; Madison, the associate concertmaster; and retired cellist Adrian Siegel, the Orchestra's photographer. (Mann Center for the Performing Arts Archives)

Soprano Beverly Sills, conductor Julius Rudel, and the Robin Hood Dell Orchestra perform on opening night of the Dell's 40th season, June 16, 1969. (Mann Center for the Performing Arts Archives)

An audience of nearly 20,000 heard conductor Julius Rudel and the Robin Hood Dell Orchestra in an all-French program featuring symphonic pieces by Berlioz, Claude Debussy, and Maurice Ravel; operatic arias sung by soprano Beverly Sills; and Sills, the Orchestra, and the Philadelphia Chorale in Francis Poulenc's 1961 piece, *Gloria*.

At intermission, Mann presented plaques to the seven longtime orchestra musicians and noted that 10 million people had heard concerts at the Dell over its 40-year history. He thanked Philadelphia Mayor Tate and the City Council for their continued support, which drew hisses from some in the audience. "Let's be grateful," Mann told them.[64] Indeed, Mann and the Dell Board had good reason to be grateful to the mayor and City Council that year.

Unlike in 1967 and 1968, there were no rock or pop shows at the Dell in 1969 after the Orchestra's season concluded. There was a major gospel concert, however. On August 28, 1969, the Dell hosted its final event of the year, "Gospel in the Dell," the grand finale of *Gospelrama*. A series the city offered as part of its "Better Break '69" summer program, *Gospelrama* offered gospel shows at various locations throughout the city over the course of the summer, culminating with a free concert at the Dell featuring a number of local gospel groups.

## A New Era, a New Name

The audience on opening night of the Dell's 41st season on June 17, 1970, saw something different in the concert program: The event was billed as "Robin Hood Dell Concerts presents The Philadelphia Orchestra—Eugene Ormandy, Music Director." The name "Robin Hood Dell Orchestra" had officially been retired, and for the first time in more than 35 years, the Dell ensemble was called "The Philadelphia Orchestra" once again. The name change signaled, at long last, the final resolution of the issues of artistic control and naming privileges that Robin Hood Dell Concerts Inc. and The Philadelphia Orchestra Association had been negotiating since 1963.

Since implementation of the Orchestra's 52-week contract in 1966, Philadelphia Orchestra Association President Wanton Balis had periodically reported to his Board that he was in discussions with Mann on the outstanding issues between the two organizations. During this time, Robin Hood Dell Concerts Inc. was reimbursing the association 87.5 percent of the cost of the musicians for the Dell concerts, since the association was now paying the musicians for the Dell summer concerts. There was no substantive progress on naming rights or artistic control, however, until April 1968, when Balis reported to the association Board that "Mr. Mann agreed to submit for the Association's approval the list of soloists and guest conductors involved with the Dell concerts. He [Mann] asked the Board to authorize [association] officers to undertake negotiations with the Dell management to the end that an agreement

■ Opening night audience, June 17, 1970, the beginning of the modern era when the Dell ensemble began performing under the name The Philadelphia Orchestra once again. Originally scheduled for June 15, the concert was rained out twice. Photograph published in *The Philadelphia Inquirer*, June 18, 1970. (From *The Philadelphia Inquirer*. © 1970 Philadelphia Inquirer, LLC. All rights reserved. Used under license. *The Philadelphia Inquirer* photograph collection, Special Collections Research Center, Temple University Libraries)

might be reached under which the Association would be granted artistic control of the Dell concerts, and the Dell would be entitled to the use of the name 'The Philadelphia Orchestra.'" Agreeing to the request, the association appointed two of its members to negotiate an agreement "with provisions satisfactory to them with respect to artistic control."[65]

It took two more years, but finally, at The Philadelphia Orchestra Association Board meeting on March 23, 1970, Balis reported:

> The Orchestra will perform under its own name for the Dell concerts this summer. The Association has entered into an agreement with Robin Hood Dell Concerts whereby the Association has full artistic control of the concerts, but control has been delegated to Mr. Fredric Mann as long as he is in charge and no drastic change is made in the format of the concerts. The arrangement is felt to be advantageous to the Association in that it puts the

imprint of The Philadelphia Orchestra on the Dell concerts, which are produced free for the public.

Richard C. Bond, who had assumed the association presidency in 1968, added that "the Dell has agreed to reimburse the association for 100% costs instead of 87½%, and the season will be five weeks instead of six."[66]

In the end, everyone appears to have gotten what they wanted. The Philadelphia Orchestra Association now had ultimate artistic control over the Dell concerts, and the name "The Philadelphia Orchestra" was prominently featured during the summer season; for his part, Mann continued to manage the Dell facility and choose the conductors, soloists, and repertoire. At the June 22, 1970, association Board meeting, five days after opening night, Bond noted that "the Orchestra is now appearing under its own name at the Dell and . . . Mr. Ormandy conducted the opening concert there. Mr. Mann is very pleased that this has been accomplished."[67]

■ Zubin Mehta leading a rehearsal at the Dell in June 1970 of Prokofiev's Piano Concerto No. 5, with pianist Jerome Lowenthal. Originally scheduled for June 18, the concert was pushed back due to weather-related rescheduling. Mehta had a prior commitment and could not lead the rescheduled program, which was held on June 19 with Daniel Barenboim conducting. (Mann Center for the Performing Arts Archives)

The decision to reduce the number of concerts in the 1970 season by eliminating the week of July 4, traditionally one of the weakest in terms of attendance, was prompted by increased costs the Dell was facing due to the new musicians' contract that year. (The season still extended over six weeks, but there were no concerts the week of July 4.) The musicians' higher pay rate, coupled with the fact that the Dell was now reimbursing The Philadelphia Orchestra Association for 100 percent of their costs for the summer concerts, brought the musicians' weekly payroll cost to the Dell to \$35,000–\$40,000 for three concerts a week. The Dell would save this amount by eliminating one week and thus reducing the season from 18 to 15 concerts. The musicians took the July 4 week as one of their paid vacation weeks.[68]

Opening night for 1970 was originally scheduled for June 15 but had to be postponed twice due to rain. On June 17, "with a nearly full moon shining on the crowd of 20,000," according to *The Philadelphia Inquirer*, Ormandy led the Orchestra in Beethoven's Eighth and Ninth Symphonies in honor of the 200th anniversary of the composer's birth, with Philadelphia's Singing City Choir providing the massed voices for the monumental Ninth Symphony.[69] Zubin Mehta, who had been scheduled to conduct on June 16 and 18, was moved to June 19 but had a prior commitment and could not lead the second of his two scheduled concerts, which was the William Kapell Memorial concert, featuring Jerome Lowenthal. Barenboim, who was scheduled to conduct three concerts the following week, flew in early from Europe to conduct Mehta's second program, in addition to his three concerts the week after. Cliburn closed the season on July 23 before an audience estimated at 30,000, a concert in which the weather was also threatening but did not disrupt the proceedings.[70] Such were the challenges of scheduling summer concerts in an open-air, uncovered arena. Freddie Mann had even more incentive to redouble his efforts to secure a new venue.

# 7.

# 1971–1975

## *Search for a New Home*

**With a resolution finally in place as of the 1970 season in** the long, at times contentious, negotiations between Robin Hood Dell Concerts Inc. and The Philadelphia Orchestra Association over management of the summer concerts, Fredric Mann could turn his attention to the Dell's other pressing issue: the need for a new home. The final week of the 1970 season proved once again how the weather could wreak havoc with the schedule in an uncovered venue, while the constant drone of traffic noise from the nearby Schuylkill Expressway continued to compromise the concert experience. "Every once in a while, in the middle of a sweet glissando at the Robin Hood Dell, comes the galump of trucks pulling up the Schuylkill Expressway," noted the *Philadelphia Daily News* in July 1966. "The galump has finally gotten to Fredric Mann, president of the Dell, and he says he's going to move the summertime series to a new site in Fairmount Park as soon as possible."[1]

In the end, "as soon as possible" turned out to be 10 years. Things looked promising for a while in 1971: A site was chosen; a renowned local architect was recruited; conceptual designs were completed; and a major fundraising campaign was announced. But the plans would fall victim to Philadelphia politics. Meanwhile, the concerts continued as Mann and the Dell Board made progress on other fronts in the early 1970s.

### Board Developments

In November 1970, the Board elected A. Leon Higginbotham to its membership, the first Black Board member in Dell history. A distinguished jurist, presidential adviser, and civil rights advocate, Higginbotham was then serving on the U.S. District Court for the Eastern District of Pennsylvania, having been appointed by President Lyndon B. Johnson in 1964 to replace retiring judge, and fellow Dell Board member, J. Cullen Ganey, who negotiated the Dell's agreement in the late 1960s with The Philadelphia Orchestra Association. While Judge Higginbotham's appointment represented a symbolic milestone for the Dell, his impact appears to have been minimal; he did not attend Board meetings or seem to play an active role in Dell affairs, at least publicly.

Rising costs continued to present a challenge. "We're skating on thin ice," Mann told the *Philadelphia Daily News* in February 1972. "Artists that used to get $1,500 now get up to $6,000." The budget that season was projected to be $320,000, of which the Dell was requesting $210,000 from the city. This amount was well over the 50 percent of the Dell budget the city traditionally provided—it had allocated $160,000 the previous three years—but Mann was optimistic the administration of new Philadelphia Mayor Frank Rizzo, an ally whose political career benefited from Mann's contributions, would be supportive.[2] Indeed, the city ended up providing $225,000 in 1972.

As he did every year, Mann stressed the need to bolster the ranks of Friends of the Dell, but there was a new focus in the early 1970s on enlisting corporate support. "We have many additional costs that can be met only by the business leaders in the Philadelphia area," Mann explained. To that end, in March 1971 he appointed longtime Board member and prominent businessman Lawrence Katz as chairman of a new corporate campaign committee "to bring the corporate community into the cultural life of the city on a fuller basis." The following year, Jack Wolgin, a major Philadelphia real estate developer, joined the Board and was added as cochairman of the committee.[*3]

The Board also authorized hiring public relations professionals to assist with "plans for broadening the base of public support" for a new home, engaging the firm of Sommers/Rosen (whose cofounder, Abe Rosen, had served as deputy city representative under Mann in the late 1950s and early 1960s).[†4] Their first job was to create a media campaign around a big announcement in the spring of 1971.

## New Home, First Attempt

On May 20, 1971, Mann and prominent local architect Vincent Kling held a press conference at the Bellevue-Stratford Hotel to unveil plans for a new Robin Hood Dell facility. Kling was a natural choice for the project. Head of Philadelphia's largest

---

* Dell financial records for this period are not extant, so it is difficult to determine how successful the committee was, but there were no announcements of major corporate donations or sponsorships in the early 1970s.

† The Dell also hired local radio and television reporter Donald Angell as a public relations representative at this time, but he soon left to join the administration of incoming Mayor Frank Rizzo.

■ *Left to right*: Mayoral hopefuls Thatcher Longstreth and Frank Rizzo join architect Vincent Kling and Robin Hood Dell President Fredric Mann at the May 20, 1971, unveiling of a model of Kling's design for the new Robin Hood Dell in West Fairmount Park. (Mann Center for the Performing Arts Archives)

architectural firm, he had designed dozens of high-profile buildings and public spaces in and around the city. Among other projects, he had been the principal architect for Penn Center, the massive redevelopment of the downtown area west of City Hall following the demolition of Broad Street Station in 1953, and he designed the adjacent Centre Square high-rise office complex (fronted by the iconic "Clothespin" sculpture, created by artist Claes Oldenburg and commissioned by the property's developer, Dell Board member Jack Wolgin). Kling also designed the U.S. Mint at 5th and Arch streets and the Annenberg Center for the Performing Arts on the University of Pennsylvania campus, while his work for the city included the Municipal Services Building, JFK (now Love) Park, Dilworth Park, and an expansion of Philadelphia International Airport. Kling was also a longtime member of the Philadelphia Art Commission, in which capacity he weighed in on almost every major architectural and landscape project in the city.

At the press conference, Mann and Kling presented a model for a new $9 million "Robin Hood Dell West" in West Fairmount Park, off Chaminoux Drive near Ford Road (about a mile and a half north of where the new facility would eventually be built). Mann announced a "vigorous" fundraising campaign to make the venue a reality. Referring to Veterans Stadium, the recently completed football and baseball venue that had just opened in South Philadelphia, Mann said, "If the city can afford a $50 million sports stadium, it can afford $9 million for the arts."[5]

Sommers/Rosen arranged for statements of support from Mayor James H. J. Tate (in his final year in office), Pennsylvania Governor Milton Shapp, and Philadelphia Orchestra Music Director Eugene Ormandy, who praised the "wonderful design" and "beautiful natural setting," noting that it "offers my colleagues in the orchestra a shield from the noises of traffic and will provide a more attractive location to bring great conductors and soloists to Philadelphia during the summer months."[6]

The press conference was held two days after the primary election in what was expected to be a heated race for mayor of Philadelphia. The two contenders—Democrat Frank Rizzo, the city's tough-talking police commissioner, and Republican Thatcher Longstreth, former city councilman and president of the Philadelphia Chamber of Commerce—attended the event and voiced their support for the project. Rizzo was the victor in November, having campaigned on a platform of law and order and a promise to shake up city government if elected. Unfortunately for the Dell, Kling was one of the new mayor's targets soon after he took office. Rizzo removed Kling from the influential Art Commission in February 1972 and later that year publicly questioned the architect's fees for the airport expansion project, which had been negotiated with the previous administration, stating that Kling would receive "no new contracts with the city as long as I am the mayor."[7] (A subsequent investigation found no wrongdoing on the part of Kling's firm.) Kling recalled the turn of events in a later oral history interview:

> When I was discharged from the Art Commission I read about it in the newspaper. . . . I never to this day have had formal notice. . . . I immediately went over to see Rizzo and said I had spent a great part of my life in this—is there something that you think I've done wrong? He said no. I just think we ought to give somebody else a chance. But in rapid succession thereafter I was relieved of my commission as architect for the airport, as architect for the new Robin Hood Dell, the work down at Society Hill, and so forth. . . . I guess when I was set aside I made room for some others to come in and do work for the city. So therefore the new Robin Hood Dell is not my design, which I had hoped to see built.[8]

Issues with Kling aside, the Chaminoux Drive site was later deemed to be just as susceptible to traffic noise as the original Dell location, and the project's $9 million price tag was considered too steep. With Kling's plans abandoned, it was back to the drawing board for Freddie Mann. Fortunately, the stars would align more favorably a couple of years later. Ironically, Rizzo was elected to the Dell Board in the midst of his dispute with Kling. At its April 11, 1972, meeting, the Board approved an amendment to its bylaws stipulating that the mayor and City Council president would be ex officio members of the Board as long as the Dell received an annual city grant equal to half its annual budget. The city did make its annual allocation to the Dell that year—$225,000, as previously noted—and Rizzo and Council President George X. Schwartz were elected to the Board accordingly. Schwartz occasionally attended meetings; Rizzo did not, although he did prove very supportive of the Dell in terms of the city's annual appropriation and subsequent efforts to build a new home.

Mann became embroiled in a legal controversy as a result of his relationship with Rizzo in this period. Mann was named treasurer of a new Mayor's Office Restoration Fund established in January 1972 to raise money to renovate the incoming mayor's City Hall office. Ostensibly set up in such a way that Rizzo would not know who the contributors were, and thus not be in a position to grant them political favors, the fund quickly drew suspicion and became part of a special state prosecutor's investigation into municipal corruption in Philadelphia. Since only Mann was supposed to know who contributed, the prosecutor attempted to get him to testify before a grand jury, even threatening him with jail if he refused, but Mann repeatedly invoked the Fifth Amendment. Ultimately, he never did testify, and the matter was dropped. No doubt Mann's loyalty to Rizzo—not to mention his contributions to Rizzo's political campaigns—helped when he needed city support for the Dell.[9]

## Artists and Repertoire in the Early 1970s

Programmatically, the early 1970s seasons saw the Dell continue its well-established practice of mixing appearances by longtime favorites with debuts by promising emerging artists. "It has always been a place where young artists can be heard," Eugene Ormandy told *The Philadelphia Inquirer* in 1972. "Freddie Mann has a great nose for new talent. Look at the conductors who have started here—Zubin Mehta, Daniel Barenboim, Lorin Maazel."[10]

For the second consecutive year, the 1971 season opened with Van Cliburn as featured soloist, performing one of his showpieces, Tchaikovsky's Piano Concerto No. 1, before an audience of 30,000 on June 20. (Five days later, Cliburn would open the Temple University Music Festival season with the same piece.) Ormandy was originally scheduled to conduct but was recovering from hip surgery. His replacement was 26-year-old Michael Tilson Thomas, making his first appearance in Philadelphia. Thomas was then serving as assistant conductor of the Boston Symphony Orchestra and was on his way to becoming one of the great American-born conductors of his generation. He would later be noted for his long tenures as music

*Left to right*: Michael Tilson Thomas, Van Cliburn, and Fredric Mann at the Dell, June 22, 1971. (Mann Center for the Performing Arts Archives)

director of the San Francisco Symphony and New World Symphony in Miami Beach (which he founded), and as principal conductor of the London Symphony Orchestra for seven years. Thomas would appear frequently at the Dell and the Mann Center throughout the 1970s.

The weather and conductors' health issues necessitated major juggling of the schedule during the last two weeks of the 1971 season. In week four, Austrian American conductor Franz Allers was scheduled to lead the first concert and Zubin Mehta, the next two, but Mehta suffered a neck injury in a car accident in Israel (he was then music adviser to the Israel Philharmonic), so Allers led the entire week. He began the week with a concert version of Franz Lehár's lighthearted operetta *The Merry Widow* and ended it with Carl Orff's dramatic cantata, *Carmina burana*, which Mehta had programmed. Both performances featured the Philadelphia Chorale. In between, the Tuesday night program included Tchaikovsky's perennially popular *1812 Overture*, with The Philadelphia Orchestra joined by the 40-piece 19th Army Band from nearby Fort Dix, New Jersey, and the Fairmount Park Police firing shotguns into metal cans backstage to simulate cannon fire.

For the fifth and final week of the 1971 season, Barenboim was scheduled to lead all three concerts, but on-and-off (mostly on) rain that week caused the postponement by one day of the first concert, which was the last Dell appearance by the great Chilean pianist Claudio Arrau, and then ultimately the cancellation of the last two concerts, the second of which was to feature violinist Pinchas Zukerman. Faced with paying the conductor, soloist, and orchestra regardless, Mann tried to have the final concert moved indoors to Convention Hall, but the musicians' union would not agree to it.[11] The cancellations notwithstanding, the 1971 season set a Dell attendance record of 371,000.[12]

Weather disruptions marked the first week of the 1972 season as well, continuing Mehta's streak of bad luck at the Dell. Ormandy was scheduled to lead the opening concert of the season on Monday, June 19, with esteemed local pianist Rudolph Serkin playing Beethoven's Piano Concerto No. 5, followed by Mehta leading the Tuesday and Thursday concerts. Rain caused postponement of the opener from Monday to Tuesday, which was Serkin's first Dell appearance in 13 years and would be his last. Mehta's concerts, pushed to Wednesday and Thursday, were also both rained out. After several days of rehearsing with the Orchestra during the day, only to have the evening concert postponed, Mehta had to leave for another commitment, so Assistant Conductor William Smith led a single Saturday night concert that was a combination of the pieces Mehta had programmed for Tuesday and Thursday.

There was also bad weather for part of the last concert of the 1972 season on July 27, featuring conductor Rafael Frühbeck de Burgos and Van Cliburn, but the rain let up at intermission, allowing Cliburn to perform another of his signature pieces, Rachmaninoff's Piano Concerto No. 3. As *The Evening Bulletin* reported, "The crowd that went wild afterward was of every age, although the youngest fans raced to the footlights, flinging roses and screaming—'play!' . . . [Cliburn] then broke all records here by playing a program of ten encores, . . . that lasted longer than the stated program."[13]

Fortunately, there were no issues with the star-studded opening night of the 1973 season, which featured the Dell and Philadelphia Orchestra debuts of Luciano Pavarotti, the dynamic 37-year-old Italian tenor who was then beginning to take the opera world by storm. The program was a concert version of Giuseppe Verdi's opera *Rigoletto*, performed by Metropolitan Opera regulars. In addition to Pavarotti, they included Met Principal Conductor James Levine (a frequent conductor at the Dell and Mann Center in the 1970s), baritone Louis Quilico, soprano Roberta Peters (a longtime Dell favorite, making her 18th appearance), and bass-baritone James Morris (who had studied at the Academy of Vocal Arts in Philadelphia, where Quilico would later teach). Also in the cast and making his Dell debut was baritone Richard Shapp, son of Pennsylvania's governor Milton Shapp. The men of Philadelphia's Singing City Choir provided the choral parts. "Pavarotti's tenor is a brilliant instrument," *The Philadelphia Inquirer* proclaimed, "tinged with excitement through its range. . . . The high notes are vibrant, true, well produced, and snapping with electricity." *The Evening Bulletin* noted that Pavarotti's arias "were done in fine style and [he] belted out the rest of his high-voltage part with the ardor of a true and very electrifying tenor."[14]

**(above)** ■ Some of the principals involved in the June 19, 1973, opening night program, featuring a concert version of Verdi's *Rigoletto*. *Left to right*: Singing City Founder and Director Elaine Brown, conductor James Levine, soprano Roberta Peters, and Dell President Fredric Mann. (Mann Center for the Performing Arts Archives)

**(right)** ■ Luciano Pavarotti in the role of the Duke in a later performance of *Rigoletto*, the role he performed at the Dell on June 19, 1973. (The Metropolitan Opera Archives)

The fourth week of the 1973 season presented yet another scenario in which an emerging, soon-to-be-famous conductor substituted for an indisposed well-known one. This time, the replacement process proved especially complicated. André Previn, then principal conductor of the London Symphony Orchestra and an Academy Award–winning film composer (and married at the time to actress Mia Farrow), was scheduled to lead all three concerts in the fourth week but had to cancel after collapsing from exhaustion while conducting the previous week in the Midwest. His replacement was 31-year-old Italian conductor Riccardo Muti, making his debut at the Dell.

Muti, recently appointed conductor of the Philharmonia Orchestra in London, had made his first U.S. appearance in Philadelphia in 1972, conducting The Philadelphia Orchestra for two weeks of concerts at the Academy of Music. On Saturday, July 14, 1973, Muti led a concert with the Boston Symphony at its summer home at Tanglewood, in western Massachusetts, then was pressed into service to substitute for Previn's Monday and Tuesday concerts at the Dell. Milton Katims, longtime music director of the Seattle Symphony, was to take Previn's Thursday concert. However, Muti fell ill himself during the Tuesday concert, and Katims, who was in attendance, took over after intermission. Fortunately, the second half of the program featured César Franck's Symphony in D minor, a Dell favorite that the Orchestra had played many times. Seven years later, Muti would succeed Ormandy as music director of The Philadelphia Orchestra. Much to Mann's chagrin, Muti did not conduct at the Mann Center very often during his 12-year tenure in Philadelphia. Previn never ended up conducting at the Dell or Mann.

Amid all the last-minute shuffling of conductors during week four of the 1973 season, Orchestra players received immunization shots at the Dell for their upcoming historic trip to China.[15] At President Richard M. Nixon's request, The Philadelphia Orchestra was scheduled to tour China in September 1973—the first Western orchestra to perform in the Asian nation—as part of a cultural exchange, the purpose of which was to lay the groundwork for the eventual establishment of diplomatic relations between the two countries. The tour was a landmark event in Orchestra history, one with enormous international cultural and political impact, and marked the beginning of the Orchestra's long-standing, close musical relationship with China.

## Other Featured Artists

In addition to those previously mentioned, the Dell concerts of the early 1970s featured many famous or soon-to-be famous conductors and soloists: singers Beverly Sills, Marilyn Horne, Jan Peerce, Richard Tucker, and Robert Merrill (Anna Moffo was scheduled in 1974 but had to cancel due to illness; she would never appear at the Dell again); violinists Itzhak Perlman, Yehudi Menuhin (who also conducted), and Isaac Stern, who closed the 1973 season with Ormandy conducting a concert "In

Commemoration of the 25th Anniversary of the Independence of the State of Israel," a cause near and dear to Mann; and pianists José Iturbi, Byron Janis, Radu Lupu, Jerome Lowenthal, Susan Starr, and André Watts (the last three all Philadelphians).

Like vocalists, pianists were especially popular at the Dell. Iturbi drew an audience of 30,000 in what was billed as his 84th Dell appearance since his debut in 1934. "After Iturbi played, many of the older people stood to give him a determined ovation," *The Evening Bulletin* reported on the 75-year-old pianist's 1971 concert. "Memories of the man past seemed to light up their smiling faces as he bowed humbly with courtesy. For a moment it made time stand still once again in a much tilting world."[16] A year later, *The Evening Bulletin* described the especially enthusiastic audience reaction to Watts's July 20, 1972, performance of Frederic Chopin's Piano Concerto No. 2 as "the kind of idolatry enjoyed by only one other pianist—Van Cliburn."[17] Cliburn himself closed the season a week later, to the frenzied audience response described earlier.

Conductors Aldo Ceccato, Stanislaw Skrowaczewski, Sergiu Comissiona, Lorin Maazel, and William Steinberg all led multiple concerts in the early 1970s. Maazel's three concerts in the second week of the 1972 season were his last Philadelphia summer appearances for many years; soon after, he began his 10-year tenure as music director of the Cleveland Orchestra. Steinberg, who since 1970 had been leading the Pittsburgh Symphony's summer concerts at the rival Temple University Music Festival in Ambler, Pennsylvania, closed out the 1974 Dell season, leading two concerts. The first featured brothers William and Joseph de Pasquale, The Philadelphia Orchestra's associate concertmaster and principal violist, respectively, in Mozart's Sinfonia concertante in E-flat, while the second featured Van Cliburn once again performing one of his audience favorites, Tchaikovsky's Piano Concerto No. 1.

June 20, 1974, was "Robert Stoltz Night," honoring the 91-year-old Viennese composer and conductor whose waltzes, songs, and light classical works in the tradition of his native city made up the program. Stoltz had conducted several times at the Dell in the 1940s and early 1950s, often leading his own pieces. He was scheduled to attend the 1974 concert in which he was honored but had to cancel due to illness. He did write a new piece for the occasion, "Philadelphia March," which was given its world premiere that night, with his fellow Austrian Walter Goldschmidt conducting.

## Highest Standards

Occasional concerts of lighter orchestral fare such as Robert Stoltz Night notwithstanding, Dell programs mostly featured the highest-level works in the Western symphonic repertoire. Mann was adamant that Dell patrons have the opportunity to hear the same high-caliber music and soloists that Philadelphia Orchestra patrons heard during the regular season at the Academy of Music. "I've always thought the Dell ought to provide music and the artists that most people can't afford to hear in the win-

■ A solitary Philadelphia Orchestra violinist warms up onstage as the audience settles in before the July 24, 1973, concert at the Dell, an all-Russian program led by conductor Andre Kostelanetz. (*The Philadelphia Inquirer* photograph collection, Special Collections Research Center, Temple University Libraries)

ter," he told *The Philadelphia Inquirer* in 1972. "We have good programs here. See the programs [The Philadelphia] Orchestra plays at Saratoga. We'd have the same thing here otherwise. Pops concerts. I hate that word."[18] He expanded on that theme a year later in an interview with *The Evening Bulletin*: "We try to serve the music lovers, the middle-income people, students, youth, the aged, the poor. These are the people who can't afford Academy of Music prices in the winter. And we don't play down to them. We keep up the same standards as the regular Philadelphia Orchestra season."[19]

## The Dell vs. Ambler

The Temple University Music Festival at Ambler continued to vie with the Dell for the summer symphonic music audience, especially after Steinberg and the Pittsburgh Symphony became the resident orchestra at Ambler in 1970. A public spat developed in 1972, when the season-opening concert at Ambler was broadcast nationally on TV, with funding provided by Pennsylvania's Tourist Development Bureau. During intermission, the audience was treated to a 15-minute state-produced promotional film titled "Sounds of Pennsylvania," which made no mention of the Robin Hood Dell. Allen Sommers, the Dell's public relations representative, wrote a letter to the state director of commerce, claiming that "not only was the Robin Hood Dell ignored visually, it was not even mentioned, while much lesser cultural subjects were given considerable play. . . . I cannot believe [the omission] was accidental in view of the considerable time—and cost—that went into the production. . . . We must take this as a slap."[20] In reporting the story, *The Sunday Bulletin* noted that Governor Milton Shapp's son, baritone Richard Shapp, was a vocal student at Temple University at the time, and the governor often attended the Ambler concerts. Adding fuel to the fire, the governor had advocated for a summer home for The Philadelphia Orchestra in the Poconos, an idea that did not sit well with Mann.[21]

## Children's Concerts

As they had since 1952, the Children's Concerts provided opportunities for promising young area musicians to perform with the summer version of the renowned Philadelphia Orchestra. There were two especially notable debuts in the early 1970s. On July 28, 1971, 10-year-old violin virtuoso Nadja Salerno-Sonnenberg, from nearby Cherry Hill, New Jersey, was the featured artist. Born in Rome, she came to the United States with her family at eight to study at the Curtis Institute. Her

Audition winners for the 1971 Robin Hood Dell Children's Concerts series pose in Silvia and Fredric Mann's apartment in May 1971. Third from the left is Nadja Salerno-Sonnenberg, the 10-year-old violinist from Cherry Hill, New Jersey, whose debut at the Dell on July 28, 1971, marked the beginning of her celebrated international performing career. (*The Evening Bulletin* photograph collection, Special Collections Research Center, Temple University Libraries)

■ These youngsters sport the proper headwear and cool off with ice cream for the July 11, 1973, Children's Concert. The Robin Hood Dell Guild supplied the visors as protection from the sun at the concerts, which were held at 10:30 on Wednesday mornings in July. (*The Philadelphia Inquirer* photograph collection, Special Collections Research Center, Temple University Libraries)

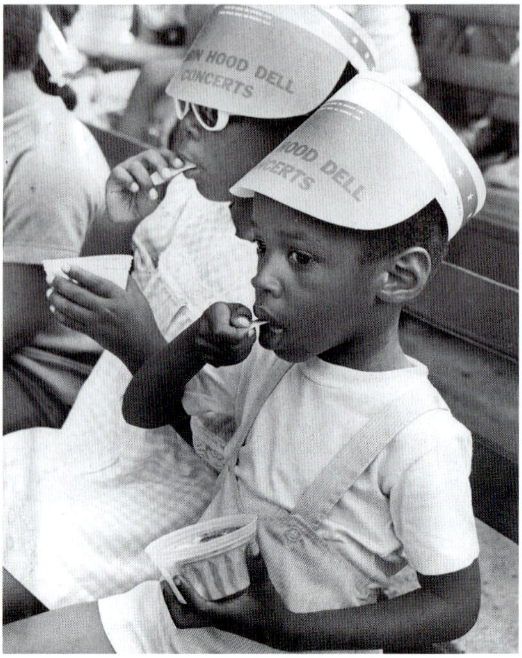


Dell debut was early in a career that would see her make the transition from child prodigy to successful international recording and concert artist, including headlining at the Mann Center four times from 1990 to 2001. On July 18, 1973, another area 10-year-old made his Dell debut: pianist Marcantonio Barone. He would go on to have a prominent career in the Philadelphia area as a teacher and recitalist, known especially for championing contemporary piano music, including premiering works by noted local composers George Crumb and George Rochberg.

The women of the Robin Hood Dell Guild helped coordinate the Children's Concerts, including choosing the selection committee, scheduling the performers' auditions (generally held at the Queen Village branch of Settlement Music School), and presenting the winners with monetary awards—usually $100, sometimes more—from the guild's scholarship fund. In 1972, the guild also sponsored professional performers at each of the Children's Concerts, presenting artists they thought young people would enjoy, from jazz combos to ballet and African dance troupes. Starting in 1973, the guild supplied audience members with visors as protection from the sun, as the concerts were held on Wednesday mornings in July. The final Children's Concert of 1973 featured local singer and guitarist George Britton, a classically trained bass-baritone who became involved in folk music in the 1950s and cofounded two long-running Philadelphia institutions: the Philadelphia Folksong Society in 1957 and the Philadelphia Folk Festival in 1962.

## James Frazier

William Smith, the longtime Philadelphia Orchestra assistant conductor who led the Dell Children's Concerts, took a leave of absence for the 1974 summer season, giving Ormandy an opportunity to advocate for James Frazier, a young Black conductor from

■ Detail from a 1974 Robin Hood Dell brochure. (Mann Center for the Performing Arts Archives)

Detroit whose career Ormandy had been helping to advance since Frazier impressed him at a conducting seminar in 1964. In January 1971, Ormandy had arranged for Frazier to become the first Black conductor to lead The Philadelphia Orchestra in a concert at the Academy of Music. Three years later, when the assistant conductor position at the Dell became available, Ormandy again interceded on Frazier's behalf. With Fredric Mann's approval, Ormandy arranged for The Philadelphia Orchestra Association to hire Frazier as assistant conductor for the 1974 Dell season. His primary responsibility was leading the Children's Concerts, but he was also required to attend all regular rehearsals and concerts and be ready to substitute for scheduled conductors if needed. (He never was.) Frazier's compensation was $2,500 for the five-week season.[22]

With an eye toward bringing diversity to the Children's Concerts, Frazier programmed a number of Black-oriented works, including excerpts from his own *12th Street: A Soul Opera*, a musical about life in his native Detroit; the soul-infused theme from the 1971 movie *Shaft*, written by Isaac Hayes; and selections from George Gershwin's opera *Porgy and Bess*, featuring four Black singers.[23]

While in Philadelphia that first summer, Frazier came to the attention of the Reverend Leon Sullivan, the great civil rights leader and social activist who was pastor of Zion Baptist Church in North Philadelphia. Sullivan invited Frazier to become music director at Zion and to develop programs to expose Black youth to classical music, something Frazier had done in Detroit and was then doing as a public-school music teacher in New York City. As Frazier told *The New York Times* in 1975:

■ James Frazier leads the July 17, 1974, Children's Concert, featuring 13-year-old cellist Carol Tashjian. (*The Philadelphia Inquirer* photograph collection, Special Collections Research Center, Temple University Libraries)

> [I have] been trying to make inner-city children realize there may be and can be possibilities for them, both esthetically and vocationally, in classical music. Blacks feel left out of the mainstream of symphonic music, removed from the classics and to understand why all you have to do is count the number of black musicians with leading orchestras. . . . I believe music can be a valuable tool in dealing with inner-city children, because it gives them an outlet for self-expression and provides a discipline.[24]

Smith returned as assistant conductor for the 1975 Dell season, but Frazier continued to conduct the Children's Concerts that year. "We are quite happy to have Mr. Frazier back with us to conduct the three children's concerts," said Mann. "His success with the sizeable children's attendance at our three 1974 concerts, his innovations in programming, and his fine musicianship indicates we can look forward to an outstanding series of concerts for children this summer."[25]

The 1975 Children's Concerts would be Frazier's last appearances at the Dell. There were no Children's Concerts the following year, when all of the attention was focused on the opening of the new facility and the U.S. Bicentennial celebrations. In all, Frazier would conduct only six Children's Concerts for the Dell over two years. He would remain active in Philadelphia after that, however, continuing his work with Reverend Sullivan both at Zion Baptist Church and in advocating for Black musicians in classical music. The two established the short-lived National Afro-American Philharmonic Orchestra, which debuted at the Academy of Music in May 1978 and was designed to give Black musicians experience in the orchestral field. Frazier died in 1985 at 44.

## Dance at the Dell

Ballet made a high-profile return to the Dell in the 1970s after rarely being programmed the previous decade. The star attractions were several Russian defectors to the West who had been members of the famed St. Petersburg–based Kirov Ballet. Natalia Makarova, former prima ballerina with the Kirov, defected in 1970 and joined American Ballet Theatre in New York City. She made her first Philadelphia appearance at the Dell on June 24, 1971, drawing an audience of some 30,000 in a program with The Philadelphia Orchestra led by Akira Endo, conductor of American Ballet Theatre. *The Philadelphia Inquirer* noted Makarova's "unerring sense of line. No movement was flat or irrelevant, but each was attacked with the kind of

Ballet dancers Natalia Makarova and Ted Kivitt, who performed together at the Robin Hood Dell on June 24, 1971. (*The Philadelphia Inquirer* photograph collection, Special Collections Research Center, Temple University Libraries)

precision and brio that makes the Kirov style seem so alive."[26] *The Evening Bulletin* was also highly complimentary but noted that the Dell stage was too small for a true ballet performance and sensed tentativeness in Makarova's dancing after she bumped into a poorly placed microphone stand on the stage.[27] (Like Van Cliburn, Makarova would perform at the Temple Music Festival later that summer.)

New York City Ballet stars Edward Villella and Patricia McBride performed at the Dell in 1973 with Andre Kostelanetz conducting, followed two years later by one of the Dell's biggest events of the 1970s: a performance by the celebrated Russian expatriate husband-and-wife duo Valery and Galina Panov. Former stars of the Kirov Ballet, the Panovs drew international attention when they were persecuted for attempting to leave the Soviet Union in 1972 to settle in Israel. (Valery Panov was Jewish; his wife was not.) Valery was expelled from the Kirov; Galina resigned in protest; and they were both prohibited from dancing and subjected to various forms of harassment, including a purported poisoning attempt on Valery. After finally being allowed to emigrate in 1974, their first performance in the free world was in November of that year in Israel at the Fredric R. Mann Auditorium in Tel Aviv. They made their American debut in Philadelphia in February 1975 at the Spectrum, the sports and entertainment arena in South Philadelphia that, in retrospect, everyone agreed was not a suitable venue for ballet, especially the eagerly awaited American debut of such world-famous dancers. Following their Spectrum performance, the Panovs danced throughout the United States before returning to Philadelphia to perform at the Dell on July 10, 1975, with Seymour Lipkin conducting The Philadelphia Orchestra.

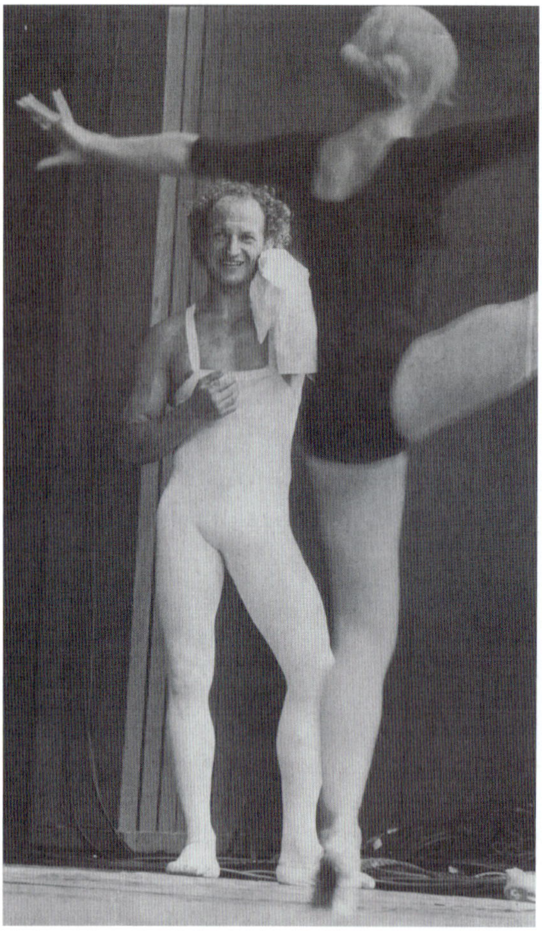

Valery Panov watches as his wife, Galina, rehearses at the Robin Hood Dell in advance of their July 10, 1975, performance. Photograph published in *The Philadelphia Inquirer*, July 11, 1975. (From *The Philadelphia Inquirer*. © 1975 Philadelphia Inquirer, LLC. All rights reserved. Used under license. *The Philadelphia Inquirer* photograph collection, Special Collections Research Center, Temple University Libraries)

Unfortunately, it began to rain at concert time. Lipkin dispensed with the orchestra-only opening selection and went straight to the dance pieces. The overhang of the Dell amphitheater shell kept the floor dry for the first half of the program, but the wind shifted after intermission and conditions worsened. "The scene was grotesque, even bizarre," *The Evening Bulletin* reported. "White sheets of light flashed over a sea of umbrellas. Rain started as a driving thing that pelted down in front of the stage. . . . The scene was something between a Dracula-Frankenstein movie and Gene Kelly dancing in the rain."[28] Mann was prepared to cancel the remainder of the program, but the Panovs insisted the concert go on. *The Philadelphia Inquirer* reported that, despite the rain,

> [the Panovs] were unstinting in their movement. Their solo variations were displays of virtuosity. [Valery] Panov fearlessly—in these circumstances, dangerously—executed long soaring leaps and air turns and lifted his partner as if she were gossamer and down. . . . It was rare dedication, and the act itself overshadowed the dance. . . . At the end, they took their bows, going far downstage to stand in the rain before the hill of umbrellas. The audience crowded the stage, picked the marigolds growing in the boxes along the apron and threw the flowers to the dancers.[29]

## Soirees and After-Parties

The women of the Robin Hood Dell Guild sponsored a number of events in the early 1970s to entertain featured Dell artists and raise money and awareness for the venue. These ranged from formal dinner dances at upscale hotels such as the Bellevue-Stratford and Barclay to smaller-scale soirees and lunches. The planning for these events often took place at luncheon meetings held at the estate of Guild President Selma Katz and her husband, Dell Board Member Lawrence Katz, in Melrose Park, just outside the city. The early 1970s saw the guild's practice of hosting a high-profile dinner dance following a concert early in the Dell season largely abandoned, primarily because, as noted in the guild's Board minutes, "most artists don't care to be entertained" in this manner anymore. Instead, guild members were encouraged to host luncheons and small dinners for Dell featured artists at their homes. The Katzes hosted Riccardo Muti and violinist Ruggiero Ricci following their concert on July 16, 1973, for example. Silvia Mann proposed an interesting alternative that the guild tried in 1974: a "cocktail soiree and mini-concert" at the Bloomingdale's department store in suburban Jenkintown, Pennsylvania. On April 30, 1974, the store decorated several of its designer showrooms; local restaurants supplied food; and tenor Richard Tucker gave a recital for invited guests. The event was deemed a great success and was repeated in 1976, with baritone Robert Merrill as featured vocalist.[30]

Separate from guild-sponsored activities, Freddie and Silvia Mann continued their tradition of hosting after-parties for Dell featured artists and others, sometimes at their swanky apartment in the Barclay Hotel on Rittenhouse Square and sometimes at area restaurants. Legendary ballet dancer Mikhail Baryshnikov, another mid-1970s Soviet exile who performed at the Mann Center in 1979 and 1981, recalled: "Freddy . . . was famous for vodka and cigars and late-night dinners that went to two or three in the morning in his Rittenhouse Square apartment after the show. Lots of laughs and booze and happiness."[31] Philadelphia TV and print journalist Marciarose Shestack, a close friend of the Manns and later a longtime Mann Center Board member, wrote about one such party in a *Philadelphia Inquirer* column. Held at Center City restaurant Frankie Bradley's following a July 7, 1975, Dell concert featuring Van Cliburn and James DePreist (an old college friend of Shestack's), the party included many of that week's Dell headliners, as Shestack recalled:

> I had a moment of personal joy watching Van Cliburn get to his feet as Jimmy and Betty DePreist approached the table. "Maestro," [Cliburn] said, embracing him, . . . "I want my mother to meet you." . . . Later, Valery [Panov] looked approvingly at the table laden with sauerkraut, pickles, and green tomatoes, and said, "This is a real Russian table." Then, raising his vodka he made a toast to Cliburn [referencing Cliburn's stunning gold medal performance at the 1958 International Tchaikovsky Competition in Moscow]: "We drink to you because you came to us in Russia without politics . . . and you conquered us." As the evening wore on into morning . . . reminiscences of the past turned to plans for the future. "Next year . . . the bicentennial year . . . will be the greatest year yet," said Freddie, lighting still another cigar. When Freddie talks about the Dell you've got to believe him.[32]

## Better Break "Second Season"

The use of the Dell for types of music other than classical that began in the late 1960s intensified in the early 1970s, when the Philadelphia Department of Recreation expanded its Better Break summer activities program to include a full series of concerts at the Dell in August, after The Philadelphia Orchestra's season had concluded. The series grew to the point that it essentially constituted a second season at the Dell, one that almost rivaled the Orchestra season in scale and popularity.

The highlight of the Better Break series in 1971 was to be a set of nine rock and pop shows produced by indefatigable local DJ and promoter Jerry Blavat, "the Geator with the Heater." Each of the concerts was to be sponsored by one of the city's leading radio stations. The top-rated Black station, WDAS, was to kick off the series with Stevie Wonder and Smokey Robinson and the Miracles headlining; other stations had big names lined up as well. But WIBG, one of the city's top rock and pop stations, threatened to sue, claiming it was not invited to participate and objecting to Blavat's proposed $20,000 fee. There was evidence that WIBG had, in fact, been invited, and Blavat claimed that WIBG was just upset that it was given the eighth concert in the series, not the first. When a WIBG attorney notified the Department of Recreation that the station was preparing to seek a court injunction against the series, the concerts were cancelled.[33] As a result, only three Better Break events were held at the Dell in August 1971: a comic opera, a ballet performance, and the always popular *Gospelrama*, the gospel-themed show featuring local choirs and singers. These were cosponsored by the Sam Goody record store chain and the nonprofit Musician's Performance Trust Fund, in conjunction with the Department of Recreation.

The department ramped up the Dell summer concert series significantly in 1972, when the new mayor Frank Rizzo provided additional support for the Better Break program; Recreation Commissioner Robert Crawford secured more corporate contributions; and Rizzo appointed his longtime ally Theodore "Ted" Jordan as deputy recreation commissioner. A retired Philadelphia police detective, Jordan had been Rizzo's bodyguard when Rizzo was police commissioner—Jordan was proud of being the first Black officer to serve in this role—and the two had grown close. When Rizzo resigned to run for mayor in 1971, Jordan also resigned to become a campaign aide and continue as Rizzo's bodyguard. After taking office in early 1972, Rizzo appointed Jordan deputy commissioner for recreation, responsible for enhancing Better Break programming, with a particular focus on increasing concerts at the Dell.

Under Jordan, the Recreation Department established an annual Better Break "August Festival" in 1972, a month-long concert series at the Dell with shows presented two nights a week. Catering to a variety of musical tastes, the concerts encompassed a wide range of genres. "We have found that over 80 percent of the people who patronize our shows don't patronize the regular [Philadelphia Orchestra] Dell shows," Jordan told the *Daily News*. "I have an audience 30, 60, 70 years old. They get dressed up to come out and have a good time. They're people nobody's catered to for years."[34]

Big band jazz was a major attraction at the August festival, with the top-name bands of Woody Herman, Lionel Hampton, Duke Ellington, Benny Goodman, Count Basie, and Maynard Ferguson all appearing. The *Gospelrama* concerts now featured famous gospel and gospel-influenced artists such as the Staple Singers, Andre Crouch, the Dixie Hummingbirds, Reverend James Cleveland, and Brook Benton, as well as various local gospel groups. Opera and operetta were presented by the Philadelphia Grand Opera Company, Philadelphia Lyric Opera Company, and Light Opera Company of Philadelphia; the Pennsylvania Ballet and Philadelphia Civic Ballet performed; Spanish Fiesta nights featured Latin music stars Tito Puente, Ray Barretto, and others; there were concerts featuring Slavic, Scottish, and other ethnic

■ *Philadelphia Inquirer* ads for Better Break concerts at the Robin Hood Dell: *upper left*, August 3, 1971; *lower left*, July 23, 1972; *right*, August 13, 1972. (All: From *The Philadelphia Inquirer.* © 1971 & 1972 Philadelphia Inquirer, LLC. All rights reserved. Used under license. Retrieved from Newspapers.com)

music; and there was a "Mummers Bicentennial Preview" concert in 1975, with several popular Mummer string bands providing the entertainment. Undeterred by his earlier disappointment, the Geator with the Heater presented "Jerry Blavat's Rock 'n Roll Revival," a 1973 concert featuring a full lineup of singers and groups that had had hits in the 1950s and early 1960s, including three local acts: the Dovells, Lee Andrews and the Hearts, and Chubby Checker. Rizzo attended the Chubby Checker concert and was applauded when introduced.[35]

The Dell was hopping on August 20, 1974, when the Better Break program presented a double bill with the great soul singer Ray Charles and jazz pianist Erroll Garner. "Ray Charles electrified the crowd with his high-voltage singing," *The Evening Bulletin* reported. "The genius of his reputation is surely not an exaggeration. . . . [H]is voice possesses an uncanny combination of power and frailty that is unforgettable. 'Busted,' 'Let the Good Times Roll,' 'Georgia on My Mind,' and the sentimental 'I Can't Stop Loving You' are his calling cards and he played [them] for all the soul that could be squeezed out of them."[36]

## "The Body" and the Deputy Commissioner

One of the performing groups that appeared often with Lionel Hampton and the other big bands in the Better Break concerts at the Dell was the Coppertone Review, a Philadelphia-based, mostly female Black dance troupe led by Hortense Allen, the wife of Ted Jordan. A popular local dancer, choreographer, and producer whose alluring physique led to her nickname, "The Body," Allen and her dance troupes were a fixture in the world of Black entertainment in Philadelphia and beyond in the mid- to late 20th century. She produced and performed in shows at legendary area venues such as the Earle Theatre, Uptown Theatre, and Club Harlem in Atlantic City. Her group began appearing as the Coppertone Review at the Dell in 1972. A *Philadelphia Inquirer* review of their August 28, 1973, performance with Hampton noted that the "17 not overly-clad girls and the two fully-costumed boys, accompanied by the band, scored in a conventional high-kicking number and a tap-dancing bit. The girls gave a good example of the precision line. . . . Ted Jordan, resplendent in white tuxedo, served as master of ceremonies."[37]

Hortense Allen was a major talent and longtime attraction in Philadelphia, so her frequent appearances at the Dell Better Break shows were not necessarily unusual. What did draw attention was the fact that these appearances commenced in 1972, the year her husband began booking the series. Jordan's stewardship of the Dell concerts came into question in early 1980, after he was replaced as deputy recreation commissioner when William J. Green succeeded Rizzo as mayor. Green's managing director, W. Wilson Goode (who would become mayor himself four years later), launched an investigation into Jordan's management of the Dell series, claiming: "There is certainly a potential here that criminality was involved. It appears that

■ Coppertone Review dancers pose at the Robin Hood Dell in August 1972. Leader Hortense Allen is sixth from the left in the bottom row. (Courtesy of the Philadelphia Folklore Project)

there were definitely conflicts of interest." Goode specifically cited the fact that the Coppertone Review had received $25,000 for 18 Dell performances during Jordan's tenure, all paid out of a special account that Jordan controlled. Jordan's boss, Recreation Commissioner Robert Crawford, was quoted at the time as saying that he had been directed by Mayor Rizzo's office not to interfere with Jordan's administration of the Dell concerts. Jordan denied any wrongdoing and was never charged with misconduct.[38]

## New Home, Second Attempt

Robin Hood Dell Concerts Inc. was not involved in the city-sponsored Better Break shows at the Dell, other than making the venue available. A private nonprofit focused solely on The Philadelphia Orchestra's summer concerts, the Dell Board of Directors was actively pursuing a new home in the early 1970s, one it could control completely and not have to share with other city agencies. Things began moving seriously in this direction in 1973, not long after the collapse of the project for the Vincent Kling–designed new Dell. The focus now was on having a new home ready in time for the

U.S. Bicentennial in the summer of 1976, when the eyes of the world would be on Philadelphia. At the March 29, 1973, Dell Board meeting, Mann noted that he was making progress in that area. William L. Rafsky, a city official and president of the Philadelphia 1976 Bicentennial Corporation, joined the Dell Board at the meeting and "affirmed his personal support of the new facility and the support of the Philadelphia Bicentennial [Corporation] to help make the new facility a reality by 1976."[39]

Two months later, Mann reported to the Board that negotiations were underway with the New York architectural firm MacFadyen-De Vido to design the new facility. John H. MacFadyen and Alfredo De Vido had recently designed two other major outdoor music venues similar in nature to what was envisioned for the Dell: Saratoga Performing Arts Center in Saratoga Springs, New York, which opened in 1966 and hosted the annual August residency of The Philadelphia Orchestra, and Wolf Trap National Park for the Performing Arts in Vienna, Virginia, just outside Washington, DC, which opened in 1971.

Mann noted that the projected cost of the new facility was now $3 million (the actual cost would be well over twice that). There would be 5,000 seats under cover and room for 10,000 more on benches and the lawn behind. Mann also reported that the Dell had engaged the New York firm of Carl W. Shaver and Company at a cost of $10,000 to do a feasibility study and make presentations to state and federal agencies for grant funding.[40]

While embarking on a capital fundraising campaign for the new venue, the Dell pursued public funding in support of its musical programming. In a May 1973 *Evening Bulletin* profile of Mann and his efforts to obtain a new Dell home, Mann lamented that the Dell did not receive a National Endowment for the Arts (NEA) grant for which it had applied, while the New York Philharmonic received $190,000 from the NEA for giving free concerts in the park, something the Dell had been doing for years. "We could have used that money for expansion of our programs," Mann noted. "The trouble is that our congressmen and senators didn't go to bat for us. I don't think any of them have ever heard a piece of music in their lives, except maybe [Congressman Joshua] Eilberg."[41] (At the time, the two U.S. senators from Pennsylvania were Republican, while all of the area's congressional representatives were Democrats, the party in which Mann was a major player and funder.) The Dell was successful in securing state funding for programming in 1974 and 1975 from the Pennsylvania Council on the Arts, the state agency that had been providing major support to the Temple University Music Festival for several years.

In that same *Evening Bulletin* article, Mann noted that "the financing for the new Dell is practically assured. We expect a $3 million loan from the city, but we'll be able to pay it off within a few years with gifts from foundations and industry. It won't cost the taxpayers one cent." (This turned out not to be true.) While a site had been selected, it had not yet been approved, and Mann did not divulge the location. He did say that it would be in West Fairmount Park "away from the noise of the expressway and the pattern of aircraft" and that the facility would be a cross between Saratoga and Wolf Trap. "I'll tell you one thing," he said. "The new Dell will be built in concert with nature, and it will be accessible to the people. Governor Shapp wants the Philadelphia Orchestra to play in the Poconos in the summer. But I say Philadelphia should have its own summer festival right here, in our own backyard."[42]

The proposed new Dell's significance to the region's musical life aside, a group of area elected officials and civic leaders envisioned the venue as part of a large-scale international exposition—a true World's Fair—they were hoping to hold in Philadelphia in conjunction with the U.S. Bicentennial in the summer of 1976. They saw the new Dell as one of several major public buildings that would open in the city that summer. However, by the early 1970s it was clear that the hundreds of millions of dollars necessary for such an ambitious undertaking would not be forthcoming from federal or private sources and that Philadelphia's Bicentennial celebration, while still robust, would have to be more modest in scale.

## George's Hill

The site chosen for the new Dell was George's Hill, a broad sloping tract on the western edge of Fairmount Park, adjacent to the neighborhood of Parkside in West Philadelphia. The site was named for the George family, local Quakers who had had extensive landholdings in the area going back to the 18th century. In 1869, Jesse George and his sister Rebecca donated the George's Hill tract to the city to become part of Fairmount Park. Seven years later, it was part of the grounds of the 1876 Centennial Exposition and housed an observation tower that offered a bird's-eye view of the sprawling Centennial complex (many extant aerial view photographs of the Centennial were taken from the George's Hill tower). As previously noted, the Fairmount Park Commission sponsored band concerts in a gazebo at George's Hill in the 1920s. In the 1940s, the site was a popular lover's lane, with a beautiful view of the city skyline from the top of the hill serving as a major attraction. None other than Freddie Mann remembered "necking like hell" in a Buick on George's Hill in his younger years, while a veteran columnist for the New Jersey newspaper the *Courier-Post* recalled it as the "fairest spot of all for couples in love. . . . Especially if the guy owned a car with a radio." The columnist waxed nostalgic about "the Hill and the moon and a very young Frank Sinatra" crooning love songs on the radio.[43]

The Fairmount Park Commission gave formal approval for construction of the new facility at George's Hill on October 10, 1973.[44] With other approvals—from the Art Commission, Planning Commission, City Council, and Mayor's Office—in hand or anticipated, Mann used his considerable political connections to secure state and city funding to build the facility. The initial plan of the city providing a long-term, low-interest loan that Robin Hood Dell Concerts Inc. would pay off over time proved impractical, as did the original $3 million estimate for the project. Costs skyrocketed as planning proceeded, a chief culprit being the price of steel, which essentially doubled during this time. The actual final cost ended up being almost $7.5 million, with the city providing more than $5 million; the state, a little more than $2 million; and private donors, almost $500,000.*[45] Although no records of the private donations survive, Mann and fellow wealthy Dell Board members such as Lawrence Katz, Jack Wolgin, and others no doubt contributed generously.

## The Public Weighs In

As the project unfolded and the price tag rose during the 1973–1975 planning phase, a spirited public debate ensued regarding the need for the new facility and the merits of investing millions in public money in it. Letters to the editors of local newspapers ranged from those who felt that the current Dell was fine or that the city had many more pressing needs than a new concert venue to those who claimed that the Dell was outmoded and problematic and that the world's top musical artists would stop coming if it was not replaced.[46]

Among those writing in favor of the new venue was Philadelphia Orchestra violinist Manuel "Manny" Roth, who had been playing at the Dell since it opened in 1930. In a July 26, 1975, letter to the editor of *The Evening Bulletin*, Roth offered an inside perspective from one who had to contend with the Dell's shortcomings:

> In the past decade or so, since the Schuylkill Expressway was constructed, artists, conductors, and musicians of the Philadelphia Orchestra have been assaulted by assorted noises, plus overhead planes. Add to this humidity, and constant threats of thunderstorms and you have an idea of what auto and truck traffic and the elements have been doing to the present Robin Hood Dell. Often communication between the conductor and soloists is lost because of these ungodly noises. And I understand many artists have objected to the noises and beg off making appearances even with our great orchestra.
>
> But, those of us who have literally grown up at Robin Hood Dell have long felt there was a need to upgrade our outdoor summer music facility to match those in Boston, Cleveland, Houston, North Jersey and Washington, D.C. Here we are with one of the world's finest symphony orchestras, and we have to worry constantly about inclement weather and postponements, and often cancellations. These are nerve twisting, and costly. . . . Those of us who help provide the music three nights a week will welcome the new Dell. And so will world-famous artists and conductors.[47]

* Different sources give slightly different figures for the final cost and how the funding sources break down, but all are in the general range given here.

■ On January 29, 1975, a model of the new Robin Hood Dell West was unveiled in the Grand Court at John Wanamaker's department store in downtown Philadelphia. Mayor Frank Rizzo (*center*) gestures to Fredric Mann (*in dark glasses, at right*) while Wanamaker's president, John Harrison (*at left*), and members of the public look on. (Mann Center for the Performing Arts Archives)

On January 29, 1975, a scale model of the new facility was unveiled in the Grand Court of the John Wanamaker department store in the heart of Center City. Ground was broken at the George's Hill site the following week.* (Unlike in 1930, there was no ceremonial groundbreaking, perhaps because work began in the dead of winter.) Public reaction to the building's modern design was mixed. One letter writer was particularly unimpressed: "Judging by the model, the new Robin Hood Dell will resemble a huge monster, and does not have an inviting appearance. Gruesome would describe it better."[48] Opinions on the aesthetics of the new structure were one thing, but a number of writers raised the more troubling issue of elitism. Whereas charges of elitism at the Dell in the late 1960s were a result of the classical music–only programming, this time they were prompted by the design of the new building. In the

---

* Ironically, the unveiling occurred the day after the death at 93 of renowned classical music impresario Arthur Judson, who was manager of The Philadelphia Orchestra from 1915 to 1935 and one of the prime movers in getting the original Dell built in 1930 (see Chapter 2).

Excavation of the site for the new Robin Hood Dell West in March 1975. The Catholic Total Abstinence Fountain is in the immediate background, with the dome of Memorial Hall beyond that. (Both were built for the 1876 Centennial and are still standing.) The Philadelphia skyline is in the distance. (*The Evening Bulletin* photograph collection, Special Collections Research Center, Temple University Libraries)

old Dell, Friends of the Dell enjoyed preferred seating, but everyone was exposed to the elements equally. In the new facility, it was anticipated that most of the 5,000 seats under cover would be taken by Friends of the Dell, leaving the 10,000 free attendees on the benches and lawn area to contend with the weather on their own. Concerts that would have been postponed or cancelled previously would now go on, with mostly just the Friends of the Dell able to enjoy them comfortably.

As in the 1960s, the response of Mann and his supporters was that the Friends of the Dell system was the only way to make the concerts free for all and that no other venue in the nation offered an entire summer season of world-class symphonic music completely free. How could this be considered elitist, they contended? Philadelphia Recreation Commissioner Robert Crawford wrote an op-ed for the July 26, 1975, *Evening Bulletin* (published along with Roth's letter), outlining the need for the new facility and the financial realities that necessitated preferential seating arrangements for contributors. Taking aim at Mann's critics, Crawford wrote: "It is rather disturbing to level accusations at Ambassador Fredric R. Mann, who singlehandedly

SLIPPER WRITES MARCH 1975 PAGE 1

GOLDEN SLIPPER CLUB SETS MELODIC SALUTE TO THE ROBIN HOOD DELL - PAST AND FUTURE

Tuesday, March 18, at 6 P.M. - Bellevue Stratford

An Evening for Music and Memories Marking the New Dell and Remembering Past Joys

Model of the new Robin Hood Dell

Ambassador
Fredric R. Mann
President
Robin Hood Dell Concerts, Inc.

And Featuring Music's Finest

World Famous
Philadelphia Concert Pianist
Susan Starr

Philadelphia's Own
Noted Concert Pianist
Jerome Lowenthal

The One and Only
Andre Kostelanetz
Famed Conductor

Israeli Singing Star
Tslila Keren
In Many Languages

■ Program from the Golden Slipper Club's March 18, 1975, tribute to the history and future of the Robin Hood Dell. The Golden Slipper Club was a local Jewish charitable organization. Susan Starr, Jerome Lowenthal, and Andre Kostelanetz were frequent guest artists at the Dell. (Mann Center for the Performing Arts Archives)

rescued the Dell from bankruptcy, and who alone developed the plan to provide free admission to the summer festival of our great Philadelphia Orchestra. Mr. Mann not only has been the guiding spirit behind these summer concert series, but has sacrificed much of his time and funds to support it from year to year."[49]

Mann himself addressed the issue the following year in a long profile piece in *The Philadelphia Inquirer*: "Elite? What is all this elite business the newspapers talk about? I just don't understand it. Where else in the entire country can a person hear great music by the Philadelphia Orchestra—FOR FREE!" City Council President George

Schwartz noted in the article that he did not think the city would support the Dell if it were not for the contributions of the Friends, which helped to make the concerts free for thousands of others: "We have at least 2,400 who are paying [and getting two seats each], and this is extremely important. You talk about elitist things. No one is admitted [for free] to the Philadelphia Orchestra at the Academy of Music, ever."[50]

## The Promoters

With an eye toward expanded programming opportunities in the new facility, and increasingly cognizant of the fact that the audience for classical music was shrinking and the Dell needed to cultivate new, younger patrons, the Dell Board authorized Mann in October 1974 to hire Philadelphia music and theater impresario Moe Septee in the new position of "executive producer."*[51] Septee would be responsible for staging special concerts and events and bringing in high-profile performing arts groups, while Mann would continue to program The Philadelphia Orchestra's concerts. Executive Director Helen Martin would manage overall operations. Septee came on board in early 1975 and sometime thereafter reached out to Larry Magid, head of Philadelphia-based Electric Factory Concerts, one of the largest rock concert promotion companies in the nation, who agreed to produce rock and pop shows at the new Dell starting in 1976. In bringing in Septee and Magid, the Dell was tapping into the talents of two of the most influential and successful music promoters in Philadelphia history.

Born Moses Septytor in Poland, Moe Septee came to America at age four with his family, who settled in Newark, New Jersey. A devout Jew—throughout his career he never worked during the Friday–Saturday evening Jewish Sabbath, even though this was prime time in his business—Septee originally studied to be a rabbi but was drawn to the entertainment field. He worked in radio, TV, and theater in his early years, then moved on to booking classical music and ballet shows in Newark in the 1950s and to producing rock and pop shows in the New Jersey beach resort town of Asbury Park starting in the early 1960s. The rock and pop shows came to be known as the "Moe Septee's Summer of Stars" series. Equally adept at promoting classical, rock, and popular music, Septee seemed to have an innate sense of what the public wanted, from presenting the Moscow Philharmonic in Symphony Hall in Newark to the Rolling Stones in Convention Hall in Asbury Park. He also produced some shows in Philadelphia in the early 1960s, including The Beatles' first appearance in the city, in 1964 at Convention Hall.

When Emma Feldman, longtime head of the All Star-Concert Forum in Philadelphia, took ill in 1966, Septee's mentor, the great New York City–based impresario

* The Board minutes initially gave Septee's title as "managing producer," but it was later changed to "executive producer."

■ Moe Septee, ca. 1983, in front of a billboard for the All Star-Forum he had been directing since 1966. (*The Philadelphia Inquirer* photograph collection, Special Collections Research Center, Temple University Libraries)

Sol Hurok, convinced him to move to Philadelphia to assume management of the series. Settling in the city, Septee became a major force in the Philadelphia performing arts world for more than 30 years. He raised the All Star-Concert Forum series to international prominence, bringing the world's top classical musicians and dancers to the Academy of Music and other venues. In the early 1970s, he began focusing on theater, taking over management of the Locust Street Theater and working to revitalize and expand the audience for the city's rather lackluster theater scene at the time. "The more intimate or off-Broadway attractions have never felt welcome in Philadelphia. Young people and blacks have never really felt welcome at our theaters, either," he said at the time. "I decided to fill the gap."[52] While offering classic theater—his production of *Waiting for Godot* was very successful—he also brought in popular Black productions such as *Bubblin' Brown Sugar* and an all-Black production of *Guys and Dolls* and made sure that young people could attend shows.*

By the time he began working for the Dell in the mid-1970s, Septee was mostly out of the rock and pop concert business, focusing mainly on classical music and

* Septee's impact on Philadelphia's performing arts continued long after his work for the Dell and in local theater. In 1979, he founded the Philly Pops and hired its musical director, Grammy Award–winning pianist and composer Peter Nero, who would have a long, celebrated career with the ensemble, and in the 1990s Septee was a driving force behind the establishment of the Avenue of the Arts, the performing arts district along South Broad Street in Center City.

theater. The rock industry had grown enormously by then; rock concerts were now big business, with huge artists' fees and expenses, but also great profits to be made for those with the resources and acumen to showcase rock music effectively. Septee knew that, when it came to putting on rock shows in Philadelphia, one promoter towered over all others: Larry Magid. Septee reached out to Magid and arranged a meeting with Freddie Mann. As devoted to classical music—and generally dismissive of rock and pop—as he was, Mann knew that if his organization were to survive, it would have to start offering such concerts when it occupied its new facility in 1976.

Magid was part of a different generation and musical aesthetic from Mann and Septee. Born in 1942 and raised in West Philadelphia, Magid came of age during the rhythm-and-blues and early rock-and-roll era. Captivated by the music but not a musician himself, he began booking bands in college venues while attending Temple University in the early 1960s. For a time he managed Len Barry, former lead singer of the popular Philadelphia doo-wop group The Dovells, who had success as a solo artist in the mid-1960s. In 1965, Magid moved to New York City to work for a high-profile talent agency, where he booked emerging rock artists on the cusp of stardom, among them Jimi Hendrix, Cream, Janis Joplin, and Van Morrison. He returned to Philadelphia in late 1967 to open the city's legendary psychedelic rock club, the Electric Factory, with the Spivak brothers—Herb, Jerry, and Allen, who owned bars and jazz clubs in the city and were beginning to promote concerts in larger venues—and another partner, Shelley Kaplan, who left after a few years. Originally a paid employee who managed the club, Magid eventually was made a full partner with the Spivaks and became the leader and public face of the company.

The Electric Factory opened in February 1968 at 22nd and Arch streets in Center City and immediately became the center for psychedelic rock and counterculture in Philadelphia. Young people flocked to the trailblazing 2,500-seat venue to see leading American and English rock bands of the day, as well as local groups, perform in a multisensory environment that included light shows, artwork, and bizarre amenities such as coffins and monkey bars. Such hippie gatherings did not sit well with Frank Rizzo, who was then Philadelphia's police commissioner and who visited several times to observe the goings-on, once bringing Mayor Tate. The two tried, unsuccessfully, to close the club down.

As the counterculture flourished and the Electric Factory prospered in the late 1960s, its owners expanded their activities. They offered free "Be-In" concerts in Fairmount Park that drew tens of thousands of young people; began staging large-scale rock concerts at the Spectrum, the new sports arena that opened in South Philadelphia in 1967; and produced the Atlantic City Pop Festival in August 1969, a three-day rock extravaganza at the Atlantic City Racetrack where some 40,000 daily attendees saw dozens of top rock artists and other acts. (The more famous Woodstock festival two weeks later featured many of the same artists.)

■ Larry Magid (*third from the right*) with his wife, Mickey, and members of the J. Geils Band backstage at the Spectrum, ca. 1973–1974. In 1976, Magid's company, Electric Factory Concerts, would begin promoting pop and rock concerts at the new Robin Hood Dell West. (Courtesy of Larry Magid)

By 1970, the economics of the rock business had changed. Top acts that could now sell out the 20,000-seat Spectrum had priced themselves out of the club market. Magid and the Spivaks closed the Electric Factory in November 1970, but they established Electric Factory Concerts, which emerged as one of the largest, most powerful rock promoters in the nation. By the mid-1970s, the company was producing dozens of shows a year at the Spectrum, which they had developed into one of America's premier rock showcases. Electric Factory Concerts also owned or operated several small to midsize area venues, including the Bijou Café, Tower Theater, and Theatre of Living Arts (TLA), and was about to start staging mega-concerts at the 100,000 seat JFK Stadium, adjacent to the Spectrum.[53]

Such was 34-year-old Magid's position in the rock concert business when he met with Septee and Mann at Mann's apartment in the Barclay Hotel sometime in 1975 or early 1976 to discuss Electric Factory Concerts' producing rock and popular shows at the new Dell. Years later, Magid described the unusual circumstances of the meeting in which the fateful deal was made, noting in particular Septee's key role in the process:

> Moe was the guy, he was the catalyst. . . . He knew that in order to make the venue successful, we had to fill in the dates [before, in between, and after

the Orchestra's scheduled programs]. They had a three-and-a-half-month schedule, and the Orchestra was to play twenty-four of those dates [with the expanded 1976 season schedule, the Orchestra actually gave twenty-three performances that year], and they probably could not have made it financially unless there were other [revenue-producing] dates. . . .

Moe called me and asked me if I would consider doing shows [at the new venue] and we talked about it and it looked like a good situation. . . . And he said, "I'd like you to meet Fred Mann." And we talked briefly, and he said, "I'd like to set a meeting for so-and-so date. . . . Can you make it?" I was going to Los Angeles that day, I had an early flight. So the meeting took place around seven o'clock in the morning at [Mann's] apartment in Rittenhouse Square.

So we talked about the [concerts] that were going to happen there. And [Mann] said, in his gruff tone, "Well, no rock and roll! I don't want any rock shows there." OK, well, that's basically what I do. And he said, "No, can't have that. And nobody standing on chairs, I won't have that! . . . I heard about concerts with people standing on chairs." And I said, "With the type of acts [soft rock and pop artists] that you're asking for, people don't do that."

So we spoke for a while, and then he said, "OK, let's solidify this deal; we're going to have a contract." And I said, . . . "Where do I sign?" And he said, "No, you don't have to sign anything. We're gonna have a drink." OK. So he opened up a chilled bottle of vodka . . . and I hadn't had breakfast; I figured I'd eat on the plane. This is really early and I had to make that plane. And he took out these three little silver glasses or goblets and made a toast to our relationship [Magid makes a gesture of drinking a shot]. I was a little bit groggy. And we talked for a little bit more and I said, "Well, I have to catch the plane." And he said, "Well, before you catch the plane, we'll have another." And I remember staggering out of his apartment, I mean *staggering*, to get a cab at eight o'clock in the morning [to get to the airport]. In those days, you could just walk on board.

And that was it, . . . that was how we made the deal. To this day, I don't know if we actually had a physical contract. I would doubt it, but if we did, it wasn't a lot [of detail]. But he took you at your word.[54]

While both were visionaries, it is doubtful that either the veteran classical music impresario or the powerful young rock promoter knew at the time that their agreement over vodka shots that morning would mark the beginning of a decades-long, inexorable transformation in which the new Robin Hood Dell West, later the Mann Center for the Performing Arts, would evolve from a primarily classical venue that offered occasional rock and contemporary music into a primarily rock and contemporary venue that offered occasional classical concerts. It was a scenario that unfolded at similar venues throughout the nation in the late 20th century, as the musical tastes of the baby boomer generation exerted an ever more powerful influence on the concert industry.

Magid laments that, while Mann's legacy has been justly celebrated, Septee's contributions to Philadelphia's cultural life have been largely forgotten:

> Moe was an unbelievable person and never, ever got the credit that he deserved. . . . He was an Orthodox Jew and if you called him on Friday afternoon, you better call him early, because that was [the beginning of the Jewish Sabbath]. And you had to respect him. . . . He was [an] engaging person, delightful guy, to be in his company. . . . It was like a yin-yang thing [with Mann and Septee], these opposites. Philadelphia wouldn't be the same without either one of them.[55]

## Farewell Season

The 46th and farewell season of The Philadelphia Orchestra at the original Robin Hood Dell location opened on June 23, 1975, with Eugene Ormandy conducting and young American violinist Eugene Fodor making his Dell debut in the annual Emma Feldman Memorial Concert. Three weeks later, Ormandy was back, leading a program with the great Russian cellist and human rights activist Mstislav Rostropovich as featured soloist. Four days earlier, Rostropovich's wife, Galina Vishnevskaya, former leading soprano at the Bolshoi Opera in Moscow, had been the soloist at the Dell, singing Tchaikovsky arias with Julius Rudel conducting. Like dancers Valery and Galina Panov, who had appeared the previous week, the Rostropoviches were a famous Russian activist couple who were persecuted in their homeland for their activities, which, in their case, included sheltering the famous Russian dissident writer Alexander Solzhenitsyn in their home for several years. They were finally allowed to leave the Soviet Union in 1974. His political activism aside, Mstislav Rostropovich was considered one of the world's greatest musicians. "He surrounds the cello," *The Philadelphia Inquirer* noted in its review of his July 21, 1975, Dell concert, "makes demands on its very existence in his playing, and produces a level of performance that is individual, sometimes outrageous, but always brimming with conviction. Few musicians can match his intensity."[56]

In addition to the famous Russian dissident couples the Panovs and the Rostropoviches, the five-week farewell season featured mostly longtime Dell favorite conductors and soloists, with a few new faces. Israeli conductor Eliahu Inbal made his only Dell appearance leading two concerts during week one, the second of which featured Roberta Peters and Robert Merrill singing medleys of operatic arias. James DePreist led the first two concerts the following week, the first accompanying Van Cliburn (it was the after-party to this concert that Marciarose Shestack wrote about

Mstislav Rostropovich, Eugene Ormandy, and Fredric Mann share a light moment during a rehearsal at the Robin Hood Dell in July 1975. (Adrian Siegel photographs, Philadelphia Orchestra Association records, Kislak Center for Special Collections, Rare Books, and Manuscripts, University of Pennsylvania)

in *The Philadelphia Inquirer*), and the second with his aunt, Marian Anderson, reprising her non-singing role as narrator in Aaron Copland's *Lincoln Portrait*. Michael Tilson Thomas led the first two concerts of week three, the first marking the Dell debut of Polish Jewish pianist Emanuel Ax in the annual William Kapell Memorial Concert and the second featuring The Philadelphia Orchestra's principal viola, Joseph de Pasquale, as soloist. Andre Kostelanetz led two concerts in week four.

Zubin Mehta conducted all three concerts in the fifth and final week, closing the season—and the Dell's 46-year history as a symphonic venue—with a spectacular concert version of Verdi's opera *Aida* on July 31, 1975, with soprano Gilda Cruz-Romo, mezzo-soprano Mignon Dunn, tenor Herman Malamood (a replacement for Veriano Luchetti), baritone Robert Merrill (replacing Douglas Lawrence), and bass James Morris, with the Mendelssohn Club of Philadelphia providing the choral parts. "Whether it was the emotion of the event or some less visible spark, Mehta made the performance an historic one, supercharged and nearly overwhelming in its sweep and color," *The Philadelphia Inquirer* reported. *The Evening Bulletin* deemed the concert "one of the finest performances in the history of outdoor music in Philadelphia," one that was "driven by terrific energy by Zubin Mehta."[57]

At intermission, Philadelphia Recreation Commissioner Robert Crawford presented a plaque from the city to Mann, honoring his many years of leadership at the

Bulletin Staff Photo by Dom Ligato

Four decades of musical strings at the Dell—left to right: David Madison, Manuel Roth and Leonard Mogill. They've played at The Dell since it opened in 1930.

Work on the new Dell had reached this stage last week

Dell, while Mann presented plaques to three Orchestra musicians who had played at the Dell since it opened in 1930: violinists David Madison and Manuel Roth and violist Leonard Mogill. (Madison and Roth had retired from the Orchestra in 1972 but continued to play the summer concerts.) Mann told the audience that he felt like the father of a bride, losing one Dell but gaining another. The evening concluded with Merrill, a Dell favorite, leading the audience in "Auld Lang Syne" as a farewell to the venue as Philadelphia's longtime summer home for symphonic music.

## Dell East Postscript

At this point, our history shifts from Robin Hood Dell East to Robin Hood Dell West. Robin Hood Dell Concerts Inc., the organization that had founded and managed the Dell since it opened in 1930, ended its affiliation with the Dell East after the July 31, 1975, concert and directed its focus entirely to the new Dell West under construction a few miles away. The Philadelphia Department of Recreation took over responsibility for booking all concerts and events at the Dell East. The department continued to offer musical events there through its Better Break program into the early 1980s, and thereafter through a similar series, "Essence of Entertainment." These concerts were primarily geared toward Black audiences, featuring mostly jazz, gospel, rhythm-and-blues, and soul artists. As the Better Break program had demonstrated, there was a loyal summer audience for this music in the original Dell's open-air setting in East Fairmount Park.

The Dell East was renamed the Dell Music Center in 2010, and there was an effort a few years later to rename it the Georgie Woods Entertainment Center, after the noted Philadelphia Black radio personality, concert promoter, and civil rights activist, but that did not happen. "The Dell," as it is still known—the Dell East/West designations were unnecessary after the Dell West was renamed the Mann Music Center in 1979—has undergone several major city-funded renovations and continues to be an important summer venue for Black music. In the 2020s it began to branch out and offer other types of music, with plans to expand the range of programming as the venue approaches its centennial in 2030.

**(facing page, top)** ■ Three Philadelphia Orchestra musicians who had played at the Robin Hood Dell since its opening season in 1930 and were playing the final symphonic concert at the venue on July 31, 1975. *Left to right*: violinists David Madison and Manuel Roth and violist Leonard Mogill. (*The Sunday Bulletin*, July 27, 1975, Scrapbook, Mann Center for the Performing Arts Archives)

**(facing page, bottom)** ■ *The Philadelphia Inquirer*, August 31, 1975. (From *The Philadelphia Inquirer*. © 1975 Philadelphia Inquirer, LLC. All rights reserved. Used under license. Scrapbook, Mann Center for the Performing Arts Archives)

# III. Mann Center

# 8.

## 1976–1979

*Robin Hood Dell West*

On May 20, 1976, as the Robin Hood Dell West was nearing completion, Fredric Mann was honored at a luncheon of the Philadelphia Public Relations Association at the Bellevue-Stratford Hotel. He told the attendees that the new venue "represents a victory. Not a personal one, but a victory of hope and the realization of a dream that the greatest music by the greatest artists may be brought to the greatest number of people."[1] Mann's self-effacing assertion aside, the new Dell was, in fact, very much a personal victory; everyone knew that it was his baby, that it was his singular vision and determination that brought the venue to fruition. Longtime Dell Executive Director Helen Martin summed it up on the eve of opening night: "Freddie did it all. . . . It was his dream. Without him, it wouldn't have happened. . . . [He] pushed, shoved, persuaded, twisted arms, pleaded, threatened. He's been incredible—hell to work with, but he got it done."[2]

Mann told his friend, journalist Marciarose Shestack, at the time that he was well aware that his style turned many people off: "Listen, I know I come on strong. I know I'm abrasive. I know I rub a lot of people in this town the wrong way. . . . You can't achieve 100% popularity when you're trying to accomplish something."[3] He told another journalist that his friends joked that he had an "edifice complex." As previously noted, 20 years earlier he had reportedly given $3 million for a new home for the Israel Philharmonic in Tel Aviv, the Fredric R. Mann Auditorium.[4]

■ Detail from a 1976 promotional brochure for the new Robin Hood Dell West.
(Mann Center for the Performing Arts Archives)

## The New Dell

As noted in Chapter 7, Mann's new, $7.5 million edifice in Philadelphia was designed by the New York architectural firm MacFadyen-De Vido, who had designed Wolf Trap and Saratoga Performing Arts Center. They worked in partnership with local architectural firm Demchick, Berger and Dash. The builder was McCloskey and Company, one of Philadelphia's (and the nation's) largest general contractors. The company's founder, Matthew McCloskey Jr.—a Dell Board member and Mann confidant for decades—had died in 1973, but his son, Matthew McCloskey III, was a longtime Dell Board member and vice president, although he was no longer involved in the family construction firm when it built the new Dell.

Mann tried creative approaches to hold down construction costs. "I worked on the idea that the Steel Institute would donate the steel and the Cement Institute would

donate the cement to have a nice place to have their products on display," he told the *Philadelphia Daily News*. "I knew they made contributions like that, but . . . they weren't interested in doing it in Philadelphia for this kind of job."[5] The skyrocketing cost of steel at the time was a major factor in the new Dell costing more than double the original estimates. The steel was made by Bethlehem Steel, the industrial giant 55 miles north of Philadelphia.

Early in the construction process, Mann told the press that the plan was to have the facility completed a month before its official opening so it could host a series of preview concerts.[6] This would give the Dell team time to fine-tune the facility and work out any technical issues well in advance of the inaugural concert, a star-studded event scheduled for June 14, 1976, that was expected to draw national attention. The reality ended up being quite different. A number of factors, including a strike by cement-truck drivers in the spring of 1976, delayed progress on the facility and took final preparations down to the wire.

## The Dell Team

Responsibility for getting the venue ready fell primarily to Mann, Martin, and a new employee who came on board in early May, less than six weeks before the opening: Gerald W. ("Jerry") Grabey. Originally hired as stage manager, Grabey would play an important role in the history of the Dell West/Mann Center, working at the venue for 40 years, eventually rising to general manager and overseeing all aspects of its operations. Grabey was a graduate of Temple University, where he had been managing director of the university theater, and had served as production manager for the Temple Music Festival at Ambler and for the University of Pennsylvania's Zellerbach Theater. He had also worked in construction when he was younger, experience that proved helpful in the predicament in which he now found himself.

Among the myriad issues Grabey and the team faced literally days before the June 14 opening were that the concrete for the balcony had not yet been poured, so the more than 800 balcony seats could not be installed (the cement-truck drivers' strike ended in late May); the sod for the lawn seating area had not been laid, and the lawn was still a field of mud; the stage lighting was wrong, and the musicians could not read their music; and the fill material in the backstage loading area was inadequate, and the tractor trailers bringing in Philadelphia Orchestra equipment were getting

■ This *Evening Bulletin* photograph from April 1976 shows the new Robin Hood Dell West still very much under construction a little more than two months before its scheduled opening. (*The Evening Bulletin* photograph collection, Special Collections Research Center, Temple University Libraries)

Philadelphia Orchestra Music Director Eugene Ormandy and Fredric Mann tour the new venue on June 1, 1976, two weeks before Ormandy would lead the Orchestra in the inaugural concert. (*The Philadelphia Inquirer* photograph collection, Special Collections Research Center, Temple University Libraries)

stuck in the gravel and mud. Somehow, the team resolved these and other outstanding issues—if not completely, at least enough to open on time.*[7]

One issue that could not be resolved satisfactorily was the venue's acoustics. German acoustician Heinrich Keilholz, whose work on high-profile symphonic venues included Philharmonic (later, Avery Fisher) Hall in New York City, Heinz Hall in Pittsburgh, and Severance Hall in Cleveland, was brought in to design the sound. He had to make compromises due to budget constraints, including reducing the size of the overhead "acoustical cloud" panels designed to project the sound, and his acoustical tests were done late in the process and under the most adverse conditions. The first test was on June 7, a week before opening night, with Metropolitan Opera baritone Robert Merrill and a small string ensemble from the Curtis Institute performing onstage while Keilholz and others tried to assess the sound amid incessant hammering by workmen, cement trucks pouring concrete, and other distractions.[8] Keilholz was not happy, and not surprisingly, there were serious problems with the sound on opening night.

* Grabey noted that Robin Hood Dell Concerts Inc. had "Substantial Completion" and "Final Completion" agreements with the City of Philadelphia. Terms of the former were met just prior to the June 14, 1976, opening; terms of the latter were met later that summer.

## The Lead Up

There was a flurry of activity and press coverage leading up to opening night, from previews of the new facility and the inaugural concert season to profiles of Mann and his accomplishments. Shestack's *Philadelphia Inquirer* article, published the day before the opening, detailed how the stellar lineup for the season reflected the esteem in which Mann was held among the world's leading concert artists:

> If Freddie wanted the first season at the new Dell to be spectacular, his wish is certainly coming true. And mostly as a testimony to him, his friends in the music world are responding to his dream as well. Mstislav Rostropovich is flying in from South America because of a promise he made Freddie two years ago. Vladimir Ashkenazy cancelled three concerts in Germany to be here for the opening. Gregor Piatigorsky, a Freddie friend for forty years, flies in from California for his first Dell appearance in 23 years. José Iturbi is flying in from Spain for a specially scheduled 80th birthday celebration concert. Beverly Sills postponed a trip to London to sing for the last concert and Daniel Barenboim is giving up his vacation so he can jet from Paris for two concerts.[9]

Other top-tier artists booked for the inaugural season—both those who had performed at the Dell often over the years and those making their debut or whose appearances were rare—included conductors Leonard Bernstein, Zubin Mehta, James Levine, Andre Kostelanetz, and Franz Allers; violinists Isaac Stern, Pinchas Zuckerman, and Pavel Kogan; pianists Jerome Lowenthal, Andre Watts, Van Cliburn, and Gina Bachauer; singers Roberta Peters and Robert Merrill; and the Mormon Tabernacle Choir. Dell press materials noted that there were 13 new artists appearing in 1976.

Opening day was a whirlwind, beginning with a proclamation from Philadelphia Mayor Frank Rizzo designating June 14 "Freddie Mann Day" in the city. Later in the day, Mann hosted a preconcert reception for members of the press at Belmont Mansion, the historic estate adjacent to the new Dell in Fairmount Park, while the ladies of the Robin Hood Dell Guild were at nearby Memorial Hall, the grand hall built for the 1876 Centennial, preparing for a lavish postconcert gala to be held there. All the while, Dell staff and contractors were working feverishly on final preparations at the venue. "The opening will be at the end of a breathless race which saw concrete construction, landscape, paving, and acoustical testing going on at a breakneck speed," *The Philadelphia Inquirer* had reported two days earlier.[10]

Not working opening day, unfortunately, was a large contingent of members of the local Transport Workers Union, who were staging a job action against the Southeastern Pennsylvania Transportation Authority (SEPTA) due to a labor dispute. As

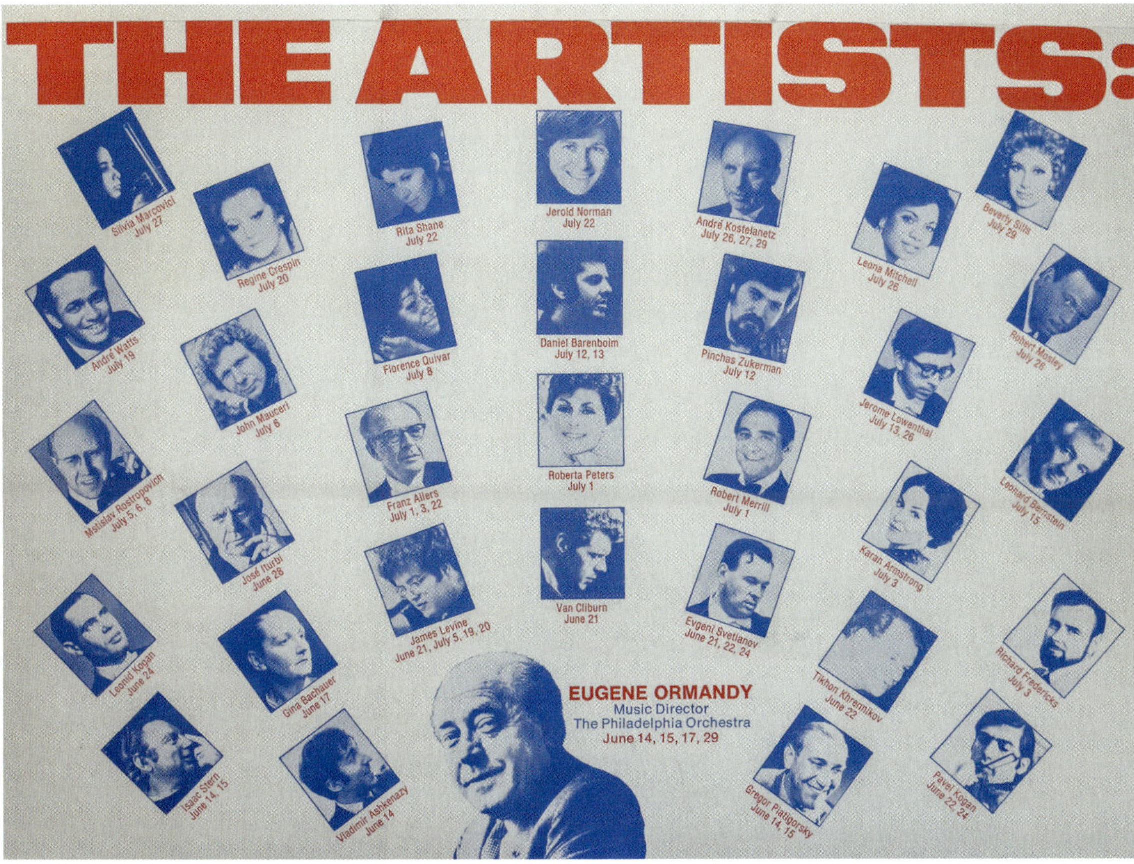


■ Promotional flyer showing featured artists for the 1976 Philadelphia Orchestra inaugural season at the new Robin Hood Dell West. (Mann Center for the Performing Arts Archives)

a result, SEPTA had to cancel several special bus routes it had scheduled to the new Dell for opening week, forcing hundreds of concertgoers to find alternative transportation to the venue. Thankfully, the new Dell had 7,000 parking spaces, versus 2,000 at the old facility.

## Opening Night

All the frantic activity and anticipation came to a head on Monday evening, June 14, 1976, when the gates opened and a capacity crowd of some 15,000 entered to marvel at the long-awaited venue and take their seats, or places on the lawn. It was 76 degrees with no rain at 8:00 P.M. as "gowned and tuxedoed Main Liners, assorted beautiful people and cultural cognoscenti in reserved boxes joined blue-jeaned and T-shirted teenyboppers, college students, and senior citizens on benches or the grass," the *Philadelphia Daily News* reported.[11]

The real moment of truth came shortly after 8:30 P.M., when Eugene Ormandy, dressed in white tuxedo jacket, black tie, and black trousers, strode to the podi-

View from behind the Orchestra on opening night of the Robin Hood Dell West, June 14, 1976. Published in *The Philadelphia Inquirer*, June 15, 1976. (From *The Philadelphia Inquirer*. © 1976 Philadelphia Inquirer, LLC. All rights reserved. Used under license. *The Philadelphia Inquirer* photograph collection, Special Collections Research Center, Temple University Libraries)

um, lifted his baton, and led The Philadelphia Orchestra in the national anthem to christen the new Robin Hood Dell West. At long last, the venue had hosted its first official musical performance. The program that followed consisted of three standard works in the Western classical canon; there were no newly commissioned pieces for the opening of the hall or American works in honor of the Bicentennial. The first half of the concert consisted of Beethoven's *Leonore* Overture No. 3 and Brahms's Concerto for Violin, Violincello, and Orchestra ("Double"), the latter featuring violinist Isaac Stern and cellist Gregor Piatigorsky, and the second half was taken up with Rachmaninoff's Piano Concerto No. 3, with pianist Vladimir Ashkenazy. In between was an intermission of speeches and congratulatory greetings by city and state officials.

Ormandy and the Orchestra rendered Beethoven's dramatic *Leonore* Overture with "great precision and polish," according to *The Philadelphia Inquirer*, but the real attraction of the night were the soloists.[12] Piatigorsky, Stern, and Ashkenazy—all Russian émigrés, like Mann—were among the top concert artists in the world. Many in the audience were especially eager to hear the legendary Piatigorsky, considered one of the greatest cellists of all time, who had been head of the Cello Department at the Curtis Institute and lived in Philadelphia from 1942 to 1951. (He lived directly across Rittenhouse Square from Fred and Silvia Mann and was their good friend and frequent guest.) At 73, Piatigorsky had not been performing in recent years and had last appeared at the Dell in 1953, when he and Stern played the Brahms concerto they would perform that evening at the new Dell West. Unfortunately, Piatigorsky was not well at this time, and his playing suffered. Critics praised Stern's playing but noted major problems with Piatigorsky's. "Stern suavely filled out Brahm's [*sic*] genial melodies with rich, even sound, . . . [but] too often, his attractive playing was undercut by Piatigorsky's labored efforts," wrote one reviewer.[13] Piatigorsky redeemed himself somewhat the following night, when he and Stern were again the featured soloists in a different program and the cellist's playing was reportedly better.

At intermission, Pennsylvania Governor Milton Shapp, Mayor Frank Rizzo, City Council President George Schwartz, and Commissioner of Recreation Robert Crawford appeared onstage to praise the new facility and congratulate Mann, who stood with them. "Without Freddy Mann, there would be no Robin Hood Dell," said Rizzo. Congratulatory letters were read from President and Mrs. Gerald Ford and the chairman of the National Endowment for the Arts. Mann thanked everyone and proclaimed that "Philadelphia is a great music center." The celebratory mood notwithstanding, Rizzo was roundly booed by the audience, although one reporter noted that the booing emanated mostly from the free bench and lawn seats, not those in the Friends of the Dell sections.[14] Rizzo was deeply unpopular among a large part of the electorate at the time, and there was a major citywide effort that summer to recall him as mayor. A petition demanding a special recall vote gathered more than 200,000 signatures, but the effort was ultimately unsuccessful.

■ Music Director Eugene Ormandy conducts The Philadelphia Orchestra with featured soloists—cellist Gregor Piatigorsky (*left*) and violinist Isaac Stern (*back to camera*)—on opening night of the Robin Hood Dell West, June 14, 1976. (*The Evening Bulletin* photograph collection, Special Collections Research Center, Temple University Libraries)

By all accounts, the highlight of the evening was a thrilling performance of the Rachmaninoff Concerto by Vladimir Ashkenazy that closed the concert and brought the audience to its feet. Praising his "clear and vibrant tone from every inch of the piano," one critic wrote that "one senses that there is nothing standing between the performer and the composer. It is as if Ashkenazy was born to be Rachmaninoff's messenger."[15] Another reviewer described how the pianist "ripped into the concluding pages of the concerto with a steely accuracy and incredible ardor that lifted the cheering audience out of their seats."[16] It was an appropriately rousing finale to the Robin Hood Dell West's opening night.

Following the concert, some 400 leading figures from the city's musical, political, civic, and diplomatic worlds descended on Memorial Hall for an elegant dinner dance in honor of Mann. The event was sponsored by the Robin Hood Dell Guild. As Mann and his wife entered, the Mark Davis Orchestra struck up the "Triumphal March" from Giuseppe Verdi's opera *Aida*. All of the evening's dignitaries and featured performers attended (except Piatigorsky), as did past and future Dell artists James DePreist, Jerome Lowenthal, Elaine Malbin, and John Green. There were congratulatory telegrams from Leopold Stokowski, Andre Kostelanetz, and others. Freddie and Silvia were reportedly still dancing at 2:30 A.M.[17]

The new venue's opening week saw Ormandy conduct all three regularly scheduled concerts, a rare occurrence. Stern and Piatigorsky returned for the second concert—Stern performing Mendelssohn's Violin Concerto in the first half of the program and Piatigorsky featured in the prominent cello part in Richard Strauss's tone poem *Don Quixote* in the second. After intermission, Stern came out and announced that it would not be right if he and Piatigorsky were on the same program and did not play something together again. They then gave an impromptu duo performance of Handel's *Passacaglia*. As the *Philadelphia Daily News* noted, "Piatigorsky's age and health did not permit him the strength available to his younger friend Stern, but their mutual love for each other and beautiful music found no obstacles."[18] It turned out to be a poignant moment indeed. After his Dell performances, Piatigorsky returned to his home in California and died three weeks later.

The third concert that week, on June 17, featured Greek pianist Gina Bachauer, whose only other Dell appearance had been in 1959. The all-Russian program included Prokofiev's Symphony No. 1 ("Classical"), Rachmaninoff's Piano Concerto No. 2 (Bachauer reportedly was mentored by Rachmaninoff in Paris in the 1930s), and Mussorgsky's *Pictures at an Exhibition*, in Maurice Ravel's orchestration. At intermission, Bachauer received a plaque from William Rafsky, Dell Board member and president of the Philadelphia 1976 Bicentennial Corporation, honoring Greek contributions to American concepts of beauty and government. It would be Bachauer's last Dell appearance as well; she died suddenly two months later, shortly before she was to appear in concert in Athens.

## Public and Critical Reaction

"Robin Hood Dell West is a great hall for a great symphonic orchestra," read an editorial in *The Philadelphia Inquirer* two days after the opening. "Summers at the Dell, a beloved Philadelphia tradition for several generations of loyal fans, will be even bigger and better than before."[19] While many shared the *Inquirer*'s sentiments, judging by a number of critical reviews and letters to the editors of local newspapers, quite a few others did not. There was general consensus that the new Dell's setting in West Fairmount Park, with its breathtaking view of the Philadelphia skyline, was beautiful, and that the interior cedar-paneled stage and brightly colored seating areas were aesthetically pleasing. Opinions on the exterior of the building varied. Some liked the modern structure that was clad in terne metal and thought it blended well with its natural surroundings; others had quite different reactions. "At first glance the new facility seems to be an armadillo crossbred with a praying mantis," wrote a *New York Times* reviewer, while *The Evening Bulletin* arts editor thought the building looked like a "Quonset hut on stilts."[20]

The American Institute of Steel Construction had a different view. It gave the structure its 1977 Award for Architectural Excellence, one of 19 buildings nationwide so honored that year. A "jury of distinguished architects" noted that "the attractive exterior envelope conforms precisely to the acoustical demands and the

Robin Hood Dell West, 1978 view. (*The Evening Bulletin* photograph collection, Special Collections Research Center, Temple University Libraries)

structural system yet identifies itself by its own distinctive architectural form. The exposed steel framing is an effective element of the architectural design."[21]

The most serious objections were with the sound and the seating arrangements, two issues that were now linked in a way they had not been before. In the old Dell, everyone was outside, exposed to the sound and the elements more or less equally. Friends of the Dell subscribers were just closer to the stage. In the new Dell, not only was there a marked physical separation between the paid undercover Friends' seats and the free seats in the open-air bench and lawn areas behind, but the sound in the latter area was much worse. Commentators lamented the obvious physical and aural separation between "the haves and the have nots" and questioned what such an arrangement said about the city and its cultural values.

In the Dell East, about 2,000 seats had been taken up with Friends of the Dell subscriptions; in the Dell West, Friends subscriptions totaled nearly 5,000 for the inaugural season, taking up virtually all the seating in the covered areas, including the 800-plus seats in the balcony. (At one point, Dell management had to stop selling subscriptions when it looked like the balcony might not be finished in time; they resumed sales when it was determined the balcony seating would be ready.)[22] The 1976 subscription cost was increased to $200 for reserved seats and $400 for box seats, which entitled the subscriber to two tickets to each of the 22 concerts in the seven-week Orchestra season. The Dell Board also gave 500 reserved tickets for each concert to Philadelphia '76 Inc., the local Bicentennial organization. To patrons on the outside, it was clear that those who could afford Friends subscriptions or had connections would be protected from the elements, while everyone else would not. The noticeable difference in sound quality only exacerbated the situation.

Those in the covered sections heard the music directly from the stage, for the most part, with some added amplification. There were some issues with the sound in those sections, no doubt exacerbated by having to reduce the size of the ceiling acoustical panels due to budget cuts, but the issues were not too serious. The balcony had the best sound. For those in the open bench and lawn areas, the sound was entirely amplified, coming through speakers embedded in the rear wall of the balcony. Due to insufficient testing time, the system performed poorly, or sometimes not at all, in the opening concerts. *The Evening Bulletin* found the amplified sound in the rear sections "tinny, muddled, often inaudible," while *The Philadelphia Inquirer* noted that "those sitting directly in line with the speakers were overwhelmed [while] those sitting off the axis, heard very little of any playing."[23] In a letter to the editor of *The Evening Bulletin*, one disgruntled patron who sat in the first row of benches wrote that "the severe distortion of the speakers made listening to the concert 'live' little better than hearing it on a transistor radio. We were disappointed and enraged, as were all the listeners around us."[24] Another wrote, "The Orchestra in Veterans Stadium would have been more visible, audible, and pleasurable."[25]

Adjustments were made as the season progressed, and the sound gradually improved, although it remained less than satisfactory for large parts of the venue throughout the season. Well aware of the problems, Mann promised a complete overhaul in time for 1977. "It may cost $200,000 but I'm starting a new sound study from my own pocket," he told *The Philadelphia Inquirer*. The original acoustician, Keilholz, had left before opening night; in addition to being unhappy with the working conditions, he reportedly had differences with Ormandy. On the advice of pianist and conductor Daniel Barenboim, Mann hired Israeli acoustician Avram Meltzer, who had installed the sound system for the Paris Orchestra, to study the venue's sound and suggest improvements.[26]

While most agreed that the acoustical problems could be worked out in time, a more troubling issue for many was the stark dividing line the balcony wall formed between the paid Friends of the Dell section and the free seating areas. One writer likened being in the free seating area to "sitting behind the 'castle walls,'" while another said, "I felt like I was peering in at someone else's party."[27] *The Philadelphia Inquirer*'s architecture critic noted that, in the free seats, "you do not feel as if you are part of the action. That is because there is a balcony in the way. . . . It doesn't block the view of the non-paying customers, it just separates them."[28] Another writer yearned for the more communal atmosphere at the Dell East:

View from the lawn area of the new Robin Hood Dell West in 1976, showing the balcony wall facing the outside seats that created a visual barrier between the covered and outside seating areas. (Mann Center for the Performing Arts Archives)

June 1976 interior view of the new Robin Hood Dell West, showing the covered seating area of the venue. (*The Evening Bulletin* photograph collection, Special Collections Research Center, Temple University Libraries)

> In time, I suppose the technological problems . . . might be corrected. Unfortunately, time is not likely to heal the injury that has been done to the concept of the Dell. . . . The "old" Dell seldom failed to produce a delightful evening. There was a feeling of democratic togetherness, a feeling of openness under the evening sky, and a sense of intimacy with the performers. At the "new" Dell, the sense of democratic partnership has been sacrificed for one of elitist privilege.[29]

As he had before, Mann countered that nowhere else in the country could 10,000 people hear an entire summer season of concerts by internationally acclaimed artists and one of the world's finest orchestras completely for free, and the only way to make that possible was through paid subscribers who were entitled to preferred seating. As in the past, subscribers' contributions were matched by city funds; the city appropriated $300,000 for the Dell West in 1976, up from $225,000 in 1975.

## Inaugural Orchestral Season

With national attention focused on Philadelphia because of the new venue and the U.S. Bicentennial, The Philadelphia Orchestra Association agreed to extend the 1976 Orchestra summer season from the usual five to seven weeks, offering 22 concerts instead of 15. Concerts were held on Mondays, Tuesdays, and Thursdays from June 14 to July 29, including the week of July 4, which the Orchestra had traditionally taken off. The Philadelphia Orchestra Association also "gifted" two additional concerts to the Dell and the public, free of charge; these were not part of the regular schedule. There would be no Children's Concerts in 1976, although they would resume in later years.

As if complaints about the sound and seating arrangements were not enough, several music critics expressed disappointment in the lack of American music programmed at the new venue for the Bicentennial. One local critic noted that "1976 may be the American Bicentennial year, but you would not know it from the Dell's unadventurous and un-American programming. . . . [A]n outsider looking over the Dell programs this year might conclude Philadelphia was celebrating either the Russian Revolution or the unification of Germany."[30] There actually was a good bit of American music offered in 1976, but it was mostly relegated to special concerts or those with a popular or light classical flavor, not integrated into the regular programming, which focused primarily on music of the European masters. "Segregating it, as the Dell does, into isolated programs only perpetuates the myth that American classical music is somehow inferior and unworthy. . . . The opportunity to present a Bicentennial retrospective of serious American music has been lost."[31]

Although segregated, American music did figure prominently at the Dell West that Bicentennial summer. On June 18, Academy Award–winning songwriter and film composer John Green, writer of the great jazz standard "Body and Soul," presented a concert billed as an "American Salute." Leading off the program with American composer Morton Gould's orchestral piece by that name, the concert featured Green as conductor, pianist, and composer in a mix of his own music—songs, movie scores, orchestral compositions and arrangements—and popular Broadway and concert pieces. "One reason I am leading the concert here," Green told *The Philadelphia Inquirer*, "is my admiration for the Bicentennial as a springboard for expression for more American artists than ever before."[32] On July 3, Franz Allers led a "Glorious Broadway" concert, with vocal soloists and the Mendelssohn Club of Philadelphia performing the music of celebrated American musical theater songwriters Cole Porter, Jerome Kern, Richard Rodgers, and Frederick Lowe. Gould's *American Salute* led off that program as well. These all-American programs were the two donated Philadelphia Orchestra concerts that were not part of the regular schedule.

Leonard Bernstein returned to the Dell on July 15 after a 20-year absence, leading a concert that mixed the serious and the popular and featured American music prominently. Also appearing in the triple role of conductor, pianist, and composer,

Leonard Bernstein performing at the Robin Hood Dell West, July 15, 1976. (*The Evening Bulletin* photograph collection, Special Collections Research Center, Temple University Libraries)

■ Leonard Bernstein in his "coat of many colors" with Fredric Mann. (Courtesy of the Mann family)

Bernstein led Tchaikovsky's Symphony No. 4; conducted and played piano in Gershwin's *Rhapsody in Blue*; and conducted selections from some of his well-known Broadway musicals, including the Overture to *Candide* and Symphonic Dances from *West Side Story*.* The audience loved it. "Brilliant Bernstein Turns Dell into Wild Inferno of Joy," *The Evening Bulletin* proclaimed.[33] Highly popular at the time, Bernstein drew the largest crowd to date at the new Dell, estimated at 17,000–20,000. Jerry Grabey remembers looking out at the mass of people and hoping nothing bad would happen that night (nothing did).[34]

"He was a very gracious person," Grabey remembers of the famous New York conductor. "He would hold court in the Green Room after the concert. He would come in dressed in what he called his 'coat of many colors,' which was just a colorful bathrobe, and would regale everyone."[35]

---

* In 1968, The Philadelphia Orchestra Association, with support from the Philadelphia-based American Philosophical Society, commissioned a new piece from Bernstein for the Bicentennial for $25,000. The plan was for the piece, which Bernstein envisioned as a song cycle, to be premiered during the Orchestra's 1976 summer season at the new Dell. After making little progress on the work and receiving urgent pleas from Ormandy for the score in the mid-1970s, Bernstein wrote to Ormandy in August 1975 that he did not have time to complete the composition and had to abandon the project: Minutes of Board of Directors of The Philadelphia Orchestra Association, 1968–1974, Organizational Governance records, Philadelphia Orchestra Association records; and Leonard Bernstein correspondence, Eugene Ormandy papers—both at Kislak Center for Special Collections, Rare Books, and Manuscripts, University of Pennsylvania.

"Serious" American concert music was the focus of two programs that mixed choral and instrumental works. On June 29, the renowned Mormon Tabernacle Choir debuted at the Robin Hood Dell, with Ormandy conducting. The program included works by John Knowles Paine, Samuel Barber, Randall Thompson, William Schuman, Aaron Copland, Howard Hanson, and Bernstein. Pieces such as Barber's *Second Essay*, Schuman's *New England Triptych*, Bernstein's *Chichester Psalms*, and Copland's *Fanfare for the Common Man* lent an air of solemnity to the evening. On July 26, Andre Kostelanetz led the annual William Kapell Memorial Concert with pianist Jerome Lowenthal, vocal soloists, and Philadelphia's Singing City Choir. The program featured Schuman's orchestration of Charles Ives's *Variations on America* (Kostelanetz had given the world premiere of the piece with the New York Philharmonic in 1964), Charles Tomlinson Griffes's tone poem *The Pleasure-Dome of Kubla Khan*, Lowenthal performing Gershwin's Piano Concerto, and excerpts from Gershwin's opera *Porgy and Bess*.

June 22 was an all-Russian program, with Yevgeny Svetlanov, then principal conductor of both the Bolshoi Theatre and the USSR State Symphony Orchestra, along with pianist and composer Tikhon Khrennikov and violinist Pavel Kogan, all making their debuts at the Dell. After opening with Tchaikovsky's Symphony No. 5, Svetlanov led the Orchestra in Khrennikov's Piano Concerto No. 2, with the composer at the piano, and then Kogan playing Khrennikov's Violin Concerto No. 1. Khrennikov was a controversial figure. As general-secretary of the Union of Soviet Composers, he wielded considerable influence over musical composition in his country and was widely seen as someone willing to bow to political pressure from the Soviet regime. Under such pressure in 1948, he famously denounced the music of his fellow Russian composers Dmitri Shostakovich and Sergei Prokofiev, an act that drew condemnation and that Philadelphia music critics noted prominently in their reviews of the 1976 Dell concert.[36]

In a season full of milestones and superstars, there were many other highlights: José Iturbi's 80th birthday celebration concert on June 28, his 85th and final appearance at the Dell, in which, like Bernstein and John Green, he appeared as conductor, pianist, composer (he conducted his own piece, *Seguidillas*, and led Mozart and Mendelssohn concertos from the piano); Mstislav Rostropovich making his Dell conducting debut, a concert in which the audience was momentarily distracted when Philadelphia's own Princess Grace of Monaco, the former Grace Kelly, took her seat in Mann's reserved box with her family; James Levine conducting programs with Rostropovich and André Watts; Barenboim conducting with violinist Pinchas Zukerman in a concert that was also supposed to feature Keith Chapman, organist at Philadelphia's famed John Wanamaker department store, but the organ did not arrive in time; Franz Allers leading his popular "A Night in Old Vienna" program; perennial favorites Van Cliburn, Roberta Peters, and Robert Merrill appearing again; and Kostelanetz leading all three concerts in the final week, beginning with the July 26 all-American William Kapell Memorial concert noted earlier, followed by violinist Silvia Marcovici featured in the Emma Feldman Memorial Concert on July 27, and closing the season on July 29 with Beverly Sills, another Dell favorite.

It was quite an inaugural season. Mann summed up its successes and challenges in a letter to Dell patrons published in the final program book of the season:

> To our Friends:
>
> Our seven-week bicentennial season at the new Robin Hood Dell West has been a notable one. We opened our new covered facility in a fanfare of nationwide publicity and acclaim.
>
> While we have encountered some problems during the opening weeks, primarily because we were barely able to begin our season on time in the face of several labor disputes, I am happy to report that our patrons enjoyed both the new facility and the outstanding programs and artists we were able to bring to Philadelphia for this unique occasion. . . .
>
> By next season, we will have ironed out the physical difficulties one always encounters when a new building is placed into use. In fact, many of these problems have already been eliminated and adjusted. The only thing we were short of this year was time itself.
>
> I want to express my gratitude to many who supported Robin Hood Dell Concerts, Inc. through the trying opening days, and went on to enjoy some of the most outstanding classical music concerts offered anywhere in the world. . . .
>
> Cordially,
> Fredric R. Mann, President
> Robin Hood Dell Concerts, Inc.

## Other Series

While The Philadelphia Orchestra concerts were the main attraction, they constituted just one of three separate sets of concerts presented in the Dell West's first season. Larry Magid and Allen Spivak's company, Electric Factory Concerts, produced a series of popular concerts from mid-July to late August, and Moe Septee, the Dell's executive producer of special events, oversaw a series of symphonic, dance, and operatic programs from early August to mid-September. Mann had minimal involvement with these non–Philadelphia Orchestra concerts, which were all paid, ticketed events. "All he really cared about was the Orchestra concerts," Grabey remembers. "He didn't care about the other stuff."[37]

Based on Magid's agreement with Mann over vodka shots months earlier (see page 243), and mindful of Mann's admonitions, Magid booked six shows by pop and soft-rock artists, avoiding anything hard-edged. The headliners for the series,

■ Advertisement in the July 4, 1976, *Philadelphia Inquirer* for the first series of rock and pop concerts at the Robin Hood Dell West, billed as the "Bicentennial Popular Series." (From *The Philadelphia Inquirer*. © 1976 Philadelphia Inquirer, LLC. All rights reserved. Used under license. Retrieved from Newspapers.com)

presented mostly on weekend nights when the Orchestra was not playing, were James Taylor, Barry Manilow, Janis Ian, the Carpenters, Linda Ronstadt, and the folk-rock group America. "They were all soft shows," Magid notes. "Nothing hard, because we knew that if we had a problem with Fred Mann, we'd be out. . . . He was great, but he was tough. . . . He reminded me: 'Nobody standing on the chairs!'"[38]

James Taylor was an ideal artist to kick off the series. A major star since his 1970 breakout album, *Sweet Baby James*, he had a loyal following that appreciated his mix of gentle, introspective ballads and engaging mid-tempo numbers. The concert was a great success. *The Philadelphia Inquirer* had effusive praise for both the new Dell West and Taylor, who would go on to become one of the most frequent and beloved guest artists at the venue over the years:

> Singer-songwriter James Taylor opened the long-awaited series of pop music concerts at the Robin Hood Dell West. There was much to rave about at Saturday evening's event—the spectacular surroundings of what looks to be the finest open-air concert venue in the country, and the superb performance of a rock superstar. . . . The clean, beautiful, and well run . . . structure is certainly a refreshing new spot for Philadelphia pop music goers to enjoy.[39]

The second Electric Factory show, two weeks later, featured pop tunesmith Barry Manilow. Mann's granddaughter Jane Gitomer remembers her grandfather being concerned about the concert: "He was very nervous about having Barry Manilow come. I said, 'Oh, you have to have him,' and he said, 'Well, are they going to rip up my place?' and I said, 'No, they won't. . . . You have to do it.' . . . Of course, I was like 20-something and I wanted to see Barry Manilow."[40] Mann attended the show, where his fears were confirmed, leading to a funny episode, as Magid recalls:

> [Mann] showed up at the second . . . show, and it was Barry Manilow. And he walks up the steps and there's people standing on the chairs. . . . It was a lot of women in their 20s, 30s, 40s—that was the audience, pretty much. And he comes up the steps and he's standing there with a big cigar, gruff guy, and he's looking, and he sees the women standing on the chairs and he says, "That's it, that's it! You're never gonna do another show. . . . You're done!" And I said, "What?" And he said, "That woman, standing on that chair!" And I said, "You mean that woman there? . . . Hold on." So I walked over to the woman, knowing who it was, and I said, "Nessa, can you turn around? Your father's standing over there." And he sees [his daughter] and he goes [Magid makes a growling sound, gesturing like he has a cigar in his mouth] and he walks down the steps, and never said another word.[41]

The rock and pop series concluded on August 30 with the folk-rock group America headlining, with special guest, singer-songwriter John Sebastian, then a solo artist who had been chief songwriter and singer for the 1960s pop-rock group The Lovin' Spoonful. "We didn't make a ton of money. . . . We did OK," Magid remembers of the inaugural series. "We were just fine, made a couple of bucks."[42] The ensuing years would yield much more than a couple of bucks for Magid and Electric Factory Concerts at the Robin Hood Dell West, a period in which the company solidified its hold on the greater Philadelphia rock and pop concert market. *The Philadelphia Inquirer* reported that Electric Factory Concerts produced 92 percent of the nonclassical concerts in the Philadelphia area in the first half of 1976.[43]

In between the rock and pop shows in early August, the new venue hosted a series of concerts that were part of the 41st Eucharistic Congress, a worldwide religious gathering of Catholics that was held in Philadelphia from August 1 to August 8 and drew more than a million visitors to the city. The Dell West hosted four concerts as part of the Congress's Performing Arts Program. Highlights included a performance by William Steinberg and the Pittsburgh Symphony Orchestra; a "Concert of Religious Jazz" featuring two giants of jazz, pianist and composer Dave Brubeck and singer Ella Fitzgerald, in a program that included a new piece by Brubeck entitled *The Gates of Justice*; and Dance Theater of Harlem's presentation of "Dance in Praise of Him," a program consisting of several dance and dramatic pieces. The dramatic pieces included *Spiritual Suite*, a new staged work written and choreographed by Dance Theater of Harlem's director, Arthur Mitchell, that was given its world premiere. *Spiritual Suite* was the first staged work presented at the new venue and featured a narrator, two singers, dancers, and a stage set. It was performed on two consecutive nights; the narrator for the second performance was Philadelphia's own Marian Anderson, who, at 76, had retired from singing but was still doing occasional spoken-word performances.

The final events of the inaugural season were two high-profile concerts held in September that represented real coups for Septee and the Dell West. On September 2, the venue hosted Zubin Mehta and the Israel Philharmonic performing Hector Berlioz's *Symphonie fantastique* and Brahms's *Violin Concerto*, the latter with Isaac Stern returning for yet another appearance that season. Mehta, who made his American debut at the Dell East in 1960, had been appointed music adviser to the Israel Philharmonic in 1969 and would be named its music director in 1977. The Israel Philharmonic, billed as "The Official Representative of the Israel Government to the Bicentennial Celebrations in the U.S.," gave the concert on a somber note. Two months earlier, Israeli commandos had conducted the famous Entebbe raid in Uganda, freeing more than 100 people who had been taken hostage on an airplane and taken to the African nation. The concert program noted that the performance was a "Benefit for the Israel Soldier's Relief Fund in memory of Lt. Col. Yonatan Netanyahu, a native of Philadelphia, who was killed in the rescue of hostages in Uganda."[44] The lone Israeli military fatality in the operation, Netanyahu was the older brother of Israel's future Prime Minister Benjamin Netanyahu, who also spent part of his youth in the Philadelphia area.

The season concluded on a grand scale on September 21, with the famous Milan-based Italian opera company Teatro alla Scala making its first appearance in Philadelphia. Music Director Claudio Abbado led La Scala Chorus and Orchestra in Verdi's monumental *Requiem*, with vocal soloists, soprano Shirley Verrett and mezzo-soprano Marilyn Horne, both Americans who had performed at the Dell before, and two Italian singers who were making their Dell debuts: tenor Veriano Luchetti and bass Ruggero Raimondi. "The climactic moments were thunderous in their effect," *The Philadelphia Inquirer* noted, "and the luminous soft, sustained passages . . . were beautifully achieved. . . . Abbado steered between the extremes in dynamics in building this tumultuous performance."[45]

So ended the Robin Hood Dell West's eventful inaugural season. Fittingly, the final concert was on the last full day of summer, a day before The Philadelphia Orchestra's regular season commenced with an opening concert and gala at the Academy of Music.

## Inaugural Season Postlude

The Robin Hood Dell Concerts Inc. Board met on November 11 to assess the first season, focusing on six areas to be addressed going into 1977: acoustics, parking, a ramp to the balcony, railings, seating changes, and the need for concession buildings. Mann said he hoped that the city would fund "substantial portions" of the needed work, but to the extent that it was unwilling or unable, the Board would have to assume the costs. The new acoustician, Avram Meltzer, was already working on the sound issues, and Mann noted that there was an agreement in place with food concessionaire Nilon Brothers, which ran the concessions at Veterans Stadium, by which the company would fund construction of a permanent concession building (a tent had been used in the first year) and be reimbursed for the expense from their gross receipts.[46]

In other action, having received a large grant from the Pennsylvania Council for the Arts, the Board voted to have a member of the state legislature serve on the Board. James D. Barber, a Black state representative from Philadelphia whose district included the Dell West, was elected, joining Judge Leon Higginbotham as one of two Black members of the Board.[47] Like Mayor Frank Rizzo and City Council President George Schwartz, ex officio Board members whose positions were contingent on continued city funding, Barber would serve as long as the state funding continued.

## Major Improvements

The entire 1976 season was essentially the Dell West's "shakedown" period, the time when a new venue's systems are tested and adjusted. Usually done during a preview phase in advance of an official opening, the Dell West shakedown, by necessity, took place during the regular summer season. Having learned valuable lessons during that often trying time, Mann and the Dell Board were well positioned to make major improvements for the second season. "If it isn't right now, I'll have to leave town," Mann joked a few days before the 1977 season opened.[48]

There were some $600,000 in upgrades, of which the city funded $200,000. For the balance, Robin Hood Dell Concerts Inc. took out a four-year $400,000 loan from First Pennsylvania Bank.[49] Acoustical improvements were the highest priority. Under Meltzer's direction, the interior shell was rebuilt substantially, including installing more and better acoustical panels and raising the ceiling so the air could move better in the space (and the musicians, who had complained about the heat the previous year, could get some relief). The amplification system was relocated and upgraded, and a sound engineer from the Hollywood Bowl was hired to operate it. Meltzer promised "high-fidelity amplification" in season two.

Outside, a 100-foot level ramp was installed for easier access to the balcony (replacing steep steps that had come to be known as "cardiac hill," since many of those with balcony seats were elderly); railings were mounted on the stairways; permanent concession buildings were erected where patrons could purchase gourmet box dinners, as well as snacks; and a 45-foot earthen berm—dubbed "Mann Mountain" by some—was built to block the intrusive sights and sounds from Parkside Avenue. There were also major changes to the parking, which, all agreed, was poorly handled in 1976. The parking area was blacktopped, and Nilon Brothers was contracted to manage parking operations.[50]

"It seems to me we have a great institution here," Mann told *The Philadelphia Inquirer*, "and what we are doing is providing great music with a balanced budget. We are not asking for money to bail us out. Sometimes I don't think people appreciate that."[51] One influential person who did was Al Guadiosi, a close ally of Mayor Rizzo who was then serving in Mann's former position as Philadelphia city representative. "I make all the concerts at Robin Hood Dell [West] that I can," Guadiosi said in 1977. "I find that after a tough day in the trenches, an evening with the Orchestra at the Dell is very relaxing."[52] Guadiosi made sure the Dell West got what it needed from the city at budget time. The city appropriation for 1977 was $385,000, which was separate from the $200,000 the city allotted for capital improvements.

## Save Our Park

On May 30, 1977, Lucinda Hudson, who lived on the 5100 block of Parkside Avenue, adjacent to the new Robin Hood Dell West in the Parkside neighborhood of West Philadelphia, had a Memorial Day cookout with her two young sons in the park area across the street from her house. Someone came up to tell her that bulldozers were coming the next day to turn that area into a parking lot for the new Dell. "That night, I took my son's crayons and made 'Save Our Park' signs, and at 7:00 A.M. the next morning the three of us marched over to the park and laid down in front of the bulldozers. The bulldozer operator said he wouldn't do anything to hurt us and needed to go call his supervisor. While he was making the call, I went knocking on neighbors' doors and rallied over 500 people to come join the protest. All the local TV stations covered it."

Hudson eventually got more than 4,000 people to sign a "Save Our Park" petition. Mann agreed to meet with representatives of the group at nearby Memorial Hall a few days later. "There was a lot of back and forth between them and us," Hudson recalled. "The last straw was when Fredric Mann offered us $10,000; we were quite insulted. We got up from the table and told him how insulting that it was; that we were leaving and if we see any bulldozers or any equipment moving forward, we will be out there protesting each and every time."

The protest worked. The park area was saved, and the effort gave birth to the Parkside Association, the local civic group that has looked after the neighborhood's interests ever since. Mann eventually became one of the association's biggest supporters. Although the initiator, Hudson did not serve as the group's president at first. "I was busy raising my sons," she said. She became president in 1997 and joined the Mann Center's Board of Directors that year. She continued on the Mann Board in the 2020s, helping to foster the constructive working relationship between the Mann Center and the Parkside neighborhood.[53]

## The Late 1970s

The Philadelphia Orchestra's extended seven-week schedule in 1976 was an exception for the Bicentennial season; the Orchestra changed to a six-week, 18-concert Dell schedule in 1977 and the years that followed, again taking off the week of July 4. Ormandy, now in his late 70s and approaching retirement, continued to lead the season-opening concerts in this period, with the world's leading conductors filling out the rest of the schedules: Leonard Bernstein, James Levine, Zubin Mehta, Rafael Frühbeck de Burgos, Klaus Tennstedt, Daniel Barenboim, Michael Tilson Thomas, and Andre Kostelanetz, among others. Likewise, renowned soloists returned, and promising up-and-coming artists made their debuts in the late 1970s.

The 1977 season featured several large-scale vocal-choral performances. Levine led Gustav Mahler's monumental Symphony No. 8 ("Symphony of a Thousand") with the Mendelssohn Club of Philadelphia, Singing City Choirs, Brooklyn Boys Chorus, and eight soloists (including soprano Kathleen Battle). Leonard Bernstein led concert versions of excerpts from Wagner's opera *Tristan und Isolde*. And the great German conductor Klaus Tennstedt made his Dell debut, closing the season with Carl Orff's stirring cantata, *Carmina burana*, with the Philadelphia College of the Performing Arts Chorus Summer Workshop and the All-Philadelphia Boys Choir. The venerable Stuttgart Ballet gave three dance performances during the week of July 4 when the Orchestra was off, while in the popular realm, Electric Factory Concerts booked another lineup of soft-edged artists, mostly singer-songwriters in the folk-rock vein. James Taylor returned, and Jackson Browne and Gordon Lightfoot made their debuts.

The opening concert of the 1978 season was a tribute to Leopold Stokowski, who had died the previous September at 95. The groundbreaking conductor had led The Philadelphia Orchestra from 1912 to 1941 and brought it worldwide fame and admiration. As previously noted, Stokowski had supported the building of the original Robin Hood Dell in 1930, and although he never conducted a full, regularly scheduled concert there during his tenure as music director, he made a few brief impromptu appearances in the early 1930s and was a frequent and very popular guest conductor in the early 1960s. On June 19, 1978, Ormandy led a program in honor of Stokowski at the Dell West that was an exact repeat of Stokowski's first concert with the Orchestra in 1912: Beethoven's *Leonore* Overture No. 3 (the same piece with which Ormandy christened the Dell West in 1976), Brahms's Symphony No. 1, Mikhail Ippolitov-Ivanov's *Sketches from the Caucasus*, and Wagner's Overture to *Tannhäuser*.

On July 15, 1978, Keith Chapman, the organist who was scheduled to appear in 1976 but had to be omitted from the program because the organ did not arrive in time, finally got to perform the piece he was originally scheduled to play—Camille Saint-Saëns's Symphony No. 3 ("Organ")—with Dutch conductor Edo de Waart leading the program. A graduate of the Curtis Institute of Music and Temple University, Chapman was appointed principal organist at John Wanamaker department store at age 20 in

1966. It was, and still is, a coveted position; the Wanamaker Organ is the largest fully functioning pipe organ in the world, and daily organ concerts in the Grand Court at Wanamaker's (later Macy's) have been a cherished Philadelphia tradition since they began in 1911.* Chapman held the position until his death in a plane crash in 1989.

## Pop, Rock, and Jazz

Popular and contemporary music figured more prominently at the Dell West in 1978, both shows produced by Electric Factory Concerts and Philadelphia Orchestra pops concerts. A new feature in 1978 included two programs that were part of the Orchestra season but billed as "In Special Concert" events. These were partly symphonic and partly pops programs featuring well-known singers performing with the Orchestra. On July 18, jazz vocalist Sarah Vaughan appeared in an all-Gershwin program, with Michael Tilson Thomas conducting. After opening the program with *An American in Paris* and the Second Rhapsody for Piano and Orchestra—the latter with Tilson Thomas leading from the piano—the second half of the concert featured Vaughan singing Gershwin songs accompanied by her trio and the Orchestra. The configuration made "the setting look like a very cool concerto grosso," according to *The Philadelphia Inquirer. The Evening Bulletin* praised Vaughan's "three-octave vocal span, infectious scatting, and sly puns such as a baroque-style fugue between the singer and various instruments."[54] Broadway legend Ethel Merman was the soloist on July 27. Despite a torrential downpour that saw rain sweeping in the open sides of the venue, the show went on, with Merman belting out classic show tunes in the inimitable style that made her a hit on Broadway for many years.

Both concerts were very well attended. "Judging by the response to Sarah Vaughan and Ethel Merman, [pops concerts] are here to stay," noted *The Philadelphia Inquirer.* One patron, a Temple University music history professor, was not happy with the introduction of such concerts, however: "No doubt they will attract audiences, but we are paying our taxes for culturally uplifting programs. There is so much popular music available in this area. Must the Dell go pops, and is this just the beginning of the deterioration in programming?"[55] No doubt much to the writer's chagrin, the Dell would indeed increasingly "go pops" in the years to come.

The Electric Factory Concerts' series was larger and more varied in 1978 as well, featuring a mix of jazz, folk, and rock, some of which had a slightly harder edge than in previous years. Headliners were Boz Scaggs; Barry Manilow; Grover Washington Jr. and Al Jarreau; Jane Oliver and Manhattan Transfer; Crosby, Stills, and Nash; Cleo Laine and Kenny Rankin; Kris Kristofferson and Rita Coolidge; Linda Ron-

* The Macy's store closed in 2025 and the daily organ recitals were suspended when the Wanamaker building was closed for renovation. The new owners have committed to reviving the recitals when the building reopens.

stadt; George Benson; Jackson Browne; and Peter, Paul, and Mary. Slowly but surely, rock and pop were becoming an integral part of programming at the new Dell.

Mann reflected on the changes on the eve of the Orchestra's opening concert in 1978: "I hate to call myself a prostitute, but we do make money with [rock and popular shows]. And why should I chase all the young people to the Spectrum [the 20,000-seat sports arena where Electric Factory Concerts booked major rock shows]? Besides, these acts fill open dates for us. And when young people come to the Dell to see Barry Manilow, we make a lot of new friends." He noted that he had his limits, though: "I've been badgered and badgered to bring in musical comedy productions. As far as I'm concerned it will happen over my dead body. . . . We're a cultural institution, not an entertainment institution [which seems to contradict his earlier statement]. The Dell is essentially the home of the Philadelphia Orchestra in the summer. I believe it should remain that way."[56] The balance between classical and nonclassical programming would shift dramatically in later years, but in its early years, the Dell West/Mann Center would be known primarily as the summer home of The Philadelphia Orchestra.

The sold-out Grover Washington Jr. and Al Jarreau concert on July 19, 1978, was marred by several incidents. Washington and Jarreau were jazz musicians who had "crossed over" and were having success on the pop charts. Washington, a native of Buffalo, New York, made his home in Philadelphia and was a local favorite. His album *Live at the Bijou*, recorded earlier in 1978 at the popular downtown club that Larry Magid and Allen Spivak owned and managed, would be released that fall and hit number one on the jazz charts. Gate-crashers—numbering in the hundreds or thousands, depending on different versions of the story—made it into the venue and took patrons' seats and, in some cases, accosted them. There was also an altercation backstage between Dell union stagehands and nonunion staff working for Washington. Dell and Electric Factory representatives downplayed the incidents as minor, while Washington and his wife described them as more serious. "We have played all over the world, and we've never had anything like this happen before," Washington said after the concert. "I've been living here [in Philadelphia] 11 years now, and it's the only place I've seen that I really want to live. I feel close to the people here. Someone just tell me why it happened." An Electric Factory representative explained: "We weren't as prepared as we should have been. . . . We tried to get back-up forces, and there were lots of plain clothes [police] there. But if you call in uniformed police, they may agitate the situation."[57] There was no word of Mann's reaction to the incidents; one can only imagine.

## Opera and Ballet

In addition to expanded pop and contemporary offerings, 1978 was the year the Dell West was finally able to present fully staged opera and ballet performances.

The Metropolitan Opera performs Verdi's *Rigoletto* at the Robin Hood Dell West on June 1, 1978. (*The Philadelphia Inquirer* photograph collection, Special Collections Research Center, Temple University Libraries)

Mann and Septee had big plans to host such productions at the new venue from the beginning, but construction delays in 1976 and major offseason improvements in 1977 made booking them too risky. The one exception was the Stuttgart Ballet performances in 1977. The following year, grand opera and ballet became big attractions at the Dell, beginning with three highly anticipated performances in early June 1978 by the Metropolitan Opera, which had not performed in Philadelphia for more than a decade. The productions represented a major expense for the Dell, reportedly taking 28 tractor trailers to transport and costing $100,000 a night. The Philadelphia Cultural Affairs Council gave the Dell a $60,000 grant to cover the costs of making the performances mostly free. As a result, the series was partly paid and partly free: Tickets for covered seating cost $15–$20, while the 10,000 uncovered seats were free to those who clipped out and mailed in coupons published in the newspaper, the same procedure used for the regular Orchestra concerts.[58]

■ The American Ballet Theatre dancers Mikhail Baryshnikov and Marianna Tcherkassky in a performance at the Robin Hood Dell West in June 1978. (*The Evening Bulletin*, June 14, 1978, Scrapbook, Mann Center for the Performing Arts Archives)

The Met's productions of Verdi's *Rigoletto* on June 1, Pietro Mascagni's *Cavalleria rusticana* and Ruggiero Leoncavallo's *Pagliacci* on June 2, and Giacomo Puccini's *Madama Butterfly* on June 3 were huge hits. While some local critics complained that the Met did not send its top-name stars to Philadelphia, the company performed to large, enthusiastic crowds. *The New York Times* reported:

> The Metropolitan Opera drew the largest live audience ever to attend one of its staged performances Thursday night. An estimated 15,000 people came to hear and see the company's production of Verdi's "Rigoletto" in Philadel-

> phia's Robin Hood Dell West. . . . What brought a record-breaking crowd to the handsome structure in West Fairmount Park was the combination of perfect weather (cloudless sky, warm temperatures), free seats for those watching from the uncovered portion of the arena, and the fact that the Met had not visited Philadelphia in ten years.[59]

High-profile stage productions continued the following week when the Dell West hosted American Ballet Theatre, which also had not appeared in Philadelphia for 10 years. The company boasted some of the biggest names in ballet, including American Gelsey Kirkland and Russians Mikhail Baryshnikov and Natalia Makarova. Baryshnikov, like Makarova (see page 225), had been a member of the renowned Kirov Ballet in Leningrad before defecting to the West and becoming internationally famous. The troupe opened the Dell West series with a program of varied shorter pieces on June 13, a cold, dreary night, and followed with the classic *Giselle* the next two nights, when the weather was much more pleasant. Kirkland was scheduled to perform the first night, but her partner suffered an injury, and she did not appear at all during the series. Baryshnikov, making his Dell debut, was in two pieces the first night; then he and Makarova were the leads in the two *Giselle* performances the following nights. His star power was huge at this time, as was his talent. "Baryshnikov astonished the audience with a brilliant dance display that combined refined technical control and aggressive athleticism," reported the *Courier-Post* after the first evening.[60] Critics were equally enthusiastic about his and Makarova's performances in *Giselle*. The two "danced . . . with astonishing technical power . . . and were incredibly strong and exciting," noted *The Evening Bulletin*.[61] The *Giselle* performances were Baryshnikov's last during his first tenure with American Ballet Theatre; he had already signed with the New York City Ballet, and the Dell West concerts were his last contractual obligations with his former company.

## Freddie's Little Summer Toy

On October 19, 1978, Zubin Mehta wrote to Eugene Ormandy about scheduling issues with his upcoming concerts. Mehta had recently become music director of the New York Philharmonic and was telling Ormandy that, because of the new position, his ongoing role as music director of the Israel Philharmonic, and other commitments, he could not squeeze in any additional conducting engagements. However, he noted that, in deference to Mann, he would still conduct at the Dell the following summer, when he was scheduled to lead all three concerts during the fifth week. "I am glad I am conducting at the Dell where I can look forward to making music with your great musicians again," he wrote to Ormandy. "The visit to the Dell is also a long standing promise to our friend Freddie Mann to help him celebrate the fiftieth anniversary of his little summer toy and I am really cutting my month's vacation to three weeks in order to make the gesture."[62] It was one of many gestures Mehta made over the years in appreciation of Mann, his longtime friend and benefactor.

The year 1979 was an auspicious one indeed for Mann's "little summer toy." Not only was it the 50th anniversary of summer concerts at the Dell (East and West), but it was the year the name of the venue was changed in his honor. In January 1979, local newspapers reported that John Taxin, owner of Philadelphia's landmark Old Original Bookbinders restaurant, sent a letter to Mayor Rizzo requesting that the Dell West be renamed in honor of Mann, calling it "a fitting recognition of the tremendous contribution (of) a gentleman who has brought a special flavor and meaning to the cultural wellbeing of the citizens of Philadelphia."[63] Others were working on the idea as well, including Magid: "I remember talking to Moe Septee and Dick Doran [an influential Philadelphia political insider and cultural leader who would later become chairman of the Mann Center Board] . . . , and I said, 'You have Robin Hood Dell West, East—too confusing. People are going to the other place; they don't know about this place. I think you should honor Fred Mann [by renaming the Dell West].'"[64]

The combined efforts worked. On June 13, 1979, a few days before the beginning of The Philadelphia Orchestra's summer series at the Dell, the Philadelphia City Council passed an ordinance that Rizzo signed into law renaming Robin Hood Dell West the Fredric R. Mann Music Center. The change happened too late for the venue's printed matter; schedules and promotional materials for the 1979 season still read "Robin Hood Dell West," and the organization itself, Robin Hood Dell Inc., did not legally change its name for several years thereafter. But for decades since, Philadelphians have referred to the beloved West Fairmount Park venue as "the Mann," whether they know the origin of the name or not (most do not). (The name change did not come with a financial endowment. While Mann poured substantial amounts of his own money into both the original Dell East and new Dell West/Mann Center over the years, there was no endowment fund to support the latter venue until a modest one was established in the 2010s.)

Continuing the tradition begun the previous year, the Metropolitan Opera opened the 1979 season. From May 28 to June 2, the company presented Puccini's *Tosca*, Wagner's *Tannhäuser*, and Verdi's *Otello*. There were no complaints this year about the Met not sending its stars. James Levine led two of the performances, Luciano Pavarotti was featured in *Tosca*, and other high-profile Met singers performed. Once again, the Philadelphia Cultural Affairs Council provided a grant that allowed for 10,000 free seats, and attendance was strong. As anticipated, Pavarotti delighted the audience and critics. One reviewer noted "the sheer beauty of his voice, the ease with which it pours out, and his sense of the long line."[65]

The night after the Met opera series concluded, Electric Factory Concerts presented the first of its popular concert series for the year. British singer-songwriter Joan Armatrading headlined, with American singer-songwriter Steve Forbert as the

Advertisement for the Metropolitan Opera's 1979 series at the Robin Hood Dell West, published in *The Philadelphia Inquirer*, May 6, 1979. (From *The Philadelphia Inquirer*. © 1979 Philadelphia Inquirer, LLC. All rights reserved. Used under license. Scrapbook, Mann Center for the Performing Arts Archives)

opening act. The venue was then dark for two weeks until The Philadelphia Orchestra's season began, with Ormandy scheduled to lead all three concerts during the first week of the 50th anniversary year.

A sellout audience of 15,000 was in attendance for the Orchestra's June 18 opening concert, an all-Beethoven program featuring the Eighth and Ninth Symphonies, the latter with the Singing City Choir and a vocal quartet. At intermission, Mann was honored with a plaque and an official citation recognizing the naming of the venue in his honor and celebrating the 50th anniversary of the summer concerts. Beethoven's great Symphony No. 9 provided a thrilling end to the program. "Ormandy's exposition of the 9th was something else, altogether," proclaimed *The*

*Philadelphia Inquirer.* "He went after it with a passion that infected his players and brought them to the limits of expression." *The Evening Bulletin* noted: "The great Ninth Symphony [was] ideal as a festive and ceremonial climax" to the evening; the "vocal quartet . . . [sang] ardently, . . . joined by Singing City Choir in a final joyous shout that crowned the historic night."[66] Remarkably, in the string section that night was violist Leonard Mogill, who had played in every Dell season since the original venue opened in 1930.

The festivities continued at a gala dinner in honor of Freddie Mann at nearby Belmont Mansion following the concert. Some 200 people attended, including Ormandy and his wife, Gretel, who made a brief appearance before leaving early. The next morning the 79-year-old conductor was taken to Pennsylvania Hospital with chest pains. Doctors determined that he had not suffered a heart attack, but they ordered rest. Associate Conductor William Smith stepped in to lead the second concert of opening week, and Polish American conductor Stanisław Skrowaczewski led the third.

A week later, another Dell veteran had to cancel his scheduled appearance after being hospitalized. Mann had engaged José Iturbi as pianist for the 50th anniversary year, in what would have been the Spanish pianist and conductor's 86th Dell appearance, in recognition of all he had done for the venue over the years. "When we were trying to bring the Dell back from bankruptcy [in the late 1940s], Iturbi played several seasons for free," Mann recalled. "I'll never forget that."[67] With Iturbi unavailable, American pianist Misha Dichter substituted, with Sergiu Comissiona conducting. The concert was in memory of Morton Howard, the retired longtime Dell general manager, who had died earlier in the year. Iturbi never made it back to the Dell/Mann Center; he died the following year at 84. His 1976 appearance turned out to be his last.

Russian ballet artists Valery and Galina Panov returned in 1979. Conditions were better than in their last appearance in 1975, when they bravely danced in heavy rain at the uncovered Dell East (see pages 226–227). Still popular in Philadelphia, they drew a sellout crowd of 15,000. Leading the Orchestra was Maurice Kaplow, longtime conductor of the Pennsylvania Ballet Orchestra, who had played viola for The Philadelphia Orchestra in the late 1950s and early 1960s, including performing in the summer concerts at the original Dell.

After six weeks of world-class conductors and soloists, Leonard Bernstein closed the 1979 Orchestra season on August 2, leading Mahler's Symphony No. 9. It would be the iconic musician's sixth and final appearance at the Dell/Mann Center. It did not begin well. Things were tense between conductor and Orchestra in rehearsal, with Bernstein telling the musicians that they were not playing at their best and that the Boston Symphony had played the piece much better when he led it the week before in Tanglewood. The Player's Committee met with Bernstein during the break and worked things out, and the concert that night went very well, ending with Bernstein "giving sweaty embraces for all the players within reach."[68]

Baryshnikov made his return to the Dell at the end of the season, leading a series of three sold-out programs in early August with Danish dancer Peter Martins and dancers from the New York City Ballet. The program was in honor of the New York City Ballet's founder and director, George Balanchine, and his contemporary, Jerome Robbins. Baryshnikov again received rave reviews and a great audience response, as did Martins, who was making his Mann/Dell debut. "Baryshnikov Has Crowd Gasping," read one *Evening Bulletin* headline.[69] The famed Russian dancer had recently announced that he was leaving the New York City Ballet after a year and a half to return to American Ballet Theatre as artistic director.

Electric Factory Concerts produced an ever wider-ranging series of popular shows in 1979. While the focus was still mostly on pop and soft-rock artists, particularly singer-songwriters—James Taylor and Gordon Lightfoot made return appearances, and Carly Simon (then Taylor's wife) and Joni Mitchell made their debuts—the trend toward slightly harder-edge rock continued. The rock group Chicago and country-rock group Poco made their debuts, while the Taylor and Mitchell concerts were more highly charged, revealing that both had evolved musically from the acoustic guitar–based styles of their early careers. Both had top-notch rock and jazz musicians in their backing bands—Mitchell had pioneering jazz fusion bassist (and Norristown, Pennsylvania, native) Jaco Pastorious in her ensemble—and gave them ample opportunities to stretch out in live performance. *The Philadelphia Inquirer* noted that many of the new songs Taylor performed at his July 27 concert were "outright hard rockers," while Mitchell's August 28 show featured rock-infused versions of her earlier well-known songs along with those from her recent jazz-influenced album *Mingus*, much of which was written with the renowned jazz bassist Charles Mingus.[70]

Also debuting in 1979 were Jimmy Buffett and the Coral Reefer Band. The term "parrot head" had not yet come into popular use to describe followers of the laid-back, tropical-themed lifestyle espoused by Buffett and his loyal fans, but he had already recorded many of his classics, such as "Margaritaville," "Cheeseburger in Paradise," and "Come Monday." The group's festive concert/party tradition was well formed by the time it first played the Mann on August 11.

Perhaps the strangest bill Electric Factory Concerts presented that year was the August 27 show that opened with Ray Charles and His Orchestra, followed by up-and-coming comedian Jay Leno, then middle-of-the-road crooner Perry Como as the headliner, backed by Charles's 28-piece orchestra. "It was a package show that I bought," Magid remembers, not one that his company put together. As *The Philadelphia Inquirer* reported, "The music harked back a couple of decades and pleased the audience of nearly all over-30s."[71]

The final classical concert of the 1979 season was a benefit for the Marian Anderson Library and Scholarship Fund. The renowned singer, born and raised in South Philadelphia, had recently donated her collection of personal papers, music, and memorabilia to University of Pennsylvania Libraries. August 22 was proclaimed

"Marian Anderson Day" in Philadelphia, and that evening the Mann Center presented Luciano Pavarotti in recital as a fundraiser to support work on the collection and establish a scholarship in Anderson's name. Promoted as "An Extraordinary Musical Event," it was actually a recital—just Pavarotti and a pianist—the first time the venue had hosted such an intimate performance. Pavarotti flew in from Italy specifically for the concert, which drew a sold-out crowd who showed great love for both the Italian tenor and the legendary Philadelphia contralto. "As a child in Philadelphia I had never dreamed that there would be a Marian Anderson Day in Philadelphia," she told the audience. "This is one of the greatest moments of my life. . . . From the bottom of my heart I shall always send all of my love to you."[72]

9.

# 1980–1997

## *Mann Music Center to Mann Center for the Performing Arts*

**In the closing years of the 20th century, the Mann Music Center would** transition from a small, tightly run enterprise—basically "a mom-and-pop operation," as one later staff member described it—to a larger, more diversified, and professionally run organization. The transition coincided with the ending of the Fredric Mann era, a 10-year process that started with Mann's death in 1987 and concluded with the retirement in 1997 of his longtime assistant Helen Martin, who had become president after his passing. In Martin's final year, the Board adopted a new vision and an expanded mission for the venue, officially renaming it the Mann Center for the Performing Arts in February 1997. Later that year, the Board hired an experienced performing arts executive from New York, who began to modernize the venue and its operations, instituting more contemporary programming and fundraising practices and undertaking long-needed upgrades to the facility.

### Sixth Decade

There were a number of sentimental moments as the Mann Music Center began the 1980 season, marking the organization's sixth decade of concerts, its fifth year in its new home, and its first full year under its new name. Eugene Ormandy's last

**(following spread, left)** ■ Brochure for the 1980 Philadelphia Orchestra summer season at the Mann. (Mann Center for the Performing Arts Archives)

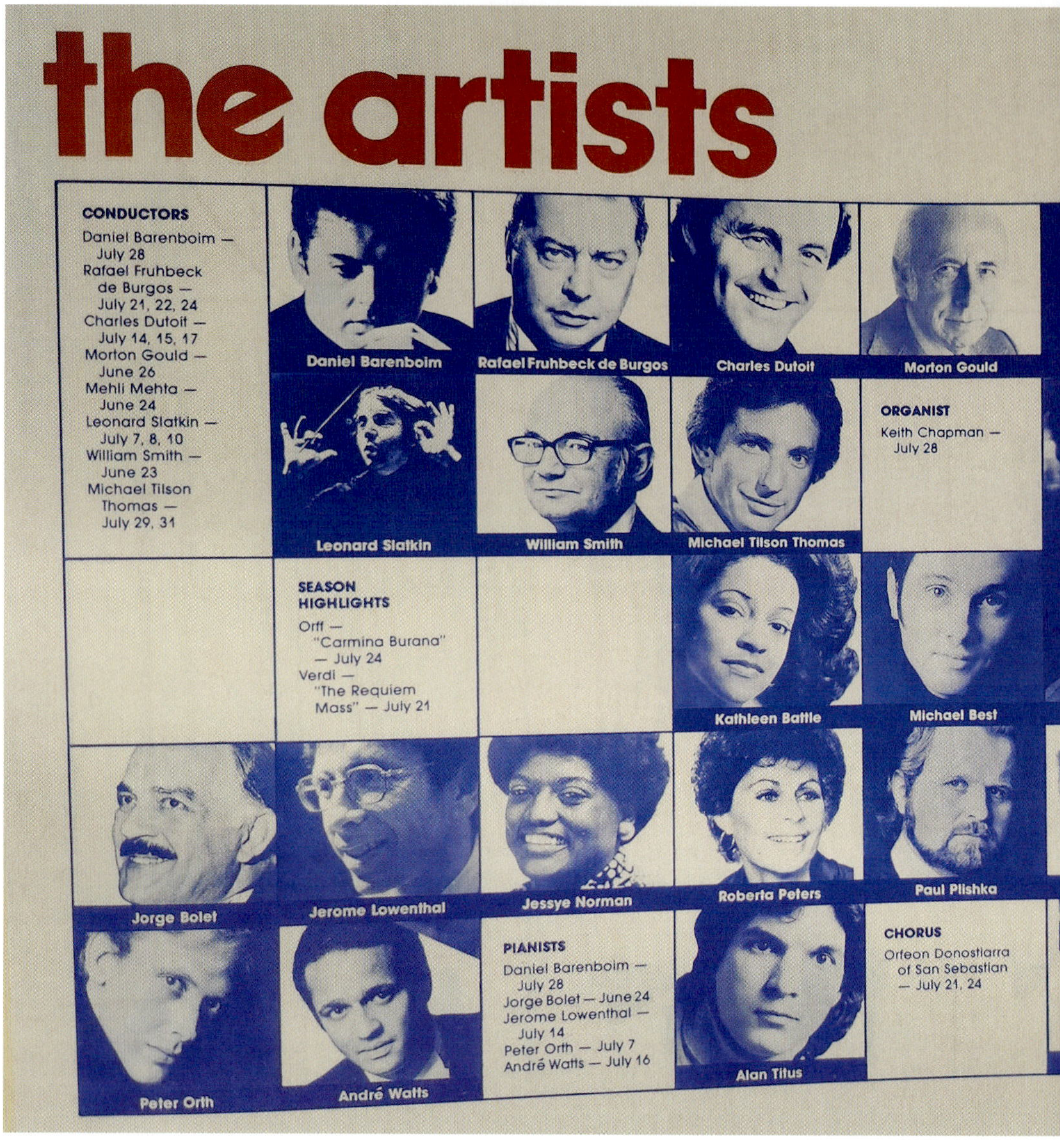


concerts in the city as music director of The Philadelphia Orchestra, soprano Beverly Sills's final performance in Philadelphia, and a tribute to recently deceased audience favorite Andre Kostelanetz were among the poignant programs in the first weeks of 1980. There were significant debuts and revivals that season as well. The New York City Opera returned after a 12-year absence; Children's Concerts resumed after a five-year hiatus; and Swiss conductor Charles Dutoit made his debut at the Mann, leading a week of concerts that would lay the groundwork for his appointment as artistic director 10 years later. At the same time, the Mann was becoming a major rock-and-roll venue.

On February 26, 1980, Sills, mostly retired from singing and now director of the New York City Opera, held a press conference in Philadelphia with her good friend Freddie Mann to announce that her company would be back in the city in

■ Beverly Sills and Fredric Mann announce on February 26, 1980, that the New York City Opera will give three different operas at the Mann Center in June of that year. Photograph published in *The Philadelphia Inquirer*, February 27, 1980. (From *The Philadelphia Inquirer*. © 1980 Philadelphia Inquirer, LLC. All rights reserved. Used under license. *The Philadelphia Inquirer* photograph collection, Special Collections Research Center, Temple University Libraries)

June to present a series of three operas at the Mann Center, prior to the Orchestra's summer season. She also shared the surprising news that she would be performing in one of the productions. As she told the attendees, "Fred . . . said if I didn't sing, he wouldn't take the company. When I first approached him about taking the company, he answered 'What are you going to sing?' So I figured what the heck. . . . I'll do it."[1] At 51, Sills sang the role of Rosina in Rossini's *The Barber of Seville* on June 9, 1980, her last performance in Philadelphia. "It was billed as her farewell," *The Philadelphia Inquirer* noted, "but it was another display of her boundless energy and charm."[2] Later in the week, her company presented Johann Strauss's *Die Fledermaus* and Giuseppe Verdi's *La Traviata*.

The following week, Ormandy opened the Orchestra season, leading all three concerts. He had announced a year earlier that he was retiring as music director of

■ Eugene Ormandy conducting in his later years. (Philadelphia Orchestra Association Digital Library)

The Philadelphia Orchestra after the 1979–1980 season. His heir apparent, principal guest conductor Riccardo Muti, would assume the position in the fall of 1980, with Ormandy taking the title of conductor laureate. His final regular-season concert as music director was May 3, 1980, at the Academy of Music; his three June concerts at the Mann would be his last in Philadelphia as music director; and his four concerts during the Orchestra's August residency at the Saratoga Performing Arts Center (SPAC) in upstate New York would be his last ones under his longtime title. Ormandy's 44-year tenure in Philadelphia was unprecedented in American orchestral music, but even more remarkable was his tenure combined with that of his predecessor, Leopold Stokowski, who joined the Orchestra in 1912—an amazing 68 years under just two music directors.

At 80, "Eugene Ormandy was back, fit and erect," to open the 1980 season, according to *The Philadelphia Inquirer.*[3] The first concert, on Monday, June 16, was a "Three B's" program featuring the music of Bach, Beethoven, and Brahms, with pianist André Watts performing Beethoven's Piano Concerto No. 4. Tuesday was an all-Sibelius program; Thursday was all-Wagner. At intermission of the Monday concert, Mann honored Ormandy and violist Leonard Mogill, the only two musicians still with the Orchestra who had played in the 1930 opening season of the Robin

Hood Dell. Mann presented Mogill with a gold watch and announced the establishment of a Eugene Ormandy Conducting Fellowship, in which a young conductor of Ormandy's choosing would lead a concert at the Mann every year.

Mogill, in an interview with *The Evening Bulletin* prior to the concert, recounted the unusual circumstances of his first Dell appearance. He was a 17-year-old student at the Curtis Institute of Music attending a 1930 Dell concert with a date when the Orchestra's personnel manager pressed him into service to substitute for a violist who was unable to perform that night. Thus began Mogill's 51 consecutive years of playing the Robin Hood Dell and Mann Center concerts. He received a permanent appointment with The Philadelphia Orchestra after graduating from Curtis in 1935 and retired in 1981. "For a kid like me, it was a real thrill," Mogill recalled of his early years at the Dell. "In the old days, we played every night for two months in a row. There were a lot of rainouts. . . . Conditions are a lot better now."[4]

Conductor Andre Kostelanetz, who had appeared at the Robin Hood Dell and Mann Center more than 40 times from 1939 to 1979, died in January 1980 at 78. His specialty in "light" classical repertoire—operetta, overtures, incidental music—was a perennial favorite with Philadelphia summer audiences. On June 26, 1980, composer and conductor Morton Gould led a Kostelanetz tribute concert featuring many of these types of pieces, although Gould's *Holocaust Suite*, written for a 1978 television miniseries on the Holocaust, was of a decidedly different mood. Featured artists were soprano Roberta Peters, another longtime favorite, who sang several popular arias, and Werner Klemperer, son of the famous German conductor Otto Klemperer, who narrated Aaron Copland's *Lincoln Portrait.* (Readers of a certain age will remember Werner Klemperer as the character Colonel Klink in the late-1960s TV sitcom *Hogan's Heroes.*)

Charles Dutoit, artistic director of the Montreal Symphony, led the fourth week of concerts. Born in Switzerland in 1936, he had musical training there and in Italy, then began playing viola in various orchestras in Europe and South America in the late 1950s. Beginning in 1959, he guest-conducted and held chief conductor posts for various orchestras in Switzerland, including leading the Bern Symphony Orchestra from 1968 to 1978. He became artistic director of the Montreal Symphony in 1977, a post he held until 2002, recording prolifically and touring regularly with them during that period.

Interviewed in Montreal prior to his July 14, 1980, debut at the Mann, Dutoit said, "This is my first big American orchestral appearance. I had conducted Mostly Mozart concerts in New York, and I will be conducting the [New York] Philharmonic in 1982 and Boston, Los Angeles, and Pittsburgh. You can image I am happy to work with the Philadelphia Orchestra."[5] Dutoit's first concert featured pianist Jerome Lowenthal in Rachmaninoff's Piano Concert No. 3; his second concert was all orchestral; and the third marked the first and only Mann appearance by soprano Jessye Norman, who sang Ravel's *Shéhérazade* and Richard Strauss's *Four Last Songs.*

Dutoit would appear with increasing frequency at the Mann throughout the 1980s and be named its music director in 1990.

Leonard Slatkin, Rafael Frühbeck de Burgos, Daniel Barenboim, and Michael Tilson Thomas were among the other notable conductors in the 1980 Mann season. In previewing the season that March, *Billboard* magazine noted the lack of Russian conductors and soloists on the schedule, an unusual situation the magazine attributed to tensions between the United States and the Soviet Union over the Soviet invasion of Afghanistan in late 1979.[6] The season ended on July 31, with Tilson Thomas conducting and soprano Shirley Verrett making her sixth appearance as guest soloist at the Dell and Mann.

A month after the 1980 Mann season ended, the Temple University Music Festival in Ambler, Pennsylvania, presented its last concert, closing after 13 years. The festival was reportedly losing about a quarter-million dollars a year at that point, while the university was facing a major budget crisis. The music institute associated with the festival had been discontinued in 1975, and Temple University made the decision to end the festival in 1980. The Mann Center would eventually adopt Temple's model of presenting a mix of classical, jazz, and popular music, sometimes in a festival format, but that would come later. For the 1980s and much of the 1990s, Mann staff would focus mostly on Philadelphia Orchestra concerts, as well as opera and ballet performances, leaving nonclassical programming to outside promoters.

## The 1980s

Riccardo Muti led the first two concerts of the 1981 season, marking his debut at the Mann as Philadelphia Orchestra music director. He had performed at the old Dell once, in 1973, leading two concerts as a late substitute for André Previn, who had fallen ill, but otherwise had never appeared in the Orchestra's summer concert series. In addition to his two 1981 concerts, he led a week of concerts in 1983, 1986, and 1988, but those were his only appearances at the Mann. He reportedly did not like leading outdoor summer concerts and did not have much of a presence at the Mann in his 12-year tenure in Philadelphia, a fact that Freddie Mann resented.[7]

Ormandy, now holding the title of conductor laureate of The Philadelphia Orchestra, led a week of concerts in 1981, a pair of concerts in 1982, and a week in 1983. His June 23, 1983, concert with violinist Cho-Liang Lin was his last at the Mann, and his January 10, 1984, concert at Carnegie Hall was his last with the Orchestra. He died on March 12, 1985, at 85. His passing was truly the end of an era. As he told *The New York Times* in 1979:

> I think I am the last one of a breed. After me, . . . the jet set conductors, they all jump from one place to another. . . . I'm from the old school, I work every day with the Philadelphia Orchestra. Today's conductors, they're the

■ Music Director Riccardo Muti leads The Philadelphia Orchestra with piano soloist André Watts at the Mann Center on June 30, 1983. (Mann Center for the Performing Arts Archives)

> jet set conductors. It's terrible in my opinion. Three weeks and after the last concert his car is waiting and it rushes him to the midnight plane to Vienna or Berlin or London. . . . They have to get from one place to another as fast as they can.[8]

While Ormandy was devoted to The Philadelphia Orchestra, his commitment to the Dell and the Mann during his 53 years of performing at the venues varied over time. He was a regular presence at the Dell from 1930 until his appointment as Philadelphia Orchestra music director in 1936; thereafter, he conducted single concerts each year in the late 1930s and early 1940s, but from 1942 until 1965 his only appearances were sets of three concerts in 1953 and 1956. He began to appear with more frequency in the early 1970s and then conducted regularly from the time the Robin Hood Dell West/Mann Center opened in 1976 until his final concerts in 1983. Like his relationship with Freddie Mann, Ormandy's presence at the Dell and Mann ebbed and flowed over time.

In terms of soloists, the early 1980s saw return appearances by many longtime favorites, along with some notable debuts. Performing for the first time in 1981 were 25-year-old American cellist Yo-Yo Ma, in the early stages of what would be an extraordinarily successful career; popular American film composer Henry Mancini, who conducted a pops program that featured some of his compositions along with other film and television music; and Irish flautist James Galway, former principal flautist with the Berlin Philharmonic, who was then enjoying major "crossover" success, appealing to both classical and popular music audiences.

## Blue Shirt Blues

Metropolitan Opera soprano Leontyne Price performed at the Mann four times from 1979 through 1986. In the Orchestra for her August 3, 1983, appearance with Dutoit and The Philadelphia Orchestra was Larry McKenna, then a local journeyman saxophonist who had gotten a call to be an extra instrumentalist for the concert. McKenna had played with Woody Herman's big band early in his career and accompanied singers such as Frank Sinatra and Tony Bennett; in his later years, he would become a respected stalwart of the Philadelphia jazz scene. But in the early 1980s, he was mostly playing weddings, bar mitzvahs, and dances, as well as in the house bands at local venues such as the Latin Casino and Valley Forge Music Fair. As he recalled in a 2021 interview, playing with The Philadelphia Orchestra at the Mann Center was a major career highlight, although at one point the engagement brought a stark reminder of the journeyman life:

> I was mostly working society gigs and weddings and such; that's basically how I was making my living. This one summer, I got a call to play at the Mann Music Center with The Philadelphia Orchestra, a very prestigious gig. Every once in a while I used to get a call, because they would add saxophones for whatever music they happened to be programming. . . . It always made me feel like a foot taller, "Hey, I'm playing with The Philadelphia Orchestra!" It was a big feather in my cap, a big honor. And a departure from playing weddings and bar mitzvahs . . . and stuff like that—what we called "playing the outside."
>
> At the time, it became fashionable . . . for musicians playing weddings and stuff to wear blue shirts with their tuxedos, instead of the usual white shirt. This particular day . . . at the Mann Center, we had to rehearse in the afternoon, and I'm thinking, "Boy, this is so nice, and such a step up from playing the outside, playing society gigs and all that stuff." And [to] rehearse with all these wonderful musicians, . . . I just felt on top of the world, feeling real proud of myself. After the rehearsal, I turn around and I see about five or six guys, all of whom were friends of mine, . . . they're wearing tuxedos with blue shirts. And I knew them all to be wedding band players, [and I'm thinking,] "What are they doing here ruining my day?" And they come up and say, "Hey, Lar, what are you doing here?" They didn't expect to see me there. I felt it was some kind of personal affront, that I was being dragged back into [the other world of] playing. . . . It turns out they were hired to play after the

concert for Freddie Mann's birthday. . . . My feeling was, "Can't I ever escape this, can't I ever get away from it?"[9]

## Ballet at the Mann

The early to mid-1980s was an especially rich period for ballet at the Mann. In August 1981, the Mann presented a two-day "Ballet Spectacular" with three of the world's premier ballerinas: Gelsey Kirkland, Natalia Makarova, and 17-year-old American sensation Amanda McKerrow, who had just won first prize in the International Moscow Ballet Competition. *The Evening Bulletin* had high praise for all three, but especially for Kirkland, a native of Bethlehem, Pennsylvania, noting her "extraordinary fluidity and almost magical ability to float in the air [that] resulted in a breathtaking performance that cannot be described—it can only be experienced."[10]

Mikhail Baryshnikov and members of American Ballet Theatre gave two performances in 1981, billed as "Mikhail Baryshnikov and Company." Baryshnikov

■ Mikhail Baryshnikov is featured prominently in this ad for a 10-day series of performances by American Ballet Theatre at the Mann Center in August 1982. (Scrapbook, Mann Center for the Performing Arts Archives)

was then artistic director of American Ballet Theatre, but the Mann programs were separate Baryshnikov productions, not official performances of the company. The full company was in residence the following year, however, for a high-profile, 10-day series of performances in August that was a great success.

The Pennsylvania Ballet (later the Philadelphia Ballet), founded in 1963 by George Balanchine's protégé Barbara Weissberger and directed by her for many years, made its Mann debut in 1984 and appeared annually through 1987. Fredric Mann, who had often been accused of following the "star system" in preferring famous New York companies to local ones, explained that a grant from the Mabel Pew Myrin Trust made it possible to present both the Pennsylvania Ballet and American Ballet Theatre in 1984. He said that money was the main reason that it took the Mann Center more than 20 years to host the Pennsylvania Ballet. "You have to understand that we won't take a loss," he said. "If Weissberger had come up with $40,000, we'd have gambled on the company. But . . . they never came up with a proposal. I always thought that the Pennsylvania Ballet was good enough to perform at the Mann, and I'm a pushover for good things. But we could never figure out a way to fund it."[11]

Weissberger, who was no longer artistic director by 1984, agreed that money had been the issue and that, while "Freddie liked us and respected us and was always very nice to me," he had urged her in the past to have famous guest dancers, which she resisted. "I tried to convince him that the guest-artist approach is passé from an artistic point of view and that, besides, it doesn't really work unless you have a Baryshnikov or a [Rudolf] Nureyev. We had different philosophies. Mann is of the old-impresario school, of the [great classical music promoter] Sol Hurok ilk. But I always thought that it was important for the company to perform there, and I'm glad it's happening now."[12]

Mann's crowning achievement in dance was bringing the legendary Kirov Ballet to his namesake venue for a series of four performances in late May 1986, the Russian company's first appearance in America in many years. It was a triumph; the performances were virtual sellouts, and the reviews were very enthusiastic. "The company . . . was magical," the *Philadelphia Daily News* reported enthusiastically, while *The Philadelphia Inquirer* noted that "one knew straight from the beginning that the Kirov dancers are without peers in classical dancing."[13]

While great Russian dancers, many of them Kirov alumni, had appeared at the Mann and Dell in the past, they were defectors or exiles. The Kirov company members were Soviet citizens and very much under the control of their Russian handlers. "Many of their production people were KGB [the Russian intelligence agency]," said former General Manager Jerry Grabey, who remembers being able to spot Soviet and American agents in the audience, all watching each other. Grabey described the plan he and Mann concocted for giving tokens of appreciation to the company members.

They decided on blue jeans, which were highly prized in Russia. Mann got the pants from the iconic Philadelphia Army-Navy store I. Goldberg, and Grabey had Mann Center patches sewn on them. He reasoned that if the jeans were later sold on the Russian black market—a distinct possibility—the Mann Center would get free advertising in the Soviet Union.[14]

## Jazz, Rock, and Pop

The Mann Center hosted the Kool Jazz Festival from 1982 to 1984, presenting many of the biggest names in jazz. Renowned promoter George Wein, founding producer of the Newport Jazz Festival in the 1950s, took the event to different cities under different corporate sponsorships in the early 1980s. In Philadelphia, it was the Kool Jazz Festival, sponsored by Kool cigarettes, with shows at the Mann, the Academy of Music, and other local venues. The list of jazz giants who performed at the Mann during the festival's three years in Philadelphia reads like a Who's Who of the genre: Miles Davis, Dizzy Gillespie, Ella Fitzgerald, and the Modern Jazz Quartet, among dozens of others. Many up-and-coming "young lions" of jazz were featured as well. "One year [1982] we had Wynton Marsalis," Grabey remembers. "He was just 21. This was before he became famous. I remember thinking, 'Wow, this guy can play!' He was friendly and respectful." The festival lost money every year, however. "They got clobbered financially," Grabey said. "It was self-promoted by [Wein's] company; the Mann didn't produce it. They couldn't afford the losses. I did get to meet George Wein, though. An incredible guy."[15]

Electric Factory Concerts, the principal promoter of rock and pop concerts at the Mann, increased its number of shows significantly in the early 1980s, a slight drop-off from 1981 to 1982 notwithstanding. In 1981, there were 20 such shows; in 1982, there were 16. Several of the 1982 shows were part of a two-week "American Music Festival" that Electric Factory coproduced that year commemorating the 300th anniversary of the founding of Philadelphia in 1682. Continuing the trend started in the late 1970s, some Electric Factory shows began to take on a harder rock edge. Singer-songwriters and soft rock artists were still a big draw—James Taylor, Carly Simon, and Jackson Browne all appeared in the early 1980s—but Mann audiences were also rocking out to groups such as the Doobie Brothers, Santana, and George Thorogood and the Delaware Destroyers. It was more a natural progression than a conscious policy change, noted Electric Factory's head, Larry Magid. "It was a matter of trust and growth. Audiences grow and change and go to see different artists in different venues. We grew with them and presented quality shows at the Mann."[16]

Many rock artists liked the vibe and natural setting of the Mann. "We've always loved playing there because Philly audiences are so passionate," said Kate Pierson, one of the singers in the B-52s, the retro/new wave group that first performed at the

■ May 1980 ad for part of Electric Factory Concerts' rock and pop lineup for the 1980 Mann season. Seven concerts were listed, with "More July & August Shows to Be Announced." (Scrapbook, Mann Center for the Performing Arts Archives)

Mann in 1982. "We've particularly enjoyed playing the Mann because it's in such a beautiful setting; it feels really homey and has great acoustics. There really are so few venues like that anymore."[17] Elton John, Ray Charles and B. B. King (together), Joni Mitchell, and Peter Gabriel were some of the big names that appeared at the Mann in the early 1980s. Hometown favorites Hall & Oates, Philadelphia-area natives Daryl Hall and John Oates, who would become the most successful duo in rock history, played the Mann in 1980 and 1983.

## Battle of the Promoters

By this time, Magid and Allen Spivak had built Electric Factory Concerts into a formidable concert promotion company, one of the most powerful in the nation. They had an especially firm grip on the Philadelphia rock and pop concert industry, including at the Mann, but other area promoters were getting a foothold. One was Black promoter Jimmy Walker, whose company, Sherjam, produced rhythm-and-blues and soul shows. Walker publicly challenged the long-running industry practice of White promoters profiting from booking Black acts. He staged a public protest at the Academy of Music in February 1981 at an Electric Factory–produced show that featured blues artists B. B. King and Bobby "Blue" Bland. To avoid getting embroiled in the conflict, the Academy of Music cancelled upcoming shows booked by Electric Factory and Sherjam, and a legal battle ensued.[18] Whether Walker's activism had something to do with it is unknown, but Sherjam began producing shows at the Mann that summer, including concerts by the Temptations, the Dells, Harold Melvin and the Blue Notes, the Stylistics, and others. Sherjam had a presence at the venue through much of the 1980s, generally producing a few shows a year.

Another local promoter who worked his way into producing shows at the Mann Center in the 1980s was future restaurateur Stephen Starr. Long before Starr Restaurants, the very successful company he established in the mid-1990s, Starr began as a music promoter in Philadelphia in the late 1970s. His cabaret club Stars in Old City and, later, his music hall Ripley's on South Street booked established and emerging musical artists, but Starr wanted to get out of running clubs and into booking concerts. "At the end of the day, those clubs couldn't really make money," he said.[19] He started promoting shows around town, and sometime around 1980 he approached Fredric Mann about doing concerts at the Mann Center. As Starr describes it, he was David going up against Philadelphia's Goliath, Electric Factory Concerts. Mann had a lucrative arrangement with Magid and Electric Factory Concerts and was reluctant to open the venue to unproven promoters. Starr recalled the circumstances in an interview years later:

> In the very beginning, when I first started my concert promoting career, it was very difficult to actually get the Mann Music Center to allow me to do shows. They pretty much exclusively dealt with Electric Factory. I met with Fredric Mann one day, who was a big, cigar-smoking guy, and he wasn't very nice to me. I was a young guy; I didn't know what I was doing. He was like a stereotypical Hollywood producer. Big cigar. I had a lot of chutzpah back then and [after the meeting] I sent him a letter from a lawyer, pretty much threatening that we would consider filing an anti-trust action if he didn't allow me to do shows. This was around 1980.

Mann subsequently relented, but Starr then had to contend with the fact that between the Orchestra concerts and Electric Factory shows, very few dates were available:

> [Mann] then called me back in and allowed me to do shows. But it was difficult getting the dates because I'd say, "How about August 5?" . . . "Nope that's booked." . . . "OK, how about August 8?" . . . "No, we got something there, too." I had to play a lot of games to get where I wanted to get.

■ Stephen Starr at his club Stars in Old City Philadelphia in 1980, around the time he began booking shows at the Mann Center. Published in *The Philadelphia Inquirer*, October 23, 1980. (From *The Philadelphia Inquirer*. © 1980 Philadelphia Inquirer, LLC. All rights reserved. Used under license. *The Philadelphia Inquirer* photograph collection, Special Collections Research Center, Temple University Libraries)

Grabey confirms the scenario: "I remember always having to tell him, 'Sorry, Stephen, those dates are booked.'"[20] Starr persisted and eventually was able to produce shows at the Mann. His biggest success was a pair of concerts in 1986 that were part of a reunion tour by The Monkees. The pop-rock group had been hugely popular in the late 1960s due to their hit TV show and then had a resurgence in the 1980s when MTV began showing reruns of the program. "The Monkees' reunion went crazy," Starr remembers. "It sold out in about 15 minutes. It was one of the more fun shows. . . . Other shows I did there were Steve Winwood, Kenny G, and Michael Bolton."

The Mann Center's relationship with Magid and Electric Factory Concerts continued to present a challenge for Starr, however:

> Larry and I are good friends now, but there definitely was a David and Goliath thing going on. I was young, he was *the* guy, and I fought for dates. What happened there and at the Spectrum [the South Philadelphia arena where Electric Factory booked major rock shows] was whoever could hold the dates got the dates. If you got word that Lionel Richie was touring in the beginning of August, if Larry found out before I did, even if it was a day, he would call the Spectrum or the Mann and hold all the dates for the first week in August. So I was kind of screwed.

> So what happened in the end, those facilities started holding the dates no longer for the promoter, but for the act. So Lionel Richie has August 1—it's either Larry or Stephen is going to get the date. And then we would compete. It was based on money, but also many times [the artists] felt more comfortable with him, because he was, you know, the godfather of promoters, the biggest.[21]

Starr's difficulty in securing open dates at the Spectrum, the Mann, and other local venues led him to pursue a project to build a new venue just across the Delaware River from Philadelphia, in Camden, New Jersey, where he would not have to compete with other promoters. While he ultimately dropped out before the project came to fruition, he helped set the wheels in motion for the new outdoor arena, which opened in 1995. As we shall see, the Camden venue would lead to a major decline in the fortunes of the Mann Center.

In 1985, Electric Factory produced some two dozen shows at the Mann Center, but much of the company's attention that summer was focused on Live Aid, the massive rock concert held on July 13, 1985, that the company coproduced with the famous San Francisco–based promoter Bill Graham. An international benefit to raise money to address world hunger, Live Aid was held at John F. Kennedy (JFK) Stadium in South Philadelphia, with a simultaneous concert at Wembley Stadium in London. Almost 90,000 people attended in Philadelphia and 72,000 in London, while a worldwide audience of almost two billion watched on television as the biggest names in rock performed at the all-day concerts. It was a signal event in the history of rock. But life also went on; that same night, Electric Factory presented jazz fusion guitarist Pat Metheny at the Mann Center. "Live Aid was produced and booked in five weeks," Magid remembers. "Metheny was booked months earlier, and they didn't want to move their show."[22]

## The Board

As in prior decades, the Mann Center Board in the 1980s included some heavy hitters: political insider Richard A. Doran, who in 1980 was appointed Philadelphia city representative and director of commerce (Fredric Mann's former position); wealthy philanthropists Meyer Potamkin and F. Eugene Dixon; businessmen Joseph Neubauer and John Bunting, chief executive officers, respectively, of Aramark and First Pennsylvania Bank, two of Philadelphia's major corporations; and, notably, Richard C. Bond and David P. Eastburn, former and current chairmen, respectively, of The Philadelphia Orchestra Association. With Bond and Eastburn on the Board, and Fredric Mann serving on the Orchestra's Board at the time, it was a period of close relations between the two organizations, which had sometimes been at odds over the years. At the April 13, 1983, Mann Center Board of Directors meeting, Mann thanked "the Philadelphia Orchestra Association, through Mr. Eastburn, for its interest in Mann Music Center."[23]

The talents and connections of the Board were needed, as Mann's long-established "Philadelphia Plan" of supporting the summer concerts through Friends of the Mann subscriptions matched by city appropriations was not keeping pace with the increasing costs of presenting the Orchestra and maintaining the venue. In 1981, the Board hired its first development director, Otis Morse, who undertook a range of fundraising activities, including securing corporate contributions and applying for federal and state grants. In January 1982, the Mann launched its first-ever public fundraising campaign, with a goal of raising $2 million. These efforts helped, but the financial situation was daunting. In September 1984, the projected deficit for the recently completed season was $178,800. Mann noted later that the deficit was less than it would have been because "a conductor and several soloists took no fees or (in one case) accepted a reduced fee."[24] In 1985, the Mann held a gala fundraising concert, with Henry Mancini conducting and James Galway as featured soloist.

## Joseph Kluger Arrives

In 1985, Joseph H. Kluger was appointed general manager of The Philadelphia Orchestra Association, having spent the previous seven years as orchestra manager of the New York Philharmonic. He would work for the Orchestra for the next 20 years, becoming president in 1989, and would play a key role in the Orchestra's relations with the Mann until his retirement in 2005:

> When I moved to Philadelphia [in 1985], . . . other than my wife's family, . . . there was only one other person in Philadelphia I knew, and that was Freddie Mann, because I had spent seven years working at the New York Philharmonic, when Zubin Mehta was music director, and Freddie was there all the time. . . . So I knew Freddie and Silvia pretty well. And I came to the [Philadelphia] position welcoming that relationship and was kind of surprised when I started that, not that there was tension, but that there was a separation [between the Mann and the Orchestra]. I was the general manager of the Orchestra, but basically people told me that for six weeks in the summer, I didn't have anything to do. . . . Freddie and Helen Martin were in charge. . . . It evolved over time, but it started out with that perception—that the Mann managed the six weeks of the Orchestra— . . . and we didn't have much to do.
>
> Six full weeks, 18 concerts, three concerts a week. [Only] three rehearsals a week, which was a source of frustration for Freddie and Helen, because it limited the kind of programming they could do. And I have to say, if you look at the guest artists who appeared—an amazing array of soloists and guest

The Great Lawn area was packed with picknickers for the June 17 opening night concert of the 1986 season, featuring violinist Itzhak Perlman, a longtime Mann favorite. (Mann Center for the Performing Arts Archives)

> conductors. You put on a program of standard classical repertoire with a big-name soloist, and you would get 5,000 people. And if you did a Beethoven Ninth [Symphony], you'd get 9,000 or 10,000 people. I don't want to say it was the "golden era," but it was an era of cultural literacy on the part of the audiences that has disappeared, not just from Philadelphia, but from pretty much everywhere.[25]

## Eventful Final Years

There is no record of Fredric Mann's personal monetary contributions to the Dell and the Mann Center over the years, but they had to have been substantial. He was quite wealthy and known to be very generous with causes that were important to him. The two venues were his passion. A hint came in an interview he gave in March 1980, in which he estimated that he had given away some $20 million in support of making classical music free. He had owned several companies and factories over the course of his business career and shared in the interview that, at 76, he was retiring from business to focus on music: "Business interferes with my music, and I've given up the business part." Admitting that he rarely tended to his one remaining factory, Mann-Kraft Box in Newark, New Jersey, he remembered how "the boys at the plant once sent me a cartoon which showed me sitting by a pool and a blonde in a bikini asks me what I do for a living. . . . [I reply that] I'm a director of 12 companies and I take a month's vacation from each."[26]

Mann was involved in a strange controversy in 1981 that brought some famous people together in a tangled legal dispute. James Robb was a Philadelphia Department of Recreation employee who managed the Robin Hood Dell East concerts and had a private organization, the Performing Arts Society, that he founded and directed. Through the Performing Arts Society, he booked the great pianist Vladimir Horowitz in 1978 for a concert, but the notoriously unpredictable Horowitz later reneged, prompting Robb to sue him for $2.5 million. Mann, a good friend of both Horowitz and Robb's boss, Recreation Commissioner Robert Crawford, offered to mediate, but Robb claimed that Mann's proposed resolution benefited only Horowitz and that Robb was being persecuted by Crawford and the Department of Recreation for not accepting it. Robb's lawyer was the notorious attack-dog attorney Roy Cohn, who made his name in the 1950s as chief counsel for the U.S. Senate anticommunist hearings headed by Senator Joseph McCarthy, the infamous "McCarthy hearings." At one point in the dispute, Cohn came to meet with Mann, who insisted that Grabey be present. When Cohn left, Grabey said he wanted to go wash the dirt off his hands, to which Mann replied, "Me first!"[27] The dispute was eventually resolved through an agreement in which the Mann Center produced a Horowitz concert at the Academy of Music and Robb got a fee.[28]

Silvia Mann threw a surprise 80th birthday party for her husband at the Mann Center following the final concert of the 1983 season on August 4. (This was the concert for which saxophonist Larry McKenna joined the Orchestra as an additional player.) Mann's birthday was actually September 13, but he and Silvia were going to be in Paris then, where Mehta was giving Freddie a party following Mehta's performance with the Israel Philharmonic. The 15,000 in attendance at the Mann on August 4 to hear Dutoit and Leontyne Price were invited to stay for ice cream and Tastykakes for all. Price sang "Happy Birthday"; 1,000 balloons were released; and there were performances by the Avalon String Band, the Mark Davis Orchestra, and a balalaika band. The festive night ended with Silvia and Freddie dancing on the Mann stage.[29]

Three months later, Mann was the subject of a highly critical special investigative report by local station KYW-TV on the management of his namesake venue. Entitled "One Mann's Empire," the program aired in November 1983 and began with the investigative reporter stating that "Fredric Mann's contribution to the cultural arts scene in Philadelphia is undeniable, but it appears that that influence has given him virtually complete control over the public theater. One man's empire may be good for Fredric Mann, but taxpayers pay a heavy price for his privilege." The report called into question various financial arrangements between the venue and the city and criticized Mann's tight control of programming at the venue, asserting that he excluded certain local performing arts groups, particularly Black companies such as Philadanco and Opera Ebony, in favor of more famous New York–based companies.

The report concluded by saying that it was the Philadelphia City Council's responsibility to investigate irregularities and unfair practices at a taxpayer-supported venue such as the Mann Center, but nothing ever came of it.[30]

The celebratory 80th birthday bash and the negative investigative report were emblematic of Mann's 40-plus years of public life in Philadelphia, a life that elicited great loyalty and appreciation, on the one hand, and often animosity and resentment, on the other. "People who have ideas and try to do things get accused of many false notions," he told the interviewer in March 1980. "There's a little bit of dictator in all of us. Fortunately, I was blessed with a disproportionately generous share."[31]

In what turned out to be his final year running the summer concert series in 1986, Mann instituted changes designed to raise the artistic quality of the concerts to an even higher level. The schedule was rearranged to provide concerts on Tuesdays, Thursdays, and Fridays, with two rehearsals on Mondays and single rehearsals Tuesdays through Fridays. This would allow considerably more time for conductors and Orchestra musicians to work on new music and fine-tune familiar repertoire. "Mann keeps probing for the way to offer quality, satisfy the audience, and please himself, since he is artistic director, fund-raiser, promoter, and provider of momentum" of the summer concerts, wrote *The Philadelphia Inquirer.* Considering the fundamental question of whether summer concerts should offer lighter fare or reflect the same high standards as the regular season, the *Inquirer* article noted that the 1986 season "seems designed to revive the image of summer music as an extension of the repertoire and quality of the winter season."[32]

This would be Mann's last major innovation at his beloved venue. The amazing life of the benevolent dictator came to an end on February 26, 1987, when Fredric Rand Mann died at 83 while in Florida. He had been ill with a heart condition and pancreatic cancer for some time, but his passing was still a shock. Grabey remembers Helen Martin calling him with the news late that night. "It was one of the worst days of my life," he said. Tributes poured in from across Philadelphia and around the world. Like the passing of his sometime friend and sometime nemesis Eugene Ormandy two years earlier, it was the end of an era in Philadelphia music. "He was the last of the great impresarios," Grabey noted.[33] The *Philadelphia Daily News* summed up Mann's life and impact in an editorial two days later:

> Fredric R. Mann was a paradox. He was loud, abrasive, and domineering, the last person in the world you'd expect to have the artistic sensitivity and exquisite taste unanimously attributed to him by giants in the world of music.
>
> The combination of these contradictory characteristics proved invaluable to Philadelphia for several decades.
>
> It was Mann who rescued Robin Hood Dell from bankruptcy and oblivion, developing a summer series of free concerts which became a model for cities all over America.

■ Fredric R. Mann. (Courtesy of the Mann family)

It was Mann who brought Philadelphians the world's greatest musical artists.

It was Mann who initiated, inspired, and helped finance—out of pocket—construction and development of what was appropriately renamed Mann Music Center.

Music wasn't Mann's only claim to fame. He was a self-made business tycoon, a philanthropist of worldwide renown, onetime ambassador to Barbados and a Philadelphia municipal official—serving as city representative and director of commerce, director of the recreation department, and chairman of the Cultural Affairs Council.

> But Mann's legacy—the one he'd like to be remembered for—lies in the continuing tradition of great music he has helped to guarantee to his fellow Philadelphians.[34]

Joseph Kluger, who knew Mann well from his days at both the New York Philharmonic and The Philadelphia Orchestra, also viewed him as a paradox:

> Freddie was a character. He struck me as gruff and crude and yet at the same time unbelievably sophisticated in terms of his relationships. It always seemed paradoxical to me. . . . And he had a big heart, a really big heart. . . . One of the questions is, "How was he able to get all these [great] artists to come to the Mann Center?" . . . Having spent a good bit of time with all these artists, they're motivated by people they care about, and they care about people who care about them as people, not as starstruck fans. And Freddie had this way of interacting with Zubin [Mehta], with Itzhak [Perlman], Pinchas Zukerman, Isaac Stern, that whole crowd. He just made them feel very comfortable and he was very gracious and entertaining.[35]

"He was cool," said his granddaughter Jane Gitomer. "He never really got old. He used to call me at 2:00 or 3:00 in the morning, just to talk."[36]

## Post-Mann Years

At its March 23, 1987, meeting, the first without Mann, the Mann Center Board began the process of reorganizing. They divided the late president's duties into two newly created positions: chairman of the Board and chief executive officer and president and chief operating officer. Helen Martin, Mann's longtime assistant who had been serving as executive vice president, was elected president and chief operating officer, and at the next meeting, on April 27, Vice President Bernard Guth was elected chairman and chief executive officer. This leadership team would guide the Mann into its new era. Joining the Board at the April 27 meeting was pianist Gary Graffman, who had been appointed director of the Curtis Institute of Music the previous year. In addition to being a Board member, Graffman would perform at the Mann in the late 1980s and early 1990s.*

Martin and Grabey had been running the show with Mann for many years, so in some ways it was business as usual in the late 1980s. The Orchestra still performed

* Graffman's performances in the 1980s and 1990s would be for piano left hand. He suffered a playing-related injury to his right hand in the late 1970s, after which his performing career focused on piano left hand repertoire only, including a number of pieces commissioned especially for him.

three nights a week for six weeks, and top-name conductors and soloists, many of them Mann's dear friends, continued to appear. The 1987 season was dedicated to Mann, and the opening concert featured his longtime friend, violinist Isaac Stern. Before playing, Stern spoke movingly to the audience about Mann, telling them that his appearance that night "was the result of promises I made to Fred Mann. . . . [He] was a special man. He adored music and he adored musicians . . . , and in the achievements of his friends he found joy. . . . He travelled the world, but his home was Philadelphia, and he wanted to build something here so you can enjoy what the city can be and can do. To him, we play. He lived fully and loved fully, and he left something to us." Stern then played the evocative Sarabande from Bach's Partita in D minor for unaccompanied violin.[37] After intermission, he performed Brahms's Violin Concerto, with Dutoit conducting. There would be an annual Fredric R. Mann Memorial Concert from 1988 to 2001, with the 1989 concert honoring both Mann and Ormandy.

June 1989 saw some major highlights at the Mann Center. For six consecutive nights that month, the venue hosted the national touring company of the record-breaking Broadway show *Cats*. It was the first time the Mann hosted a Broad-

■ *Left to right*: Chairman of the Mann Center Board of Directors Bernard Guth and President and Chief Operating Officer Helen Martin with violinists Itzhak Perlman and Pinchas Zukerman and conductor Zubin Mehta at the August 2, 1988, Fredric R. Mann Memorial Concert at the Mann. (Mann Center for the Performing Arts Archives)

way show, and the series was very successful. Two days after *Cats* left, the Orchestra season commenced, on June 19, with a gala concert in honor of Ormandy and Mann, featuring the first public concert in 11 years by pianist Van Cliburn, who had taken a hiatus from performing but returned to play in support of the Mann Center and in honor of his two good friends. Cliburn's return made national news. *The Washington Post* reported, "It became obvious, before Van Cliburn played a single note here tonight, that his concert, with Stanislaw Skrowaczewski conducting the Philadelphia Orchestra—Cliburn's first appearance at a public concert since 1978—would be a triumph."[38]

In the rock and pop realm, Electric Factory Concerts and other promoters presented almost 30 shows at the Mann in 1989, one of the most active seasons ever to that point for nonclassical music at the venue. These shows were an important source of revenue for the Mann, which continued to face daunting financial challenges. Costs were increasing significantly in all phases of the venue's operation—presenting the Orchestra was expected to cost the Mann $150,000 more in 1990 than it had in 1989—and income was not keeping pace. The $2 million endowment campaign launched years earlier had raised only a quarter of its goal by October 1989.[39] Annual deficits were in the hundreds of thousands. On a positive note, in the spring of 1990 the Fairmount Park Commission funded the installation of 4,500 new seats in the open area just beyond the covered seating, replacing the 15-year-old benches with stadium-style seating.[40]

There was a potentially disastrous development in the early 1990s, however. Since the venue opened in 1976, the Robin Hood Dell/Mann Center Board had leased the property from the Fairmount Park Commission for $1 per year under a concession agreement. Leases were generally for four years, more or less coinciding with the terms of city mayoral administrations. When Edward G. Rendell assumed office as mayor in January 1992, Philadelphia was in financial crisis and on the verge of bankruptcy. With the Mann Center running six-figure deficits, the venue costing the Fairmount Park Commission some $300,000 in yearly maintenance, and the city appropriating hundreds of thousands of dollars annually to match the Friends of the Mann subscriptions, the new administration viewed the Mann as an unnecessary financial burden on the taxpayers.

At its March 10, 1993, meeting, the Fairmount Park Commission voted to lease the venue to the Mann Center Board for another year, but it also voted to invite proposals from other entities to take it over and operate it. "We are hoping for a new bidder to relieve us of some of the financial burden," said commission member Robert N. C. Nix III.[41] Such a vote would have been inconceivable during Mann's chairmanship of the commission, or that of his successor, his protégé and longtime friend Robert Crawford, but they were now gone—one deceased; the other retired. The Mann Board was navigating a very different political landscape. Electric Factory Concerts and Spectacor, the sports and entertainment company that owned the

Spectrum, reportedly expressed some interest in leasing the venue, but nothing ever developed with finding a new tenant.[42] The Mann Center Board continued to lease and operate the venue.

## The Dutoit Years

The Board had been discussing the need for a music director for the summer concerts for several years before Mann's death, but after his passing, the need became acute.[43] It was time for someone to bring a singular artistic vision to the summer series—to plan the programs, conductors, and soloists, as Mann had done—and to lead a substantial number of the concerts. Charles Dutoit had been helping Martin in this capacity unofficially since Mann's passing; at the same time, his profile with The Philadelphia Orchestra was rising. When the Orchestra's music director for its August residency at Saratoga (SPAC), Dennis Russell Davies, resigned in 1988, it created an opportunity for a cooperative arrangement. On March 10, 1989, The Philadelphia Orchestra and the Mann Music Center held a luncheon at the Academy of Music to announce that they had engaged Dutoit to serve as artistic director and principal conductor for both summer series in 1990 and 1991, with an option for 1992. Dutoit would hold the Mann position until 1999 and the SPAC position until 2010.

Kluger, then the Orchestra's general manager but soon to be named president, said in a later interview that, from a practical standpoint in terms of maximizing rehearsal time, Dutoit having the dual role "was really convenient, really a good solution, given the lack of rehearsals. . . . Some of the programs were different [between SPAC and the Mann], but a lot of them were repeated. . . . It really worked out well." Kluger noted, however, that Dutoit thought the appointments put him in a position to be the Orchestra's next music director when its current one, Wolfgang Sawallisch, retired.[44] When this did not happen, there was a major fallout at the Mann. But that would take place 10 years later. For most of the 1990s, the relationship between Dutoit and the Mann was a harmonious one.

The Dutoit years at the Mann were successful artistically, if not financially. The Swiss-born conductor presided over many notable concerts from 1990 to 1999. July 9, 1990, saw the return of violinist Nadja Salerno-Sonnenberg, now an international star, who grew up in Cherry Hill, New Jersey; studied at the Curtis Institute of Music; and made her debut at a Robin Hood Dell Children's Concert in 1971 at age 10 (see pages 221–222). The Fredric R. Mann and William Kapell memorial concerts continued with a variety of featured artists, Gary Graffman and André Watts among them.

Dutoit was on the podium for part of the program when the great soul singer Aretha Franklin made her debut at the Mann on July 3, 1992, in a "Sounds of Freedom" concert presented as part of the city's July 4 celebrations that year. Dutoit led the first part of the all-American concert, which included local television sportscaster (and, later, news anchor) Ukee Washington narrating Aaron Copland's *Lincoln*

■ Charles Dutoit, Mann Center music director from 1990 to 1999. (Mann Center for the Performing Arts Archives)

■ Flyer for a 1998 Peter Nero and the Philly Pops concert at the Mann Center. (Mann Center for the Performing Arts Archives)

*Portrait*, after which Franklin's musical director led the Orchestra in accompanying Aretha, who sang many of her hits. At one point, Franklin brought out another great soul singer, Philadelphia native Teddy Pendergrass, who had been one of the most successful vocalists in the "Philly Soul" style of Black popular music in the 1970s and early 1980s, to sing with her. Pendergrass was at the height of his fame when he was paralyzed in a car accident on Lincoln Drive in Philadelphia in 1982. He made a successful comeback several years later, singing from a wheelchair—his first return appearance was at Live Aid in 1985—and was warmly welcomed when he sang with Aretha at the Mann.

In 1993, German conductor Wolfgang Sawallisch replaced Riccardo Muti as music director of The Philadelphia Orchestra. Like Muti, Sawallisch would rarely conduct at the Mann. He led three concerts in 1995 and a memorable September 11 benefit concert in 2001, but he otherwise did not appear at the venue. As noted in the Mann Center Board minutes, however, before one of his 1995 concerts, "Maestro Sawallisch visited the picnickers at the top of the hill."[45]

Dutoit programmed a number of pops concerts during his tenure, which were a big draw. Local favorite Peter Nero, longtime director and pianist of the Philly Pops, brought his ensemble to the Mann for multiple shows in 1992 and 1998. Born in Brooklyn in 1934, Nero had been in the spotlight since he was featured on national television with Paul Whiteman at 17 performing

■ Brochure announcing the 1997 PNC Summer Concert Series at the Mann Center, the third year of PNC Bank's sponsorship of the concerts. (Mann Center for the Performing Arts Archives)

Gershwin's *Rhapsody in Blue*. Performing engagements, recording sessions, and TV appearances followed, and he won a Grammy for best new artist in 1961. When Moe Septee established the Philly Pops in 1979, he chose Nero as founding musical director. "Peter Nero and the Philly Pops" were a ubiquitous presence in Philadelphia during his 34-year leadership of the ensemble. They played the Mann many times, where Nero's mix of top-notch jazz piano skills and engaging pops conducting were always a hit.

Composer Marvin Hamlisch led pops concerts at the Mann in 1994 and 1997 as well. Hamlisch had had great success since the 1970s as a songwriter and Broadway and film composer and was doing quite a bit of conducting in the 1990s. He was named principal conductor of the Pittsburgh Symphony Pops in 1995.

Genre-bending vocalist Bobby McFerrin conducted three Philadelphia Orchestra concerts at the Mann in the mid-1990s. Appearing as conductor and vocalist in 1995 and 1996, he led the Orchestra in traditional symphonic repertoire while also displaying his amazing vocal and improvisatory skills in a range of vocal pieces, many of them made up on the spot. In 1997, he led the Orchestra and a chorus of regional singers in a concert performance of Gershwin's opera *Porgy and Bess*. McFerrin toured this version of *Porgy and Bess* in honor of his father, Robert McFerrin Sr., who was the first Black man to sing at the Metropolitan Opera in 1955 and who dubbed the singing parts for actor Sidney Poitier, who portrayed Porgy in the 1959 film version of the landmark opera.

Jerry Grabey rarely booked concerts at the Mann himself, focusing mainly on his duties as general manager. But with Septee's help, he booked "In the Fiddler's

House," a concert on July 29, 1997, that featured violinist Itzhak Perlman and several Klezmer groups, ensembles that played lively, ancient Jewish instrumental dance and celebration music. While a respected classical artist, Perlman was versatile. "He could play anything," said Grabey. "Classical, bluegrass, klezmer—you name it."[46]

The Mann received a financial boost in 1994 when PNC Bank took on sponsorship of the Orchestra concerts, the first time in the organization's 64-year history that its summer series had a named corporate sponsor. On January 10, 1994, PNC President and Chief Executive Officer Richard L. Smoot, Dutoit, and Kluger announced that the concerts would now be called the "PNC Bank Summer Concert Series." "We intend to make a significant contribution," said Smoot, noting that he envisioned a long-term relationship and that PNC would "distribute Mann tickets at our 81 branches, create a scholarship grant, and offer our marketing expertise."[47] PNC's sponsorship continued until 2002.

## More Pop, Rock, and Soul

Nonclassical concerts became a key part of the Mann's programming in the 1990s, as well as a continued important source of income. During the six-week symphonic season, Electric Factory and other promoters would squeeze shows in between Orchestra concerts when they could, but in August, after the Orchestra series had concluded, the Mann was essentially a rock and pop venue. Many of the biggest names in contemporary music made the Mann a stop on their summer tours. Bonnie Raitt headlined three shows in the early 1990s. She had lived in Philadelphia in the late 1960s and started her professional career in the city. After having moderate success as a recording and touring artist in the 1970s and 1980s—including headlining Mann shows in 1981 and 1982—her breakthrough 1989 album *Nick of Time* won four Grammy awards and sold more than five million copies, propelling her to superstardom. Her Mann concerts in 1990, 1994, and 1995 were very successful. James Taylor was another perennial favorite, doing a total of seven concerts at the Mann in the 1990s. Bob Dylan appeared in 1988 and 1997. "Dylan got off his tour bus, did his show, and got back on the tour bus; didn't use the dressing room or Green Room," remembers Grabey.[48]

Many top-name Black artists performed at the Mann in this period as well. Barry White; Earth, Wind, and Fire; the Isley Brothers; Salt-N-Pepa; and Frankie Beverly and Maze with Gladys Knight were among the soul and rhythm-and-blues artists to headline shows in the 1990s. These were all Electric Factory–produced concerts, however; there were very few Black promoters at the Mann at this time. (Sherjam Concerts stopped producing shows at the venue at some point in the 1980s.) One major exception was the June 5, 1994, concert by James Brown, the "Godfather of Soul," his one and only appearance at the Mann. That concert was produced by the great Philadelphia DJ Georgie Woods, "the Guy with the Goods," who had produced the shows at the legendary Uptown Theater on North Broad Street, Philadelphia's premier Black music venue in the 1950s and 1960s. Radio station WIOQ's fifth annual Q-102 Monster Jam, held on September 25, 1993, saw the Mann debut of the West Philadelphia rap duo DJ Jazzy Jeff and the Fresh Prince (Jeff Townes and Will Smith), who had catapulted to fame five years earlier on the strength of their platinum-selling second album, *He's the DJ, I'm the Rapper.*

The Mann also became a favorite stop for jam bands in the 1990s. The term *jam band* came into general use in the 1980s to describe rock bands whose music is characterized by extended improvisational passages that often fuse rock with elements of jazz, blues, folk, country, and electronic music. Their audiences are composed of loyal followers who revel in the extended jams and give the concerts a festive, communal atmosphere. The jam-band style dates to the late 1960s when groups such as the Grateful Dead and Allman Brothers developed dedicated fan bases with live shows that featured lengthy instrumental passages. The style came into more widespread popularity in the 1990s with groups such as Phish, the Dave Matthews Band, and others achieving commercial success as touring and recording artists. The ambiance of the Mann—its beautiful natural setting, ample room to spread out, and varied concession areas—made it an ideal venue for the celebratory communal gatherings of jam-band shows.

The Grateful Dead, the grandfathers of the jam-band movement, never appeared at the Mann as a full band before disbanding following the death of the group's guitarist Jerry Garcia in 1995, but Garcia had brought his side group, the Jerry Garcia Band, to the Mann in 1984, and Bob Weir, another Grateful Dead founding member, performed with his frequent partner, bassist Rob Wasserman, in 1991 and 1992. The Allman Brothers appeared every year from 1990 to 1994. In 1992, the group Blues Traveler initiated the HORDE (Horizons of Rock Developing Everywhere) Festival, a traveling collective of jam bands that played the Mann in 1994 and 1995. Perhaps more than any other group, Phish, the Vermont-based band led by guitarist Trey Anastasio, inherited the mantle of the Grateful Dead and became the preeminent jam band of the 1990s. Phish appeared at the Mann every year from 1992 to 1995, the last a sold-out two-concert series. Both the Grateful Dead and the Allman Brothers also spawned spin-off bands that played the Mann at one time or another.

## Challenge from Camden

Of the many challenges the Mann Center faced in the 1990s, the one that had the biggest long-term impact came from the opening in June 1995 of the Blockbuster-Sony Music Entertainment Centre, popularly known as the "E-Centre" in its early years, on the Delaware riverfront in Camden, just across the river from Philadelphia. (The venue went through several corporate sponsorships and name changes over the years; in 2022, it was rechristened the Freedom Mortgage Pavilion.) The new venue had minimal effect on the Mann in its first year, but things would change dramatically starting in 1996.

As previously noted, it was Stephen Starr who initiated the Camden venue project. The riverfront area of Camden was poised for a major revitalization around 1990. A park area had been created along the river, and there were plans for an aquarium and Minor League Baseball stadium (which opened in 1992 and 2001, respectively). With its attractive waterfront location, convenient access from Philadelphia, and beautiful view of the city skyline, it seemed an ideal location for an outdoor music venue. "I'm the one who did the Camden facility; I negotiated the deal, all in an effort to have my own amphitheater that I could control," said Starr. "I was David, they [Electric Factory] were Goliath, and I was trying to win. . . . I made a deal with Sony [and] Pace [Entertainment Group, a Texas-based concert promotion company], brought them into Camden with the developer of the project there, to do the amphitheater."[49]

But in 1990, as the project was starting to come together, Starr sold his concert business to Electric Factory Concerts. "[The Camden amphitheater] was in part the catalyst, I think, that caused Electric Factory to want to buy [my company]," Starr said.[50] As he told the *Daily News* at the time—prophetically, as it turned out—he felt that "the concert business was going in a direction that was not positive for the small promoter. It seems the big corporations across the country will be the promoters of the future."[51] Starr left the Camden project, and the concert world in general, and began to focus on the restaurant business. One of Electric Factory Concerts' chief competitors was now no longer a factor, but a few years later the E-Centre would present a more serious challenge to the powerful rock concert company, and then present an intriguing opportunity.

The Mann and the E-Centre were both large outdoor concert venues near downtown Philadelphia, but the E-Centre held 25,000 people versus the Mann's 14,000, and the Mann was owned by the City of Philadelphia and run by a nonprofit. It did not have the resources or institutional flexibility of the privately owned E-Centre, backed by Sony and Pace, a deep-pocketed Texas promoter. The Mann Center–Electric Factory partnership battled the E-Centre for the rock and pop audience in 1995, then the E-Centre made Electric Factory an offer. Magid shared his perspective on the turn of events in a later interview:

> We had a battle on our hands. We were battling a company, [Pace,] based in Houston, Texas, that was formidable, they had a lot of money. They owned [the E-Centre]. . . . At that point, I was pretty well situated, known. Our company did great shows. We had done Live Aid. [We had] great relationships with managers, agents, acts. But we knew we weren't going to be able to have everybody [play the Mann]. The amphitheater in Camden was double the size of the Mann. . . . When you're bidding for an act and somebody offers them twice as much money, you know, friendship a lot of times just goes out the door. And you understand that; that's reality. But we fought them pretty good.

Larry Magid at JFK Stadium in South Philadelphia in September 1988, preparing for the star-studded Human Rights Now! concert. Magid's company, Electric Factory Concerts, was the main promoter of rock and pop concerts at the Mann Center from 1976 to 1995. (*The Philadelphia Inquirer* photograph collection, Special Collections Research Center, Temple University Libraries)

> At the end of the [first] season, they were pretty bloodied. They lost millions of dollars. . . . We didn't make a lot of money, but we held them at bay.

After the E-Centre's first season, Pace approached Electric Factory Concerts with a lucrative offer to be the exclusive promoter of shows at the new venue. Magid went to Richard Doran, chairman of the Mann Center Board, about getting a better deal at the Mann, but, as detailed later, the Mann was deep in debt, in the midst of difficult negotiations with the city regarding its lease of the venue, and in deliberations with The Philadelphia Orchestra, to which it owed more than $1 million. It was in no position to sweeten Electric Factory's deal. Magid picks up the story:

> After that [first] year, [Pace] came to us and offered us a deal. And I had gone back to Dick Doran, who was the head of the [Mann] Board at that time, and we said, "Look, we'll stick around, we'll fight this out." But the only way we can fight it out is if we can get a better deal, negotiate a better deal . . . with any revenue stream we can possibly get. We wanted to be the loyal company, but we're not going to be able to do that with the money that's on the table. We were only going to be able to go so far. We went back and forth. There were four meetings that the Board had, and I had gone to the Board with a proposal.

> [But] because they were supporting the Orchestra, and any money that would have come to us was money that would have gone to the Orchestra, and even though they were a non-profit, it wasn't enough to do both things.
>
> We had to choose, and we went to Camden, made a deal with Pace [in 1996]. Went there and put them on the map, as we did with other venues. It was the right choice, at the time. It was never [going to be] viable [at the Mann], it just couldn't be. You don't make up for double the size, so we chose. . . . We were able to maintain the relationships with our acts, which was crucial to our business. We were told that in no uncertain terms by the agents.

Electric Factory did not completely abandon the Mann; it still produced some concerts there. "Some shows just belong there," Magid said. But starting in 1996, the overwhelming majority of its summer bookings would be at the E-Centre. "It just stands to reason, you're going to make more money with doubling the size [of the venue]."[52]

As Electric Factory phased out at the Mann, a new company, New Park Entertainment, began booking shows there in 1997. New Park was a group of four partners who had all worked for Electric Factory for long periods and recently left. They booked the Indigo Girls, Iggy Pop, Pat Benatar, Styx, and other groups in their first year at the Mann.[53] Electric Factory actually sued New Park to prevent the group from using "trade secrets and confidential information" they learned while working for Electric Factory. Like Starr's company, New Park Entertainment was a competent promoter but paled in comparison with the power and influence of Electric Factory Concerts. The loss of Electric Factory's bookings was a major blow to the Mann Center.

## New Name, New Direction

Richard Doran succeeded Bernard Guth as chairman of the Mann Center Board in February 1995, just as the E-Centre was about to open. While his term lasted only two years, he set in motion profound changes at the institution. This was an especially trying time for the Mann, as issues that had been brewing over the years were coming to a head while the Board was in the midst of difficult negotiations with the city over a new concession agreement for operating the venue. Doran told the Board at one point that the city was "attempting to drive a 'hard bargain' because of fiscal issues" at the Mann. At the same time, the Board was negotiating with The Philadelphia Orchestra Association over its mounting debt to the Orchestra, which had grown to more than $1 million. To complicate matters, the city was requiring the Mann to resolve its financial issues with the Orchestra before it would enter into a concession agreement with the organization.[54] While all of this was happening, attendance at Orchestra concerts was declining and, as noted earlier, Electric Factory Concerts was shifting its focus to the E-Centre, significantly reducing the number of concerts it booked at the Mann and depriving the Mann of an important revenue stream.

The terms of the city lease agreement were hammered out in the fall of 1996, and the agreement was signed in early 1997. That resolved one major issue, but breaking out of the cycle of shrinking audiences, declining revenues, and mounting debt required a bold reimagining of the Mann's future and its role as a performing arts venue. Doran outlined his vision for this future in a 12-point memo he presented to the Mann Board at its January 2, 1997, meeting. The memo opened with the following three recommendations:

1. It is proposed that The Mann be officially renamed "The Mann Center for the Performing Arts" and that a full program of cultural, artistic, and related events be scheduled between the months of May and September.
2. The core program will be the six week Philadelphia Orchestra season but will also contain a full array of popular concerts and other events which can produce revenue, recognition, and attendance across a wide segment of the public: Broadway shows in concert; rock concerts; ballet; contemporary dance; chamber music; country and western; opera staged or in concert; special events. . . .
3. In order to achieve this goal, an aggressive marketing and promotional campaign must begin now for the 1997 season and beyond.

Doran concluded the memo with an inspirational call to action:

> To me, the bottom line is that I view the Mann as potentially one of the best, if not the best, summer performing arts venue in the country. I have no doubt that it can succeed along the lines I have outlined. To do so, however, will take the commitment, determination, and support of the Board, the staff, the city, the Orchestra, and its other present and potential stakeholders. The time to begin that process is now.[55]

The Board unanimously adopted the memo "as the strategic plan for the Mann Music Center" at the January 2 meeting.[56] At the next meeting on February 3, Doran resigned from the Board and Craig Millard, owner of a major real estate firm, was elected to replace him. Millard told the Board that he "believes there is now a consensus where the Mann must go in order to stay in existence. He said that the Mann is in 'deep trouble' and this should not be 'candy coated.' He believes we need to negotiate a new relationship with the Orchestra; we need to renegotiate the Concession Agreement with the City, and we need to work on popular bookings."[57]

Immediately following the meeting, Mann leadership held a news conference at the Four Seasons Hotel at which Millard announced the new name and new direction for the venue. Among those in attendance were Dutoit, Mayor Rendell, Silvia Mann, and President Richard Smoot of PNC Bank, which was still sponsoring The

Helen Martin, Beverly Sills, and Van Cliburn at a fundraising event for the Mann Center. (Mann Center for the Performing Arts Archives)

Philadelphia Orchestra's summer concerts.[58] With the public now informed of the changes, Millard's next priority was finding a replacement for Helen Martin, who had told the Board during the planning process that she was retiring after the 1997 season. Having worked at the Robin Hood Dell and Mann Center in various capacities for more than 50 years, the last 10 as president, Martin had done remarkable things for the institution, but it was time for someone else to take the helm and lead the institution into the new era. She would stay on in a consulting capacity after her retirement, however.

Debbie Lobel, who began as production manager at the Mann in 1996, remembers Martin as "an amazing woman who was a well-known figurehead in the classical music world. There weren't very many women around in her position. . . . She had a good command of the classical world, and people really respected her."[59]

## The Peter Lane Era

In July 1997, the Mann announced that Peter B. Lane had accepted the position of president and chief executive officer at the Mann. Lane had been an orchestral musician early in his career, playing bass with the San Francisco Opera and Ballet, and since 1988 he had been executive director of the New York Pops Orchestra at Carnegie Hall. He had taken the Pops from an ensemble with a $200,000 annual budget to one of several million dollars. In an interview prior to starting at the Mann, he told *The Philadelphia Inquirer* that he was well aware of the challenges he would be facing: "It's a critical situation, but I came in here with my eyes wide open." He said that the Mann must focus on "creating programs that enrich, excite, and entertain. They need to reflect the diversity of the community. . . . Freddy Mann's vision was for a community resource. We need to build on that vision."*[60]

Lane officially began on September 1, 1997. As he shared in an interview years later, the situation when he started was bleak: "We had all but three staff members when I arrived. With Helen [Martin] gone, there were [only] a couple of people left. We had seasonal staff like [Production Manager] Debbie Lobel, who was there, and Jim McCafferty running the box office, but in terms of internal staff, administrative staff, it was basically Jerry Grabey and I and one or two other people. Jerry . . . was one of the key people still there as the continuity."[61]

Martin, although retired, would continue to book conductors and soloists for Music Director Charles Dutoit, at both the Mann and The Philadelphia Orchestra's other summer home, the Saratoga Performing Arts Center. As Lane recalled, Dutoit and Martin had been booking artists together at the two venues for several years, and Dutoit wanted to continue the arrangement. "Helen was asked by Charlie to stay on because at that time . . . he was dual music director for both SPAC and for the Mann."[62] The arrangement worked for a couple of years, but it would eventually lead to friction between Dutoit and the Mann.

Lane was coming on board as the fallout was setting in from Electric Factory Concerts' decision in 1996 to largely abandon the Mann and set up shop at the E-Centre in Camden, upending the financial model under which the Mann had been operating. As Lane described it: "The Friends of the Mann . . . were the subscription base; they paid for the right to be [under cover], down in the center [at the Orchestra concerts] . . . and at one point it may have paid for the free [lawn] tickets, but that was when we were doing 25 rock-and-roll shows a year and it was paying the bills. . . . That's what financed the Orchestra; it wasn't the seats in the front." Referencing the "Rock pays for Bach" formula, Lane noted, "When the rock went away, we couldn't pay the Bach. We couldn't pay The Philadelphia Orchestra. . . . And so, in essence, if you look at the opening of the Electric Factory [concerts in] Camden, it was the beginning of the demise of the business model. And hence, when I got there, we had to do a refresh."†[63]

"Refresh" was putting it mildly; radical changes were coming to the Mann.

---

* Lane was the nephew of Peter Benoliel, who was chairman of The Philadelphia Orchestra Association Board at the time. However, Benoliel was not involved in the search process that resulted in Lane's hiring.

† Lane's "rock went away" statement is referring to the major drop in revenue when Electric Factory moved most of its concerts to Camden. Rock and pop concerts did not stop at the Mann; New Park Entertainment stepped in to produce concerts in the late 1990s, but its shows did not produce anywhere near the revenue that Electric Factory's did.

# 10.

## 1998–2007

*Millennial Challenges, Expanding Mission*

"Visitors to the Mann Center for the Performing Arts this summer will find a new attitude," proclaimed the *Philadelphia Daily News* on the eve of the 1998 season, "from the way you're greeted to the way they entertain you, feed you and finally send you blissfully into the night." It was the first season under new President and Chief Executive Officer Peter Lane, who noted, "We've literally rethought the operation from the ground up—from the parking to the programs to the visitor amenities."[1]

Indeed, the changes were major. The number of programs was essentially doubled, from about 30 in 1997 to almost 60 in 1998, with a striking level of variety in the musical offerings. There was a new food court and an upscale preconcert buffet dinner service, both under the direction of a new concessionaire, Steve Poses, proprietor of the innovative Frog Commissary in Center City. "Come for Dinner, Stay for the Show" was the motto. And the policy of offering free outdoor tickets to the entire Orchestra season, a hallmark since Fredric Mann instituted it in 1953, was dramatically reduced. The newspaper–coupon clipping system for free lawn seats was kept for just six of the 18 Orchestra concerts; for the other 12, the Mann distributed blocks of tickets to local nonprofits. The old system was "basically [being] exploited by the same well-heeled demographic that buys the indoor tickets," Lane noted. PNC Bank continued to sponsor the orchestra series, with season passes offered at the very affordable rate of $75, about $4 per concert.[2]

## Performing Arts for the People

But the biggest change was in the music itself—both the orchestral concerts and the popular and contemporary shows. On the orchestral side, Charles Dutoit, working under a new mandate, programmed a lot of pops concerts and lighter symphonic fare. Peter Nero and the Philly Pops did four concerts: "Broadway Bound" and "Night at the Oscars" programs and concerts featuring singer and actress Bernadette Peters and trumpeter Doc Severinsen. "The Pops can do a Broadway- or Hollywood-themed concert with a soloist like Bernadette Peters or Doc Severinsen for a lot less than the $70,000 we pay the orchestra for a night's work," said Mann Board Chairman Craig Millard.[3] Peters was then a major Broadway and film star, and Severinsen was known to millions from his time as bandleader for *The Tonight Show Starring Johnny Carson* from 1967 to 1992. To draw more diverse audiences, there were themed Philadelphia Orchestra concerts such as "A Latin Extravaganza," "A Gospel Salute," and "A Gershwin Celebration."

There was also a conscious effort to present more young, emerging soloists and conductors, as opposed to established stars, again to save money. Fredric Mann's vision of offering summer audiences a full season of world-renowned artists and "serious" repertoire along the lines of the Orchestra's regular-season concerts at the Academy of Music was not abandoned completely—Van Cliburn, Pinchas Zukerman, and Martha Argerich (Dutoit's ex-wife) all appeared in 1998, and Dutoit programmed Beethoven, Schubert, and Mendelssohn, among other great masters—but such artists and repertoire were more the exception than the rule now. "When you think of concerts outside in the summer, you think pops," said Lane. "Clearly, Charlie [Dutoit] has taken a direction I'm very pleased with. I think we're doing what we need to be doing, to identify ourselves as distinct from the programming down at Broad and Locust [the location of the Academy of Music]."[4]

Among the emerging classical artists who appeared at the Mann in 1998 were Hilary Hahn and Leila Josefowicz—Hahn making her debut; Josefowicz, her second appearance—two violinists in their late teens who had studied at the Curtis Institute of Music and were on the cusp of international careers. Pianist Marcus Roberts, who had been in Wynton Marsalis's jazz group in the 1980s and who, like Marsalis, was adept in both jazz and classical music, debuted at the July 2 "Gospel Salute" concert. Led by The Philadelphia Orchestra's assistant conductor André Raphel Smith, the program featured all Black performers, with Roberts in Gershwin's *Rhapsody in Blue* and performances by two local choral groups—Chorus of Regional Singers and Joy Unlimited Youth Mass Choir—directed by choral conductor Donald Dumpson.

Showcasing emerging artists had long been a tradition at the Mann and Robin Hood Dell, but it was now an economic necessity. Fredric Mann was no longer around to support appearances by top-name artists (or get them to appear for free);

Peter Nero, Peter Lane, and Doc Severinsen at the Mann Center in July 1998. (Courtesy of Peter Lane)

the city ended its annual subsidy in 1997; and the ticket-buying audience for symphonic music had declined. PNC's sponsorship helped, but it was not enough. "We ended last year $1.4 million in the hole," Lane noted. "We were perilously close to losing the crown jewel of Fairmount Park and Philadelphia's summer cultural season."[5] The Mann was built as the summer home of The Philadelphia Orchestra, and this would always be a key part of its identity, but Mann leadership increasingly looked to popular and contemporary music to keep the enterprise going. That was much more difficult now, with Electric Factory Concerts and the E-Centre monopolizing the biggest rock artists, but the Mann managed to carve out a place in the Philadelphia concert landscape with its mix of classical and contemporary programming.

The variety of programs in the 1998 season was impressive. "The aim is diversity," Chairman Millard declared. "We want to be all things to a whole lot of people."[6] The Mann partnered with the Philadelphia Clef Club of Jazz and Performing Arts, the jazz education institution that had recently opened an impressive new facility in

South Philadelphia, on a new "Jazz at the Mann" series. The series included concerts by Wynton Marsalis and the Lincoln Center Jazz Orchestra, the Count Basie Orchestra, the Preservation Hall Jazz Band, and double bills of Nancy Wilson with Joe Williams and Dave Brubeck with Betty Carter.

New Park Entertainment, the promotion company composed of former Electric Factory employees, booked almost 20 rock, pop, and folk shows in 1998. Among others, they included Ani DiFranco, Dan Fogelberg, blues guitarists Buddy Guy and Jonny Lang, Culture Club and the Human League, Irish artists Sinead O'Connor and the Chieftains, and "An Evening of Real Live Songs," with singer-songwriters Richard Thompson, Dar Williams, and Bruce Cockburn. The Irish artists and "Real Lives Songs" concerts were package shows that New Park put together that debuted at the Mann and went on to other cities. The key was finding the right artists for the venue, said New Park's Larry Ahearn. "Maybe [heavy metal band] Metallica shouldn't be playing here, but there are a lot of acts who appreciate and deserve the Mann's more intimate atmosphere and better sound."[7] The 1998 season concluded with a very successful two-week run by the popular Irish dance show *Riverdance*.

In the midst of the eclectic season, the Mann hosted a gala concert capping off daylong celebrations honoring singer, actor, and civil rights activist Harry Belafonte with the inaugural presentation of the new Marian Anderson Award. Anderson herself had established the award in 1943 to support worthy young singers, and it had gone through different incarnations and dormant periods over the years before being revived in 1998 to honor notable humanitarians. The June 27, 1998, concert featured mezzo-soprano Florence Quivar, singer and pianist Harry Connick Jr., and the Marian Anderson Award Chorus, whose members were drawn from the choir at Union Baptist Church, the South Philadelphia congregation where Anderson began singing.

## Raising Money, Reducing Debt

The Mann's operating budget increased from $2.5 million in 1997 to $4.7 million in 1998 to support the dramatically expanded programming.[8] In April 1999, Lane hired Nancy Newman as director of development and tasked her with building a fundraising program capable of supporting his and the Board's ambitious vision for the Mann. A graduate of the University of Pennsylvania and former coordinator of membership and development for Friends of Independence National Historical Park in Philadelphia, Newman would be a key player in the Mann's resurgence in the early 21st century, eventually rising to executive vice president. "Bringing Nancy Newman on board was a game changer," said Lane.[9] Together, he and Newman began to expand the donor base and cultivate private, foundation, and government funders. "Nancy and Peter were a dynamic fundraising team," Jerry Grabey remembers. "They raised a lot of money."[10]

There was also a fundamental restructuring in 1999 of the financial arrangement between the Mann and The Philadelphia Orchestra Association for the Orchestra's

■ Nancy Newman and Peter Lane. (Courtesy of Peter Lane)

summer concerts. Until that year, the Mann had produced and assumed financial responsibility for the concerts, paying the Orchestra to perform at the venue. This had become a major money-losing situation for the Mann, resulting in a large and growing debt to the Orchestra. As Lane shared in a later interview:

> The Orchestra was charging us full freight for their services to come out and play the 18 concerts, and we were obligated to pay the music director, Charles Dutoit. . . . It was clear that the money we . . . owed, amounting to a couple of million dollars, was not sustainable. . . . We needed a refresh; we needed to rethink how we were approaching this completely. . . . (A) We could not pay The Philadelphia Orchestra the price they were asking; (B) We couldn't afford to continue to give away free tickets to a product that was certainly worth a lot of money. . . . The business model was broken. . . . We needed to stabilize the ship with the Orchestra.
>
> I . . . went and renegotiated with [Orchestra President] Joe Kluger. I said, "Going forward, we need to be equity partners together in this. . . . If [playing at the Mann] is what you need [as a summer residency for the Orchestra], you need to help me. So let's do it together." Reluctantly, . . . they said yes, because they really didn't have much of a choice. I wasn't going to pay them, so we figured out an arrangement.[11]

Kluger confirmed the turn of events in a 2024 interview, offering his perspective on how things had gotten to that point and how they resolved the situation, although not completely:

> A whole bunch of things changed after Helen Martin retired [in 1997]. The financial structure of the Mann was for many years [before the mid-1990s] quite successful. The Orchestra concerts were selling well. . . . Larry Magid was putting on rock-and-roll shows, sharing the profits with the Mann, and those profits were used to underwrite the Orchestra concerts. You had those free lawn seats. . . . [Then] there was a confluence of events sometime in the mid-1990s that disrupted this financial equilibrium. [Kluger detailed the departure of Electric Factory Concerts to Camden; the city cutting its annual subsidy; and the Pew Charitable Trust ending a multiyear grant it had been giving the Mann.] And the Mann ended up with a huge operating deficit. . . . And they were not paying the Orchestra. We became their banker. And that led to a restructuring of the relationship . . . where essentially the Mann and the Orchestra became partners. We did a joint venture. And that worked sort of OK, but really it didn't.[12]

Under the new arrangement, the Orchestra would essentially present itself at the Mann, assuming 90 percent of the financial risk for the summer concerts, with the Mann responsible for 10 percent. The two parties also agreed on a plan to gradually reduce the Mann's accumulated debt to the Orchestra (although eventually the Orchestra ended up just forgiving most of it).[13] The new agreement prompted the Orchestra to reconsider the number of concerts it gave at the Mann. As Lane recalls, "When the Orchestra became a partner, they said, 'We can't afford 18 [concerts].' . . . I said, . . . 'Nobody can. Let's cut it back a little bit.' So it went to fifteen [in 2000]." This was the beginning of the process of the Orchestra gradually reducing its presence at the Mann over time. "I tried to keep it to around twelve, so you had some semblance of a season," said Lane, "but you booked other things around it to create revenue. I think when I left [in 2007] . . . we were doing 10."

## Second Season

The 1999 season, Lane's second as president and chief executive officer, continued the "all things to a whole lot of people" programming approach. There were jazz and orchestral pops series again, and New Park Entertainment continued to book rock and pop acts. "They [had] a hit once in a while," Lane remembers. "If we had one or two of those big shows land, they would help pay for a lot of [the Mann's] initiatives." But New Park could not compete for the top-level rock acts Electric Factory Concerts was booking in Camden; revenues from New Park shows at the Mann would never approach those that Electric Factory generated.

■ Promotional materials from the late 1990s. (Mann Center for the Performing Arts Archives)

The Mann hosted the second annual Marian Anderson Award concert on June 26, 1999, honoring actor Gregory Peck. It was the last time the award concert would be held at the venue. Marvin Hamlisch returned that year also. "I was very close to Marvin Hamlisch," said Lane. "He worked for me a lot when I ran the New York Pops at Carnegie Hall." Hamlisch appeared on August 3 with the Mann Festival Orchestra, an ensemble the Mann created that year for pops-type concerts. "It was a freelance band, we put it together," said Lane. "We hired the contractor for the Philly Pops and augmented where we wanted to. We called it the 'Mann Festival Orchestra,' and we used it for all kinds of shows. Again, to create content."[14] The "Tchaikovsky Spectacular," featuring the thrilling *1812 Overture* with fireworks, returned that year, on its way to becoming one of the Mann's most popular annual events. *Riverdance* closed the season once again.

Due to public criticism, the Mann revised the restricted free ticket policy for the Orchestra series that it had introduced in 1998. In the new plan, 1,500 free tickets (but with a $2 per ticket service charge) were made available to the public for each Orchestra concert on a first-come, first-served basis. Another 3,500 free lawn tickets to each concert were distributed to nonprofit organizations. Single day-of-show tickets were available for $8.[15]

The 18 Orchestra concerts in 1999 included several eclectic programs designed to attract new audiences. Innovative conductor Marin Alsop led an all-American program that featured Aaron Copland's ever popular *Fanfare for the Common Man* paired with Joan Tower's 1993 composition *Fanfare for the Uncommon Woman*, along with songs and vocal pieces by award-winning Broadway soprano Audra McDonald. Bobby McFerrin, vocalist extraordinaire making his fourth Mann conducting appearance, led the Orchestra in standard symphonic works while also being featured in "Vocal Improvisations." Dutoit led the last six concerts of the season. The second-to-last was a space-themed program on July 21 celebrating the 30th anniversary of the 1969 moon landing. The sold-out concert, featuring Women of the Mendelssohn Club of Philadelphia, included film composer John Williams's *Star Wars Suite* and Gustav Holst's *The Planets*, the latter with narration by astronaut Edwin "Buzz" Aldrin, the second man to walk on the moon, along with NASA footage projected on a screen. The Orchestra season ended on July 22 with Dutoit conducting the Orchestra, the Mendelssohn Club of Philadelphia, and the American Boychoir in Leonard Bernstein's *Chichester Psalms* and Carl Orff's *Carmina burana*. At intermission, Dutoit had a surprise announcement.

## Dutoit Resigns

Charles Dutoit had adapted to the new programming policies and austerity measures at the Mann, but he did not like them. Things came to a head at the end of the 1999 season, as Lane recounts:

> Charlie wasn't happy with the fact that we were reducing the number of shows at the Mann from 18 to 15, . . . [and] he made it difficult because he used Helen [Martin] to book the concerts up in Saratoga and he asked if Helen could also book the artists [at the Mann]. I said, "She can book, but they have to be cleared through me. I don't want her making obligations on behalf of the Mann Center without it being approved by me." Charlie didn't like that; he wanted to just book the artists with Helen, and I said, "It's not going to work that way. . . . You're not obligating the Mann to artists and fees if I don't have the opportunity to negotiate those fees. And I'm not letting Helen do that as a non-employee. It doesn't make any sense."
>
> He didn't conduct all 18 concerts [each summer]. . . . We would sit down and come up with a list of guest conductors, and I said, "Charlie, I'm not

spending $25,000 on a guest conductor to do one show where I'm already losing $30,000 for the show. . . . We're going to find a conductor that can do it, that's competent" [and affordable]. I'd give him a list of five or six artists, and he didn't like any of them. And I said, "Well, here's the price range." And he didn't like that. He had full authority with the Mann Center in the past and he wanted to have that [still], and I was the guy who said no.

There was a deeper issue going on with Dutoit at this time as well: He had been considered a strong candidate to replace Riccardo Muti as music director of The Philadelphia Orchestra when Muti left in 1992, but the post went to Wolfgang Sawallisch. (Joseph Kluger relates that Dutoit told him that Kluger's predecessor, Philadelphia Orchestra Executive Director Stephen Sell, had promised Dutoit that he would be appointed music director when Muti left and that Dutoit harbored considerable resentment when that did not happen.)[16] When Sawallisch signaled in the late 1990s that he would be stepping down in the coming years, indications were that Dutoit was being passed over once again. According to reports, he was deeply disappointed by this.[17]

Following intermission on July 22, the final concert of the 1999 Mann orchestral season, Dutoit announced from the stage that he was resigning as the Mann Center's music director. He had informed Lane and Kluger shortly beforehand, but the audience and the musicians were stunned. In an interview 10 days later, Dutoit cited a heavy summer workload and a "very shaky" and "very difficult" situation at the Mann as the reasons for his decision.[18] He claimed that the music director position did not factor into his decision, but most people familiar with the situation (including Lane and Kluger) think otherwise. Dutoit would continue as music director for the Orchestra's summer series at the Saratoga Performing Arts Center until 2010 but would never conduct at the Mann Center again. His sudden resignation in 1999 "was a shocking and not very pleasant experience," said Kluger. "I'll leave it at that."*[19]

## Moving On

As for the fallout from Dutoit's departure, Lane says: "I was ready to move on, and so was the [Mann] Board. Because we had been seeing this coming, I said to the Board, 'If Charlie walks, we can still make this work. It will be cheaper, and we can make it work.'" Dutoit's per concert conducting fee at the Mann was about $15,000.[20] "We did very imaginative programming [following Dutoit's departure,]" Lane continued:

* In 2017, multiple women came forward with allegations of sexual harassment against Dutoit. Many of these accusations were deemed credible, and several orchestras severed ties with him, including The Philadelphia Orchestra, which in December 2017 announced the discontinuation of its relationship with Dutoit and the revocation of the title of conductor laureate it had bestowed on him in 2012.

> We did *Bugs Bunny on Broadway*, *Lord of the Rings* with choir, . . . a lot of very inventive programs, some of which he had blessed, begrudgingly, and some that he didn't. And we had a couple of assistant conductors from the Orchestra come out and they got to burnish their chops, and we still had Itzhak Perlman coming and Yo-Yo Ma. So at the end of the day, as long as those artists are still showing up, people are going to show up.[21]

Lane credits Silvia Mann, Fredric's widow, as being especially helpful in supporting the organization's new direction and helping to maintain its relationships with some of the renowned artists from the past. "She legitimized the direction we were going, even when Charlie [Dutoit] got upset, because she represented Freddie Mann and [his] vision. And when it came time to celebrate [the Mann's 25th] anniversary [in 2001], she helped to get Zubin Mehta and the Israel Philharmonic to come and do that concert. . . . And it was a big success. . . . She was very close with André Watts . . . , and I booked André numerous times [at the Mann]."

## September 11

The Israel Philharmonic concert was held on August 27, 2001. The following week, *Riverdance* had a five-day run, from September 5 to September 9. Two days later, virtually all public performances nationwide were halted following the horrific attacks of September 11, 2001. The people of America were in a state of shock and sadness; it was not a time for entertainment or large public concerts. But from the tragedy came some of the Mann's finest moments.

The Mann had a show scheduled for Friday, September 14, with Marvin Hamlisch and Broadway star Linda Eder and faced the dilemma of whether to cancel it or proceed as planned. As Lane recalls, "Marvin was in Cincinnati visiting his mother-in-law, and Linda was in upstate New York. Marvin called me and said, 'Can I do the show? What do you want to do?'" Lane conferred with Peter Gould, chairman of the Mann Board; Gould picks up the story:

> It was another one of those really precarious years here [at the Mann]; we were kind of on the edge financially. And we had a very large commitment to Marvin Hamlisch and Linda Eder under a contract that, had we cancelled the show, we would've had to pay them anyway, and that might well have pushed us over the cliff. So, we're in this difficult ethical situation, 'cause the show was scheduled for September 14. And Peter and I talked and said, "All right, let's figure out what's acceptable. Can it be done? And should it be done?" He basically worked the industry. He called everybody in the industry, everywhere in the country, trying to understand it. Everything was shut down; there were no venues open. Broadway was shut down; everything

was shut down. And I worked the politicians, and said, "What would be the consequences if we opened?" And we went back and forth on [September] 12, talking to all these people trying to figure out what to do. . . .

And then . . . Marvin decided that he wanted to do the show and reframe it as a patriotic event. So he gets a car and puts his music director in the car, and the music director is driving him to Philadelphia on [September] 13, with Marvin sitting in the passenger seat restructuring the entire show, changing everything. Linda Eder is in New York, and her husband says to her, "If you don't get out of the house now, you'll never leave again." So he gets her in a car and brings her down here. So everybody arrives here on [September] 14. Peter somehow got the Orchestra members to come out, the Mann Festival Orchestra, . . . and so we made the decision. The politicians all said, "Not a bad idea." The industry said, "Somebody's gotta go first." We had artists ready to do an appropriate kind of show, who were really emotionally attached. Marvin really wanted to do this show. So we said, "All right, it's a go," and we announced that we were going to go ahead on September 14.[22]

Debbie Lobel, director of production at the Mann, remembers that Eder was still apprehensive about performing and recalls how Hamlisch convinced her that it was the right thing to do:

We were all here. We started rehearsing, and Linda Eder . . . had concerns about how do we go out onstage and perform when we're in such mourning? I don't remember the [exact] words that Marvin said to her, but I remember standing outside of the stage door and listening to him talk to her about how important it was to help the country heal by providing . . . this music, and we'll be sure it's done tastefully, and [he] convinced her that it was something we should do. . . . The show went on, and it was a beautiful evening.[23]

Peter Gould concurs:

We were the first venue in the country to reopen. We had a few thousand people. . . . And it was an incredibly emotional show. I got up and explained to the crowd why we were doing this and why Marvin and Linda wanted to come . . . ; [that] we had to pick up and go on—that is what you did in these circumstances. And the concert was an incredible success. Everybody went home feeling like it was the right thing to do.[24]

Two days later, on September 16, the Mann partnered with The Philadelphia Orchestra and local public television station WHYY to present a free September 11 benefit concert, with audience donations going to the American Red Cross and the Twin

Towers Relief Fund. A hastily assembled, all-volunteer effort, the concert was one of the nation's first September 11 memorial events. It drew some 6,500 attendees and was broadcast locally on WHYY and picked up by TV stations in several other cities. It was a moving event for all concerned, as Kluger remembered some 23 years later:

> I've had this career in the arts for 40 years, and when people ask me what are the top 10 events, that's on the list of really special moments. It came together unbelievably quickly. . . . I was talking to Bill [William J.] Marazzo [the president and chief executive of WHYY]; we were just commiserating with each other shortly after 9/11, how horrible it was, what can we do to help the community through this, and we came up with this idea of doing a free performance of Beethoven's Ninth at the Mann. Sawallisch was stuck in Germany, because planes weren't flying. And I called and asked him if he would do it, and he said yes, absolutely, if he could get on a plane. I think he got on the first flight out of Europe to the United States. . . . And, of course, we gave the tickets away.

Lane recounts how the concert came together on his end:

> Joe [Kluger] said, "I think we want to do a benefit concert. Can we do it at the Mann?" I said, "Absolutely. . . . What do you think you want to do?" He said, "I've got Sawallisch, I think we want to do it with a choir. One rehearsal, we'll just do the show." I said, "Here's the thing, Joe. We're not paying anybody." And he said, "No, we're not going to pay anybody." And I said, "OK, I'll talk to my team, and I'll get back to you in a few hours." So I went to my team and I said, "We have two choices: We can try to make this work and know that we'll have bumps, or we can just say no." And to a person, they all said, "We have to do something." So Marazzo got WHYY all geared up, the Orchestra, our team . . . you know, we were three unions at the time. Every single person donated their time.* . . . They did a rehearsal in the morning.
>
> What was fascinating to me was the outpouring of people who came to the show and were just dying for something other than watching [coverage of the events on TV]. . . . People came to the box office—there were no tickets, just show up, sit anywhere. They were stuffing cash under the window—"Please, take this"—because our concert was a benefit concert specifically for the families of victims of 9/11.

---

* Lane notes that it was "probably the only event I can recall in my career where [almost] every single person involved did it for free." Of the hundreds who participated, he remembers that only one required payment: the director of the TV program. Lane heard later that that director never worked for WHYY again: Peter Lane, interview by the author, April 15, 2024.

Wolfgang Sawallisch rehearses The Philadelphia Orchestra on September 16, 2001, for the benefit concert that evening for the September 11 relief fund. (Philadelphia Orchestra Association Digital Library)

**Wolfgang Sawallisch leads the concert performers.** The benefit at the Mann was broadcast last night locally on WHYY radio and TV, and carried by PBS stations in New York, Boston, Washington and Long Island.

*The Philadelphia Inquirer*, September 17, 2001. (From *The Philadelphia Inquirer.*  Retrieved from Newspapers.com)

The 90-minute concert included Copland's *Fanfare for the Common Man*, Samuel Barber's Adagio for Strings, the Philadelphia Singers performing a movement from Brahms's *A German Requiem*, and the Wilmington-Chester Mass Choir performing Philadelphia native Carol Antrom's solemn, gospel-infused choral piece "Sovereign." While the original plan was for Beethoven's Ninth Symphony to anchor the program, the team later decided that its theme of joy was inappropriate for the occasion, so it was not included.

"We were one of the first benefit concerts," Lane recalled. "I was really proud of our team, proud of our organization and the Mann for doing that. . . . Those are things you always remember." Kluger is still moved by the experience years later: "I still get choked up talking about it. It's one of the most moving things you can possibly do in the face of such tragedy."

## Millennial Highlights

Reviewing the early 2000s at the Mann, Lane notes, "We did some ambitious programming. We brought the Houston Grand Opera in to do *Pagliacci* [2000] and *Carmen* [2001]. . . . We brought the Bolshoi Ballet in [2005]. . . . We brought the Royal Ballet in [2007]. . . . We really just tried to do creative things." The Bolshoi performances stand out in the memories of Mann staff. "They were spectacular," remembers Nancy Newman. "That was one of our proudest moments, having the Bolshoi."[25] Lobel recalls: "Their leaps! They could jump like no other ballet artists I've ever seen. They're amazing."[26] While acknowledging their artistry, Lane remembers a different aspect of the Russian troupe's time at the Mann: "At intermission, you go out the back door and it was just a cloud of smoke, with dancers and French horn players all smoking together. [I'm thinking,] 'How do you *do* that?'"[27]

While the Bolshoi and Royal Ballet performances were artistic triumphs, they were major money losers for the Mann. Another financial blow in this period came when PNC Bank ended its nine-year sponsorship of the Orchestra's summer series after the 2002 season, opting instead to support a series of winter concerts in the Orchestra's new regular-season home, the Kimmel Center for the Performing Arts. PNC's support in 2002 amounted to $175,000.[28] While this certainly did not cover the cost of the full Orchestra series, it helped defray some of the costs and allowed the Mann to keep the ticket prices low so more people could afford the concerts.

The Mann hosted multi-night runs of Broadway shows such as *Rent* and *Fiddler on the Roof* in the early 2000s.* It also hosted iconic American singers such as Tony

* Lobel remembers inadvertently locking Fiddler on the Roof's star, Theodore Bikel, in his dressing room one night when she closed the facility after the show. It was only when she encountered Bikel's driver outside that she realized he was still inside. "I remember running down the hall and hearing him banging on the door": Debbie Lobel, Mann Moments Interview, June 10, 2024.

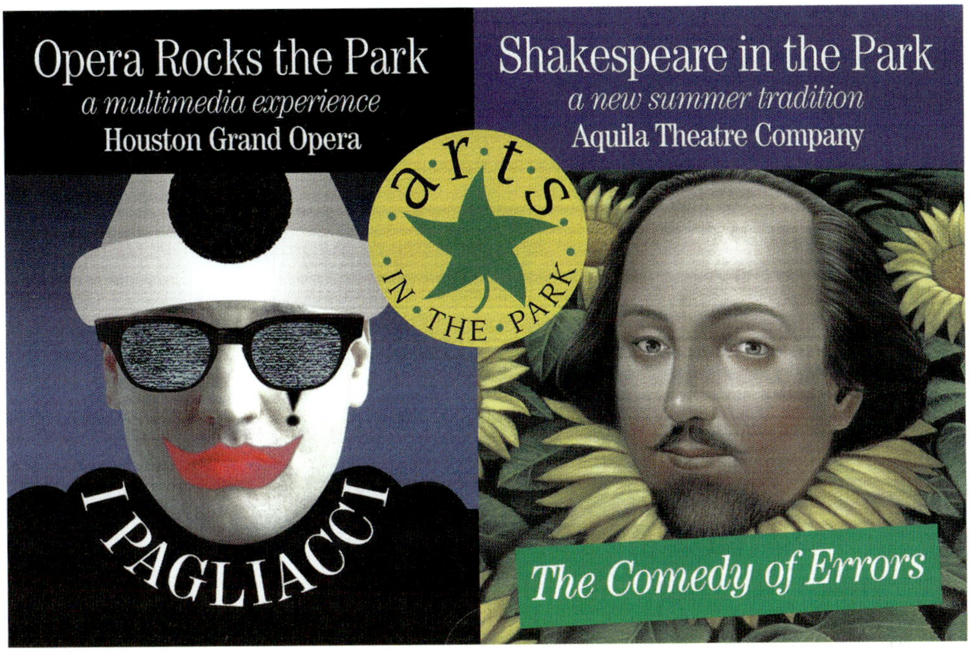


■ Opera and theater performances were part of the Mann's "Arts in the Park" series in 2000. (Mann Center for the Performing Arts Archives)

Bennett, Dolly Parton, and Ray Charles. John Williams, the great film composer, made his debut at the Mann on July 15, 2003, conducting The Philadelphia Orchestra in a "John Williams Salutes the Silver Screen" program. The concert featured selections from his beloved scores for such iconic films as *E. T. the Extraterrestrial*, *Star Wars*, *Raiders of the Lost Ark*, and *Harry Potter and the Sorcerer's Stone*. It was a traditional music-only concert, however, not accompanied by screenings of the films. It would be several years before the technology would evolve to a point where entire films could be shown to live orchestral accompaniment.*

New Park Entertainment, which had been booking rock and pop shows at the Mann since 1997, dissolved after a few years and was replaced by BRE Presents, founded by one of New Park's principals, Bill Rogers. Based in Haddonfield, New Jersey, BRE would be the primary contemporary music presenter at the Mann in the early 2000s. As had been the case with New Park, acts that BRE promoted at the Mann would not rival the top-name artists Electric Factory Concerts was presenting in Camden, but every now and then BRE had a hit. Such was the case with Norah Jones in 2003. When her show was booked, Jones was a promising up-and-coming artist whose performance fee was relatively modest. Then her 2002 album *Come*

* The Philadelphia Orchestra had performed to early-era silent movies in the 1980s and 1990s, but they did not involve the sophisticated synching technology required to accompany modern sound films.

■ Three longtime key figures at the Mann in the early 2000s. *Left to right*: Gilda Rand Mann Ellis, daughter of Fredric Mann; Jerry Grabey, general manager of the Mann Center; and journalist Marciarose Shestack, a Board member. (Courtesy of Peter Lane)

*Away with Me*, featuring the hit song "I Don't Know Why," swept the Grammy's in February 2003 and propelled her to stardom. Her June 20, 2003, show at the Mann was a big success.

## Time for Three

One of the more remarkable events at the Mann in the early millennial period occurred in late July 2003, when a chance thunderstorm helped launch the career of Time for Three, a trio of young string players from the Curtis Institute of Music. Violinists Zachary DePue and Nicolas Kendall and double bassist Ranaan Meyer formed the group while at Curtis as an outlet for playing a genre-blending mix of bluegrass, jazz, classical, and roots music. On July 31, 2003, while Kendall was in Vermont playing chamber music at Marlboro Music, DePue and Meyer were substitutes with The Philadelphia Orchestra at the Mann Center, getting ready to play an all-Beethoven program with conductor Neeme Järvi. The highlight of the concert was to be Beethoven's Symphony No. 9, with the Philadelphia Singers Chorale and vocal soloists.

During the concert, lightning struck a generator in the area, causing the power to go out. Lane told the near-capacity audience that the power should be coming back shortly and to please wait. Meantime, he and Orchestra musicians prevailed on DePue and Meyer, constituting two-thirds of Time for Three, to entertain the audience with their unique repertoire. As Meyer later recalled:

> Zach looked at me kind of wide-eyed and said, "Are we gonna do this?" And I said, "We're gonna do this!" . . . And we made our way out on center stage, and we played for about 20 minutes. It was completely surreal. They gave us an ovation. We went backstage, and then [Peter Lane] asked us to come back out, because they wanted a little more, and we played another 20 minute set. Our lives were kind of built up by this experience at the Mann Center.
>
> You gotta understand . . . the odds of having a successful career are quite limited. So you do your thing, and you love what you do, and you try real hard, but you look for these opportunities to seize. And after this happened, we got national and international press. We started getting calls from other conductors for orchestras. . . . And a career was really born because of the Mann Music Center.[29]

Time for Three went on to tour and record successfully, returning to the Mann as featured artists in 2004, 2005, and 2023 (a concert scheduled for 2020 was cancelled due to COVID-19). DePue left the group in 2015 after being appointed concertmaster of the Indianapolis Symphony Orchestra; he was eventually replaced by Charles Yang. Time for Three's sixth album, *Letters for the Future*, recorded with The Philadelphia Orchestra and conductor Xian Zhang, won the Grammy award in 2023 for Best Classical Instrumental Solo.

## Expanded, Improved Campus

One of Lane's lasting legacies at the Mann was a dramatic expansion and redesign of the campus. He began to focus on the physical landscape in the early 2000s, after spending his first few years addressing the venue's more pressing programming and financial issues. Lane recalls:

> The Mann was very tired [when I arrived] in 1997. It was . . . chain-link fences; it was just not very appealing. . . . After a few years, [when] we finally got our feet under us . . . , we did a $13 million capital campaign to refresh the grounds. We moved the road at the top of the hill, gained all that space, we put the new entry plaza at the bottom, put the box office over there, redid concessions, built an education center, all of that.

■ View of the Philadelphia skyline from Crescendo, a tented, open-air dining and event space that opened on the hill at the Mann in 2008, one of many new amenities made possible by the early 21st-century expansion and renovation of the Mann campus. (Mann Center for the Performing Arts Archives)

Helping to envision and guide the transformation was Alan Greenberger, a principal in the Philadelphia architectural and design firm MGA Partners, which was engaged to oversee the project. Greenberger remembers that when they began in 2002,

> the Mann facility was an isolated entity within [Fairmount] Park. . . . The fences that surrounded it were very tight to the big house; they had a smallish space on the far side of the stage house that they used for donor events. . . . But for the public, you came in through a chain-link fence and you were right there at the entrance to the house. . . . It was all very tight in. We said, "We need more parkland to create a campus out of this. There was no generosity to the public experience."[30]

Lane and Greenberger considered similar performing arts venues elsewhere, such as Wolf Trap, Tanglewood, and Saratoga, and found that they were all "in a . . . park environment that is effectively part of the venue and the hospitality the venue presents." Such was not the case with the Mann, said Greenberger:

> The Mann was not like that at all. It was completely the opposite. So the design work said, "We have to turn this thing into a campus. We have to have a

proper place to welcome people, to sell merchandise; better places to do food; proper ticketing that is not in the stagehouse itself; an accessible way to get up the hill." . . . It was really a great venue with a very inhospitable environment. We were able to convince [Fairmount] Park . . . that the boundaries of the Mann campus needed to grow. We absorbed the hill . . . to the right of the venue. This hill was critical to the Mann campus, . . . and when you get to the top of the hill, that was the sweet spot. The top of the hill had a great view of Philadelphia. What an asset! We have to take advantage of this asset.

Over the next six years, Greenberger oversaw implementation of a grand vision for an expanded and improved campus. "They did what they could do in phases," he notes, and the Mann is now "a vastly improved venue from what it was when we started the project." Greenberger left MGA in 2008 to join the new administration of Philadelphia Mayor Michael Nutter, first as head of the Planning Commission and later as deputy mayor for planning and economic development. In the latter capacity, he proved a key ally for the Mann during some difficult times.

## New Artistic Director

When the newly renovated campus opened in 2006, the Mann Center had a new artistic director, Philadelphia Orchestra Associate Conductor Rossen Milanov. A native of Bulgaria, Milanov had studied in his home country and at Duquesne University, the Julliard School, and the Curtis Institute. He was appointed assistant conductor of The Philadelphia Orchestra in 2000, associate conductor in 2004, and artistic director of the Orchestra's summer series at the Mann Center in March 2006. Like his predecessor, Charles Dutoit (who continued to lead the Orchestra in Saratoga), Milanov would conduct most of the Orchestra's concerts at the Mann and would advise on the programming of the others. However, this was a period when the Orchestra was significantly reducing its number of concerts at the Mann, so Milanov's impact ended up being minimal. His appointment ended after the 2010 season.

## Education and Community Outreach

Another of Lane's legacies was instituting education and community outreach programs. For many in the primarily Black neighborhood of Parkside, where the Mann is located, the venue had been a monolithic presence that brought traffic, noise, and trash to the neighborhood, but little else. Lane hired Rhoda Blount as director of education and community outreach to better connect the Mann with the neighborhood and develop programs to provide young people from Parkside and beyond with experiences in performing arts. "Rhoda Blount ran education; she was a jazz aficionado," said Lane. "She had a concept of 'all these kids in these summer programs

■ Rhoda Blount, the Mann Center's director of education and outreach, profiled in the July 28, 2005, *Philadelphia Daily News.* (From *The Philadelphia Inquirer.* © 2005 Philadelphia Inquirer, LLC. All rights reserved. Used under license. Retrieved from Newspapers.com)

need a place to come and get educated on arts and culture, and let's do it in a way that relates to them.' . . . With those free summer programs, the kids were bussed in. . . . We spent a lot of money on that, and it worked really, really well."

Offering "Global Dance Rhythms," band festivals, jazz workshops, and other activities, Blount brought tens of thousands of young people to the Mann annually to see, hear, and connect with performing artists. She told the *Philadelphia Daily News* that after one of her education programs, a 2004 jazz workshop with bassist (and Philadelphia native) Stanley Clarke, then an international jazz star, Clarke came up to her with tears in his eyes, telling her how happy he was to be teaching the young people. "He said to me as he looked out at the kids, 'Rhoda, that was me 30 years ago.'"[31]

With funding from the Joseph and Marie Field Foundation, the Mann built the Field Education Center in 2006 to host its educational activities, including performances, lectures, demonstrations, master classes, and preconcert workshops. The Field Center also served as a pre- and post-concert donor reception space and for artist meet-and-greet sessions over the years.

## Peter Lane Departs

In September 2007, Lane left the Mann to become chief executive officer of the Bethel Woods Center for the Arts in Bethel, New York, site of the famous 1969 Woodstock Festival. He left that position after a year to become president and chief executive officer of the Walton Arts Center in Fayetteville, Arkansas, where he remained in the mid-2020s. By all accounts, Lane did an amazing job reviving the Mann in his 10 years leading the organization. He diversified its programming and audiences, significantly expanded and improved the campus, and introduced innovative community engagement programs, all of which made the Mann a more vital and valued institution in Philadelphia. In hindsight years later, Lane noted:

> I loved the Mann and felt it was a crown jewel in the cultural fabric of Philadelphia. It deserved the care and feeding of any great institution. . . . Yet at the time that I made the decision to leave, I felt that no matter what we did regarding strategy and fundraising, we were not going to be in control of our destiny. We could work harder and out-fundraise others, but the opportunity to have revenue-generating programs was not going to be in our control. Why? The Kimmel Center [the multivenue performing arts complex that opened downtown in 2001] was going to be the lead presenter of Broadway and major touring attractions at the Academy of Music and Verizon Hall. They had the resources and capacity to really make a year-round difference. And contemporary concerts were controlled by two large companies [Electric Factory Concerts and Live Nation, which would eventually merge], neither of whom were interested at that time in putting shows into

> the Mann. Unfortunately, we were at the mercy of the changing strategies of promoters who had numerous venue options that made them more money. The Mann was not in a position to get the "rock revenue" it needed to help justify our expensive artistic and educational undertakings.[32]

This inherent challenge, together with other issues that arose in the years following Lane's departure, would put the Mann Center into crisis mode a few years later. But as has happened throughout its history, resourceful individuals would step in to lead the institution out of crisis and into a period of stability and creative resurgence.

# 11.

## 2008–2024

*The Mann Flourishes*

**The Mann Center entered a golden age in the 2010s and 2020s,** reclaiming its place as one of the nation's premier outdoor performing arts centers. Its concerts and programming expanded significantly in this period; audiences flocked to its shows; its facilities were upgraded and enhanced; and its finances were stabilized. But to reach this enviable state, the institution had to overcome two major challenges: a financial crisis in 2008–2009 that tested its very survival, and the unprecedented disruption of the COVID-19 pandemic in 2020 that forced the cancellation of the entire concert season and required painful budget cuts and operational adjustments. In each case, the Mann weathered the storm and emerged a stronger, more dynamic organization, largely due to the leadership of President and Chief Executive Officer Catherine M. Cahill and her resourceful Board and staff.

The Mann enjoyed an enviable degree of stability in its Board and senior staff leadership in the early 21st century. At the Board level, there was a 20-year period with the chairmanship held by just two people: attorney Justin P. Klein (2005–2013) and corporate executive Christopher L. Bruner (2014–mid-2020s). The president and chief executive officer position was even more stable. A brief interim period aside, Peter Lane and Cahill served for a combined 27 years and counting: Lane held the position from 1997 to 2007, Board member William Leonard served in an interim capacity in 2007–2008, and Cahill was appointed in 2008 and continued to lead the Mann in the mid-2020s. At the senior staff level, General Manager Jerry Grabey served from 1976 to 2016; Director of Production Debbie Lobel, from 1996 to 2021;

■ Audience gathers at the Mann Center gates for a July 2015 concert by singer and actress Idina Menzel. (Mann Center for the Performing Arts Archives)

and Executive Vice President Nancy Newman, from 1999 to 2019—a combined 85 years of service. This stability in leadership would be crucial in helping the Mann navigate difficult times.

## Enter Catherine Cahill

A native of Ewing, New Jersey, about 40 miles north of Philadelphia, Catherine M. Cahill came to the Mann Center in June 2008 with an impressive résumé and a familiarity with the Philadelphia classical music scene from her college and graduate school days 25 years earlier. A cellist, she received a bachelor of music in performance from Temple University in 1980 and a master's degree in arts administration and arts management from Drexel University in 1983. She was a management fellow of the American Symphony Orchestra League in 1983–1984, which included assignments with the venerable Chicago Symphony, and from 1986 to 2008 she held high-level positions with musical organizations in several different cities: associate artistic director of Santa Fe Chamber Music, festival director and artistic director of the Grant Park Music Festival in Chicago, general manager of the New York Philharmonic, executive director of the Toronto Symphony, and chief executive officer of the Brooklyn Philharmonic Symphony Orchestra. She held the Brooklyn position from 2000 until she came to the Mann Center in 2008.

In Cahill's office is a framed ticket to a June 26, 1978, concert she attended with her college beau at the time at what was then called Robin Hood Dell West. The

■ Singer and actress Julie Andrews with Mann Center President and Chief Executive Officer Catherine Cahill in August 2008. Andrews was featured in a program the Mann co-commissioned titled "The Gift of Music," presented on August 7, 2008. Cahill had started at the Mann just two months earlier. (Mann Center for the Performing Arts Archives)

concert featured conductor Andre Kostelanetz and violinist Yehudi Menuhin. "I remember sitting on the lawn becoming completely enchanted with that experience," she said.[1] Thirty years later, she was back as president and chief executive officer of the venue. The timing was not fortuitous. Not only was the Great Recession of 2008 in full swing and the economy in deep decline, but, as she would discover, the Mann's finances were in a perilous state; its relationship with its resident ensemble, The Philadelphia Orchestra, was at a low point; and there were serious facilities issues. Keeping the Mann going would be a formidable task, she soon realized:

> What I found was that the facilities conditions were seriously challenged. . . . It had been quite some time since there had been any proper . . . maintenance or infrastructure investment. In the early 2000s, Peter Lane did a really great job with a local architectural firm [MGA] to create a new master plan [that resulted in significant renovations to the campus]. So there had been some very needed improvements. Amen to that! But there were other things that were a major concern. . . . Backstage, . . . you would literally need an umbrella, because there were so many leaks in the roof. . . . And I would go out and the maintenance staff would be watering the grass on the Great Lawn. . . . And I said, "Good afternoon, why are you gentlemen out here watering, can you please tell me, where's the sprinkler system?" And they would start laughing, "There is no sprinkler system." I said, "What do you mean there's

> no sprinkler system? It's the 'Great Lawn' from 1976 and it's 2008 and you still don't have a sprinkler system?" Nope, they're out there with the hoses.
>
> So there were issues, particularly around facilities. . . . But equally there was tremendous opportunity and promise. Knowing somehow that we would get through this debilitating recession, . . . we buckled up and determined that we were going to figure this out. That said, there were serious challenges ahead. . . . So we had to jump-start trying to figure out cash flow and how much money we were in arrears, etc. . . . Additionally, there were a number of major administrative things that needed attention. And the finances were candidly pretty frightening. . . . It took us a while to get our hands around that, figure out what the operating model should be, what kind of debt we were in, etc.

The story of how the Mann had reached such a perilous state highlights the difficulties inherent in stewarding a major urban performing arts center. When Lane left, budgets had been balanced in his last years, at least on paper, and the Mann's operations, while lean, appeared stable. Because money was tight and the venue's physical footprint had been expanded dramatically, some aspects of maintenance were necessarily deferred. Especially troublesome was the later discovery that the metal roof of the amphitheater had not been properly sealed when it was installed in 1976—the terne metal panels should have been double-crimped together but were only single-crimped—and the huge structure was starting to leak. Repairing this defect would be extremely expensive. But most troubling was the discovery that the financial reports Lane and the Board had been receiving in his later years were inaccurate. The full extent of the institution's financial condition did not come to light until Cahill arrived and began to investigate. What she found was an institution that was, in fact, in extreme financial distress:

> When I began to realize how concerning the fiscal conditions were, . . . I said to the chair of the Board at the time, Justin Klein, "We're really going to have to examine if we're a going concern, are we going to be able to survive, what are the bankruptcy lawyers going to tell us?" . . . And Justin and I brought together key members of the Executive Committee and said, "We have to examine, at least [from] what little I can determine here, . . . if there is a pathway forward."
>
> We agreed in spirit that [the Mann] was too big to fail, . . . too important for the city to let it go down. So we went on a quest to get our shop in order, stop the hemorrhaging of recent operating deficits which had been developing. . . . Our Board rallied under Justin's steadfast leadership. We did the best we could with the information we had . . . and determined . . . let's just figure out what we have to do to get it right.

In addition to Cahill and Klein, the key team members who came together to navigate the crisis were Director of Development Nancy Newman and Board members Barbara Austell, Peter Gould, William Leonard, and Christopher Bruner. Gould had served as chairman in 2001–2002; Leonard had served as interim president in 2007–2008; and Bruner would become chairman in 2014. "They were incredible," Cahill recalls. "Excellent listeners, great problem solvers, and not afraid to roll up their sleeves. There was many a Sunday morning when my phone would ring, and it was Justin checking in. He was an amazing leader who cared about the Mann, and to my great fortune, me." The group launched a "Stabilization Campaign" to keep the Mann going and determine a sustainable pathway forward.

"It was a very challenging time," Klein remembered. "The recession was especially hard on arts organizations; they suffered the most. The group came together, got some funding, and guided the Mann through the crisis. [Philanthropist] Gerry Lenfest was very generous in contributing funds and [Philadelphia Mayor] Michael Nutter was helpful. Not one Board member left during the crisis; they all stayed and were supportive." Klein notes that it was primarily Cahill and Newman who pulled the organization through: "Cathy and Nancy really did it. They were just not going to fail. . . . Whatever happened, they [were going to] work through it and be successful."[2]

Michael A. Nutter took office in January 2008, five months before Cahill arrived, and would prove to be an important ally. For 14 years prior to becoming mayor, Nutter had been the city councilman for Philadelphia's 4th councilmanic district, which included the Mann Center. He knew and loved the venue. Nutter had to make painful cuts in the city budget when he took office because of Philadelphia's own, very challenging financial situation, but Cahill and Newman remember that he was supportive of the Mann during this difficult period, both in allocating capital city money and encouraging support from other donors. Also invaluable were two Nutter appointees: Alan Greenberger and Michael DiBerardinis. Greenberger, the architect who had overseen the Mann's recent expansion, was appointed head of the city's Planning Commission and, later, deputy mayor for planning and economic development. DiBerardinis served as commissioner of parks and recreation, and later, under Mayor Jim Kenney, as city managing director. Upon retirement, he joined the Mann's Board of Directors.

Cahill and Newman made a determined effort to cultivate these elected and appointed officials in soliciting help from the city, which had ended its annual appropriation to the Mann several years earlier and hadn't provided substantive support in quite a while. "We worked very hard for a long time at building relationships . . . with City Council members, with the mayor. That was ongoing," remembers Newman. "We walked up and down those halls of City Hall for a long time, let me tell you!" She and Cahill spent many hours meeting with city officials, hosting them at Mann events and at private dinners.[3]

■ Mann Center President and Chief Executive Officer Catherine Cahill (*left*) and Executive Vice President Nancy Newman with Philadelphia Orchestra Music Director Yannick Nézet-Séguin at a gala event celebrating Nézet-Séguin's June 24, 2019, debut at the Mann. (Mann Center for the Performing Arts Archives)

Cahill credits her partnership with Newman, who began as director of development in 1999 and would retire as executive vice president in 2019, as a key factor in the Mann's turnaround:

> She was fearless, doggedly committed to the Mann, and someone who seemed to know everyone in Philadelphia. Nancy made it her mission to make sure I succeeded at the Mann. We truly locked arms together and charted a pathway forward for the Mann. . . . [Having] a resolute partner constantly championing the way forward, while simultaneously opening up many doors for me, well you couldn't ask for anything or anyone better.

## Orchestra Issues

In 2007, The Philadelphia Orchestra began a summer residency at Bravo! Vail, an outdoor festival established in 1987 in Vail, Colorado. The new commitment prompted the Orchestra to reduce its presence at the Mann even further. Because the Orchestra was now presenting itself at the Mann—unlike at Vail and Saratoga, where the venues were the presenters and the Orchestra was paid a fee for performing, with no monetary risk for the concerts—the Mann concerts had become a financial burden to the Orchestra, which had its own financial crisis looming. As Cahill recalls:

> By the time I got here [in 2008], the Orchestra [had cut] back to three weeks because they had started a residency at Vail. . . . Vail had emerged onto the scene, and they were attracting major orchestras: the New York Philharmonic, Philadelphia Orchestra, Dallas Symphony, Rochester Philharmonic. When Philadelphia got that engagement, it was a financial win for them. So they were determined to reallocate their services from the Mann to Vail. . . . Unfortunately, the Mann was not seen as valuable at that point in the relationship. . . .
>
> My second year on the job, I received a call to please go over to the Orchestra offices. . . . The gentleman in charge at the time was an interim president, a businessman named Frank Slattery, who called me into his office in March [2009] and said, "We're not coming." And I said, "You're talking about next summer, correct?" We had a three-year contract; we were in year two. And he said, "No, this summer." I said, "Frank, I have a brochure for the upcoming season at the printer as we speak." And he was clear, "Nope, we're not coming." Well, long story short, that did not materialize; they did come.

The Orchestra ended up giving only five concerts at the Mann that year. In 2011 it went on a summer tour of Europe and gave only three performances at the Mann. Cahill remembers how she and her staff arranged for other orchestras to fill in:

> We'll bring in another great Pennsylvania orchestra, the venerable Pittsburgh Symphony; we'll invite the Curtis Institute Orchestra to come and perform, as they, too, have a fine orchestra; and that particular summer the Russian National Orchestra was out in California, and we said, "Might you stop here on your way home?" So we were able to resurrect three weeks of classical concerts by inviting other esteemed ensembles.

The 2010s was a difficult period for the Mann and the Orchestra, individually and in terms of their relationship. In 2011, the Orchestra took the unprecedented step of filing for bankruptcy in an effort to restructure its obligations and develop a new financial model. (The Mann had also considered bankruptcy at one point but was able to avoid that drastic step.) The Orchestra maintained a fairly low profile at the Mann in this period, usually performing about six concerts a year; it was not until the late 2010s that the two institutions had each gotten into a better position and could become valued partners with each other once again.

## The Strategy

One person with a unique vantage point on Cahill's efforts to steer the Mann through its many challenges was former Philadelphia Orchestra Association President Joseph Kluger. After retiring from the Orchestra in 2005, he became a consultant to arts organizations, and in 2013 he was hired to do an institutional assessment of the Mann and help develop its strategic plan. Kluger notes: "The key things that Cathy did to turn things around were, first, reestablishing a semi-exclusive relationship with a popular event promoter. First it was AEG [Anschutz Entertainment Group]; eventually it [switched to] Live Nation. That was the first pillar of the turnaround. And second, [she made] a dramatic investment in education and community engagement programming—not just token 'Let's send some musicians into the schools,' but really in-depth serving of community needs." Third, as Kluger notes later, was undertaking major improvements to the campus and facilities.

Kluger said that by connecting with its neighbors in Parkside, hiring local residents for jobs at the venue, and offering educational programs for local young people, the Mann was able to demonstrate to government, foundation, and private funders that it was not just a concert presenter but was really benefiting the community. It was not an insular organization "serving the declining classical music audience," Kluger noted, or "presenting rock and roll shows for people who were trashing" the neighborhood, but an institution "focused on outwardly serving the community."[4] It was not only the right thing to do, but it proved to be a very effective strategy for fundraising.

With increased financial support, the Mann was able to undertake major capital improvements to the facilities and grounds, making visiting the venue a much more enjoyable experience for both audiences and artists. This was a third key component of the Mann's turnaround, according to Kluger: Having modern facilities and amenities to entice top-level contemporary artists and their audiences would help generate the income necessary for the Mann to sustain itself as a viable performing arts center.

## New Promoters at the Mann

For the first decade of the 21st century, the Mann was caught in the middle of a highly competitive Philadelphia concert promotion market that can best be described as "cut-throat." "It's a really tough town," noted Cahill. As Stephen Starr had discovered in the 1980s, Electric Factory Concerts was the Goliath among the Davids trying to gain a foothold in the local industry. Electric Factory's principals, Larry Magid and Allen Spivak, presented the best artists and most lucrative shows in Camden (the facility was renamed the Susquehanna Bank Center in 2008 and would be renamed several times thereafter), and industry practices being what they were, this prevented the Mann from hosting these artists and their large audiences.

Electric Factory still occasionally produced shows at the Mann with artists it felt were better suited to the venue's more intimate ambience than to the much larger Camden facility. One such show was James Taylor in June 2008, a concert that Cahill remembered especially well: "My first day on the job was June 1, 2008, and it was a concert with James Taylor. It was sold out; it was a beautiful night. And I remember saying to Justin Klein, my Board chair, . . . [as] I'm sitting in the box with him: 'Is this like it is every night here?' Little did I know! . . . That was a Larry Magid presentation. He was one of the few last impresarios to hold out against the Live Nation machine."

As Cahill noted, the industry was changing at this time. The nationwide network of independent regional promoters such as Electric Factory Concerts was consolidating into mega-promoter companies. SFX Entertainment emerged as the first industry giant in the late 1990s; then it was purchased by the radio conglomerate Clear Channel Communications for $4.4 billion in 2000. Magid and Spivak sold Electric Factory Concerts to SFX around this time. In 2005, Clear Channel spun off its concert business to the company that became Live Nation. In 2010, Live Nation merged with the ticketing company Ticketmaster to become Live Nation Entertainment, a behemoth that dominated the concert industry worldwide. Magid was a senior executive at Clear Channel and then at Live Nation until 2010, when he left to form Larry Magid Entertainment, which focused mainly on producing Broadway shows but also occasionally promoted concerts.

In the midst of all this change, a new promoter was establishing itself on the Philadelphia scene that would come to the Mann's rescue: AEG, a sporting and entertainment company that was one of many businesses owned by billionaire entrepreneur Philip Anschutz. The connection was made by Ed Kasses of Princeton Entertainment, an innovative producer Cahill hired in 2010 to help revitalize the Mann's programming. Cahill said:

> We needed a producer . . . who was really on the cutting edge and could figure out nontraditional ways to engage audiences. [Kasses] came in for a number of years and worked with us. He was really my liaison . . . with AEG, because the rock industry was not my strength. I was a classically trained cellist.
>
> AEG had gotten the Trocadero [a small theater in the Chinatown section of Center City] and . . . the Keswick [a medium-size theater in nearby Glenside, Pennsylvania] and I talked to them, because Larry Magid was not interested in a formal relationship with the Mann. . . . And they said, "We love the Mann!" . . . And they came in and they did a great job for us. And

they saved the Mann. I can go on record saying that, at that time—2010, 2011, 2012—Mark Shulman, Jon Hampton, and others at AEG, they helped save the Mann. Because they started bringing talent to our stages. We had a very good deal with them. . . . They were great colleagues.

In its first year at the Mann, AEG presented a mix of up-and-coming and veteran rock artists such as Faith No More, Rufus Wainwright, Squeeze and Cheap Trick, and the Grateful Dead spinoff group Further, helping to put the Mann back on the map as a viable rock and pop venue. BRE Presents, the company that had been the primary contemporary music presenter prior to AEG, would have a much-reduced role going forward but would not be out of the picture completely; it would present or co-present occasional shows at the Mann into the 2020s, working with artists with whom it had developed long-standing relationships.

On the classical side, Kasses brought in interesting orchestral programs in 2010 as well: Cellist Yo-Yo Ma's Silk Road Ensemble; *Planet Earth Live*, with The Philadelphia Orchestra playing to film footage of scenes of nature from the BBC television series; *Songs from the Heart* by the Irish group Celtic Woman; and TV hosts Regis and Joy Philbin narrating Prokofiev's *Peter and the Wolf*.

But the event that attracted the most attention that season was The Philadelphia Orchestra concert on July 27, 2010, led by Rossen Milanov that featured the unusual double bill of Aretha Franklin and former U.S. Secretary of State Condoleezza Rice. A classical pianist, Rice performed the middle movement of Mozart's Piano Concerto No. 20 in D minor, while Franklin performed many of her hits, along with several opera arias. Attendance was estimated at 10,000. As Cahill remembers:

> We dubbed it "the Diva and the Diplomat." It made international news. I am here to tell you, that performance . . . began the transformation of the Mann garnering international attention, including the full front page of *The Philadelphia Inquirer.* It launched a belief that the Mann was resurrecting itself from a number of dormant years. . . . Sadly, [they were] years where we were just not perceived to be a major player in this market.

Debbie Lobel, the Mann's director of production, remembers that Rice was "incredibly gracious and a wonderful musician [but] so nervous, and then she went and played a beautiful show."[5]

On June 23, 2012, hometown favorite Jill Scott brought her "Summer Block Party" tour to the Mann, making her debut at the venue. A North Philadelphia native who attended Philadelphia High School for Girls and Temple University, Scott emerged from the city's vibrant Black music scene in the early 2000s and went on to become one of most popular vocalists in the "Neo-Soul" style of that period, as well as a successful actress and poet. The concert also featured the return of DJ Jazzy Jeff to the Mann. Six years later, radio station WDAS sponsored the 2018 Summer Block Party at the Mann on June 30, featuring an all-Philadelphia lineup, with Scott and Jazzy Jeff sharing the bill with top-selling vocal group Boyz II Men and singer Bilal, the latter two making their Mann debuts.

## Deeper Community Engagement and Education

The 2010 Diva and the Diplomat concert was a benefit for the Mann's educational and community engagement programs, one of the pillars of Cahill's strategy for making the Mann a relevant and sustainable organization. As previously noted, the Mann had been offering free Children's Concerts since the 1950s, and Peter Lane and Rhoda Blount instituted an active educational program in the late 1990s, but Cahill, Blount, and Mann staff took it to another level in the 2010s. While continuing to provide traditional performing arts education experiences for young people, the Mann began to focus more specifically on the needs of the community, what it could do to address those needs, and what kind of impact it could have on the area's young people. "Every young person, I don't care where you live, what your Zip code is, really deserves the opportunity to grow and excel and have a full life and meaningful employment and be able to feed a family and prosper and give back," noted Cahill. "So we started to really try to figure out, where does the Mann fit in that equation?"

To connect with the community, the Mann hosted "Philly on Parade" events in which it opened its gates for the public to come and enjoy a variety of free performances and activities. It engaged Black composer and producer Nolan Williams Jr.

■ Joseph Conyers, Philadelphia Orchestra principal bass and education and community ambassador, conducts a session of the All City Orchestra Summer Academy at the Mann in July 2019. (Mann Center for the Performing Arts Archives)

■ Vocalist Al Jarreau was the Mann Center's 2015 artist in residence, leading a series of workshops in partnership with the Philadelphia Clef Club of Jazz and Performing Arts. (Mann Center for the Performing Arts Archives)

to produce a series of festivals around socially conscious themes such as "Philadelphia Freedom," "Liberty: Unplugged!" and "The Three Kings" (Reverend Martin Luther King Jr., Frederick Douglass, and Nelson Mandela). Williams also presented "A Space Odyssey," a 2017 concert honoring astronaut and West Philadelphia native Guion Bluford, the first African American in space. Focusing especially on collaborative initiatives, the Mann partnered with Moore College of Art, The Franklin Institute, the Philadelphia Zoo, and the Free Library of Philadelphia on various programs and in 2023 began hosting a biennial HBCU (Historically Black Colleges and Universities) Festival, which is free and open to all. All of these activities were designed to "break down barriers [and] change the image of the Mann," according to Cahill, "and say [to the community,] 'Come. Participate.'"

In 2012, the Mann initiated a master class program in which it engaged internationally acclaimed musicians and dancers to serve as artists in residence who led multiday, immersive classes with selected music, art, and dance high school students. Often done in conjunction with Philadelphia's High School for Creative and Performing Arts or the Philadelphia Clef Club of Jazz and Performing Arts, these programs featured such renowned artists as Debbie Allen, Al Jarreau, Ladysmith Black Mambazo, Branford Marsalis, Terence Blanchard, and Chris Botti.

In 2017, the Mann commissioned an in-depth study to assess its educational and community engagement programs and determine how they could better serve the community. The study identified three key areas of need: afterschool and summer music programs, workforce development opportunities, and creative placemaking. Responding to these needs, the Mann partnered with the nearby Global Leadership Academy charter school to establish an afterschool Motion & Music Academy; worked with the Philadelphia School District and The Philadelphia Orchestra to create an All City Orchestra Summer Academy (ACOSA) program based at the Mann; and established a Music Industry Training Program in partnership with the school district and Overbrook High School. As in all of its educational programs, the focus was on community impact: What could the Mann, as a music presenter based in West Philadelphia, do to help address the needs of its community?

Overseeing these programs was Chief Education, Community Engagement Officer, and Vice President Naomi Gonzalez, who joined the Mann in 2018 after Blount retired. Having previously served as manager of collaboration and access at The Philadelphia Orchestra and lead teaching artist for the music education organization Play On Philly, Gonzalez expanded the Mann's community engagement and education programs significantly. In addition to launching and managing the HBCU Festival, the Motion & Music Academy, ACOSA, and the Music Industry Training Program, she initiated "Voices of Hope," an annual event celebrating Black excellence, and the Mann Music Room, a free digital platform that offered a wide range of online performing arts, educational, and community engagement content.

"It is critical that the Mann have a good relationship with the community," noted former Board Chair Justin Klein. "Peter [Lane] and Cathy [Cahill] both realized that, and Mann leadership has been incredibly thoughtful about it. Naomi and Rhoda were inspirational in terms of what they wanted to give back to the community. The community engagement and education programs have grown dramatically over the years."[6]

Lucinda Hudson, president of the Parkside Association, which was founded in 1977 when Hudson led a protest to stop the Mann from paving a local green space for a parking lot (see page 275), joined the Mann Board in 1997 and served as a longtime neighborhood liaison to the venue. She witnessed Cahill's outreach to Parkside firsthand, including times when Cahill was treated somewhat harshly at community meetings. Hudson was impressed that Cahill continued to show up and engage with the neighborhood and appreciated gestures such as the Mann offering to pay for parking passes for area residents affected by parking issues on concert nights. Hudson remembers Cahill and Tom Metz, the Mann Center's chief operating officer, personally coming out one morning to clean up trash left in the neighborhood after a rock concert. And she was especially grateful for the annual appreciation dinner the Mann hosted for her in recognition of her efforts on behalf of the Parkside community and her service to the Mann Center.[7]

## New, Improved Facilities

The Mann added an important new performance space in 2012: the Skyline Stage, a general admission, open-air space at the top of the hill in the rear area of the campus. The three-and-a-half-acre area provides a communal, festival-type atmosphere for young audiences to see and hear artists who would not fill the main stage amphitheater. Icelandic ambient group Sigur Rós opened the new space on July 29, 2012, and returned several times in the succeeding years, one of many groups that found the intimate facility ideal for its music and audiences. For the first 10 years, the Skyline Stage was a temporary scaffolding structure; a permanent stage and support facilities were built in 2023.

The addition of the Skyline Stage was part of a broader upgrade of the campus and facilities the Mann initiated in the 2010s, after getting the institution's finances stabilized. The campus footprint was expanded; the slope of the lawn area was regraded to provide a better view of the stage; a sprinkler system was added; and a new sound system and lawn video screens were installed. The sound system and screens were specifically designed to improve the audience's experience of film screenings with live orchestral accompaniment that were becoming very popular. From 2017 to 2019 major renovations were made to the main amphitheater as well, including new seating, walkways, lighting, and air systems and repairs to the roof and gutters, which, as noted earlier, had been leaking. Corporate and foundation sponsorships helped support some of these projects, and the City of Philadelphia, which owns the property and facilities, contributed. In recognition of their institutional support, the main stage was named the Presser Foundation Stage in 2016; the amphitheater was rechristened the TD Pavilion at the Mann in 2019; and the Skyline Stage was named the Highmark Skyline Stage in 2024. The Mann also fully renovated its backstage area in 2024 to meet the expectations of 21st-century artists and their crews.

Another new concert setting, Downstage @ the Mann, debuted in 2022. Bringing audiences and artists together on the Presser Foundation Stage for up-close,

■ Young people await the start of a concert at the Highmark Skyline Stage in July 2024. (Mann Center for the Performing Arts Archives)

in-the-round performances, the intimate setting offered a new level of engagement and immersion in the performance experience. Downstage @ the Mann debuted on April 29, 2022, with *Deep Blue Sea*, a new dance piece created and directed by acclaimed choreographer Bill T. Jones that was originally commissioned by the Mann Center. Downstage @ the Mann programs in 2023 focused on the 50th anniversary of hip hop, and in 2024 on the theme of "Acceptance," highlighting works that told stories of LGBTQ+ individuals and offered reflections on the ongoing journey toward inclusivity and understanding.

Dining options also expanded dramatically at the Mann in the early 21st century. While picnicking on the Great Lawn remained a cherished tradition, new concession and bar areas were added, offering many more food and drink choices. New al fresco dining spaces also debuted, including Crescendo, a tented open-air space on the hill that opened in 2008, providing a buffet-style preconcert dinner option with spectacular views of the Philadelphia skyline (see page 338). The original manager of Crescendo was a familiar face, Stephen Starr, who, as previously noted, began booking shows as a music promoter at the Mann in the 1980s before abandoning the

■ Lawn audience at the Mann in the 2010s. At far right is Crescendo, the open-air tented dining space that opened in 2008. (Mann Center for the Performing Arts Archives)

concert business for a very successful career as a restauranteur. In 2019, the Mann opened the Acclaim VIP Lounge, a tented, intimate outdoor oasis with a private bar, concessions, and various amenities. In conjunction with these improvements, the Mann expanded its facility rental program, making its varied campus spaces available for graduations, weddings, corporate functions, and other events.

## Movies at the Mann

The Mann was a pioneer in the mid-2010s in showing full-length feature films with live orchestral accompaniment, a new way of presenting symphonic music that would prove enormously popular and help to broaden the audience for classical music. Film scores, originally dismissed by highbrow conductors and critics as light entertainment with minimal artistic merit, began showing up on orchestra programs with some frequency in the early 21st century. At first, just the music was presented, with no film accompaniment. That was the case when celebrated film composer John Williams made his conducting debut at the Mann in 2003 (see page 335). By the early 2010s, the technology had developed to the point that an orchestra could play along with clips from films. The Pittsburgh Symphony Orchestra performed selections from three Pixar films at the Mann in 2013 as clips from the movies were shown on a large screen, and that same summer The Philadelphia Orchestra played selections from the Disney animated film *Fantasia* (for which it had recorded the original soundtrack in 1941) as parts of the film were shown. None of these concerts entailed continuous, uninterrupted showings of the full movies, however; rather, they were performances of individual pieces from the film scores, synced to specific movie clips.

Screenings of complete, uninterrupted films with live orchestral accompaniment began in earnest in 2014, when for three nights in July the Mann presented Movie Nights @ the Mann, with The Philadelphia Orchestra performing the full scores to *Gladiator*, *West Side Story*, and *Star Trek: Into Darkness* as the movies were shown on giant screens. The concerts were a big hit, and in 2015 the Mann upgraded the sound system in the lawn area and added jumbo screens on each side of the stage for Philadelphia Orchestra performances to screenings of *The Godfather* and *Lord of the Rings: The Fellowship of the Ring*. By that time, accompanying live films had become a staple of the Orchestra's summer repertoire at the Mann. In 2016, the Mann introduced "Movies @ the Mann" as a tagline for these concerts, which continued to be among its best-attended symphonic programs into the mid-2020s.

Cahill remembers that she faced some resistance initially from the Orchestra about having the ensemble perform movie scores to film screenings:

> When I approached Orchestra management about it at the time, they were not too open to it because the Orchestra was accustomed to playing classical music. . . . And I said, "I understand that. I'm only going to ask you to play epic film scores by only the greatest composers, whether it's John Williams, for his blockbuster movies . . . or . . . *Gladiator*, the great epic score by Hans Zimmer." And I said, "As an example, the musicians of The Philadelphia Orchestra are among the very few who can really do justice to Bernstein's *West Side Story* in just one rehearsal." . . . I was very clear and honest that we would only ask them to play the finest music in the film world.
>
> And then we secured the world premiere to the original [score of the] *Harry Potter* movie, with an option for all eight films in the series . . . to do that at the Mann with The Philadelphia Orchestra [in 2016]. I couldn't believe it; we sold out in just two days—12,000-plus tickets. . . . Then we presented the *Lord of the Rings* series. Talk about a Howard Shore score that is beyond brilliant. We had never staged something with that size orchestra and chorus. For approximately four hours the stage was filled with over two 200 people [including the Mendelssohn Club of Philadelphia and the Phil-

■ Advertisement for the 2016 Orchestra series at the Mann. By this time, performances of movie scores accompanying showings of films had become a major part of the Mann's orchestral season. In addition to The Philadelphia Orchestra, the Philly Pops and the Pittsburgh Symphony Orchestra appeared at the Mann that year. (Mann Center for the Performing Arts Archives)

■ The Philadelphia Orchestra performs the score to a screening of *Harry Potter and the Sorcerer's Stone* at the Mann Center on June 23, 2016. (Mann Center for the Performing Arts Archives)

> adelphia Boys Choir]. It was incredible. People went crazy for it, absolutely crazy for it.
>
> And now [in 2024,] when [the Orchestra is] on the Mann stage and 10,000-plus people are cheering—not just for the film—they cheer for our Orchestra when it comes out, when the credits run at the end of the movies. I'd say 75 percent or more of the audience stay in their seats. They wait for the final chord, the final downbeat, and they're leaping to their feet and cheering like it's a baseball game after a grand slam. . . . To witness our musicians onstage, that an evening like this would mean so much to our collective audience, was enlightening.

For Christopher Bruner, who became chair of the Mann Center Board in 2014, one of his favorite experiences at the venue took place in July of that year when he and his wife attended a showing of the movie *The Gladiator*, with The Philadelphia Orchestra performing the score. "It was ideal weather—a beautiful clear sky, not too hot or humid," he said. "We had dinner at Crescendo, with the phenomenal view of the Philadelphia skyline. Then went down to our seats for the concert, which was great. It was the most unique dinner-and-a-movie date ever."[8]

## Aretha's Farewell

Aretha Franklin gave one of the last full concerts of her career at the Mann Center in 2017. She had been battling a slowly progressing cancer since 2010, and by the mid-2010s it had begun to affect her ability to perform. She embarked on a series of concerts in the summer of 2017 that were billed as a farewell tour, with most of the shows spaced several weeks to a month apart. But even that schedule was proving too much; she had to cancel some of the concerts, and others were touch and go until the last minute. Thankfully, she was able to perform as scheduled at the Mann on August 26, 2017.

The 90-minute show was filled with many of Franklin's hits, along with some less well-known numbers and a spirited 10-minute gospel medley. She introduced the medley by noting that the songs were made popular by "one of my mentors, who comes from the City of Brotherly Love . . . Clara Ward and the Ward Singers. They were so bad [i.e., good], it was ridiculous." Later, while noodling at the piano as she was about to sing "Brand New Me," she reminisced, "You know I started, really, in Philadelphia. I played all over Philadelphia," giving shout-outs to local jazz and rhythm-and-blues (R&B) clubs such as Peps and the Cadillac Club. She closed the show with a lively version of her 1985 hit "Freeway of Love," followed by her

Aretha Franklin performing at the Mann Center on August 26, 2017, one of the last full concerts of her career. (Mann Center for the Performing Arts Archives)

enduring anthem, "Respect," as an encore. After singing the final verse, she slowly danced her way off the stage—gingerly, but with obvious joy—as the band closed the song out. (Video of the concert is available on YouTube.) Franklin did only two more public performances after her August 2017 Mann concert and died a year later.

## Moving Forward with the Orchestra

The Mann and The Philadelphia Orchestra deepened their relationship in the late 2010s, with each of the two institutions now on a more sound financial footing and able to work together more effectively. Symbolizing the revitalized relationship, on June 24, 2019, Philadelphia Orchestra Music Director Yannick Nézet-Séguin made his debut at the Mann, continuing the long-standing tradition of his predecessors, all but one of whom (Christoph Eschenbach) had performed at the Mann or the Robin Hood Dell.

A native of Montreal, "Yannick," as he is known to all, became music director of The Philadelphia Orchestra in 2012, exactly 100 years after groundbreaking conductor Leopold Stokowski had assumed that post and began building the Orchestra into one of the world's greatest symphonic ensembles. As in the Stokowski era, Yannick and the Orchestra forged a level of artistry together that garnered worldwide acclaim and respect. In 2018, Yannick became music director of the Metropolitan Opera in New York City, giving him leadership of two of the world's greatest orchestral arts institutions. He had been music director since 2000 of Orchestre Métropolitain in his hometown of Montreal, which in 2019 appointed him "Music Director for Life," and he served as music director of the Rotterdam Philharmonic Orchestra in the Netherlands from 2008 to 2018.

The program for Yannick's 2019 debut at the Mann exemplified the new direction the Mann and The Philadelphia Orchestra were taking in connecting with the broader Philadelphia community and expanding their audiences. Yannick opened the concert by leading the Philadelphia Youth Orchestra in Beethoven's Overture to *Egmont*, then Nolan Williams conducted excerpts of *Philadelphia Community Mass*, a piece the Mann commissioned that was loosely based on Leonard Bernstein's *Mass* and was cowritten by four Philadelphia-based Black composers under Williams's direction. (Williams had led the piece two months earlier at Mother Bethel African Methodist Episcopal Church in Philadelphia.) The concert concluded with Yannick leading The Philadelphia Orchestra in Beethoven's stirring Ninth Symphony. It was an inspirational evening that symbolized the renewed relationship between the Orchestra and the Mann and their mutual commitment to engaging wider, more diverse audiences while continuing the Orchestra's great symphonic tradition at the Mann.

Matias Tarnopolsky became president and chief executive officer of The Philadelphia Orchestra in 2018 and oversaw its 2021 merger with the Kimmel Center for the Performing Arts to form The Philadelphia Orchestra and Kimmel Center Inc. In

Philadelphia Orchestra Music Director Yannick Nézet-Séguin leads the Orchestra in Beethoven's Ninth Symphony at the Mann on June 24, 2019, his debut at the venue. (Mann Center for the Performing Arts Archives)

2024, the organization introduced the brand name Ensemble Arts Philly as a unifying identity for the Orchestra and multivenue Kimmel Cultural Campus. Reflecting that year on the close relationship and deeply intertwined history of the Orchestra, Mann Center, and Robin Hood Dell since 1930, Tarnopolsky noted:

> The Philadelphia Orchestra and the Mann Center are of each other's DNA and part of Philadelphia's DNA. We are so much part of each other's origin story, and history, and present and future, for so many reasons. Obviously, in 1930 Philadelphia was very different than it is in 2024, and in these almost 100 years the relationship has mirrored the evolution of not just our great city, but also of America—in all its forms, good and bad. But the most important thing is the love for music and the civic pride in both institutions as expressed not just by the people of Philadelphia but by the people who would come from elsewhere to hear The Philadelphia Orchestra, at the Dell or the Mann. And of the legendary artists for whom their relationship with The Philadelphia Orchestra was manifest by their performances at [the Dell and Mann]. . . . Our histories and our futures are inextricably linked.[9]

Cahill expressed her appreciation for the close, cooperative relationship between the two institutions:

> I cannot say enough good things about Matias, [Executive Director] Ryan Fleur, and their core team. It is a true pleasure working with such wonderful professionals who possess such a profound love of classical music. They have been consistently welcome partners and colleagues who understand the inherent value of this long-standing relationship between both organizations, harking back to 1930. They respect and embrace that legacy while also being champions of innovation and creativity. As one example, having The Philadelphia Orchestra as a key partner in our All City Orchestra Summer Academy each year at the Mann was warmly embraced by them from the very outset. What a blessing to find colleagues who share many of the same goals to enrich the lives of our young people through the gift of music.*

Justin Klein, whose chairmanship of the Mann Board from 2005 to 2013 included some of the more difficult periods in the institution's relationship with the Orchestra, noted, "It's been a struggle at times, but it's been incredibly important to say that the Mann is the summer home of The Philadelphia Orchestra. That has always been a part of our credo."[10]

## Changing Promoters

The promotion company AEG continued to book rock and pop artists at the Mann through the 2010s. Hometown jam band the Disco Biscuits, formed at the University of Pennsylvania in 1995, staged its City Bisco festival—two days of jam bands, DJs, and electronic music—at the Mann in 2012 and 2013, while its 2014 festival was a three-day series at three different local venues that concluded with a grand finale at the Mann. Phish, the premier jam band of the era, had been on hiatus for much of the early 2000s but returned for sold-out multi-night series in 2014, 2015, and 2016. The mid-2010s were an especially active period for rock and pop music, with shows several nights a week and many top artists gracing the Mann stages. "By 2016, we had one of our biggest seasons ever," said Cahill. "We had Bob Dylan. We had Paul Simon. We had sellouts. [In 2015] we presented Ed Sheeran."

But by 2020 it was time for a change, according to Cahill:

> After 2016, the promoting world began to change, and Live Nation became more dominant in our market. They opened the Fillmore [a 2,500-capacity venue in Fishtown that debuted in 2015]; were opening the Met [the histor-

* In December 2024, Tarnopolsky left The Philadelphia Orchestra to become president and chief executive officer of the New York Philharmonic. Replacing him as president and chief executive officer was longtime Philadelphia Orchestra and Ensemble Arts Executive Director Ryan Fleur.

■ Audience at the August 12, 2018, Gladys Knight and O'Jays concert. (Mann Center for the Performing Arts Archives)

> ic 3,500-seat Metropolitan Opera House on North Broad Street that Live Nation renovated and opened in 2018]; and still had Camden. The long and the short of it, we had to make a change. We were able to exit, respectfully, with AEG, who'd been a good partner, and bring in Live Nation, who were dominating this market by then. [Live Nation could bring in] talent that really should [have been] at the Mann . . . but were all in Camden, because Live Nation couldn't play [at the Mann]. They were excluded because AEG and Live Nation were business rivals. . . . Basically, in our market, if you were a Live Nation artist, you couldn't come into an AEG house, and if you were an AEG artist, they wouldn't let you into a Live Nation house.

Realizing that if it wanted to present really top-level artists it would have to make a change, the Mann entered into an exclusive booking arrangement with Live Nation in March 2020, just as the entire concert world was shutting down.

## The Pandemic

On February 20, 2020, the Mann Center hosted its annual "Voices of Hope" event celebrating Black excellence. Ironically, the theme that year was health issues in

Black communities. It was the last in-person event the Mann would host for more than a year, as the COVID-19 pandemic was about to disrupt everything.

Few events in American history have had the wide-ranging impact on people's lives and livelihoods that the COVID-19 pandemic had in 2020 and 2021. Reports of the looming crisis began to surface in January 2020, and by mid-March, with infection rates rising rapidly, shutdowns were ordered across many sectors of public life. The Mann, which had been planning its 2020 season with its new promoter, Live Nation, had to rethink everything. By late spring, it had become obvious that the pandemic would be a prolonged phenomenon, and on June 10 the Mann announced that it was cancelling the entire 2020 season. Cahill remembers the difficult period:

> During the pandemic, it was rough, as it was for everybody, but we survived it. It gave us some time to step back and think, although no one knew when we got to the other side, what it would look like. We launched a $3 million resiliency fund . . . to "Save the Music." We were successful in that. It tided us over. We cut every expense we could; we put the entire campus in mothballs. We said, "Don't spend a nickel." . . . There were some consequences to putting the place in mothballs, but we just couldn't spend any money.
>
> [One of the consequences was that] birds nested in the highest rafters [of the amphitheater]. They're hard to get out once they nest up there. [But] we're in a public park and we didn't want to do anything to harm them. We're very conscious of our environment.

The pandemic was a difficult time for everyone at the Mann. All staff took pay cuts; some were laid off or furloughed; and everyone had their hours reduced. The skeleton staffing lasted from June 2020 until the start of the Mann's next fiscal year in March 2021. During this time, the Mann pivoted to virtual programming, offering the All City Orchestra Summer Academy online and presenting the Mann Music Room, a series of virtual performance and discussion sessions that connected audiences with teachers and artists during the summer season. The Philadelphia Orchestra, unable to perform indoors, videotaped a series of concerts on the Mann stage—with a small, socially distanced ensemble and no audience—and broadcast the performances virtually.

Things got complicated when it came time to plan for reopening for the 2021 season: Would patrons have to wear masks? Would vaccination cards need to be checked? What were the social distancing requirements? What would the staffing needs be to manage such requirements? Cahill remembers the challenges at the time:

> So coming out of that, it really became apparent that it was a new day. We had to start figuring out what were all the restrictions we had to contend

> with. . . . In 2021, we didn't even know if we were going to be open. . . . We were very much in touch with the city, and they were very good in keeping us informed with what was happening and changing.

At one point that spring, the city said it was going to require a six-foot separation between seated patrons, which would have reduced the Mann's seating capacity by 80 percent, making it financially impossible to produce concerts. But in May 2021, the city relaxed the social distancing rules, making it feasible for the Mann to proceed with scheduling the season, albeit with responsibility for implementing some cumbersome safety measures.

On May 5, 2021, in partnership with Opera Philadelphia, the Mann presented *The Drama of Tosca*, the venue's first concert before a live audience since 2019. (It was also Opera Philadelphia's debut at the Mann.) Cahill remembers, "We had people literally in tears . . . , [saying,] 'It's the first time I've been out of the house, I can't believe I'm here.' It was heartbreaking and heartwarming at the same time."

Ten days later, on May 15, 2021, Nézet-Séguin led The Philadelphia Orchestra in a program at the Mann titled "Hail to the Heroes: A Concert of Gratitude." It was the Orchestra's first post-pandemic concert before a live audience and was presented for free to frontline and essential workers in appreciation for their service during the pandemic. "What joy everyone at the Mann, onstage and in the audience, felt that evening, to be together again," Nézet-Séguin remembered.[11]

During the pandemic, the Mann co-commissioned *SoundWalk*, an immersive self-guided sound art installation tailored to the landscape of the historic Centennial District of Fairmount Park in which the venue is located. Created by composer and sound artist Ellen Reid and activated by a GPS-based mobile app, *SoundWalk* presents original compositions, recorded by musicians of The Philadelphia Orchestra and others, that are carefully crafted to harmonize with the different areas listeners encounter as they travel about the Centennial District of the park.

One of the things that helped the Mann get through this challenging time, when many people were legitimately concerned about large gatherings and concert attendance was down dramatically, was revenue from increased rentals of the facility for college and university graduations. With its outdoor setting and seating arrangements that could be tightly controlled, the Mann created a "Turn Your Event Inside Out" promotional pitch that was successful in prompting area educational institutions to rent the facility during the COVID-19 period.

## The Roots Picnic

The Roots Picnic became one of the more iconic events at the Mann when it moved to the venue in 2019. Produced by Philadelphia's beloved hometown hip-hop-and-beyond ensemble The Roots, who curate and perform at the event, the Roots Picnic

■ 2019 Roots Picnic Poster, the first year the picnic was held at the Mann. The Roots celebrated the 20th anniversary that year of their 1999 breakthrough album *Things Fall Apart* by performing the album at the picnic. (Mann Center for the Performing Arts Archives)

is a high-profile, multiday celebration of Black music and culture that attracts tens of thousands of attendees for performances on multiple stages at the Mann and its environs.

The Roots were formed in 1987 by drummer Ahmir "Questlove" Thompson and rapper Tariq "Black Thought" Trotter, then students at the Philadelphia High School for Creative and Performing Arts. The group evolved over the years into an eclectic ensemble that charted a unique, influential course in hip hop and popular music. The Roots gained widespread exposure when they became the house band for the NBC television show *Late Night with Jimmy Fallon* in 2009 and then the *Tonight Show Starring Jimmy Fallon* in 2014.

The group started the Roots Picnic in 2008 as a one-day music event at Festival Pier at Penns Landing on the Delaware River. Since moving to the Mann Center in 2019, it has grown into a wide-ranging two-day festival, with added pre-picnic workshops and events, a vendor village, and other attractions that have made it an important national event in hip hop and Black music. Due to the pandemic, the 2020 picnic was a virtual event, and the 2021 picnic was cancelled. The 2020 virtual picnic had a "Get Out the Vote" theme in advance of the U.S. presidential election that year. It kicked off with a message from The Roots and former First Lady Michelle Obama, who cohosted the opening show on behalf of her organization, When We All Vote. Mrs. Obama and several of the artists appeared virtually from different locations throughout the country, while the Roots performance was recorded on the Presser Foundation Stage in the TD Pavilion at the Mann.

The Roots Picnic returned as an in-person event in 2022 and grew even larger and more diverse. It extended the Mann's footprint beyond the 22-acre space within the venue gates to encompass adjacent sections of Fairmount Park in a 54-acre "expanded campus" setting. "The Roots Picnic is a celebration that's endured," Black Thought told *The Philadelphia Inquirer* on the eve of the 2024 picnic. "And it's Philadelphia-centric. . . . The Roots Picnic is a brand that was ideated and created and carefully built—gardened and nurtured—in the city of Philadelphia. And I think the city is fiercely protective of that."[12]

## Artists and Curators in Residence

Performing at the first Roots Picnic at the Mann in 2019 was local rapper Eric "Chill" Moody, who grew up just blocks from the venue. (He had been performing at the Roots Picnic since 2016; the 2019 Picnic was the first one in his neighborhood.) In 2023, Moody was named the inaugural Community Artist in Residence at the Mann, a new position created to integrate the Mann's programming more deeply into the local community. In addition to being involved in the Mann's Music Industry Training Program at Overbrook High School (his alma mater) and participating in activities such as Voices of Hope and the HBCU Festival, Moody helped curate and performed in three special programs in 2023 in recognition of the 50th anniversary of hip hop.

The three anniversary programs included *One Night Only: Hip-Hop x Rock x Visual Art*, a rock, hip hop, and art mash-up with local rock group Low Cut Connie that, among other activities, featured visual artist Gianni Lee painting a Cadillac Escalade onstage; "Darin Atwater's Black Metropolis," a concert that featured Moody and The Philadelphia Orchestra performing Atwater's composition *Black Metropolis*, along with members from Atwater's Soulful Symphony and DJ Wendel Patrick; and *The Art of Storytelling*, which featured Moody and Time for Three, the string trio whose career took off after an impromptu performance during a power failure at the Mann 20 years earlier (see pages 336–337). *One Night Only* was presented as part of the Downstage @ the Mann series; the *Art of Storytelling* was produced in conjunction with WXPN, the University of Pennsylvania's adult alternative radio station, and was part of the Mann's "Party in the Park" gala fundraiser.

Also in 2023 the Mann created a new jazz curator position, naming bassist Gerald Veasley to the role. A longtime area jazz musician and educator, Veasley was appointed in 2018 as the inaugural president of Jazz Philadelphia, an organization whose mission is to nurture Philadelphia's rich jazz scene and promote the city as an international jazz destination. Veasley had performed at the Mann in the 1980s as part of the Kool Jazz Festival and again in 2002 as part of the Mellon Jazz Festival. As jazz curator, Veasley oversaw the Mann's "Jazz Under the Stars presented by Cadillac" series, which began in 2021. He was responsible for selecting the artists for the series and performing with them in the intimate Crescendo tent. As he noted:

> Jazz music has strong roots in Philadelphia, but it's so important to also focus on the vitality that the genre and jazz community holds today. I'm looking forward to showcasing this incredibly talented group of musicians . . . through my curation of Jazz Under the Stars. I can't wait to celebrate this music with our jazz community at the Mann and work to foster a love for jazz with new audiences, including the young people in the Mann's educational programs.[13]

## Special Memories

Longtime Mann staff have fond memories of getting to know artists who appeared often at the venue. "Diana Ross was a lot of fun," remembered Debbie Lobel. "Riverdance [was here] for many years and . . . we became like family. . . . Tony Bennett was amazing, and he told me I was pretty. It was so sweet."[14] Jerry Grabey, whom Freddie Mann hired a few weeks before the venue opened in 1976, became friends with the English rock group The Moody Blues; with the husband-and-wife jazz team of Cleo Laine and John Dankworth; and especially with Bonnie Raitt, whom he knew from having managed her shows when he worked at the Temple Ambler Music Festival in the early 1970s and then when she began appearing at the Mann in the early 1980s.[15] Nancy Newman remembered the famous artists she observed giving generously of their time and attention:

> Some of the great artists that came to the Mann were as fabulous backstage as they were onstage. . . . Sometimes the bigger they are, the bigger they are [as people]. And they were gracious. When I think of Yo-Yo Ma, Itzhak Perlman, Zubin Mehta, Tony Bennett, Harry Belafonte. When I think of how . . . warm they were, how much time they took in speaking with people, people who were lining up to talk with them . . . , they were really with that person in that moment.

One of Newman's fondest memories is of how caring James Taylor was with a special fan:

> I received a phone call about someone who adored James Taylor. This young man had cerebral palsy and was quite handicapped. He had attended many James Taylor concerts with his mother, who had passed away. The individual

who called me wanted to know if this young man could possibly meet Taylor. To that end, we arranged for him to attend a rehearsal. James Taylor's rehearsals are completely closed, so we were the only ones in the house, sitting in my box. When the rehearsal was over, Taylor came out to the box, introduced himself to this young man, came and sat down, [and] had the most heartwarming conversation. . . . Taylor then asked if this young man had ever been on a stage, which he had not. So we managed to get him up on the stage; and as Taylor showed him the sound board, the band came out to say hello. They all knew this young man's name. At the end of this fabulous conversation, James Taylor turned to the young man and his aunt, who was with him, and said, "How would you like to have dinner with me in the Green Room after the concert?" . . . For me, that is one of my favorite stories of being at the Mann.[16]

Interviewed on the Mann stage in July 2023, prior to his 21st appearance at the venue, Taylor spoke fondly of the Mann and his long history with Philadelphia audiences:

> As time goes by, I'm grateful that places like this exist. . . . This one in particular, because it's in Philadelphia, it's really an important place for us to play. Early on, when I was just a solo act touring with a guitar, I played out at the Main Point [a legendary folk club in the Philadelphia suburbs] a lot and at other smaller clubs in Philadelphia, and I had an early and very important, to me, audience in Philadelphia. . . . It always has the sense of being a special place to play; the audience is like none other. Philadelphia is a music-loving city, and it's generated such great music, too. You feel that when you summon an audience here in Philadelphia, . . . they're alive, and they catch anything you pitch. It's a great place to play.[17]

## The Mann Team

Managing such a dynamic, multifaceted performing arts center that functions on such a high level as the Mann Center takes an engaged, resourceful Board of Directors and a committed, talented staff. Cahill had high praise for both. She acknowledged "the Board of Directors who have been most generous and who are passionate and supportive of all we do," noting especially the important role of the two Board chairs during her tenure: Justin Klein and Christopher Bruner. "They have both been stalwart leaders, generous with their time, excellent thought partners, and sounding boards who have helped me immeasurably in leading the organization. . . . They have each been so impactful as leaders in this organization, ensuring our legacy of excellence lives on."

■ Mann Center staff pose at the campus in November 2023. (Mann Center for the Performing Arts Archives)

In 2013, the Board created a Chairman's Council, composed of former Board members who had rotated off the Board but wished to stay involved, as well as individuals who wanted to play a role but were not ready or in a position to join the Board. Between the Board of Directors and the Chairman's Council, the Mann had the benefit of more than 100 Board and Board-affiliated individuals supporting the institution in various capacities.

The executive staff that managed the Mann under Cahill's leadership in the mid-2020s included Vice President of People Operations and Chief Operating Officer Anthony Boyd-Slade; Senior Vice President and Chief Advancement Officer Joan Roebuck-Carter; Vice President of Artistic Planning and Chief Innovation Officer Toby Blumenthal; Vice President of Marketing and Chief Brand Officer Kelly Schempp; Vice President and Chief Financial Officer Megan O'Shea; Chief Education, Community Engagement Officer, and Vice President Naomi Gonzalez; Vice President of Special Projects Pat Sanders; and General Manager Evan Rogers. Together with their departmental staff, they kept the Mann Center going day to day while helping it achieve its broader institutional goals and objectives. "I cannot say enough about each of these treasured individuals and their unfailing commitment to excellence in all they do," Cahill noted in appreciation. "Their esprit de corps is unmatched in the city of Philadelphia, in my judgment. Collectively, they are a force that is unbeatable. They excel, they celebrate together, and they succeed beyond anyone's expectations."

The Board and staff of the Mann had much to be proud of in the mid-2020s: major improvements to the venue's physical landscape and facilities; expanded and diversified concert offerings; large, enthusiastic audiences; deeper, more wide-ranging community engagement and education programs; a diverse Board and staff; and the institution

■ Phish performs at the Mann on July 20, 2022. The group is a longtime Mann favorite, having played many epic, sold-out shows since their debut at the venue in 1992. (Mann Center for the Performing Arts Archives)

operating on a firm financial footing—"all the hallmarks of a functioning, healthy, vibrant, world-class performing arts center in a city of Philadelphia's unique and historic character," according to Cahill. When she started at the Mann in 2008, there were eight full-time staff; the annual operating budget was approximately $6 million; and there was no endowment or cash reserves. As of 2024, there were more than 45 full-time staff; the annual budget was $45 million; and there were sufficient cash reserves and a modest but growing endowment. "The Mann is a real success story," noted Justin Klein. "Cathy Cahill has guided the Mann to prosperity with aplomb and skill."[18]

## Live Nation

Critical to the Mann's success in this period was its partnership with Live Nation Entertainment. By the time the two organizations signed an exclusive booking agreement in 2020, Live Nation had grown into the world's largest entertainment company, a multinational enterprise that included concert promotion, ticketing (as a result of its 2010 merger with Ticketmaster), artist management, and branding and sponsorship. In Philadelphia, Live Nation owned or managed most of the major music venues in and around the city—from the 1,000-capacity Theatre of Living Arts (TLA) on South Street to the 25,000-seat Freedom Mortgage Pavilion (originally the E-Centre) in Camden—and it booked large-scale concerts at the South Philadelphia sports arena and stadiums. Adding the Mann to its roster gave Live Nation a unique, flexible venue that could accommodate a wide range of concerts and events in a beautiful natural setting in Fairmount Park.

Geoff Gordon, longtime president of Live Nation Philadelphia and later president of Live Nation Northeast, expressed his fondness for the Mann in 2024:

> The Mann Center for the Performing Arts is a Philadelphia treasure. People from the greater Philadelphia region gather with friends and family to enjoy live music under the stars in Fairmount Park, creating unforgettable moments. The Mann's incredible atmosphere and the breathtaking view of Philadelphia add to its charm, making it a favorite among music fans, artists, and musicians. It's a very special place and we're very fortunate to work with the incredible team at the Mann and present countless memories for so many.[19]

Cahill conveyed her appreciation for the Live Nation team and how they helped elevate the status of the Mann:

> At the end of the day, it's always about the strengths and talents of the people involved. Having brought Live Nation on as exclusive booking partner, we at the Mann are the fortunate beneficiaries of the remarkable creativity and dedication of their team: President Geoff Gordon, Senior Vice President Jon Hampton, Director of Marketing and Programming Jen Corsilli, and others in the Philadelphia office, along with Matt Prieshoff and Matt Rogers at the national level. Their artistic influence is the envy of the industry, and their leadership and vision have helped bring world-class artists of all genres to our stages. Our partnership ensures that the Mann remains one of the nation's best outdoor venues and a premier concert destination in our region. As we look to the future, we envision a long-term relationship with Live Nation, whose local staff have become like family to many of us here at the Mann.

## Looking Forward

The Mann Center has come a long way since the organization was established in 1930 by a group of music lovers and civic leaders who came together with the dream of building a summer home for The Philadelphia Orchestra. They fulfilled their dream in July of that year with the opening of the Robin Hood Dell in East Fairmount Park. Forty-six years later, led by the indefatigable Fredric R. Mann, the organization real-

■ Aerial view of the Mann Center during the September 9, 2023, One Fine Day Festival presented by Sting and Shaggy. The all-day, multi-artist event made its festival debut at the Mann that day. The Philadelphia skyline is in the background. (Live Nation drone photograph by Steve Garfinkel)

ized a new dream with the opening of the Robin Hood Dell West, later renamed the Mann Music Center and still later the Mann Center for the Performing Arts.

The changes that have unfolded, across the nation and the world, since the organization was founded have been nothing short of revolutionary—in music, technology, media, entertainment, and society at large. Through it all, the fundamental mission has been the same: to provide high-quality music and an enriching experience to the people of the Philadelphia area in a beautiful natural setting. There have been many setbacks along the way in fulfilling that mission, and several times the institution faced crises that threatened its very existence, but each time it emerged stronger and more dynamic than ever. The Mann has survived and thrived largely because it is both *in* and *of* the city it serves—an integral part of Philadelphia's cultural fabric, a vital community asset, and a beloved gathering place for lovers of music and the performing arts.

As this history has demonstrated, the Mann will inevitably face challenges in the years ahead—another economic downturn at some point, unforeseen changes in audience tastes and expectations, perhaps an upheaval in the concert industry or a totally unprecedented development such as the COVID-19 pandemic. But the Mann is an especially strong and stable institution in the mid-2020s and seems well positioned to meet any challenges that may lie ahead.

Chairman of the Board Christopher Bruner notes:

> People who come to the Mann, both new patrons visiting for the first time and those who have not been here in a while, are blown away by the beautiful campus and the great programs we offer. . . . We have all kinds of artists now: rock, classical, popular, country, soul, R&B, jazz, and hip hop. . . . The Mann

has to be creative and thoughtful in determining who its audience is and in providing them with the kind of programs they want.

Bruner cited three Board priorities for ensuring that, going forward, the Mann maintains the level of excellence and success it has enjoyed in the early 21st century: strategic capital spending on the campus, strengthening the Board, and continued and enhanced fundraising to make it all possible.[20] To that end, a $70 million campaign announced in 2025 will fund a major renovation of the Mann campus, along with ambitious artistic programming and public engagement in the Mann's rich history—all to be unveiled in 2026.

The Mann Center for the Performing Arts celebrates two major milestones within a few years of the publication of this book: the 50th anniversary in 2026 of the opening of the current venue and the centennial in 2030 of the founding of the organization. "The former commemorates a sense of place, celebrating a handsome venue in a historic, beautiful section of West Fairmount Park," Cahill said, "while the latter honors a remarkable 100-year institutional legacy." As the Mann approaches these key moments, its vibrant community—its Board of Directors, Chairman's Council, staff, patrons, artists, volunteers, neighbors, and the people of Philadelphia and beyond—can be proud and thankful for the special place that is the Mann Center for the Performing Arts. Here's to another "Century of Music Under the Stars"!

# Acknowledgments

In acknowledging the many people who have played a role in producing this book, I must start at the top, with Mann Center for the Performing Arts President and Chief Executive Officer Catherine M. Cahill. Her passion for the history of the organization she leads has inspired a number of Mann Center history projects, including this book. It is one thing to love the history of your organization; it is quite another to actually invest in the work of documenting and sharing that history, which Cathy has done many times. The book is one of several Mann history projects that she initiated on which I have had the good fortune to work. My relationship with the Mann began when Cathy hired me as consulting archivist in 2016 to begin the process of organizing and preserving the Mann's institutional archives. In 2019, the Mann hired a full-time archivist and digital asset manager to take on that work, and I transitioned to the role of Mann historian. In this capacity I have written a series of historical blogs; curated a permanent timeline exhibit; interviewed key individuals in Mann history; and written this book. My sincere thanks to Cathy for supporting these important initiatives and for her many words of encouragement during the writing of the book.

Helping to shape the content and style of the book has been a group of reviewers who read drafts along the way and offered valuable feedback. The group was composed of both internal Mann staff and outside experts. The Mann Center reviewers, in addition to Cathy Cahill, included Senior Vice President and Chief Advancement Officer Joan Roebuck-Carter, Vice President of Marketing and Chief Brand Officer Kelly Schempp, Archivist and Digital Asset Manager Sarah Leu, and 50th Anniversary Adviser Evans Mirageas. Senior Project Manager of Programming Brandon Ehrenreich and Vice President of Artistic Planning and Chief Innovation Officer Toby Blumenthal weighed in occasionally with helpful feedback. The outside experts included Darrin Britting, Director of Publications and Content Development for The Philadelphia Orchestra/Ensemble Arts; Theresa Stuhlman, Preservation and Development Administrator, Philadelphia Parks and Recreation; Sam Katz, documentary film producer and Philadelphia civic entrepreneur; and Joseph Horowitz, cultural historian and expert on classical music in America. Their collective input improved the book immeasurably.

Of this group, Darrin Britting, Sarah Leu, and Theresa Stuhlman merit special recognition for their in-depth readings of my drafts and their many detailed edits and suggestions. They each brought a wealth of expertise to the endeavor: Darrin in Philadelphia Orchestra history and classical music artists and repertoire; Sarah in Mann Center history; and Theresa in Fairmount Park history. They went above and beyond in giving of their time, sharing their expertise, and helping to make the book as accurate possible.

In preparation for the Mann's 50th anniversary in 2026, we conducted a series of "Mann Moments" interviews with individuals who have played a significant role in the institution's history. The production team for these interviews included Brandon Ehrenreich, Sarah Leu, Evans Mirageas, Mann Center Videographer Shawn Hatten, Communications Consultant Katherine Blodgett, and me. These interviews were an especially important source of information for the book.

A group of Mann staff helped select and secure permissions to use more recent photographs for the later chapters of the book. The group included Kelly Schempp, Sarah Leu, Shawn Hatten, Director of Creative Services Phil Welcome, and Senior Director of Creative Strategy Jenna Brower. Shawn did quite a bit of photography and photo editing for the book, and he and Sarah spent considerable time tracking down images in the Mann Archives. Some of the 21st-century photos were taken by Mann house photographers Jordan August, Derek Brad, and Dan Drufovka, and by a contracted photographer, Mike Oswald. Toby Blumenthal and Kelly Schempp helped secure permissions from performing artists and concert promoters for use of their images.

Mann Center Vice President of People Operations and Chief Operating Officer Anthony Boyd-Slade served as project manager for the book for the Mann, overseeing the finances and schedule and coordinating the publishing agreement with Temple University Press. Manager of Board of Director Relations and the President's Office Alison Larkin was most efficient in managing communications and sharing files for the project.

Special thanks to the team at Temple University Press, including Editor-in-Chief Aaron Javsicas, Editorial Assistant and Rights and Contracts Coordinator Will Forrest, Senior Production Editor Ashley Petrucci, and Director Mary Rose Muccie. As editor of the book, Aaron was especially insightful in reviewing my drafts and serving as a sounding board while managing the project overall and keeping it (and me) on track. Will's expertise in image quality and formats and rights and reproduction issues was invaluable, as was Ashley's help in the editorial process. My thanks also to Temple University Dean of Libraries Joe Lucia, who helped facilitate the agreement that allowed the use of dozens of images from *The Philadelphia Inquirer* photograph collection housed at Temple Libraries' Special Collections Research Center (SCRC). Representatives of the *Inquirer*, Temple University Press, and SCRC came together to work out the details of that agreement. The group included Aaron, Will, and Mary Rose from Temple University Press; Vice President and Associate General Counsel Suzanne Mitchell Parillo and Chief Operating Officer and Chief Financial Officer Andrew Harrison from *The Philadelphia Inquirer*; Associate Archivist Brenda Galloway-Wright and Coordinator of Public Services and Outreach Josué Hurtado from Temple Libraries' SCRC; and me.

The book has benefited tremendously from the firsthand accounts of those who sat for videotaped Mann Moments interviews and those I interviewed individually. The former include Nancy Newman, Gilda Mann Rand Ellis and Jane Gitomer, Marciarose Shestack, William Leonard, Peter Gould, Larry Magid, Jerry Bates, James Taylor, Chill Moody, the group Time for Three, Gerald Veasley, Frank and Ditta Hoeber, Susan Slawson and Facetta Greene, Debbie Lobel, and Anthony Parnther. Zubin Mehta and Jerome Lowenthal were interviewed by Zoom. Catherine Cahill sat for two lengthy one-on-one interviews with me that were exceptionally important, and my Zoom interview and follow-up emails with Peter Lane were equally informative. Between Cathy and Peter, I had the benefit of firsthand insights of the two Mann presidents since 1996. Others I interviewed individually include Jerry Grabey, Larry Magid, Justin Klein, Christopher Bruner, Joseph Kluger, Matias Tarnopolsky, Alan Greenberger, Stephen Starr, and Lucinda Hudson. Larry Magid, Jerry Grabey, Nancy Newman, and Jane Gitomer were among those whom I consulted multiple times over the course of writing the book. My thanks to all.

Research in archival collections formed the other key part of this book, and I am indebted to the archivists, curators, and reference staff at historical repositories who provided assistance. In addition to the Mann Center for the Performing Arts Archives, repositories whose collections I used extensively and whose staff were most helpful include Temple University Libraries' SCRC; the University of Pennsylvania Libraries' Kislak Center for Special Collections, Rare Books, and Manuscripts; the Free Library of Philadelphia Print and Picture Collection; and the Philadelphia Parks and Recreation Archive. I also spent a week examining the 77 boxes of Fredric R. Mann papers at Yale University's Irving S. Gilmore Music Library, whose staff were very helpful and accommodating.

Of the foregoing, a number of people merit special mention for their efforts on behalf of the book. In 2022, The Philadelphia Orchestra Association transferred the Orchestra's extensive archives to the Kislak Center, which then commenced a multiyear project to process the records to make them available for research. I had used the records often when I served as consulting archivist for the Orchestra from 2011 to 2022, but access to them now was more difficult, since some of the materials were actively being processed while others were in storage awaiting processing. Orchestra Executive Director Ryan Fleur and Darrin Britting authorized my access to the records, and Kislak staff were very accommodating in getting me the materials I needed. My thanks to Sean Quimby, John Pollack, Sarah Heim, Holly Mengel, Eri Muzikane, and, especially, Anna Juliar, processing archivist for the Orchestra records, who was most helpful in arranging for me to examine records on which she was working. Katia Strieck and Joseph Fishman at Penn's remote records storage facility LIBRA were very accommodating also.

At Kislak, I also consulted the Eugene Ormandy papers, photographs, and oral history interviews, and accessed Kislak's online sources for photographs from the Marian Anderson Collection and the Oliver Daniel research collection on Dimitri Mitropoulos. John Pollack procured the Marian Anderson and Oliver Daniels images. Darrin Britting, as he has been throughout the project, was most helpful in providing access to archival records that were still in the Orchestra's possession, as well as images in the Orchestra's Digital Library.

Another major repository of which I made extensive use was Temple University Libraries' SCRC, which houses the voluminous *Philadelphia Inquirer* and *Evening Bulletin* photograph and clippings files. These were invaluable sources of information. My thanks to former SCRC Director Margery Sly and current staff members Brenda Galloway-Wright, Josué L. Hurtado, Ann Mosher, and John Pettit for being so helpful with my many research visits and scanning requests, which were numerous and sometimes urgent. As previously noted, Brenda and Josué were part of the group that negotiated the agreement for permission to use *Philadelphia Inquirer* photographs.

The outstanding collections of the Free Library of Philadelphia were another important resource. I thank Chief of Special Collections Janine Pollock and, especially, Curator of the Print and Picture Collection Laura Stroffolino and the staff of the Reproductions Department, who accommodated my many (sometimes urgent) image requests. Curator of Music Special Collections Gary Galván and former Supervisor of the Music Department Willhem Echevarria were helpful resources as well. An image from the Free Library Map Collection also appears in the book. The Philadelphia Parks and Recreation Archives, which houses important materials on Fairmount Park history, was yet another key source of images for the book. Theresa Stuhlman, in addition to reviewing drafts of the book, provided these images.

Staff at other archival repositories that provided images or access to collections for research purposes include Barbara Benedett at the Curtis Institute of Music Archives; Kristina Wilson at the Athenaeum of Philadelphia; Joshua Blay at the Philadelphia City Archives; Lexy Nilles at the Historical Society of Pennsylvania; John

Tomasicchio at the Metropolitan Opera Archives; Celia Caust-Ellenbogen at Friends Historical Library, Swarthmore College; Judith Andrews at the National Museum of African American History and Culture; and Emil Corb at Williams College Special Collections, Paul Whiteman Collection. The book also includes images from the online digital libraries of the Philadelphia Museum of Art; New York Public Library; David Rumsey Map Collection, Stanford Libraries; Library of Congress Prints and Photographs Division and Music Division; Wikipedia Commons; and various historical newspapers through Newspapers.com.

Several institutions that are not archival repositories also provided images. My thanks to Mia Kang of the Philadelphia Folklore Project; Antoinette Follett of the American Federation of Musicians; Edward S. Condra of the *Main Line Times and Suburban*; and Paul Steinke of the Preservation Alliance for Greater Philadelphia. Margaret Jerrido, consulting archivist for *The Philadelphia Tribune* (and other institutions) was helpful in searching for *Tribune* images.

Equally important were owners of private collections who provided images for the book. I am indebted to Jane Gitomer, granddaughter of Fredric Mann; Joan Mackie, daughter of Mary Binney Montgomery; Keely Stahl, longtime partner of the late Jerry Blavat; Larry Magid and his assistant Andrea McFadden; and Peter Lane for their personal images. An image from my personal collection also appears in the book.

To all of the aforementioned individuals and institutions, my sincere thanks for your many contributions to this book.

Finally, thanks to my wife and partner in history, Patty O'Connor McCarthy, an excellent historian in her own right, who supports me in all my endeavors and tolerates the crazy schedules and pressing deadlines my work often entails.

# Sources

Most of the information contained in this book was gathered from two main primary sources: recent interviews with those who played a role in the history of the Robin Hood Dell or Mann Center for the Performing Arts and research in original archival collections. The interviews include a series of videotaped Mann Moments sessions led by a team of Mann Center staff beginning in late 2022 and separate one-on-one interviews conducted by the author in person, online via Zoom, or by telephone. (Note that the Mann Moments interviews continued beyond fall 2024, but interviews after that were not done in time to be consulted for the book.)

Listed here are the interviews that were conducted and key archival collections that were consulted. Other sources that were consulted—published materials, other archival collections—are noted in the endnotes to the book.

## Mann Moments Interviews

Nancy Newman, December 16, 2022
Gilda Mann Rand Ellis and Jane Gitomer, December 17, 2022
Marciarose Shestack, March 17, 2023
William Leonard, March 18, 2023
Larry Magid, May 2, 2023
Peter Gould, May 5, 2023
Jerry Bates, May 5, 2023
Zubin Mehta, interviewed via Zoom, May 24, 2023
James Taylor, July 1, 2023
Chill Moody, August 10, 2023
Frank and Ditta Hoeber, October 4, 2023

Susan Slawson and Facetta Greene, October 4, 2023
Gerald Veasley, October 7, 2023
Time for Three, October 11, 2023
Debbie Lobel, June 10, 2024
Anthony Parnther, June 20, 2024
Jerome Lowenthal, interviewed via Zoom, October 10, 2024

## Interviews by the Author

* All interviews conducted by Zoom or telephone except March 2024 Catherine Cahill interviews, which were done in person. Several interviewees did both Mann Moments interviews and separate interviews with the author.

Jerry Blavat, October 2021
Jerry Grabey, March 16, 2023, and May 2, May 6, and May 29, 2024
Patsy Baxter Rowe, June 6, 2023
Catherine Cahill, March 12, March 28, and June 25, 2024
Joseph Kluger, April 2, 2024
Peter Lane, April 15, 2024
Alan Greenberger, April 18, 2024
Stephen Starr, April 25, 2024
Debbie Lobel, May 1, 2024
Joan Mackie, May 9, 2024
Matias Tarnopolsky, May 23, 2024
Lucinda Hudson, May 24, 2024
Larry Magid, May 28, 2024
Justin Klein, June 23, June 25, and July 14, 2024
Christopher Bruner, July 13, 2024

## Key Archival Collections Consulted

Mann Center for the Performing Arts Archives
Fredric R. Mann papers, Irving S. Gilmore Music Library, Yale University
Philadelphia Orchestra Association records, Kislak Center for Special Collections, Rare Books, and Manuscripts, University of Pennsylvania
Eugene Ormandy papers, Kislak Center for Special Collections, Rare Books, and Manuscripts University of Pennsylvania
*Philadelphia Inquirer* photographs and clippings and *Evening Bulletin* photographs and clippings, Special Collections Research Center, Temple University Libraries
American Federation of Musicians, Local 77 Records, Special Collections Research Center, Temple University Libraries
Print and Picture Collection, Free Library of Philadelphia
Philadelphia Parks and Recreation Archives (Fairmount Park Archives)
Philadelphia City Archives, Department of Records, City of Philadelphia
Philadelphia newspapers consulted via Newspapers.com

# Notes

## Preface

1. Patsy Baxter Rowe, phone call and emails with the author, May–June 2023.

2. Miller, quoted in "An Inspiring Leader," *Philadelphia Orchestra* (blog), November 20, 2019, accessed March 2024; Worley, quoted in "The Kimmel Center's Verizon Hall to Be Renamed for Philadelphia Legend Marian Anderson," *The Philadelphia Inquirer*, February 28, 2024.

3. "Orchestra to Cut Summer Concerts at Mann," *The Philadelphia Inquirer*, April 8, 2009.

## Chapter 1

1. Nicholas Wainwright, ed., "The Diary of Samuel Breck," *Pennsylvania Magazine of History and Biography*, vol. 102, no. 4, October 1978, 477.

2. *Second Annual Report of the Commissioners of Fairmount Park* (Philadelphia: King and Baird, 1870), 16, 58, 63, Records of Fairmount Park Commission, City of Philadelphia, Department of Records, City Archives.

3. Annual Reports, 1871–1874, Records of Fairmount Park Commission, City of Philadelphia, Department of Records, City Archives.

4. "Zoological Garden," *The Philadelphia Inquirer*, August 22, 1874.

5. James McClelland and Lynn Miller, *City in a Park: A History of Philadelphia's Fairmount Park System* (Philadelphia: Temple University Press, 2015), 151.

6. Henry T. Fink, *Wagner and His Works: The Story of His Life, with Critical Comments*, vol. 2 (New York: Charles Scribner's Sons, 1907), 509.

7. Rose Fay Thomas, *Memoirs of Theodore Thomas* (New York: Moffat, Yard, 1911), 121.

8. "Centennial Musical Festival," *The Philadelphia Inquirer*, September 11, 1876; "Centennial Musical Festival," *Philadelphia Times*, September 12, 1876.

9. "Fairmount Park Band," *The Philadelphia Inquirer*, February 11, 1899.

10. "Free City Concerts to Begin Tomorrow," *The Philadelphia Inquirer*, July 16, 1922.

11. "Lemon Hill Concert Broadcast by WFI," *North American*, August 1, 1924.

12. "High Taste of Philadelphians Expressed in Park Concert," *The Philadelphia Inquirer*, September 8, 1922.

13. "A Suggested Location for Summer Concerts," *Public Ledger*, March 25, 1930.

14. "Fritz Scheel Collapsed on Eve of Concert," *The Philadelphia Inquirer*, February 9, 1907.

15. "City Payroll Survey Is Placed in the 1930 Budget," *The Philadelphia Inquirer*, November 21, 1929.

16. "Third Annual Report of Harry A. Mackey, Mayor of Philadelphia: Reports of Departments, 1930," 569, City of Philadelphia, Department of Records, City Archives.

17. Records of the Philadelphia Arts Association from the early 1930s, held by the Athenaeum of Philadelphia, document the evolution of the project.

## Chapter 2

1. Abbott's initial meeting with Judson and their subsequent work laying the groundwork for the summer concerts series are detailed in "Third Annual Report of Harry A. Mackey, Mayor of Philadelphia: Reports of Departments, Philadelphia, 1930," 569–583, City of Philadelphia, Department of Records, City Archives.

2. Minutes of Meeting of Local No. 77, American Federation of Musicians, February 4, 1930, American Federation of Musicians, Local 77 records, SCRC 827, Special Collections Research Center, Temple University Libraries.

3. Elizabeth A. Fones-Wolf, "Sound Comes to the Movies: The Philadelphia Musicians' Struggle Against Recorded Music," *Pennsylvania Magazine of History and Biography*, vol. 118, 1994, 3–32.

4. Minutes of Board of Directors of The Philadelphia Orchestra Association, March 18, 1930, Organizational Governance records, Philadelphia Orchestra Association records, Kislak Center for Special Collections, Rare Books, and Manuscripts, University of Pennsylvania.

5. Charter Book 127, 567–569, City of Philadelphia, Department of Records, City Archives.

6. Minutes of Executive Committee of Local No. 77, American Federation of Musicians, March 5, March 19, March 22, and March 29, 1930, American Federation of Musicians, Local 77 records, SCRC 827, Special Collections Research Center, Temple University Libraries.

7. "Third Annual Report of Harry A. Mackey," 569–583.

8. Ibid.

9. "Sites for Concerts in Park Selected," *Public Ledger*, April 26, 1930.

10. Minutes of Committee on Superintendence and Property, April 25, 1930, Fairmount Park Commission Records, City of Philadelphia, Department of Records, City Archives.

11. "Summer Concerts in Park Assured," *Evening Ledger*, April 26, 1930.

12. "$22,500 Is Pledged for Park Concerts," *The Philadelphia Inquirer*, April 30, 1930.

13. Ibid.

14. "Concert Tickets on Sale Tomorrow," *The Philadelphia Inquirer*, May 11, 1930.

15. Finding aid to Philadelphia Federation of Women's Clubs and Allied Organizations (PFWC) records, Collection 3050, Historical Society of Pennsylvania, accessed April 2024, https://hsp.org/sites/default/files/legacy_files/migrated/findingaid3050pfwc.pdf.

16. "Clubwomen Back Park Orchestra," *The Philadelphia Inquirer*, May 16, 1930.

17. "Activities of Week in Women's Clubs," *The Philadelphia Inquirer*, May 25, 1930.

18. "Lauds Bringing Music to People," *The Evening Bulletin*, June 2, 1930.

19. "World's Best Music Pledged by Mackey for People of Phila[delphia]," *Philadelphia Record*, May 30, 1930.

20. "Ground Broken in Park for Orchestra's Shell," *Public Ledger*, June 3, 1930; "Excavations Begun for New Band Shell," *Philadelphia Record*, June 3, 1930.

21. Building agreement between Wark Company and Summer Concerts Association, June 3, 1930, Fairmount Park records, Philadelphia Parks and Recreation Archive, City of Philadelphia, Parks and Recreation.

22. "Philadelphia Orchestra Opens Summer Series," *Musical Courier*, July 19, 1930.

23. Letter to the editor signed "Apollon Musagetes," *Philadelphia Record*, May 27, 1930.

24. Untitled article, *The Evening Bulletin*, July 8, 1930.

25. "10,000 Hear Opening of Concert Series," *The Evening Bulletin*, July 9, 1930.

26. "Open Music Dell," *Philadelphia Daily News*, July 9, 1930.

27. "Third Annual Report of Harry A. Mackey," 583.

28. "First Concert in Dell Stadium Delights Throng of 12,000," *The Evening Ledger*, July 9, 1930.

29. "12,000 Enthralled by Concert in Dell," *Public Ledger*, July 9, 1930.

30. "10,000 Music Lovers Hear First Concert in Robin Hood Dell," *The Philadelphia Inquirer*, July 9, 1930.

31. "Philadelphia Launches Summer Concerts," *Musical America*, July 1930.

32. "10,000 Music Lovers Hear First Concert in Robin Hood Dell."

33. "A Midsummer Night in Robin Hood Dell," *Evening Public Ledger*, July 10, 1930.

34. "Men and Things," *The Evening Bulletin*, undated clipping, probably July 9, 1930.

35. "Sunday Music to Be Changed in Character," *Public Ledger*, August 2, 1930.

36. "Novelty Wins Favor at Concert in Dell," *The Philadelphia Inquirer*, August 30, 1930.

37. "Large Dell Crowd Shows Enthusiasm," *The Philadelphia Inquirer*, August 29, 1930.

38. "In Philadelphia," *Musical Digest*, September 1930.

39. "Ormandy Triumphs at Concert in Dell," *Public Ledger*, July 22, 1930.

40. "Ormandy Delights in Concert at Dell," *Public Ledger*, July 24, 1930.

41. "Ormandy and Orchestra Open Dell's 41st Season," *The Philadelphia Inquirer*, June 18, 1970.

42. "Long, Patient Line in Dell Nightly," *The Evening Bulletin*, July 22, 1930.

43. *The Philadelphia Inquirer*, July 20, 1930; *Philadelphia Record*, August 14, 1930; *Public Ledger*, August 17, 1930.

44. "Local Musicians Win Dell Concert Honors," *The Philadelphia Inquirer*, August 31, 1930; "Nelson Eddy Wins Triumph at Dell," *Public Ledger*, September 1, 1930.

45. *Musical Digest*, September 1930; *Musical America*, September 1930.

46. Minutes of Board of Directors of The Philadelphia Orchestra Association, October 21, 1930.

47. Third Annual Report of Harry A. Mackey, Mayor of Philadelphia: Reports of Departments, 1930, 577.

48. Minutes of Board of Directors of Philadelphia Orchestra Association, October 21, 1930.

49. "Twenty-seventh Annual Report of the Women's Committees of The Philadelphia Orchestra to the Philadelphia Orchestra Association," Minutes of Board of Directors of The Philadelphia Orchestra Association, May 26, 1931.

50. "For the Information of the Editor—Questions Concerning the Financial Status of the Philadelphia Orchestra's Summer Concerts in Robin Hood Dell" is a six-page typed document in the form of a series of questions and answers. The only known copy is in the George D. McDowell *Philadelphia Evening Bulletin Clippings*, Special Collections Research Center, Temple University Libraries. No author is listed, but the document was likely written by Judson, Tily, or Abbott for distribution to the local press.

51. Minutes of Executive Committee of Local 77, American Federation of Musicians, October 18, 1930.

52. "Twenty-seventh Annual Report of the Women's Committees of The Philadelphia Orchestra to the Philadelphia Orchestra Association."

## Chapter 3

1. "A Feast of Fine Music Under a Starlit Sky," *Public Ledger*, July 8, 1931.

2. "Concerts Stalked by Financial Woe," *Philadelphia Record*, July 5, 1931.

3. "Concerts in Dell May Be Curtailed," *Public Ledger*, July 2, 1931.

4. "Mme. Samaroff Lauds Dell Music," *The Evening Bulletin*, April 13, 1931.

5. "Women Help Summer Concerts Association at Dell," *Jewish Exponent*, July 11, 1931.

6. "Summer Concerts at Dell Were Generally Successful," *Public Ledger*, October 16, 1932. The 77 percent figure is reported in the November 17, 1932, meeting minutes of The Philadelphia Orchestra Association Board, Organizational Governance records, Philadelphia Orchestra Association records, Kislak Center for Special Collections, Rare Books, and Manuscripts, University of Pennsylvania.

7. "Stokowski Directs Park Dell Concert," *The Philadelphia Inquirer*, July 16, 1931.

8. "Stoki in Dell Leads Memorial," *The Philadelphia Inquirer*, July 21, 1933.

9. "Iturbi in Dell Debut Delights," *The Philadelphia Inquirer*, July 19, 1934.

10. Eugene Ormandy to Adrian Siegel, March 3, 1934, Adrian Siegel papers, Philadelphia Orchestra Association records, Kislak Center for Special Collections, Rare Books, and Manuscripts, University of Pennsylvania.

11. Mary Sue Welsh, *One Woman in a Hundred: Edna Phillips and The Philadelphia Orchestra* (Urbana: University of Chicago Press, 2013), 91.

12. "Illness No Flaw to Dell Concert," *The Philadelphia Inquirer*, August 21, 1933.

13. "Negro Singers Again Delight Dell Crowd," *The Philadelphia Inquirer*, July 26, 1931.

14. "Record Dell Crowd Hears Negro Choir," *The Philadelphia Inquirer*, July 29, 1932.

15. "Well Known Folks Hear Johnson's Choir in Fairmount Dell," *The Philadelphia Tribune*, August 10, 1933.

16. "Hall Johnson, 1888–1970," *The New York Times*, May 24, 1970.

17. Montgomery and Stokowski's relationship is recounted in David Nelson Wren, *Adrossan: The Last Great Estate on the Philadelphia Main Line* (New York: Bauer and Dean, 2017), 154–155. Montgomery's daughter Joan Mackie shared further information in a May 9, 2024, phone conversation with the author.

18. "Music: Dancing Philadelphians," *Time*, July 19, 1937.

19. "Many Conductors Scheduled for Robin Hood Dell," *The Philadelphia Inquirer*, June 16, 1935.

20. "Dell Season Ends While 7,000 Cheer," *The Philadelphia Inquirer*, August 31, 1933. *School for Scandal* was premiered at the final concert of the 1933 Dell season.

21. Barbara B. Heyman, *Samuel Barber: The Composer and His Music* (New York: Oxford University Press, 1992), 91.

22. "Wagner Operas for Dell Later, Says Smallens," *The Philadelphia Inquirer*, June 4, 1933. Smallens and Dell officials said at the time that, although the Dell would be presenting operas in 1933, they were not quite ready for the large-scale productions of Wagner operas.

23. Minutes of meeting of Local 77, American Federation of Musicians, May 23, 1931, Local No. 77, American Federation of Musicians records, Special Collections Research Center, Temple University Libraries.

24. Minutes of the Annual Meeting of The Philadelphia Orchestra Association, May 24, 1932, Organizational Governance records, Philadelphia Orchestra Association records, Kislak Center for Special Collections, Rare Books, and Manuscripts, University of Pennsylvania.

25. Ibid.

26. Minutes of the Annual Meeting of The Philadelphia Orchestra Association, May 28, 1935, Organizational Governance records, Philadelphia Orchestra Association records, Kislak Center for Special Collections, Rare Books, and Manuscripts, University of Pennsylvania.

27. "Officials to Decide Dell Concert Fate; Audience Aid Asked," *The Philadelphia Inquirer*, July 21, 1934.

28. "Concert Season at Dell Will Close Wednesday," *The Philadelphia Inquirer*, August 12, 1934.

29. "Dell Sets a New Record with 9,300," *The Philadelphia Inquirer*, August 15, 1934.

30. The relationship between Stokowski, Judson, and The Philadelphia Orchestra Association is detailed in Oliver Daniel, *Stokowski: A Counterpoint of View* (New York: Dodd, Mead, 1982), and James M. Doering, *The Great Orchestrator: Arthur Judson and American Arts Management* (Urbana: University of Illinois Press, 2013).

31. Minutes of Meeting of Local 77, American Federation of Musicians, January 8, 1935, Local No. 77, American Federation of Musicians records, SCRC 827, Special Collections Research Center, Temple University Libraries.

32. "Iturbi and Smallens to Conduct Opening Robin Hood Dell Concerts," *The Philadelphia Inquirer*, June 23, 1935.

33. "Music: Summer Nights," *Time*, July 8, 1935.

34. "Letters," *Time*, July 22, 1935.

35. "Great Music Jeopardized by Jazz?" *The Philadelphia Inquirer*, October 13, 1935.

36. Minutes of The Philadelphia Orchestra Association meetings, February 11, February 18, May 24, 1935, Organizational Governance records, Philadelphia Orchestra Association records, Kislak Center for Special Collections, Rare Books, and Manuscripts, University of Pennsylvania.

37. Minutes of The Philadelphia Orchestra Association meeting, December 30, 1935, Organizational Governance records, Philadelphia Orchestra Association records, Kislak Center for Special Collections, Rare Books, and Manuscripts, University of Pennsylvania.

38. August 1935 program, Robin Hood Dell program books, Music Department, Free Library of Philadelphia.

## Chapter 4

1. June 1936 program, Robin Hood Dell program books, Music Department, Free Library of Philadelphia.

2. "Iturbi Soon to Play; Injuries Not Serious," *The Philadelphia Inquirer,* April 15, 1936. The accident was covered in all the major newspapers at the time.

3. Reginald Allen to Eugene Ormandy, letter, August 10, 1937, Eugene Ormandy papers, Kislak Center for Special Collections, Rare Books, and Manuscripts, University of Pennsylvania.

4. "Iturbi's Changes Cut Dell Off Air," *The Philadelphia Inquirer,* August 10, 1937; "Iturbi Balks, Stops Popular Broadcast," *Daily News* (New York), August 11, 1937; "Music Ends but Row Lingers On," *The Philadelphia Inquirer,* August 11, 1937.

5. "Hurled Chair Shatters Calm of Dell as Arts Collide," *The Philadelphia Inquirer,* August 20, 1936.

6. Dorothy Miller's programs are housed in the Print and Picture Collection of the Free Library of Philadelphia. Her biographical information was provided to library staff in July 2023 by her daughter, Joanne Green, who donated the programs to the library.

7. "Plan Committee of 400 to Assure Dell Concerts," *The Philadelphia Inquirer,* April 28, 1939.

8. Agreement between Robin Hood Dell Concerts Inc. and Local 77, American Federation of Musicians, May 15, 1939, Minutes of Board of Directors of Robin Hood Dell Concerts Inc., Mann Center for the Performing Arts Archives.

9. "5000 Sign to Save Dell," *The Philadelphia Inquirer,* May 4, 1939; "Events of the Day," *The Philadelphia Inquirer,* May 26, 1939; "Dell Opens $45,000 Ticket Campaign," *The Philadelphia Inquirer,* June 4, 1940.

10. "Flautist, Violinist—and Now Cannonist," *The Philadelphia Inquirer,* May 23, 1940.

11. "Bombardier Named by Dell Group," *The Philadelphia Inquirer,* May 28, 1940.

12. "Baby Cannon Salvo Opens Dell Season," *The Philadelphia Inquirer,* June 19, 1940.

13. "Anderson Sets New Dell Mark," *The Philadelphia Inquirer,* July 19, 1940.

14. Ibid.

15. "6,000 at Dell Hear Robeson," *The Philadelphia Inquirer,* August 2, 1940.

16. "Social Glances," *The Philadelphia Tribune,* July 17, 1941; "10,000 Zealots Acclaim Marian Anderson in Brilliant Robin Hood Dell Song Recital," *The Philadelphia Tribune,* July 11, 1942.

17. "Jose Iturbi in Rage over Benny Goodman," *The New York Times,* June 27, 1941; "Music: Turbulent Iturbi," *Time,* July 7, 1941.

18. *K Catalog: Annotated Catalog of Works and Work Editions of Igor Stravinsky till 1971,* accessed May 19, 2024, https://www.kcatalog.org.

19. "10,000 at Dell Hear Goodman in 3 Roles," *The Philadelphia Inquirer,* July 11, 1941.

20. "Paul Robeson, Benny Goodman, and Colored Stars Delight Big Robin Hood Dell Crowds," *The Philadelphia Tribune,* July 17,1941.

21. Ibid.

22. Larry Adler, *It Ain't Necessarily So: An Autobiography* (New York: Grove, 1987).

23. "Judy Garland Sets New Dell Record," *The Philadelphia Inquirer,* July 2, 1943.

24. "Judy Garland Enraptures Dell Crowd," *The Philadelphia Inquirer,* July 3, 1943.

25. Ibid.

26. Harl McDonald and Frances Wister, correspondence, July 1943, Administrative records, Philadelphia Orchestra Association records, Kislak Center for Special Collections, Rare Books, and Manuscripts, University of Pennsylvania.

27. "Boy, 14, in Ormandy Role," *The New York Times*, January 7, 1945; 1944–1945 Season Scrapbook, Philadelphia Orchestra Association records, Kislak Center for Special Collections, Rare Books, and Manuscripts, University of Pennsylvania.

28. *The Philadelphia Tribune*, July 29, 1944.

29. "Sinatra in Surprise Dell Visit, Sings on Dinah Shore Program," *Philadelphia Record*, July 7, 1945.

30. Ibid.

31. "Record Crowd at Dell for Jeanette MacDonald," *The Philadelphia Inquirer*, July 21, 1945.

32. Correspondence in the Administrative records of The Philadelphia Orchestra Association document the exchanges between Hocker and McDonald and the Orchestra's support of the Dell in the 1940s: Administrative records, Philadelphia Orchestra Association records, Kislak Center for Special Collections, Rare Books, and Manuscripts, University of Pennsylvania.

33. F. H. Strawbridge to Orville Bullitt, letter, May 4, 1942, Administrative records, Philadelphia Orchestra Association records, Kislak Center for Special Collections, Rare Books, and Manuscripts, University of Pennsylvania.

34. Strawbridge to McDonald, letter, May 25, 1942, Administrative records, Philadelphia Orchestra Association records, Kislak Center for Special Collections, Rare Books, and Manuscripts, University of Pennsylvania.

35. McDonald to Hocker, letter, May 22, 1945, Administrative records, Philadelphia Orchestra Association records, Kislak Center for Special Collections, Rare Books, and Manuscripts, University of Pennsylvania.

36. "Recording Dispute Settled," *The Philadelphia Inquirer*, May 13, 1945. David Hocker and Harl McDonald, correspondence, 1940s, Administrative records, Philadelphia Orchestra Association records, Kislak Center for Special Collections, Rare Books, and Manuscripts, University of Pennsylvania.

37. "Cheers for Dell," *The Philadelphia Inquirer*, September 19, 1944.

38. As recounted in William Trotter, *Priest of Music: The Life of Dimitri Mitropoulos* (Portland, OR: Amadeus, 1995).

39. Amram's reminiscences are in ibid., 215–216.

40. "Prokofiev Symphony Receives Premiere at Robin Hood Dell," *The Evening Bulletin*, June 26, 1947.

41. "Mitropoulos Plays Piano and Leads Dell Orchestra," *The Philadelphia Inquirer*, July 4, 1947.

42. Minutes of Board of Directors, Robin Hood Dell Concerts Inc., June 8, June 24, 1948, Mann Center for the Performing Arts Archives.

43. Ibid. (June 24, 1948); "WFIL to Air Dell Music Tonight," *The Philadelphia Inquirer*, June 28, 1948.

44. "Hazel Scott at Dell Concert Plays Beethoven and 'Boogie,'" *The Philadelphia Inquirer*, June 30, 1948.

45. Quoted in Trotter, *Priest of Music*, 224.

46. Minutes of Board of Directors of Robin Hood Dell Concerts Inc., July 8, 1948, Mann Center for the Performing Arts Archives.

47. Ibid., July 15, July 22, 1948, Mann Center for the Performing Arts Archives. The September 1948 minutes of The Philadelphia Orchestra Association detail its negotiations with the union: Organizational Governance records, Philadelphia Orchestra Association records, Kislak Center for Special Collections, Rare Books, and Manuscripts, University of Pennsylvania.

48. Ibid. (July 22, 1948).

49. "Dell in Red, Season Will End Tonight," *The Philadelphia Inquirer*, July 17, 1948.

50. Ibid.

51. "We Must Save It," *The Evening Bulletin*, August 15, 1948.

52. "For Hillbilly Tunes," *The Evening Bulletin*, August 15, 1948.

53. "Says People Want to Be Amused, Not Educated," *The Evening Bulletin*, August 15, 1948.

54. "Mitropoulos Bows Out," *The Philadelphia Inquirer*, July 22, 1948.

55. Gilda Rand Mann Ellis, Mann Moments Interview, December 17, 2022.

56. Minutes of Board of Directors of Robin Hood Dell Concerts Inc. (July 22, 1948).

57. Ibid.

58. "Mann Named New Dell Head in Move for '49 Season," *The Philadelphia Inquirer*, July 23, 1948.

## Chapter 5

1. "The Man Behind the Mann," *Broad Street Review*, September 3, 2016, accessed May 2024, https://www.broadstreetreview.com/essays/on-the-mann-centers-40th-anniversary-remembering-fredric-r-mann.

2. "Fredric R. Mann, Arts Patron," obituary, *The New York Times*, February 27, 1987.

3. Fredric Mann to Joseph Clark, letter, May 26, 1952, Fredric R. Mann papers, Irving S. Gilmore Music Library, Yale University.

4. Crawford recounts his career in Robert Wilson Crawford, *Reflections of a Recreation Professional* (Arlington, VA: National Recreation and Parks Association, 1993).

5. Ibid., 160.

6. Zubin Mehta, Mann Moments Interview, May 24, 2023.

7. Jane Gitomer, Mann Moments interview, December 17, 2022.

8. Daniel Barenboim, 1997 interview, Fredric R. Mann papers, Irving S. Gilmore Music Library, Yale University.

9. "Mann Fights Use of Park for Carriage Trade," *The Philadelphia Inquirer*, January 31, 1952; "Mann Explores New Sites, Ideas for Dell," *The Philadelphia Inquirer*, June 4, 1972.

10. "Robin Hood Dell's Season Has Auspicious Prospects," *The Philadelphia Inquirer*, June 26, 1949; "Fine Music for Four Cents," *WFLN Program Guide*, June 1961, scrapbook, Mann Center for the Performing Arts Archives.

11. "Renovated Dell Opens 20th Year before 10,000," *The Philadelphia Inquirer*, June 28, 1949.

12. "16,000 Hear Iturbi in Final Concert," *The Philadelphia Inquirer*, August 6, 1949.

13. Resolution of the Robin Hood Dell Orchestra, August 1, 1949, framed document on display in the Mann Center offices, Mann Center for the Performing Arts Archives.

14. "16,000 Hear Iturbi in Final Concert."

15. Duke Ellington, *Music Is My Mistress* (Garden City, NY: Doubleday, 1973), 474.

16. "Billy Rowe's Notebook," *Pittsburgh Courier*, August 6, 1949; "Duke Ellington Concert Heard by 13,000," *The Evening Bulletin*, July 26, 1949.

17. "The Dell Comes of Age," *The Philadelphia Inquirer Magazine*, June 18, 1950.

18. "Movable Aluminum Roof Planned for Dell Concerts," *The Philadelphia Inquirer*, July 23, 1950; "Dell Women Sponsor Fete for Roof," *The Philadelphia Inquirer*, September 24, 1950; "Show Raises $12,000 for Roof over Dell," *The Philadelphia Inquirer*, October 11, 1950.

19. "Dell Strikes Outdoor Note for Children," *The Philadelphia Inquirer*, July 16, 1952.

20. "Prices at Dell Will Be Cut This Season," *The Philadelphia Inquirer*, May 30, 1951.

21. "City to Play Host at Three Free Concerts at the Dell," *The Philadelphia Inquirer*, June 10, 1951.

22. "All Dell Concerts to Be Given Free," *The Philadelphia Inquirer*, February 25, 1953.

23. "Philly Windfall," *Chicago Tribune*, February 25, 1953; "Box Office Banished," *The New York Times*, March 8, 1953.

24. "All Dell Concerts to Be Given Free."

25. "17,000 Attend Opening of Dell Season," *The Philadelphia Inquirer*, June 23, 1953.

26. "Comments by Fredric R. Mann about William Kapell for the Australian Broadcasting Commission," June 1983, Fredric R. Mann papers, Irving S. Gilmore Library, Yale University.

27. Correspondence, Fredric R. Mann papers, Irving S. Gilmore Library, Yale University.

28. "Mann Is Pianist's 'Surrogate Father,'" *The Sunday Bulletin*, June 16, 1974.

29. Ibid.

30. "Concert at Dell Pays Respects to Late William Kapell," *The Philadelphia Inquirer*, July 14, 1954.

31. Jerome Lowenthal, Mann Moments Interview, October 10, 2024.

32. Minutes of Board of Directors of The Philadelphia Orchestra Association, June 11, 1952, Organizational Governance records, Philadelphia Orchestra Association records, Kislak Center for Special Collections, Rare Books, and Manuscripts, University of Pennsylvania.

33. Minutes of Board of Directors of The Philadelphia Orchestra Association, 1953, Organizational Governance records, Philadelphia Orchestra Association records, Kislak Center for Special Collections, Rare Books, and Manuscripts, University of Pennsylvania.

34. Edward Arian, *Bach, Beethoven, and Bureaucracy: The Case of the Philadelphia Orchestra* (Tuscaloosa: University of Alabama Press, 1971), 64.

35. Minutes of Board of Directors of The Philadelphia Orchestra Association, June 25, 1956, Organizational Governance records, Philadelphia Orchestra Association records, Kislak Center for Special Collections, Rare Books, and Manuscripts, University of Pennsylvania.

36. Arian, *Bach, Beethoven, and Bureaucracy*, 64.

37. Richardson Dilworth to Leonard Dill, letter, November 21, 1956, Fredric R. Mann papers, Irving S. Gilmore Music Library, Yale University.

38. Arian, *Bach, Beethoven, and Bureaucracy*, 62.

39. Eugene Ormandy to Fredric Mann, letter, October 1, 1942, Eugene Ormandy papers, Kislak Center for Special Collections, Rare Books, and Manuscripts, University of Pennsylvania.

40. Eugene Ormandy to Wanton Balis, letter, July 18, 1958, C. Wanton Balis Jr. papers, Philadelphia Orchestra Association records, Kislak Center for Special Collections, Rare Books, and Manuscripts, University of Pennsylvania.

41. Arian, *Bach, Beethoven, and Bureaucracy*, 54–57.

42. "Philadelphia Orchestra Interview with Honorable Fredric R. Mann—November 14, 1984," Philadelphia Orchestra Association correspondence, Fredric R. Mann papers, Irving S. Gilmore Music Library, Yale University.

43. Joseph Kluger, interview by the author, April 2, 2024.

44. "Contracts Let for New Dell," *The Evening Bulletin*, June 21, 1955.

45. "Construction Half Completed on Rebuilding Robin Hood Dell," January 26, 1956, unidentified newspaper clipping filed in *Philadelphia Inquirer* newspaper clippings, Special Collections Research Center, Temple University Libraries.

46. "New Dell Opens with Explosion and Beethoven," *The Philadelphia Inquirer*, June 19, 1956.

47. "Dell Presents Singing City," *The Philadelphia Inquirer*, June 23, 1955.

48. "Szell's Cleveland Orchestra Opens Dell Season," *The Philadelphia Inquirer*, June 15, 1958.

## Chapter 6

1. "Financier in the Dell," *The New York Times*, June 19, 1960.

2. Minutes of Board of Directors of Robin Hood Dell Concerts Inc., May 17, 1960, Mann Center for the Performing Arts Archives.

3. "Stokowski Signed for Dell Program; Novelties Promised," *The Philadelphia Inquirer*, April 24, 1960; "Robin Hood Dell Opens Its 31st Season," *The Sunday Bulletin*, June 19, 1960; "Dell Opens June 20 with Operatic Gala," *Philadelphia Daily News*, April 23, 1960.

4. "And Now Our Dell," *Philadelphia Jewish Exponent*, June 17, 1960.

5. Ibid.

6. "Young Dell 'Alumni' to Meet," *Philadelphia Daily News*, July 17, 1961; "Reunion for Children at Dell," *The Philadelphia Inquirer*, July 16, 1961.

7. "Robin Hood Dell Opens Its Season," *The New York Times*, June 21, 1960.

8. "Quiet at the Dell," *Philadelphia Daily News*, July 12, 1960.

9. "Dell's 31st Season Is Acclaimed as Record Breaker," *The Philadelphia Inquirer*, July 31, 1960.

10. Bakhtiar K. Dadabhoy, *Zubin Mehta: A Musical Journey* (Gurugram, India: Penguin, 2016), 76–77.

11. "Israel Philharmonic Returns to Mann," *The Philadelphia Inquirer*, August 29, 2001.

12. Zubin Mehta, *The Score of My Life* (New York: Amadeus, 2006), 37.

13. "31,000 Acclaim Stokowski," *The Philadelphia Inquirer*, July 22, 1960.

14. "Fine Music for Four Cents," *WFLN Radio Guide*, June 1961, 13, scrapbook, Mann Center for the Performing Arts Archives.

15. "Stokowski's Skill and Temper Delight 31,000 at Dell," *The Evening Bulletin*, July 22, 1960; "31,000 Acclaim Stokowski."

16. "Dell Delighted Stokowski; May Be Back," *The Sunday Bulletin*, July 31, 1960.

17. Minutes of Board of Directors of Robin Hood Dell Concerts Inc., October 31, 1960, Mann Center for the Performing Arts Archives.

18. "All Clear at the Dell," *The Philadelphia Daily News*, August 3, 1960.

19. "Dell's 31st Season Is Acclaimed as Record Breaker."

20. Anshel Brusilow, interview conducted by Sharon Eisenhour, February 16, 1992, Eugene Ormandy Oral History Collection, Kislak Center for Special Collections, Rare Books, and Manuscripts, University of Pennsylvania.

21. Brusilow chronicles his career with The Philadelphia Orchestra and Robin Hood Dell Orchestra in Anshel Brusilow and Robin Underdahl, *Shoot the Conductor: Too Close to Monteux, Szell, and Ormandy* (Denton: University of North Texas Press, 2015).

22. "Van Cliburn Triumphs in Combined Role as Conductor, Pianist," *The Philadelphia Inquirer*, August 3, 1963.

23. Brusilow and Underdahl, *Shoot the Conductor*, 171–175.

24. "Solomon's Technique Is Teamed Well with Pianist Watt's Skill," *The Philadelphia Inquirer*, July 7, 1964.

25. "Anna Moffo Won't Hunt Seat for Her Dell Debut Tonight," *The Evening Bulletin*, July 2, 1964.

26. "Anna Moffo Makes Stunning Dell Debut," *The Philadelphia Inquirer*, July 3, 1964.

27. "Dell General Manager Retires with Memories," *The Evening Bulletin*, August 2, 1964, scrapbook, Mann Center for Performing Arts Archives.

28. "Stokowski Rehearses but Dell Awning Hits Chord of Discontent," *The Philadelphia Inquirer*, June 21, 1965.

29. "Miss Anderson, Fiedler Draw 27,000 Fans," *The Philadelphia Inquirer*, July 4, 1967.

30. "All-Time Record Set at Dell by Van Cliburn," *The Philadelphia Inquirer*, July 30, 1965.

31. "A Delightful Season," *Philadelphia Daily News*, August 10, 1965.

32. "A Permanent Conductor for Each Dell Season?" *The Evening Bulletin*, July 26, 1964.

33. "New Format at Dell as Bowl Opens," *The Philadelphia Inquirer*, June 19, 1966.

34. Eugene Ormandy to Fredric Mann, letter, March 26, 1966, Eugene Ormandy papers, Kislak Center for Special Collections, Rare Books, and Manuscripts, University of Pennsylvania.

35. All quotes are from Frank and Ditta Hoeber, Mann Moments Interview, October 4, 2023.

36. Samuel Grafton, "Trouble in Our Symphony Orchestras," *McCall's*, vol. 88, no. 2, November 1960, 84.

37. Minutes of Board of Directors of Robin Hood Dell Concerts Inc., October 23, 1963, Mann Center for the Performing Art Archives.

38. Minutes of Board of Directors of The Philadelphia Orchestra Association, September 23, 1963, Organizational Governance records, Philadelphia Orchestra Association records, Kislak Center for Special Collections, Rare Books, and Manuscripts, University of Pennsylvania.

39. "Dell, Orchestra near Terms," *The Philadelphia Inquirer*, June 10, 1964.

40. Statement of Agreement between Philadelphia Orchestra Association and Robin Hood Dell Concerts Inc., November 1, 1964, Organizational Governance records, Philadelphia Orchestra Association records, Kislak Center for Special Collections, Rare Books, and Manuscripts, University of Pennsylvania.

41. Wanton Balis to J. Cullen Ganey, letter, November 12, 1964, C. Wanton Balis papers, Philadelphia Orchestra Association records, Kislak Center for Special Collections, Rare Books, and Manuscripts, University of Pennsylvania.

42. Minutes of Board of Directors of Philadelphia Orchestra Association, December 27, 1963, Organizational Governance records, Philadelphia Orchestra Association records, Kislak Center for Special Collections, Rare Books, and Manuscripts, University of Pennsylvania.

43. Edward Arian, *Bach, Beethoven, and Bureaucracy: The Case of the Philadelphia Orchestra* (Tuscaloosa: University of Alabama Press, 1971), 78.

44. Minutes of Board of Directors of Philadelphia Orchestra Association, April 22, 1963, September 9, 1963, and February 24, 1964, Organizational Governance records, Philadelphia Orchestra Association records, Kislak Center for Special Collections, Rare Books, and Manuscripts, University of Pennsylvania; "Orchestra Gets Bid to Open '66 Poconos Fete," *The Philadelphia Inquirer*, April 2, 1964.

45. "New York Starts Work on Saratoga Center," *The Philadelphia Inquirer*, July 1, 1964.

46. "Ormandy Has High Praise for SPAC," *The Saratogian*, August 4, 1966.

47. "Dell Season in Retrospect," *The Philadelphia Inquirer*, July 31, 1966.

48. "PTC Plans Special Buses to Robin Hood Dell Concerts," *The Evening Bulletin*, June 16, 1967.

49. "Park Board Nixes Pop Series at Dell," *The Philadelphia Daily News*, April 27, 1967.

50. "Jazz Is an Outlaw at Robin Hood Dell," *The Philadelphia Tribune*, May 13, 1967.

51. "Broaden Dell Use or Face Suit, Foglietta Warns Mann," *Philadelphia Daily News*, June 21, 1967.

52. "Dell War Short, Too," *Philadelphia Daily News*, June 27, 1967.

53. "Only Two Events Booked at Dell after Concerts," *The Philadelphia Inquirer*, July 25, 1967.

54. Jerry Blavat, telephone call with the author, October 2021.

55. All quotes are from "25,000 Teenagers Cheer at Dell 'Rock Jamboree,'" *The Evening Bulletin*, August 9, 1967.

56. Minutes of Board of Directors of Robin Hood Dell Concerts Inc., October 16, 1967, Mann Center for the Performing Arts Archives.

57. Minutes of Board of Directors of The Philadelphia Orchestra Association, June 23, 1969, Organizational Governance records, Philadelphia Orchestra Association records, Kislak Center for Special Collections, Rare Books, and Manuscripts, University of Pennsylvania.

58. "Why So Few Negroes at the Dell?" *The Evening Bulletin*, July 16, 1965.

59. "Concerts in Ghettos: A Musician's View," *The Sunday Bulletin*, July 28, 1968.

60. "City Is Opposed to Extending Dell Season," *The Philadelphia Inquirer*, November 30, 1967.

61. "Ambassador Beams as Cliburn Wows 28,000 at Dell," *Philadelphia Daily News*, June 19, 1968.

62. "Mann Hopes to Save Dell Concerts This Summer," *The Evening Bulletin*, February 12, 1969.

63. "Dell May Survive City's Culture Cuts," *The Philadelphia Inquirer*, February 23, 1969.

64. "Beverly Sill Stars as 40th Season Opens with Concert of French Music," *The Philadelphia Inquirer*, June 17, 1969.

65. Minutes of Board of Directors of The Philadelphia Orchestra Association, April 22, 1968, Organizational Governance records, Philadelphia Orchestra Association records, Kislak Center for Special Collections, Rare Books, and Manuscripts, University of Pennsylvania.

66. Ibid., March 23, 1970, Organizational Governance records, Philadelphia Orchestra Association records, Kislak Center for Special Collections, Rare Books, and Manuscripts, University of Pennsylvania.

67. Ibid., June 22, 1970, Organizational Governance records, Philadelphia Orchestra Association records, Kislak Center for Special Collections, Rare Books, and Manuscripts, University of Pennsylvania; Statement of Amendment of Agreement Dated November 1, 1963, July 15, 1969. (The agreement governing the Dell concerts starting in 1970 was structured as an amendment to the 1963 agreement.)

68. "Cost Rise Forces Dell to Cut 3 Concerts This Summer," *The Sunday Bulletin*, April 5, 1970.

69. "Ormandy and Orchestra Open Dell's 41st Season," *The Philadelphia Inquirer*, June 18, 1970.

70. "Van Cliburn Plays Weather—and Wins," *The Philadelphia Inquirer*, July 24, 1970.

## Chapter 7

1. "Mann Seeks New Home for Dell," *The Philadelphia Daily News*, July 23, 1966.

2. "Robin Hood Dell Seeks More Green Notes from City Friends," *Philadelphia Daily News*, February 15, 1972; "Constellation of Stars Lined Up for Dell," *The Philadelphia Inquirer*, February 15, 1972.

3. "Additional 'Friends' Sought by Dell," *Downtown Record*, March 18, 1971. Robin Hood Dell Concerts Inc. Board Minutes, 1970–1972, clipping and minutes in Mann Center for the Performing Arts Archives.

4. Minutes of Board of Directors of Robin Hood Dell Concerts Inc., November 2, 1970, Mann Center for the Performing Arts Archives.

5. "$9 Million Theater Planned in Fairmount Park," *The Philadelphia Inquirer*, May 21, 1971; "Proposed New Dell Center Draws Raves," *Philadelphia Daily News*, May 21, 1971.

6. Press release statements in Mann Center for the Performing Arts Archives.

7. "Jury Probes Architect's $10 Million Airport Job," *Philadelphia Daily News*, December 12, 1972.

8. Vincent Kling, interview by Walter Massey Phillips, February 13, 1979, Walter Massey Phillips Oral Histories, Temple University Libraries.

9. The controversy was covered extensively in the local press, including "'Anonymous' Donors Are Refurbishing Rizzo's Suite," *The Philadelphia Inquirer*, January 12, 1972; "Mann Given Immunity," *The Philadelphia Inquirer*, December 14, 1974; "Contempt Warrant Sought for Mann," *Philadelphia Daily News*, December 19, 1974; "Judge Explains Why He Didn't Arrest Mann," *Philadelphia Daily News*, February 27, 1975.

10. "Curtin Opens Temple Festival; Ormandy and the Dell in Reunion," *The Philadelphia Inquirer*, June 18, 1972.

11. "Robin Hood Dell Seeks More Green Notes from City Friends."

12. "Dell Attendance Sets Record," *The Evening Bulletin*, August 4, 1971.

13. "Cliburn: A Wild Farewell Concert," *The Evening Bulletin*, July 28, 1972.

14. "30,000 Attend Dell Opener," *The Philadelphia Inquirer*, June 19, 1973; "Splendid 'Rigoletto' Opens Dell's 44th Season," *The Evening Bulletin*, June 19, 1973.

15. "How about a TV System for the Dell? Orchestra Gets Its China Shots Today," *The Evening Bulletin*, July 17, 1973.

16. "Iturbi Draws 30,000," *The Evening Bulletin*, July 13, 1971.

17. "A Chopin Close to Perfection," *The Evening Bulletin*, July 22, 1971.

18. "Mann Explores New Sites, Ideas for Dell," *The Philadelphia Inquirer*, June 4, 1972.

19. "It May Mean a Fight, but Dell Will Be Ready," *The Evening Bulletin*, May 11, 1973.

20. "Summer Discords: Dell and Ambler," *The Sunday Bulletin*, July 2, 1972.

21. Ibid.

22. Philadelphia Orchestra Manager Boris Sokoloff to James Frazier, letter, October 22, 1973, Eugene Ormandy papers, Kislak Center for Special Collections, Rare Books, and Manuscripts, University of Pennsylvania.

23. "Dell's Concert Has Four Blacks," *The Philadelphia Tribune*, June 22, 1975.

24. "A Black Conductor Pushes the Cause of Music," *The New York Times*, November 30, 1975.

25. "James Frazier Has Returned to the Robin," *The Philadelphia Tribune*, April 12, 1975.

26. "Ballet Russian-Style Returns to the Dell," *The Philadelphia Inquirer*, June 26, 1971.

27. "A Cautious Makarova on a Cramped Stage," *The Evening Bulletin*, June 25, 1971.

28. "Valiant Panovs Weather the Storm," *The Evening Bulletin*, July 11, 1975.

29. "The Panovs Dance, Despite the Downpour," *The Philadelphia Inquirer*, July 11, 1975.

30. Minutes of Board of Directors of Robin Hood Dell Concerts Inc., January 9, March 13, May 6, 1974, Mann Center for the Performing Arts Archives.

31. "An Oral History of the Mann Center," *Philadelphia Magazine*, June 2012.

32. "Dell's Friends in the Sky," *The Philadelphia Inquirer*, July 11, 1975.

33. "Rock Concert Flap Fuels Range War in Radioland," *Philadelphia Daily News*, August 20, 1971; "Better Break? Not for Dell Concerts," *The Evening Bulletin*, August 20, 1971.

34. "For Whom the Dell Tolls," *Philadelphia Daily News*, July 25, 1975.

35. "Night at the Dell with Francophonic Frank," *The Evening Bulletin*, September 11, 1972.

36. "Charles and Garner Wow Dell Crowd," *The Evening Bulletin*, August 21, 1974.

37. "Lionel Hampton Keeps Crowd Hopping at Dell," *The Philadelphia Inquirer*, August 29, 1973.

38. The controversy was covered in several local newspaper articles, including "Robin Hood Dell Was Poorly Run, Phila[delphia] Aide Says" and "City Assails Operation of Dell East," *The Philadelphia Inquirer*, April 30, 1980; "Aide's Wife Got $24K for Dell Shows," *Philadelphia Daily News*, May 2, 1980.

39. Minutes of Board of Directors of Robin Hood Dell Concerts Inc., March 29, 1973, Mann Center for the Performing Arts Archives.

40. Minutes of Board of Directors of Robin Hood Dell Concerts Inc., May 31, 1973, Mann Center for the Performing Arts Archives.

41. "It May Mean a Fight, but Dell Will Be Ready."

42. Ibid.

43. "Freddy Mann and His World," *Philadelphia Daily News*, June 14, 1976; "Where Many a Couple Made Music: Now Concert Dell," *Courier-Post* (Camden, NJ), March 24, 1976, scrapbook, Mann Center for the Performing Arts Archives.

44. "New Site Is Approved for Dell Amphitheater," *The Philadelphia Inquirer*, October 11, 1973.

45. "Stereo Dells Tax Imagination," *Philadelphia Daily News*, June 11, 1976; "The New Dell: A Brief for the Defense," *The Philadelphia Inquirer*, October 17, 1976.

46. "The New Dell: Asset or Liability," *The Evening Bulletin*, July 26, 1975.

47. Ibid.

48. "'Gruesome' Dell," *The Evening Bulletin*, February 5, 1975.

49. "Better Amphitheater Needed, Official Says," *The Evening Bulletin*, July 26, 1975.

50. "The Music Mann," *The Philadelphia Inquirer*, October 17, 1976.

51. Minutes of Board of Directors of Robin Hood Dell Concerts Inc., October 29, 1974, Mann Center for the Performing Arts Archives.

52. "Moe's Insight Fills Theater Gaps," *Philadelphia Daily News*, April 28, 1972.

53. The history of the Electric Factory club and Electric Factory Concerts is recounted in Larry Magid with Robert Huber, *My Soul's Been Psychedelicized: Electric Factory, Four Decades in Posters and Photographs* (Philadelphia: Temple University Press, 2011).

54. Larry Magid, Mann Moments Interview, May 2, 2023.

55. Ibid.

56. "Cellist Brings Bold Sounds to the Dell," *The Philadelphia Inquirer*, July 22, 1975.

57. "A Brilliant 'Aida' Ends an Epoch at the Dell," *The Philadelphia Inquirer*, August 1, 1975; "Mehta's 'Aida' Is Fitting Farewell to Dell Site," *The Evening Bulletin*, August 1, 1975.

## Chapter 8

1. "Mann Gets Medal for Dell Role," *The Evening Bulletin*, May 21, 1976; "French President's Visit Goes at Whirlwind Pace," *The Sunday Bulletin*, May 23, 1976.

2. "Music Mann Is Trumpeted," *The Philadelphia Inquirer*, June 13, 1976.

3. Ibid.

4. "Freddy Mann and His World," *Philadelphia Daily News*, June 14, 1976.

5. "Stereo Dells Tax Imagination," *Philadelphia Daily News*, June 11, 1976.

6. "Construction to Start on New Dell," *The Philadelphia Inquirer*, January 31, 1975.

7. Jerry Grabey, telephone conversation with the author, March 16, 2023.

8. "Robert Merrill Sings at New Dell Just to Test Acoustics, They're OK," *The Evening Bulletin*, June 8, 1976; "New Dell Is Worth Seeing, Not Hearing . . . Yet," *Courier-Post*, June 8, 1976.

9. "Music Mann Is Trumpeted."

10. "The Dell West Opens for Bicen[tennial], with Big Hopes," *The Philadelphia Inquirer*, June 13, 1976.

11. "New Dell Opens to Rave Reviews," *Philadelphia Daily News*, June 15, 1976.

12. "The New Dell Upstages the Performance," *The Philadelphia Inquirer*, June 15, 1976.

13. Ibid.; "The New Dell West Is a Great Success," *Courier-Post*, June 15, 1976.

14. "New Dell Opens to Rave Reviews"; "The Scene," *The Philadelphia Inquirer*, June 16, 1976.

15. "Three Notables Help Open New Dell," *Philadelphia Daily News*, June 15, 1976.

16. "The New Dell West Is a Great Success."

17. "Triumphal March Caps Homage to Fred Mann at Dell Gala," *The Evening Bulletin*, June 15, 1976; "For Fred Mann, Post-Dell Party Is an Artistic Success, Too," *The Philadelphia Inquirer*, June 17, 1976.

18. "Stern Revisits Dell to Make Beautiful Music with Maestro," *Philadelphia Daily News*, June 16, 1976.

19. "Welcome to the New Dell," *The Philadelphia Inquirer*, June 16, 1976.

20. "Ormandy's First Concert in New Dell," *The New York Times*, June 16, 1976; "New Dell Opens with Problems," *The Evening Bulletin*, June 15, 1976.

21. "Robin Hood Dell West Receives Award for Architectural Excellence," *The Philadelphia Inquirer*, February 26, 1978.

22. "Friends of the Dell's Rolls Will Be Increased to 5,000," *The Philadelphia Inquirer*, May 29, 1976.

23. "New Dell Opens with Problems"; "The New Dell Upstages the Performance."

24. "Dell Opening Marred," *The Evening Bulletin*, June 20, 1976.

25. "Dell Opening," *The Evening Bulletin*, June 22, 1976.

26. "Dell's Sound System Gets a Second Hearing," *The Philadelphia Inquirer*, June 30, 1976.

27. "Dell Is Losing Its Real Friends," *The Philadelphia Inquirer*, July 1, 1976; "New Dell Disappoints Music Fans," *The Philadelphia Inquirer*, June 20, 1976.

28. "Dell West—Beautiful but a Disappointment," *The Philadelphia Inquirer*, June 16, 1976.

29. "Some Friends of the 'Old' Dell," *The Philadelphia Inquirer*, June 28, 1976.

30. "New Robin Hood Dell Un-American?" *Courier-Post*, June 26, 1976.

31. Ibid.

32. "Green's New Symphony Is All Red, White, and Blue," *The Philadelphia Inquirer*, June 17, 1976.

33. "Brilliant Bernstein Turns Dell into Wild Inferno of Joy," *The Evening Bulletin*, July 16, 1976; "Bernstein Plays Three Roles Well," *The Philadelphia Inquirer*, July 17, 1976.

34. Grabey, phone conversation, March 16, 2023.

35. Ibid., May 2, 2024.

36. "Russians Perform Brilliantly at the Dell," *The Philadelphia Inquirer*, June 23, 1976; "Svetlanov's Conducting at Dell Is Masterful," *The Evening Bulletin*, June 23, 1976.

37. Grabey, phone conversation, March 16, 2023.

38. Larry Magid, Mann Moments Interview, May 2, 2023.

39. "James Taylor's Sound Is Right at Home at the New Dell," *The Philadelphia Inquirer*, July 19, 1976.

40. Jane Gitomer, Mann Moments Interview, December 17, 2022.

41. Magid, Mann Moments Interview.

42. Ibid.

43. "He's the Muscle Behind the Music," *The Philadelphia Inquirer*, May 1, 1977.

44. Concert program booklet, Mann Center for the Performing Arts Archives.

45. "As in Milan, Almost as in Dell West," *The Philadelphia Inquirer*, September 22, 1976.

46. Minutes of Board of Directors of Robin Hood Dell Concerts Inc., November 11, 1976, Mann Center for the Performing Arts Archives.

47. Ibid.

48. "Acoustics Are Improved at the Dell West," *The Philadelphia Inquirer*, June 17, 1977.

49. Minutes of Board of Directors of Robin Hood Dell Concerts Inc., May 19, 1977, Mann Center for the Performing Arts Archives.

50. Ibid.; "Acoustics Are Improved at the Dell West"; "What's Doing at the Dell," *Philadelphia Daily News*, June 17, 1977.

51. "Acoustics Are Improved at the Dell West."

52. "Al Gaudiosi Is Keeping Rizzo High on Culture," *The Philadelphia Inquirer*, May 22, 1977.

53. Lucinda Hudson, telephone call and emails with the author, May 24–25, 2024.

54. "Sarah Vaughan: A Session with Orchestra," *The Philadelphia Inquirer*, July 19, 1978; "A Sock of Gershwin Goodies," *The Evening Bulletin*, July 19, 1978.

55. "Joining the Crowd: The Dell Goes Pops," *The Philadelphia Inquirer*, July 30, 1978; "Do Pop Concerts Dilute the Dell?" *The Sunday Bulletin*, June 25, 1978. While characterizing the change as "deterioration" is a matter of opinion, the 1978 concerts did indeed mark the beginning of a long-term trend toward more popular programming of Philadelphia Orchestra summer concerts.

56. "The Dell West Is for Culture, and Manilow," *The Sunday Bulletin*, June 18, 1978.

57. "Grover Washington Jr. vs. Dell West," *The Philadelphia Daily News*, July 31, 1978.

58. "Opera, at the Dell, amid Dispute," *The Philadelphia Inquirer*, May 28, 1978.

59. "Met Perform 'Rigoletto' Outdoors in Philadelphia," *The New York Times*, June 3, 1978.

60. "Cold Night of Dance at the Dell," *Courier-Post*, June 14, 1978.

61. "Baryshnikov, Markarova Star in 'Giselle,'" *The Evening Bulletin*, June 16, 1978.

62. Zubin Mehta to Eugene Ormandy, letter, October 19, 1978, Eugene Ormandy papers, Kislak Center for Special Collections, Rare Books, and Manuscripts, University of Pennsylvania.

63. "Rename the Dell?" *The Evening Bulletin*, January 24, 1979.

64. Magid, Mann Moments Interview.

65. "The Met Returns to the Dell with Puccini's 'Tosca,'" *Main Line Times*, May 31, 1979.

66. "Beethoven and Mann Saluted at Dell Opener," *Philadelphia Daily News*, June 19, 1979; "15,000 Hail Dell's 50th Year," *The Evening Bulletin*, June 19, 1979.

67. "Iturbi Cancels; Misha Dichter to Fill In," *The Philadelphia Inquirer*, June 21, 1979.

68. "Last Notes of a Lush Summer of Music," *The Philadelphia Inquirer*, August 19, 1979.

69. "As Apollo, Baryshnikov Has Crowd Gasping," *The Evening Bulletin*, August 8, 1979.

70. "Taylor Returns to the Rock He Left," *The Philadelphia Inquirer*, July 29, 1979.

71. Larry Magid, email with the author, April 8, 2004; "Fans Purr as Como Croons Their Tunes," *The Philadelphia Inquirer*, August 28, 1979.

72. "Marian Anderson: A Living Philadelphia Monument," *The Philadelphia Tribune*, August 24, 1979.

## Chapter 9

1. "For an Opener, a Phila[delphia] Farewell," *The Philadelphia Inquirer*, February 27, 1980.

2. "Beverly Sills Makes a Memorable Farewell at the Mann Center," *The Philadelphia Inquirer*, June 10, 1980.

3. "Memories amid the Music," *The Philadelphia Inquirer*, June 17, 1980.

4. "No Romance, Strictly Love," *The Evening Bulletin*, June 15, 1980.

5. "Bowing In: An Old World Man in a New World Symphony," *The Philadelphia Inquirer*, July 16, 1980.

6. "Philadelphia Season Has 'New Look,'" *Billboard*, March 30, 1980.

7. "Philadelphia Orchestra Interview with Honorable Fredric R. Mann—November 14, 1984," Philadelphia Orchestra Association Correspondence, Fredric R. Mann papers, Irving S. Gilmore Music Library, Yale University.

8. "As Maestro Nears 80, Philadelphians Contemplate Post-Ormandy Era," *The New York Times*, February 18, 1979.

9. Melissa Gilstrap, prod., "Blue Shirt Blues," *After the Gig: Tales from Larry McKenna*, tale no. 5, posted February 20, 2021, accessed August 2024, https://www.youtube.com/watch?v=ATm1bQ99ohM&list=PLW_OT4kWXJCSwJCw7pFvleHPdTBxugS4M&index=5.

10. "A Definite Gold-Medal Performance," *The Evening Bulletin*, August 13, 1981.

11. "PA Ballet: Something New at the Mann," *The Philadelphia Inquirer*, August 5, 1984.

12. Ibid.

13. "Leningrad's Kirov Dances 'Swan Lake,'" *Philadelphia Daily News*, May 29, 1986; "The Kirov, in Opening, Lives Up to Reputation," *The Philadelphia Inquirer*, May 29, 1984.

14. Jerry Grabey, interview by the author, March 16, 2023.

15. Ibid., May 2, 2024.

16. Larry Magid, interview by the author, May 28, 2024.

17. "An Oral History of the Mann Center," *Philadelphia Magazine*, June 28, 2012.

18. "Promoters' Dispute Cancels Concerts," *The Philadelphia Inquirer*, February 10, 1981.

19. "Stephen Starr and Pierre Robert on Music in Philadelphia," *Philadelphia Magazine*, October 22, 2014.

20. Grabey interview, May 2, 2024.

21. Stephen Starr, Zoom interview by the author, April 25, 2024.

22. Larry Magid, email with the author, May 28, 2025.

23. Minutes of Board of Directors of Mann Music Center, April 13, 1983, Mann Center for the Performing Arts Archives.

24. Ibid., September 25, November 5, 1984.

25. Joseph Kluger, interview by the author, April 2, 2024.

26. "Business Interferes with Philanthropy," *Observer-Reporter* (Washington, PA), April 1, 1980, scrapbook, Mann Center for the Performing Arts Archives. The interview was published in several small Pennsylvania regional newspapers in late March and early April 1980.

27. "Dell's Ex-Manager Blames Mann for Loss of His Title," *The Philadelphia Bulletin*, August 18, 1981; "The Man Behind the Mann," *Broad Street Review*, September 3, 2016, accessed May 2024, https://www.broadstreetreview.com/essays/on-the-mann-centers-40th-anniversary-remembering-fredric-r-mann.

28. Grabey interview, May 2, 2024.

29. "Party for 15,000," *The Philadelphia Inquirer*, August 9, 1983.

30. "One Mann's Empire," KYW-TV, aired November 3, 1983, KYW-TV Collection, Special Collections Research Center, Temple University Libraries.

31. "Business Interferes with Philanthropy."

32. "Music at the Mann in Its Summer Style," *The Philadelphia Inquirer*, June 15, 1986.

33. Grabey interview, March 16, 2023.

34. "A Paradox," *Philadelphia Daily News*, February 28, 1987.

35. Kluger interview.

36. Jane Gitomer, conversation with the author, May 21, 2024.

37. "Stern Helps Orchestra Open Season in Memory of Mann," *The Philadelphia Inquirer*, June 10, 1987.

38. "Van Cliburn's Triumphant Return," *The Washington Post*, June 20, 1989.

39. Minutes of Board of Directors of Mann Music Center, October 5, 1989, Mann Center for the Performing Arts Archives.

40. Ibid., March 28, 1990.

41. "New Operator to Be Sought for Mann Center," *The Philadelphia Inquirer*, March 11, 1993.

42. Ibid.

43. Minutes of Board of Directors of Mann Music Center, March 28, 1990, Mann Center for the Performing Arts Archives.

44. Kluger interview.

45. Minutes of Board of Directors of Mann Music Center, September 15, 1995, Mann Center for the Performing Arts Archives.

46. Grabey interview, May 29, 2024.

47. "Mann Flashes Bankroll," *The Philadelphia Inquirer*, January 11, 1994.

48. Grabey interview, May 2, 2024.

49. Starr, Zoom interview.

50. Ibid.

51. "Starr Ends Battle with Electric Factory," *Philadelphia Daily News*, December 6, 1990.

52. Larry Magid, Mann Moments Interview, May 2, 2023.

53. "There Are New Kids on the Concert Block," *The Philadelphia Inquirer*, June 1, 1997.

54. These developments are detailed in Minutes of Board of Directors of Mann Music Center, 1996–1997, Mann Center for the Performing Arts Archives. Doran's "hard bargain" statement is in the January 30, 1996, meeting minutes.

55. Memo to "Members of the Board of Directors, the Mann Music Center," January 2, 1997, Minutes of Board of Directors of Mann Music Center, Mann Center for the Performing Arts Archives.

56. Ibid.

57. Ibid., February 3, 1997, meeting.

58. "Summer at the Mann," *The Philadelphia Inquirer*, February 6, 1997.

59. Debbie Lobel, Mann Moments Interview, June 10, 2024.

60. "Former Head of New York Pops Named Director of Mann Center," *The Philadelphia Inquirer*, July 2, 1997.

61. Peter Lane, interview by the author, April 15, 2024.

62. Ibid.

63. Ibid.

## Chapter 10

1. "To Attract More Fans, a Fresh Mann Approach," *Philadelphia Daily News*, June 12, 1998.

2. Ibid.

3. Ibid.

4. "For Summer, Mann Programs More Pops," *The Philadelphia Inquirer*, April 15, 1998.

5. Ibid.

6. "Mann Orchestrates New and Improved Summer Lineup," *The Philadelphia Inquirer*, April 16, 1998.

7. "To Attract More Fans, a Fresh Mann Approach."

8. "Mann Orchestrates New and Improved Summer Lineup."

9. Peter Lane, interview by the author, April 15, 2024.

10. Jerry Grabey, interview by the author, May 29, 2024.

11. Ibid.

12. Joseph Kluger, interview by the author, April 4, 2024.

13. "Some New Tunes at the Mann," *The Philadelphia Inquirer*, March 17, 1999.

14. Lane interview.

15. "Some New Tunes at the Mann."

16. Kluger interview.

17. "Dutoit's Departure a Puzzle," *The Philadelphia Inquirer*, July 24, 1999.

18. "Dutoit Cites Pressure of Too Many Concerts for His Quitting," *The Philadelphia Inquirer*, July 31, 1999.

19. Kluger interview.

20. "Dutoit's Departure a Puzzle."

21. Lane interview.

22. Peter Gould, Mann Moments Interview, May 5, 2023.

23. Debbie Lobel, Mann Moments Interview, June 10, 2024.
24. Gould, Mann Moments Interview.
25. Nancy Newman, Mann Moments Interview, December 16, 2022.
26. Lobel, Mann Moments Interview.
27. Lane interview.
28. "Orchestra Drops Free Concert," *The Philadelphia Inquirer*, June 20, 2003.
29. Time for Three, Mann Moments Interview, October 11, 2023.
30. All quotes by Alan Greenberger are from his interview by the author, April 18, 2024.
31. "Children 'Meet and Greet' performers," *Philadelphia Daily News*, July 28, 2005.
32. Peter Lane, emails with the author, June 2024.

## Chapter 11

1. All quotes by Catherine Cahill in this chapter are from her interviews with the author on March 12, March 28, and June 25, 2024, as well as follow-up emails in July and August 2024.
2. Justin Klein, interviews with the author, June 23, July 14, 2024.
3. Nancy Newman, Mann Moments Interview, December 16, 2022.
4. All quotes by Joseph Kluger in this chapter are from his interview by the author, April 2, 2024.
5. Debbie Lobel, Mann Moments Interview, June 10, 2024.
6. Klein interview, July 14, 2024.
7. Lucinda Hudson, interview by the author, May 24, 2024.
8. Christopher Bruner, interview by the author, July 13, 2024.
9. Matias Tarnopolsky, interview by the author, May 23, 2024.
10. Klein interview, July 14, 2024.
11. See Yannick Nézet-Séguin, Foreword, page x.
12. "Black Thought on Why the Roots Picnic Is the Philly Music Festival That Endures," *The Philadelphia Inquirer*, May 24, 2024.
13. "Jazz Under the Stars Returns to the Mann," press release, Mann Center for the Performing Arts, July 18, 2023, https://manncenter.org/pressroom/jazz-under-stars-returns-mann-gerald-veasley-jazz-curator.
14. Lobel, Mann Moments Interview.
15. Jerry Grabey, interviews with the author, May 2, May 6, 2024.
16. Newman, Mann Moments Interview.
17. James Taylor, Mann Moments Interview, July 1, 2023.
18. Klein interview, June 25, 2024.
19. Geoff Gordon statement provided to the Mann Center by Live Nation Philadelphia, September 2024.
20. Bruner interview.

# Index

Page numbers in *italics* refer to illustrations.

**Jack McCarthy** is a longtime Philadelphia archivist and historian who has held leadership positions at several area historical institutions and directed a number of major archives and public history projects. He has written extensively on the history of Philadelphia music, industry in Philadelphia, and Northeast Philadelphia. He is the author of *In the Cradle of Industry and Liberty: A History of Manufacturing in Philadelphia* and numerous articles for the *Encyclopedia of Greater Philadelphia* and was a major contributor to *The Philadelphia Music Book: Sounds of a City.* He has served as consulting archivist and historian for The Philadelphia Orchestra, the Mann Center for the Performing Arts, and the Philadelphia Jazz Legacy Project.